Stefani Scherer, Reinhard Pollak, Gunnar Otte,
Markus Gangl (eds.)

From Origin to Destination

Trends and Mechanisms in Social Stratification
Research

Essays in honour of Walter Müller

Campus Verlag
Frankfurt/New York

Distribution throughout the world except Germany, Austria and Switzerland by

The University of Chicago Press
1427 East 60th Street
Chicago, IL 60637

Bibliographic Information published by the Deutsche Nationalbibliothek.
Die Deutsche Nationalbibliothek lists this publication in the Deutsche Nationalbibliografie;
detailed bibliographic data are available in the Internet at http://dnb.d-nb.de.
ISBN 978-3-593-38411-5

Copyright © 2007 Campus Verlag GmbH, Frankfurt/Main
Printing office and bookbinder: PRISMA Verlagsdruckerei GmbH
Printed on acid free paper.
Printed in the United States of America

For further information:
www.campus.de
www.press.uchicago.edu

Content

II. Special issues in current stratification research

Preface

This volume has been prepared to honour Walter Müller for his lifetime contribution in the sociological fields of education, social mobility, and the unequal distribution of life chances. All the authors of this book have collaborated with Walter Müller in one way or another, some over a long period, some more recently. Their prominence reflects the central position of Walter Müller in the international research on social stratification. We, the editors, initiated this book project to express our gratitude and the intellectual debt we owe him.

But this volume is more than a *Festschrift*. As Walter Müller has always striven for high-level sociological research, we are very proud that the internationally outstanding scholars we assembled for this book did not hesitate to contribute state-of-the-art research with fresh theoretical ideas and new empirical results. Their contributions are positioned at the cutting edge of social stratification research and are meant to stimulate the discussion about historical trends and social mechanisms underlying educational inequalities and processes of social mobility.

We would like to express our thanks to the contributors of this volume. All chapters have undergone a review process. As external reviewers, we thank Paolo Barbieri, Carlo Barone, Louis-André Vallet, and Jörg Rössel for their helpful comments. On biographical information about Walter Müller's academic career we benefited from Karl Ulrich Mayer and Johann Handl. And we are most grateful to Beate Rossi who did the entire layout of the book and never lost patience with four editors in four different locations.

Parts of the chapters were presented at a conference to honour Walter Müller in Mannheim, January 26, 2007. We thank the Mannheimer Zentrum für Europäische Sozialforschung (MZES) for hosting this meeting and for contributing to the publication of this volume.

Milan, Berlin, Leipzig, and Mannheim, January 2007   The Editors

Introduction: from origin to destination

Reinhard Pollak, Gunnar Otte, Stefani Scherer, Markus Gangl

From origin to destination: the sociological perspective

This edited volume is meant to guide its readers through a sociological pathway from a person's social ›origin‹ to their – preliminary – ›destination‹ within a society. The position of the parental family – the origin – and the position individuals eventually achieve over their life course – the destination – is usually expressed, particularly among European sociologists, by some notion of a social class position to describe a person's relative position in a given society – a concept which will largely be applied in the subsequent chapters of this volume. The comparison of an individual's class position at her or his origins with the class position achieved over the life course is of fundamental interest for sociologists. In fact, it goes to the core of sociological research since it not only informs about the amount of inequality at two points in time (or for two generations), but also enlightens about the opportunities for an individual to move between different class positions, therefore revealing the openness or rigidity of a given society. It is no surprise, then, that merely descriptive studies on social mobility attract much attention.

Sociologists distinguish between absolute and relative rates of social mobility. The former refer to observed mobility rates, i.e. to class changes individuals actually experience (e.g. a son or a daughter of a farmer becomes a clerical worker), while the latter serve as a measure of ›social fluidity‹ and control for the fact that class distributions may differ due to changes in the marginal distributions of classes (e.g. declining farm sector, expansion of clerical occupations). For absolute mobility rates, the latest comparative study by Breen and Luijkx (2004) reports some gradual convergence among European countries towards a common level of absolute mobility rates for men as well as for women. However, this is a moderate trend towards convergence, which itself is »by no means complete« (Breen and Luijkx 2004: 49, see Erikson and Goldthorpe 1992 and Lipset and Zetterberg 1959 for previous influential studies). Much more dispute arises on differences in relative rates between countries and the development of relative rates within countries. On the basis of functionalist ideas, what might be labelled the »liberal theory of industrialism« (Kerr et al. 1960, Dunlop et al. 1975, Treiman 1970) stated that societies will experience an ongoing shift towards meritocratic selection processes which lead to a declining impact of ascriptive assets and an increase in the importance of achieved assets. Hence, effects of social origin on class destination are expected to diminish over time. In contrast to this expectation, Featherman, Jones and Hauser (1975) formulated their renowned ›FJH‹ hypothesis on genotypical patterns of mobility (i.e. social fluidity), which are expected to be »basically the same« in industrial societies with a market economy and a nuclear family system (Featherman et al. 1975: 340).

In the mid-1980s, John Goldthorpe, Walter Müller and Robert Erikson initiated a large-scale *Comparative Analysis of Social Mobility in Industrial Nations* (CASMIN) to test the ›FJH‹ hypothesis. Based on cross-sectional data of the late 1960s to the mid 1970s from a selection of nine countries, they found basic similarities in the patterns of social fluidity – with a few exceptions (Erikson and Goldthorpe 1992). However, at roughly the same time, Ganzeboom, Luijkx and Treiman (1989) published another large-scale study on social mobility from 1947–1986, including data from 35 countries. Their results showed a strong increase in social mobility over time, largely supporting the hypothesis put forward by the liberal theory of industrialism (Ganzeboom et al. 1989). In subsequent years, several studies focussed on patterns and developments of social fluidity (DiPrete and Grusky 1990, Jonsson and Mills 1993, Vallet 1999), adding to a more general picture of social mobility in industrialized countries that became less supportive of the FJH hypothesis. A new large-scale comparative study of social mobility in Europe using data from the last quarter of the 20th century, initiated by Richard Breen, aimed at providing a comprehensive assessment of recent trends in social mobility. The results show that, in fact, models of no difference over time and between countries fit the data quite well (Breen and Luijkx 2004). However, Breen and Luijkx do report evidence for variations in social fluidity between countries, for different temporal trends in certain countries, and for decreasing variation between countries. The results, therefore, do not support either of the two trend hypotheses on social mobility – neither the liberal theory of industrialism, nor the hypothesis put forward by Featherman, Jones, and Hauser. The comparative study by Breen and Luijkx (2004) looked at the development of social fluidity over survey periods. However, it can be questioned whether this approach is indeed the most suitable one, or if it is more appropriate to study social mobility in a cohort perspective, assuming that social change affects mainly certain cohorts and, hence, social change takes place through the replacement of successive birth cohorts (Mannheim 1954). Indeed, Breen and Jonsson (forthcoming) demonstrate for the Swedish case that all change found in a period perspective can be attributed to successive cohort replacement, thus strengthening the argument for a cohort rather than for a period perspective. Likewise, Müller and Pollak (2004a) show for Germany how a cohort perspective is able to reveal certain historically specific conditions that affected only few cohorts in their social fluidity pattern, which would have remained undiscovered by a period approach.

The potential benefits of a cohort perspective on social mobility will be further elaborated in two chapters in this volume. Karl Ulrich Mayer and Silke Aisenbrey use data from the German Life History Study with narrowly defined birth cohorts. They replicate the general findings by Müller and Pollak (2004a) and point to specific cohort developments that are only visible with narrowly defined cohorts. For more recent cohorts, they are able to show that the trend towards more social fluidity in Germany has indeed reversed, for men and for women alike. Given the detailed structure of their data, they are also able to show that results of social mobility analyses are sensitive to the age at which an individual's destination class is measured.

Richard Breen and Ruud Luijkx test for two countries (Great Britain and Germany) whether the idea of social change resulting from successive cohort replacement can be extended beyond the Swedish case. For Great Britain, they find rather little change over time, in period as well as in cohort perspective. Only farm inheritance becomes more pronounced, but since there are very few people in this sector it is of minor importance for the British social structure. For Germany, however, Breen and Luijkx are able to identify a moderate trend in periods towards more social fluidity, which, in fact, can be attributed – like in the Swedish case – to successive cohort replacement.

Researchers of social mobility have extended their interest beyond the description of trends in social fluidity and are increasingly interested in modelling the pathways individuals take from their origins to their current positions in society, i.e. more studies focus on the mechanisms that create existing inequalities (Morgan et al. 2006). A recent theoretical approach to a comprehensive theory of social mobility by John Goldthorpe (2007) argues that families do as much as they can to avoid downward mobility of their children compared to the family's class position. Families with different class positions apply different strategies to avoid downward mobility. A crucial component of these strategies is the amount of schooling parents provide for their children. In order to secure positions at the top of the class distribution, it is in the best interests of the family to invest as much as possible in a child's education, whereas for middle class or working class children it might be sufficient to strive for an intermediate educational qualification to secure a middle or working class position. In fact, in all contributions to the mechanisms of social mobility (or social immobility), education is of eminent importance along the pathway from social origins to destinations, and therefore for the reproduction and the creation of social inequality. We will therefore break down the origin-destination pathway into two parts, one from social origin to education, and another from education to an individual's destination.

Class-based educational inequality has attracted many theoretical and empirical sociological studies. Most of these studies can be related to two very different theoretical approaches for class-based educational inequality. Pierre Bourdieu's idea – roughly – bases on the concept of *habitus*, i.e. a set of dispositions, orientations, and modes of conduct which a child acquires and adopts during her or his upbringing and which will hardly change later in life. A crucial component of the formation of a *habitus* is the ›cultural capital‹ that a child accumulates in the family. Since school environments are usually formed by the dominant class, it is the dominant class' *habitus* that reigns at schools. Students with a dominant class background will therefore be preferred and rewarded in school compared to students with a working class background, simply because they can better relate to what teachers say. In addition, students with a favourable parental background are able to use their ›cultural capital‹ in order to do better in school (Bourdieu and Passeron 1977). Raymond Boudon (1974), in contrast, distinguishes between primary and secondary effects in the creation of class differentials in educational participation. Primary effects refer to the academic ability of children, which certainly differs with social background. Secondary effects refer to the propensity to continue education, *given* academic ability, i.e. although students are equally talented, they choose different educational routes, selective by social origin. As it turns out, Bourdieu's approach has some empirical support for the effect of ›cultural capital‹ on educational attainment (de Graaf et al. 2000, Sullivan 2001), but it also faces some serious empirical refutations (Halsey et al. 1980). One could argue that Bourdieu's approach contributes to the understanding of the generation of Boudon's primary effects.

While Bourdieu's empirical record is at least contested, there are several further refinements and empirical studies favourable of Boudon's idea of primary *and* secondary effects. The concept was picked up by several rational action based models of educational attainment (Erikson and Jonsson 1996a, Breen and Goldthorpe 1997). In these models three components typically contribute to making middle class students more likely than working class students to continue to higher levels of education: They can more easily bear the costs of higher education; they expect higher rates of success in education; and they have more incentives to continue to higher education because by doing so they avoid the risk of downward mobility. Therefore it is much more likely that the benefits outweigh the costs of more education in the middle than in the working classes (Breen et al. 2005). In fact, a growing body of literature reports empirical support for these models (Breen and Yaish 2006, Stocké forthcoming, Becker 2003).

In the present volume, two chapters address these different approaches of educational inequality. John Goldthorpe critically discusses the concept of ›cultural capital‹ in Bourdieu's work. His remarks are embedded in a larger assessment of Bourdieu's theory of social reproduction, with some recommendations of how researchers could make use of what Goldthorpe would rather label ›cultural resources‹. Robert Erikson addresses Boudon's distinction between primary and secondary effects. Referring to collaborative work on British data (Jackson et al. 2006), he assesses the importance of primary and secondary effects for different transitions in the Swedish school system and for similar transitions over time, comparing different school cohorts. He identifies primary and secondary effects operating differently at different transitions. Whereas for the transition to upper secondary education primary effects – and probably also secondary effects – are found to decline over time, they work in opposite directions at the transition to university and probably balance each other out. Robert Erikson's work contributes greatly to the cumulative knowledge of the strength of primary and secondary effects over time at different transitions and between countries.

In this context of cross-national comparisons, it is well-known that national education and training systems vary substantially in the amount to which they reproduce the social structure or offer access to favourable positions on a meritocratic base. An educational system, thereby, establishes not only the overall distribution of educational attainment (with regard to levels and tracks), but, more importantly, shapes the distribution of educational qualifications along more or less ascriptive characteristics. Several studies demonstrated considerable differences in the amount of educational inequality between countries (e.g. Jonsson et al. 1996, Baumert et al. 2006), a finding that is generally attributed to different institutional arrangements and that is largely agreed upon. Much more dispute is found when it comes to trends of educational inequality within countries. In their seminal book on *Persistent Inequality* in educational attainment, Shavit and Blossfeld (1993) demonstrated in a meta-analysis of 13 countries that despite of dramatic educational expansion during the twentieth century, all but two countries (Sweden and the Netherlands) »exhibit stability of socioeconomic inequalities of educational opportunities« (Shavit and Blossfeld 1993: 22). These results, however, have been challenged by a number of country studies (Müller and Haun 1994, Vallet 2004, Kuo and Hauser 1995, Shavit and Westerbeek 1998) as well as by comparative studies on educational inequality (Rijken 1999, Jonsson et al. 1996). A recent large-scale study of eight European countries by Richard Breen, Ruud Luijkx, Walter Müller, and Reinhard Pollak reported declining educational inequality for six countries and revitalized the debate on trends in educational inequality (Breen et al. 2005).

In their contribution to this volume, Yossi Shavit, Meir Yaish, and Eyal Bar-Haim take up this debate in a more general context of educational expansion and educational inequality. With a thorough discussion on the choice of the dependent variable (educational transitions vs. educational attainment), with critical remarks on measures of social origin and statistical modelling, and with consideration of specific historical circumstances, the authors qualify previous empirical findings and discuss the direction in which future research will probably be most rewarding.

Education is certainly the single most important determinant for a destination outcome (e.g. Ganzeboom et al. 2005). In general, higher educational qualifications lead to higher occupational prestige and to higher chances for service class positions; vocational training programmes are usually better entrance cards for skilled labour positions than general educational programmes at a similar level. Regarding tertiary education, unemployment risks are lowest and, at the same time, the marginal returns are higher than marginal returns at lower levels of education (Kogan and Schubert 2005, Müller and Shavit 1998). There are indications that the strong association between education and destination declines in various countries over time, i.e. education is less of a guarantee of successful status attainment or successful avoidance of downward mobility (Handl 1996, Vallet 2004, Jonsson 1996, Jackson et al. 2005, Breen and Goldthorpe 2001). Walter Müller and colleagues have found modest declines in absolute returns to education. At the same time, however, more highly educated students were able to even further expand their relative advantages over lower educated students, and vocational education also gains importance over time (Brauns et al. 1997, Brauns et al. 1999, Müller et al. 2002). According to these analyses, trends in returns to education depend on the detailed operationalisation of the ›return‹ variable, i.e. the measure of an individual's destination (Müller 1998a). It would be of great interest to assess the association between education and destination class with a more recent cross-national comparative study of returns to education over the life course. A study like this would shed more light on this part of the pathway from origin to destination, having also in mind Mayer and Aisenbrey's finding of different mobility patterns across ages.

The mediating effect of education on the pathway from origin to destination is well-established (e.g. Blau and Duncan 1967, Treiman and Yip 1989). It is less clear, however, how educational *expansion* and – for some countries – declining educational inequality play out in the overall association between class of origin and destination class (Müller 1998a). Does educational expansion lead to an overall reduction of this association, i.e. do we find more social mobility from generation to generation due to educational expansion? And does less educational inequality lead to more social mobility? Breen and Jonsson (forthcoming) demonstrate for the Swedish case that it is mainly a compositional effect that drives increasing social mobility. This is based on the fact that the (net) association between origin and destination is lower at higher levels of education. A medical student, for example, has good opportunities to become a medical professional, regardless of class of origin, whereas, say, a mechanic might have to rely on origin effects to achieve a skilled worker position or even a position as a technician. Due to a comprehensive expansion of the educational sector, and due to declining educational inequality in Sweden, more people reach higher levels of education. Thus, fewer individuals – on average – have to rely on origin effects, which leads to an overall (or gross) decline in the association between origin and destination, i.e. to more social mobility. The effect of the educational expansion is of a much greater relevance and consequence than the reduction in educational inequality. In an earlier study on France, Vallet (2004) found similar results. In order to explain increasing social fluidity in France, he identified a compositional effect (like Breen and Jonsson), but declining educational inequality and declining returns to education also contribute substantially to the decline in the overall association between an individual's origin and destination.

Richard Breen and Ruud Luijkx devote the second part of their chapter to the analysis of compositional effects in Germany and Great Britain. These two countries are indeed interesting test cases for the compositional mechanism: In Germany, there is a particularly strong link between the educational system and the labour market (Shavit and Müller 1998), so one could ask whether there are indeed substantial differences in the association between origin and destination for different levels of education (3-way interaction effect). For the British case, it is interesting to see why there is no trend towards more social mobility despite the fact that the educational system expanded substantially. Breen and Luijkx discuss in detail the importance of a compositional effect for Germany and its absence in Great Britain. In both countries, the educational system expanded markedly. But it is only in Germany where higher educational degrees interact with lower effects of social origin regarding destination class placement, whereas in Britain, they find no clear pattern of the 3-way interaction effect.

The importance of educational qualifications for the pathway from origin to destination is of an entirely different character when it comes to children of self-employed parents who inherit the family business. For older cohorts, it was mainly the farm sector that showed high rates of inheritance (Erikson and Goldthorpe 1992). However, the scope and the structure of self-employment has changed over time (Arum and Müller 2004). While we observe a general decline of the farm sector in industrialized countries, the share of self-employment in non-agricultural sectors increased in most OECD countries over past decades (OECD 2000), and forms of self-employment became more heterogeneous. Arum (1997) observed an increase in the proportion of well-paid free-lancing professionals as well as an increase in mostly unstable, marginal unskilled activities. In his contribution to this volume, Richard Arum provides a thorough review of the state-of-art in self-employment research. He points out the changes in the structure of self-employment and discusses the changing importance of education for certain self-employed activities. He uses new data to sketch an even more recent picture of the development of self-employment in the United States. His contribution is an important supplement to the general literature of social mobility, since it addresses the alternative route to the maintenance and attainment of social positions reliant on familial resources.

The vast majority of individuals, however, enter the labour market as employees. For them, it is mainly the structure of the educational system and the degree of labour market regulations that exert a decisive impact on their transition from the educational system to an employed position in the labour market (Müller 2005, Müller and Gangl 2003, Kogan and Müller 2003). Employers use the level and the content of educational qualifications as signals for an individual's anticipated productivity (Becker 1964, Spence 1973). The educational systems differ in the extent to which they are able to provide clear signals for employers. Standardized qualifications, stratified curricula and vocational training programmes, either in vocational schools or in apprenticeships, are indicators employers can use to overcome the screening problem of applicants. Thus, the shape of the educational system, together with labour market regulations, generates distinctive labour market attributes. Probably the most prominent distinction is between *occupational labour market* and *internal labour market* systems, the former being characterized by an educational system providing occupationally specific skills which match (more or less) the demands of employers, whereas the latter is characterized mainly by training-on-the-job arrangements and the employer's reliance on the work experience of an applicant (Marsden 1990). This dichotomy, however, is probably too simplistic to sufficiently describe the main labour market properties in various countries. For the EU-15 countries, for example, Gangl (2003a) identifies at least three clusters of labour market systems for labour market entrants, noting that these clusters still show considerable within-cluster variation. Nevertheless, labour market characteristics are important conditions for successful labour market entries, and therefore crucial conditions for an individual to reach a first own (class) destination.

Irena Kogan, Marge Unt and Ellu Saar address the necessity to have detailed knowledge about the labour market characteristics for the placement of individuals in various destination classes. In their chapter, they tie in with previous analyses by Gangl (2003a) and Kogan and Müller (2003) and expand these analyses to educational systems and labour markets in post-socialist Central and Eastern Europe countries (CEE). The transformations of educational systems and labour markets of CEE countries after 1990 provide an important testing ground for theories about the importance of the educational system and the labour market regulations for the transition of young people from school to work. Empirical results show that we cannot speak of a single Eastern European school-to-work transition pattern. The mechanisms in the new EU member states follow largely those of the well documented old member states, but with some exceptions. While most CEE countries show characteristics that resemble either an internal labour market pattern (e.g. Baltic states) or a Southern European pattern (e.g. Poland), it is mainly Slovenia and the Czech Republic which cannot be adequately grouped into one of these categories.

So far, we have been focussing on the effects of class of origin on destination class, with a detailed discussion of (potentially) mediating effects of educational attainment. Besides the effects of class of origin, however, there are, of course, other relevant characteristics of an individual that influence her or his destination class, and thus the social stratification of a society. We restrict our discussion of other influences to ethnic and to gender inequalities, which are probably two characteristics with the largest (gross) effects in our societies.

Ethnic stratification is a permanent characteristic of most European countries. Ethnic inequalities not only exist for first generation migrants, but persist, to a lesser extent, in the second generation (Granato and Kalter 2001). The basic question is whether the intergenerational transmission of ethnic disadvantages is due to general mechanisms of social inequality, or whether there is something specifically ›ethnic‹ about them. In their chapter on second generation structural assimilation in Germany, Frank Kalter, Nadia Granato and Cornelia Kristen use the pathway from origin to education and destination, but add migration background as an additional starting point. They show that at least for the situation of labour migrant descendants in Germany, general social inequality tells almost the whole story: First, disadvantages in the educational system can largely be attributed to the socio-economic background of young second generation migrants, and, second, labour market disadvantages of this group virtually disappear when the authors control for educational qualifications. Thus, for Germany, they report a clear and persistent trend towards assimilation with regard to the structural situation of the second generation. Direct effects of migration background are on the decline and, in fact, are of minor importance, because the main (gross) disadvantage for second generation migrants comes from disadvantaged social origins. Kalter, Granato and Kristen's contribution is one of the first papers that let traditions of social mobility research and migration research flow together, providing insights and encouraging further research along these lines.

Gender inequalities with respect to labour market participation receive much attention, both in public and in academic debates. In general, women participate less often in the labour market, they have a much higher risk of discontinuous employment, they are less often full-time employed, they have less favourable career prospects, and they suffer under a gender wage gap (e.g. Hakim 1996, Petersen and Morgan 1995). Although these disadvantages are almost universal in industrialized countries, the patterns and magnitudes of gender inequalities vary substantially (Charles and Grusky 2004). Though much focus is put politically on female employment rates, efforts in this direction increasingly take into account the existing and persisting patterns of sex segregation in jobs, occupations and sectors. In fact, occupational sex segregation can be seen as the »smoking gun that accounts for many other forms of gender-based advantages and disadvantages« (Charles and Grusky 2004: 7). The concept of occupational sex segregation is well-studied but disputed, especially when it comes to an appropriate measure of occupational sex segregation (Jacobs 1993). The Index of Dissimilarity, various refinements of it as well as measures within the framework of log-linear modelling compete for the best or most suitable measure. Johann Handl and Stephanie Steinmetz take up the debate on appropriate measures of occupational sex segregation. After an overview of trends and discussions in the field, they argue in their chapter that the concept of occupational sex segregation itself contributes to the confusion that different measures of occupational sex segregation produce. They compare the methodological problems in research on occupational sex segregation to the problems in social mobility research and adapt the concepts of social mobility and social fluidity to the field of occupational sex segregation. With the concepts of ›occupational chances‹ and ›sex-typing‹, they examine developments in the 1990s using European Labour Force data.

Their empirical results largely support previous findings of relatively high levels of sex segregation in Nordic countries and low levels in Southern European countries.

We conclude our volume on the pathway from origin to destination with two chapters which both address – from very different perspectives – the problem of adequate units of analysis in social mobility, and more generally, in social stratification research. Hans-Peter Blossfeld starts his chapter with a short review of research traditions with regard to the unit of analysis for class or (socio-) economic positions. Until the 1980s, much of the research in social stratification relied on a male-breadwinner model in which the male household head is taken to determine the class position for the entire household or family. This »male bias« in stratification research was eventually replaced by a more individualistic approach in which men and women are treated separately with regard to their own employment situation. However, there are good reasons to treat a family or household as an economic and social entity with shared economic, social and cultural resources that determine a child's future prospects in terms of educational success and labour market placement (e.g. Miller 1998). Ultimately, it is an empirical question whether either or both parents contribute additively or multiplicatively to the resources within a family (e.g. Korupp et al. 2002). Hans-Peter Blossfeld, however, is more interested in general trends of prospective social inequality. He opens up a new perspective when he discusses the influence of increasing educational homogamy and increasing numbers of dual-earner couples on social inequality and social stratification. Reviewing two cross-national comparative studies which he directed, he describes recent trends towards more educational homogamy and towards gender-symmetric incomes, and relates cross-national differences in the share of dual-earner households to general features of welfare state regimes. Most importantly, he assesses expected changes in the familial resources due to these developments and discusses these developments in the light of potential trends in social inequality and social mobility.

The final – truly innovative – chapter by Ulrich Kohler shifts the attention from the household or family level to the unit of analysis in cross-national research. Kohler examines which level of inequality – national or European – is related to various day-to-day-life outcomes and attitudes. He starts with the criticism by Beck and Grande (2004) of current research in social stratification for its failure to take the European dimension of inequality into account. Kohler offers an interpretation of Beck and Grande's claim in order to derive and formulate empirically testable hypotheses. He identifies four ideal types of how social inequality in Europe can be viewed: the container model is related to relative vertical positions within a given society (the state-of-the-art model), absolute vertical positions characterize the model of supra-national inequality, the national solidarity model refers to differences between, but not within countries, and finally the individualisation model, related to Beck's individualisation hypothesis, considers the general well-being of a society. With data from the European Social Survey, Kohler tests these models against three indicators of living conditions. His results are quite puzzling for the predominant research tradition. None of the four ideal types of social inequality is able to describe the distributions of living conditions across Europe exhaustively. But the container model of social inequality performs worst in mapping living conditions cross-nationally within Europe.

An edited volume on current trends and mechanisms in social mobility and social stratification research can, of course, only offer a selection of the most interesting and innovative issues. Other questions on the pathway from origin to destination remain after reading this volume. It would be probably most important and desirable to come up with an integrated micro-based theory of social mobility. Goldthorpe (2007) sets out a very promising outline of a theory of social mobility. This approach needs to be empirically assessed and, in parts, further developed, in particular when it comes to filling destination class positions. The role of employers, as already studied by Jackson, Goldthorpe, and Mills (2005), needs to be better understood, especially with regard to selection criteria based on social origin rather than on educational achievement or other test-based assets. At the same time, based on general strategies from above or below (Goldthorpe 2007), one would have to identify and explicitly model specific strategies adopted by students or applicants to achieve their mobility goals. It would be not sufficient to focus on the effect of education for labour market entrants, but one would have to follow the impact of (formal) education over an individual's work career. In addition, such a general theory of social mobility should be able to account for different institutional settings and their varying effects on the associations between origin and education, education and destination, and for direct inheritance regulations from origin to destination (for example for the self-employed).

A more indirect, but probably highly rewarding way to increase our understanding of social mobility processes is to learn from neighbouring disciplines. Synthesizing different economic and sociological approaches into one single study with different concepts and measures of class positions (Breen 2004, Jonsson et al. forthcoming) and permanent income (for an overview: Solon 2002) might reveal distinct mobility mechanisms that could foster the development of a general theory of social mobility.

From origin to destination: the biographical perspective

As stated at the start of this chapter, this volume is meant to guide its readers along the pathway from a person's social origin to her or his – preliminary – ›destination‹. With this compilation of essays at the current frontier of sociological research in education, stratification and social mobility, we commemorate Walter Müller's lifetime contribution to the evolution of these fields. As one of the key players in the field of European stratification research, he initiated numerous international projects and built up a very strong international network of researchers who have greatly contributed to the state-of-the-art in the field. We therefore conclude this chapter by guiding the reader along the personal pathway of Walter Müller's scientific achievements – from his origins to his present ›destination‹ on his 65th birthday.

Walter Müller has demonstrated outstanding social mobility. He was born in Twerenegg/Menznau, Switzerland, in 1942 as one of twelve children of self-employed small farmers. He was the first person from the village in which he grew up ever to attend university. After studying philosophy, sociology, social psychology and economics at the Universities of Löwen, Belgium, and Cologne, Germany, he worked as a research fellow at the University of Konstanz, Germany, from 1968 to 1974.

In collaboration with Karl Ulrich Mayer, he developed the »Konstanz mobility project« which had been initiated by Ralf Dahrendorf. The purpose of the project was to gain primary data in order to study social mobility in a way it had not previously been possible in Germany. One of the main features was the constant age and thus career-stage of respondents. Additionally, first steps were made to measure the full spectrum of occupational positions in a more differentiated way than in prior research. The Konstanz mobility data, collected in 1969, consisted of all accessible 33-year-old male inhabitants of the city, contained detailed information about their social origins and educational and occupational careers – i.e. it viewed mobility processes dynamically – and combined these »objective« parameters with respondents' »subjective« perceptions and evaluations. The project marks the starting point for the cumulative research programme that Walter Müller has established in collaboration with others since the mid-1970s with the ZUMABUS and ALLBUS general social surveys as well as for the German Life History Study that Karl Ulrich Mayer built up (Mayer 1990, forthcoming). The Konstanz dataset – supplemented by some others – formed the basis of Walter Müller's first publications (Mayer and Müller 1971a, 1971b; Müller 1972) and the doctoral thesis he completed in 1973 (Müller 1975).

Looking at these early works, several things are remarkable. First, they already show the main theme of Walter Müller's lifetime contributions very clearly, namely the interplay of social origin, education, occupational attainment, and the life chances involved with structural positions in the stratification system. This theme is summarized in the title of his dissertation: »Family, School, Occupation: Analyses of Social Mobility and Status Attainment in the Federal Republic of Germany«. Secondly, two decisive breaks with prior research traditions become apparent. On the *national* level, Müller and Mayer belong to the scholars bringing stratification and mobility research back on the sociological agenda and, at the same time, they dissociate themselves from others like Bolte (1959) and Kleining (1971) by introducing recent methodological innovations discussed at the session on Theory, Research and Simulation Studies on Social Mobility at the Seventh World Congress of Sociology in Varna, Bulgaria, 1970. By employing the methodological framework set up by Blau and Duncan (1967), Goodman (1969), and others, Müller and Mayer are, on the *international* level, part of a »revolt« against the »old guard« of mobility research within Research Committee 28 of the International Sociological Association – as represented by, among others, Carlsson (1958) and Svalastoga (1959). One of the early »brothers-in-mind« is John H. Goldthorpe who visited Konstanz in January 1970 to give an influential lecture on mobility research and became one of Walter Müller's lasting collaborators. This methodological paradigm – developed out of a cross-nationally comparative research effort – proved to be extraordinarily fruitful and, setting aside minor modifications, is still employed in recent mobility studies, such as Erikson and Goldthorpe (1992) and Breen (2004), as well as in several chapters of the present volume.

A third feature of Walter Müller's early works is the analytical rigour that has become a trademark of his research. For example, if we look at his article in the very first issue of today's co-leading German sociology journal, the Zeitschrift für Soziologie, we find a very thorough discussion of the role of further education as an intervening variable between respondents' first job and their current job and the implications of these findings for potential bias in the key work of Blau and Duncan (1967), who did not distinguish between general education and further education attained later during employment (Müller 1972: 75ff.): In the Konstanz data further education of a technical and vocational kind proves to be a mechanism to reduce social reproduction that takes place via the general education system. In this article, as in all his other publications, the thoughtful and balanced conclusions Walter Müller draws from his research findings are exemplary – particularly for those numerous scholars who tend to read far-reaching, but unsupported implications into their data.

Looking back to the early 1970s, there was a striking scarcity of suitable data for analyzing social mobility and educational attainment in Germany. Certainly, one of Walter Müller's prime merits has been his ambition to build up a solid data base and research infrastructure for cumulative sociological research on social inequalities. The first step towards this goal was his participation in the questionnaire design of the micro-census supplementary survey »*Berufliche und soziale Umschichtung der Bevölkerung*«, 1971, containing a differentiated schema of occupational positions and a rudimentary longitudinal perspective on lifetime mobility (Handl et al. 1977). A further step was his involvement in establishing social indicators' research and social reporting on living conditions and quality of life in Germany. Much of this work started in the project »*Sozialpolitisches Entscheidungs- und Indikatorensystem*« (SPES), based at the Universities of Frankfurt and Mannheim and led by Wolfgang Zapf (Zapf 1977, Glatzer and Zapf 1984). These efforts were continued, a few years later, in SFB 3 »*Mikroanalytische Grundlagen der Gesellschaftspolitik*« and were institutionalized in two ongoing survey projects, the Wohlfahrtssurvey (starting in 1978) and the Sozioökonomisches Panel (SOEP, starting in 1984). The SPES group was Walter Müller's home from 1974 to 1979. In 1976, he was responsible for placing innovative measurement instruments in the ZUMABUS survey, the predecessor of the German general social survey, ALLBUS (with its first round in 1980). The ZUMABUS 1976 can be seen as the starting point of cumulative stratification research with survey data and of cohort analyses of social mobility in Germany (Pappi 1979).

In 1980, after his *habilitation* (Müller 1978), Walter Müller was appointed professor at the University of Mannheim (chair since 1982), which has remained the centre of his career ever since. Already a renowned site for empirical social research in Germany, Mannheim became a national and international hub for quantitative and comparative research in social stratification during the 1980s and 1990s – institutionalized in the Department of Social Sciences, the Zentrum für Umfragen, Methoden und Analysen (ZUMA), the Institut für Sozialwissenschaften, and, since 1989, the *Mannheimer Zentrum für Europäische Sozialforschung* (MZES). In Mannheim, from 1979 to 1984, VASMA (»Vergleichende Analysen der Sozialstruktur mit Massendaten«) was the first major project led by Walter Müller. Its main objective was to employ data of official statistics to reconstruct structural changes of the labour market over time. Special consideration was given to the changing role of female labour from 1880 to 1980 (Müller et al. 1983). Two contributors to our volume, Johann Handl and Hans-Peter Blossfeld, were heavily engaged in this project (see Blossfeld 1985, Handl 1988) and, as can be seen in their chapters, are still working on the interplay of gendered labour markets and the family.

Having started with a view on the *historical* development of the stratification system, Walter Müller, in close cooperation with John H. Goldthorpe and Robert Erikson, turned to an explicitly *comparative* perspective in the CASMIN project (»Comparative Analysis of Social Mobility in Industrial Nations«) from 1983 to 1988. The main objective was to analyse patterns and trends in social mobility regimes in the light of cross-nationally different economic, political, and institutional settings. For twelve countries, the three principal investigators brought together the best national data bases available (in co-operation with country-specific experts) and combined them in the »International Mobility Superfile« (IMS). This data set contained the CASMIN educational classification and class schema, which became widely used for international comparisons of the causes and effects of educational attainment and class position (Müller et al. 1989, Braun and Müller 1997, Brauns et al. 2000, Brauns et al. 2003). The influential comparative volumes on social mobility, written by Erikson and Goldthorpe (1992), and on education, edited by Erikson and Jonsson (1996b) as well as Shavit and Müller (1998), are a direct outcome of – or draw heavily on – the CASMIN project (see also Kurz and Müller 1987,

Lüttinger 1988, Müller et al. 1989, König 1990, Müller and Karle 1993, Müller and Haun 1994, Ishida et al. 1995).

The central role that the University of Mannheim has played in the international research effort associated with CASMIN was further strengthened by the foundation of the MZES in 1989. Already heavily involved in the founding process, Walter Müller was director of the research areas on »Social Structure and the Welfare State« (1990–1992, 1996–1999) and on »European Societies and their Integration« (1999–2002) as well as MZES Director (2002–2005). Several comparative research projects initiated and led by Walter Müller have been carried out over the years, the most important probably being »Educational Expansion and Social Reproduction in Europe« (Shavit and Müller 1998, Brauns 1998, Brauns et al. 1999, Steinmann 2000, Scherer 2004), »Labour Market Processes and Structural Change« (Gangl 2003b), »Comparative Analysis of Transitions from Education to Work in Europe« (Müller and Gangl 2003, Müller 2005), »Socio-Economic Development of Self-Employment in Europe« (Arum and Müller 2004) and the ongoing project on »Social Selectivity in Tertiary Education and Labour Market and Stratification Outcomes« (Mayer et al. forthcoming, Müller and Pollak 2004b). For his analysis of class patterns in voting behaviour, he was awarded the Fritz Thyssen Award for the best paper in German (Müller 1998b). In recent years, several new collaborators have appeared, among them contributors to our volume: Walter Müller has worked with Irena Kogan on educational systems and labour markets in Central and Eastern Europe, with Frank Kalter and Cornelia Kristen on longitudinal studies for education reports (Kristen et al. 2005), and with Stephanie Steinmetz on women's labour market participation and sex-specific occupational segregation in Europe.

For his pioneering work on the international comparison of educational systems, the measurement of educational qualifications, and the role of education for individual life chances and social mobility, Walter Müller was awarded honorary doctorates from Stockholm University in 2004 and from the University of Bern in 2006. His longstanding research efforts being crowned with these degrees, we should not overlook his merits in two other fields. Since the early 1970s, Walter Müller has been very successful in improving the cooperation between sociological research and official statistics agencies, making large-scale data sets like the micro-census available for scientific use (Müller et al. 1991, Kommission zur Verbesserung der informationellen Infrastruktur zwischen Wissenschaft und Statistik

2001). Not surprisingly, he wrote the introductory chapter of the first edition of the biennial Datenreport, a sociological data handbook addressed to scientific researchers, but even more so to the general public (Müller 1983). Secondly, both personally and also on behalf of hundreds of others, we wish to emphasize Walter Müller's merits for teaching several cohorts of undergraduate and graduate students in sociology, sociological research methods, and statistics. Today, former students of the »Müller school« are to be found in many social research institutes, market research departments, and official statistics offices in Germany and abroad. The high level of his teaching and the resulting quality of empirically oriented seminar papers and diploma theses led Walter Müller to the quite unique idea to edit a book on social inequality consisting exclusively of contributions of his current graduate students (Müller 1997). In fact, three of us – Stefani Scherer, Gunnar Otte and Markus Gangl – started their scientific career with a publication in this volume.

Although Walter Müller has now formally reached retirement status, he continues to direct, co-ordinate, stimulate and initiate multiple research projects and networks. As sociologists, we can happily say that he has only arrived at a ›preliminary‹ destination. We are very much looking forward to continuing our fruitful collaboration with him, and we are curious to learn about his prospective research in the fields of social mobility and social stratification.

References

Arum, R. (1997). »Trends in male and female self-employment: growth in a new middle class or increasing marginalization of the labor force«, *Research in Social Stratification and Mobility*, vol. 15, pp. 209–238.

Arum, R./Müller, W. (eds.) (2004). *The Reemergence of Self-Employment. A Comparative Study of Self-Employment Dynamics and Social Inequality*, Princeton: Princeton University Press.

Baumert, J./Stanat, P./Watermann, R. (eds.) (2006). *Herkunftsbedingte Disparitäten im Bildungswesen. Differenzielle Bildungsprozesse und Probleme der Verteilungsgerechtigkeit. Vertiefende Analysen im Rahmen von PISA 2000*, Wiesbaden: VS Verlag für Sozialwissenschaften.

Beck, U./Grande, E. (2004). *Das kosmopolitische Europa*, Frankfurt/Main: Suhrkamp.

Becker, G. S. (1964). *Human Capital. A Theoretical and Empirical Analysis with Special Reference to Education*, New York: Columbia University Press.

Becker, R. (2003). »Educational expansion and persistent inequalities of education. Utilizing subjective expected utility theory to explain increasing participation rates in upper secondary school in the Federal Republic of Germany«, *European Sociological Review*, vol. 19, pp. 1–24.

Blau, P. M./Duncan, O. D. (1967). *The American Occupational Structure*, New York: Wiley.

Blossfeld, H.-P. (1985). *Bildungsexpansion und Berufschancen. Empirische Analysen zur Lage der Berufsanfänger in der Bundesrepublik*, Frankfurt/Main: Campus.

Bolte, K. M. (1959). *Sozialer Aufstieg und Abstieg. Eine Untersuchung über Berufsprestige und Berufsmobilität*, Stuttgart: Enke.

Boudon, R. (1974). *Education, Opportunity and Social Inequality*, New York: Wiley.

Bourdieu, P./Passeron, J.-C. (1977). *Reproduction in Education, Society and Culture*, London: Sage.

Braun, M./Müller, W. (1997). »Measurement of education in comparative research«, *Comparative Social Research*, vol. 16, pp. 163–201.

Brauns, H. (1998). *Bildung in Frankreich. Eine Studie zum Wandel herkunfts- und geschlechtsspezifischen Bildungsverhaltens*, Opladen: Leske + Budrich.

Brauns, H./Müller, W./Steinmann, S. (1997). *Educational expansion and returns to education. A comparative study on Germany, France, the UK, and Hungary*, MZES Working Paper, Research Department I, vol. 23, Mannheim: Mannheim Centre for European Social Research.

Brauns, H./Steinmann, S./Kieffer, A./Marry, C. (1999). »Does education matter? France and Germany in comparative perspective«, *European Sociological Review*, vol. 15, pp. 61–89.

Brauns, H./Steinmann, S./Haun, D. (2000). »Die Konstruktion des Klassenschemas nach Erikson, Goldthorpe und Portocarero (EGP) am Beispiel nationaler Datenquellen aus Deutschland, Frankreich und Großbritannien«, *ZUMA-Nachrichten*, vol. 46, pp. 7–42.

Brauns, H./Scherer, S./Steinmann, S. (2003). »The CASMIN educational classification in international comparative research«, in: J. H. P. Hoffmeyer-Zlotnik/C. Wolf (eds.), *Advances in Cross-National Comparison. A European Working Book for Demographic and Socio-Economic Variables*, Amsterdam: Springer, pp. 196–221.

Breen, R. (ed.) (2004). *Social Mobility in Europe*, Oxford: Oxford University Press.

Breen, R./Goldthorpe J. H. (1997). »Explaining educational differentials: towards a formal rational action theory«, *Rationality and Society*, vol. 9, pp. 275–305.

Breen, R./Goldthorpe, J. H. (2001). »Class, mobility and merit: the experience of two British birth cohorts«, *European Sociological Review*, vol. 17, pp. 81–101.

Breen, R./Jonsson, J. O. (forthcoming). »Explaining change in social fluidity: educational equalization and educational expansion in twentieth century Sweden«, *American Journal of Sociology*, vol. 112, no. 4.

Breen, R./Luijkx, R. (2004). »Social mobility in Europe between 1970 and 2000«, in R. Breen (ed.), *Social Mobility in Europe*, Oxford: Oxford University Press, pp. 37–75.

Breen, R./Luijkx, R./Müller, W./Pollak, R. (2005). *Non-Persistent Inequality in Educational Attainment: Evidence from Eight European Countries*, Paper presented at the meeting of the ISA Research Committee on Social Stratification and Mobility, Los Angeles (USA).

Breen, R./Yaish, M. (2006). »Testing the Breen-Goldthorpe model of educational decision making«, in S. L. Morgan/D. B. Grusky/G. S. Fields (eds.), *Mobility and Inequality: Frontiers of Research in Sociology and Economics*, Stanford: Stanford University Press, pp. 232–258.

Carlsson, G. (1958). *Social Mobility and Class Structure*, Lund: Gleerup.

Charles, M./Grusky, D. B. (2004). *Occupational Ghettos. The Worldwide Segregation of Women and Men*, Stanford: Stanford University Press.

de Graaf, N. D./de Graaf, P. M./Kraaykamp, G. (2000). »Parental cultural capital and educational attainment in the Netherlands: a refinement of the cultural capital perspective«, *Sociology of Education*, vol. 73, pp. 92–111.

DiPrete, T. A./Grusky, D. B. (1990). »Structure and trend in the process of stratification for American men and women«, *American Journal of Sociology*, vol. 96, pp. 107–143.

Dunlop, J. T. et al. (1975). *Industrialism and Industrial Man Reconsidered. Some Perspectives on a Study over Two Decades of the Problems of Labor and Management in Economic Growth*. Final Report of the Inter-University Study of Labor Problems in Economic Development, Princeton: Inter-University Study of Human Resources in National Development.

Erikson, R./Goldthorpe, J. H. (1992). *The Constant Flux. A Study of Class Mobility in Industrial Societies*, Oxford: Clarendon.

Erikson, R./Jonsson, J. O. (1996a). »Explaining class inequality in education: the Swedish test case« in R. Erikson/J. O. Jonsson (eds.), *Can Education be Equalized? Sweden in a Comparative Perspective*, Boulder, Col.: Westview Press, pp. 1–63.

Erikson, R./Jonsson, J. O. (eds.) (1996b). *Can Education be Equalized? Sweden in a Comparative Perspective*, Boulder, Col.: Westview Press.

Featherman, D. L./Jones, F. L./Hauser, R. M. (1975). »Assumptions of social mobility research in the U.S.: the case of occupational status«, *Social Science Research*, vol. 4, pp. 329–360.

Gangl, M. (2003a). »The structure of labour market entry in Europe: a typological analysis«, in W. Müller/M. Gangl (eds.), *Transition from Education to Work in Europe. The Integration of Youth into EU Labour Markets*, Oxford: Oxford University Press, pp. 107–128.

Gangl, M. (2003b). *Unemployment Dynamics in the United States and West Germany: Economic Restructuring, Institutions and Labor Market Processes*, Heidelberg: Physica.

Ganzeboom H. B. G./Kreidl, M./Treiman, D. J. (2005). *Trends in Occupational Returns to Education*. Paper presented at the meeting of the ISA Research Committee on Social Stratification and Mobility, Los Angeles (USA).

Ganzeboom, H. B. G./Luijkx, R./Treiman, D. J. (1989). »Intergenerational class mobility in comparative perspective«, *Research in Social Stratification and Mobility*, vol. 8, pp. 3–84.

Glatzer, W./Zapf, W. (eds.) (1984). *Lebensqualität in der Bundesrepublik. Objektive Lebensbedingungen und subjektives Wohlbefinden*, Frankfurt/Main: Campus.

Goldthorpe, J. H. (2007). *On Sociology. Volume 2* (2nd edition), Stanford: Stanford University Press.

Goodman, L. A. (1969). »How to ransack social mobility tables and other kinds of cross-classification tables«, *American Journal of Sociology*, vol. 75, pp. 1–40.

Granato, N./Kalter, F. (2001). »Die Persistenz ethnischer Ungleichheit auf dem deutschen Arbeitsmarkt. Diskriminierung oder Unterinvestition in Humankapital?«, *Kölner Zeitschrift für Soziologie und Sozialpsychologie*, vol. 53, pp. 497–520.

Hakim, C. (1996). »Labour mobility and employment stability: rhetoric and reality on the sex differential in labour-market behaviour«, *European Sociological Review*, vol. 12, pp. 1-31.

Halsey, A. H./Heath, A. F./Ridge, J. M. (1980). *Origins and Destinations. Family, Class, and Education in Modern Britain*, Oxford: Clarendon Press.

Handl, J. (1988). *Berufschancen und Heiratsmuster von Frauen. Empirische Untersuchungen zu Prozessen sozialer Mobilität*, Frankfurt/Main: Campus.

Handl, J. (1996). »Hat sich die berufliche Wertigkeit der Bildungsabschlüsse in den achtziger Jahren verringert? Eine Analyse der abhängig erwerbstätigen, deutschen Berufsanfänger auf der Basis von Mikrozensusergebnissen«, *Kölner Zeitschrift für Soziologie und Sozialpsychologie*, vol. 48, pp. 249–273.

Handl, J./Mayer, K. U./Müller, W. (1977). *Klassenlagen und Sozialstruktur. Empirische Untersuchungen für die Bundesrepublik Deutschland*, Frankfurt/Main: Campus.

Ishida, H./Müller, W./Ridge, J. (1995). »Class origin, class destination and education: a cross-national study of ten industrial nations«, *American Journal of Sociology*, vol. 101, pp. 145–193.

Jackson, M./Erikson, R./Goldthorpe, J. H./Yaish, M. (2006). *Primary and Secondary Effects in Class Differentials in Educational Attainment: the Transition to A-Level Courses in England and Wales*. Unpublished Manuscript.

Jackson, M./Goldthorpe, J. H./Mills, C. (2005). »Education, employers and class mobility«, *Research in Social Stratification and Mobility*, vol. 23, pp. 3–34.

Jacobs, J. A. (1993). »Theoretical and measurement issues in the study of sex segregation in the workplace: research notes«, *European Sociological Review*, vol. 9, no. 3, pp. 325–330.

Jonsson, J. O. (1996). »Stratification in post-industrial society: Are educational qualifications of growing importance?« in R. Erikson/J. O. Jonsson (eds.), *Can Education be Equalized? Sweden in a Comparative Perspective*, Boulder, Col.: Westview Press, pp. 113–144.

Jonsson, J. O./Grusky, D. B./Di Carlo, M./Pollak, R./Brinton, M. C. (forthcoming). *Micro-Class Mobility – Social Reproduction in Four Countries*, MZES Working Paper, Mannheim: Mannheim Centre for European Social Research.

Jonsson, J. O./Mills, C. (1993). »Social mobility in the 1970s and 1980s: a study of men and women in England and Sweden«, *European Sociological Review*, vol. 9, pp. 229–248.

Jonsson, J. O./Mills, C./Müller, W. (1996). »Half a century of increasing educational openness? Social class, gender and educational attainment in Sweden, Germany and Britain« in R. Erikson/J. O. Jonsson (eds.), *Can Education be Equalized? Sweden in a Comparative Perspective*, Boulder, Col.: Westview Press, pp. 183–206.

Kerr, C. et al. (1960). *Industrialism and Industrial Man. The Problems of Labor and Management in Economic Growth*, Cambridge, Mass.: Harvard University Press.

Kleining, G. (1971). »Struktur- und Prestigemobilität in der Bundesrepublik Deutschland«, *Kölner Zeitschrift für Soziologie und Sozialpsychologie*, vol. 23, pp. 1–33.

König, W. (1990). *Berufliche Mobilität in Deutschland und Frankreich: Konsequenzen von Bildungs- und Beschäftigungssystemen für Frauen und Männer 1965–1970*, Frankfurt/Main: Campus.

Kogan, I./Müller, W. (eds.) (2003). *School-to-Work Transitions in Europe: Analyses of the EU LFS 2000 Ad Hoc Module*, Mannheim: Mannheim Centre for European Social Research.

Kogan, I./Schubert, F. (2003). »Youth transitions from education to working life in Europe: a general overview«, in I. Kogan/W. Müller (eds.), *School-to-Work Transitions in Europe: Analyses of the EU LFS 2000 Ad Hoc Module*, Mannheim: Mannheim Centre for European Social Research.

Kommission zur Verbesserung der informationellen Infrastruktur zwischen Wissenschaft und Statistik (2001). *Wege zu einer besseren informationellen Infrastruktur. Gutachten der vom Bundesministerium für Bildung und Forschung eingesetzten Kommission zur Verbesserung der informationellen Infrastruktur zwischen Wissenschaft und Statistik*, Baden-Baden: Nomos.

Korupp, S. E./Ganzeboom, H. B. G./Van der Lippe, T. (2002). »Do mothers matter? A comparison of models of the influence of mothers' and fathers' educational and occupational status on children's educational attainment«, *Quality and Quantity*, vol. 36, no. 1, pp. 17–42.

Kristen, C./Römmer, A./Müller, W./Kalter, F. (2005). *Longitudinal Studies for Education Reports: European and North American Examples. Report commissioned by the Federal Ministry of Education and Research* (Education Reform, vol. 10), Berlin: Federal Ministry of Education and Research (BMBF).

Kuo, H.-H. D./Hauser, R. M. (1995). »Trends in family effects on the education of black and white brothers«, *Sociology of Education*, vol. 68, no. 2, pp. 136–160.

Kurz, K./Müller, W. (1987). »Class mobility in the industrial world«, *Annual Review of Sociology*, vol. 13, pp. 417–442.

Lipset, S. M./Zetterberg, H. L. (1959): »Social mobility in industrial societies«, in S. M. Lipset/R. Bendix (eds.), *Social Mobility in Industrial Society*, Berkeley: University of California Press.

Lüttinger, P. (1988). *Integration der Vertriebenen. Eine empirische Analyse*, Frankfurt/Main: Campus.

Mannheim, K. (1952). »'The problem of generations«, in P. Kecskeméti (ed.), *Essays on the Sociology of Knowledge*, London: Routledge and Kegan Paul, pp. 276–322.

Marsden, D. (1990). »Institutions and labour mobility: occupational and internal labour markets in Britain, France, Italy and West Germany«, in R. Brunetta/C. Dell'Aringa (eds.), *Labour Relations and Economic Performance*, Houndmills: Macmillan, pp. 414–438.

Mayer, K. U. (1990). »Lebensverläufe und sozialer Wandel. Anmerkungen zu einem Forschungsprogramm«, in K. U. Mayer (ed.), *Lebensverläufe und sozialer Wandel. Kölner Zeitschrift für Soziologie und Sozialpsychologie Sonderheft 31*, pp. 7–21.

Mayer, K. U. (forthcoming). »Retrospective Longitudinal Research: The German Life History Study«, in S. Menard (ed.), *Handbook of Longitudinal Research: Design, Measurement and Analysis*, San Diego: Elsevier.

Mayer, K. U./Müller, W. (1971a). »Progress in social mobility research? Some comments on mobility analysis and new data on intergenerational mobility in West-Germany«, *Quality and Quantity*, vol. 5, no. 1, pp. 141–178.

Mayer, K. U./Müller, W. (1971b). »Trendanalysen in der Mobilitätsforschung – Eine Replik auf Gerhard Kleinings ›Struktur- und Prestigemobilität in der Bundesrepublik Deutschland‹«, *Kölner Zeitschrift für Soziologie und Sozialpsychologie*, vol. 23, no. 4, pp. 761–788.

Mayer, K. U./Müller, W./Pollak, R. (forthcoming). Institutional Change and Inequalities of Access in German Higher Education, in Y. Shavit et al. (eds.): *Stratification in Higher Education: A Comparative Study*, Stanford, Cal.: Stanford University Press.

Miller, R. (1998). »The limited concerns of social mobility research«, *Current Sociology*, vol. 46, pp. 145–163.

Morgan, S. L./Grusky, D. B./Fields, G. S. (eds.) (2006). *Mobility and Inequality: Frontiers of Research in Sociology and Economics*, Stanford: Stanford University Press.

Müller, W. (1972). »Bildung und Mobilitätsprozeß – Eine Anwendung der Pfadanalyse«, *Zeitschrift für Soziologie*, vol. 1, pp. 65–84.

Müller, W. (1975). *Familie, Schule, Beruf: Analysen zur sozialen Mobilität und Statuszuweisung in der Bundesrepublik*, Opladen: Westdeutscher Verlag.

Müller, W. (1978). *Klassenlage und Lebenslauf: Untersuchung zu Prozessen sozialstrukturellen Wandels in der Bundesrepublik Deutschland* (Habilitationsschrift), Mannheim: University of Mannheim, Faculty of Social Sciences.

Müller, W. (1983). »Gesellschaftliche Daten – Wissen für die Politik«, in: Federal Statistical Office (ed.), *Datenreport. Zahlen und Fakten über die Bundesrepublik Deutschland*, Bonn: Schriftenreihe der Bundeszentrale für Politische Bildung, pp. 17–31.

Müller, W. (ed.) (1997). *Soziale Ungleichheit. Neue Befunde zu Strukturen, Bewußtsein und Politik*, Opladen: Leske + Budrich.

Müller, W. (1998a). »Erwartete und unerwartete Folgen der Bildungsexpansion«, in *Kölner Zeitschrift für Soziologie und Sozialpsychologie*, special issue 38, pp. 81–112.

Müller, W. (1998b). »Klassenstruktur und Parteiensystem: Zum Wandel der Klassenspaltung im Wahlverhalten«, *Kölner Zeitschrift für Soziologie und Sozialpsychologie*, vol. 50, pp. 3–47.

Müller, W. (2005). »Education and youth integration into European labour markets«, *International Journal of Comparative Sociology*, vol. 46, no. 5–6, pp. 461–485.

Müller, W./Blien, U./Knoche, P./Wirth, H. (1991). *Die faktische Anonymität von Mikrodaten*, Stuttgart: Metzler/Poeschel.

Müller, W./Brauns, H./Steinmann, S. (2002), »Expansion und Erträge tertiärer Bildung in Deutschland, Frankreich und im Vereinigten Königreich«, *Berliner Journal für Soziologie*, vol. 12, pp. 37–62.

Müller, W./Gangl M. (2003). *Transition from Education to Work in Europe. The Integration of Youth into EU Labour Markets*, Oxford: Oxford University Press.

Müller, W./Haun, D. (1994). »Bildungsungleichheit im sozialen Wandel«, *Kölner Zeitschrift für Soziologie und Sozialpsychologie*, vol. 46, no. 1, pp. 1–42.

Müller, W./Karle, W. (1993). »Social selection in educational systems in Europe«, *European Sociological Review*, vol. 9, no. 1, pp. 1–22.

Müller, W./Karle, W./König, W./Lüttinger, P. (1989). »Class and education in industrial nations«, *International Journal of Sociology*, vol. 19, no. 3, pp. 3–39.

Müller, W./Pollak, R. (2004a). »Social mobility in West Germany: the long arms of history discovered?«, in R. Breen (ed.), *Social Mobility in Europe*, Oxford: Oxford University Press, pp. 77–113.

Müller, W./Pollak, R. (2004b). »Weshalb gibt es so wenige Arbeiterkinder in Deutschlands Universitäten?«, in R. Becker/W. Lauterbach (eds.): *Bildung als Privileg? Erklärungen und Befunde zu den Ursachen der Bildungsungleichheit*, Wiesbaden: VS Verlag für Sozialwissenschaften, pp. 311–352.

Müller, W./Shavit, Y. (1998). »The institutional embeddedness of the stratification process: a comparative study of qualifications and occupations in thirteen countries«, in Y. Shavit/W. Müller (eds.), *From School to Work. A Comparative Study of Educational Qualifications and Occupational Destinations*, Oxford: Clarendon Press, pp. 1–48.

Müller, W./Willms, A./Handl, J. (eds.) (1983). *Strukturwandel der Frauenarbeit 1880–1980*, Frankfurt/Main: Campus.

Organisation for Economic Cooperation and Development (OECD) (2000). *The Partial Renaissance of Self-Employment* (OECD Employment Outlook), Paris: OECD.

Pappi, F. U. (ed.) (1979). *Sozialstrukturanalysen mit Umfragedaten. Probleme der standardisierten Erfassung von Hintergrundsmerkmalen in allgemeinen Bevölkerungsumfragen*, Königstein/Taunus: Athenäum.

Petersen, T./Morgan, L. (1995). »Separate and unequal: occupation-establishment sex segregation and the gender wage gap«, *American Journal of Sociology*, vol. 101, no. 2, pp. 329–365.

Rijken, S. (1999). *Educational Expansion and Status Attainment. a Cross-National and Over-Time Comparison*, Amsterdam: Thela Thesis (ICS dissertation).

Scherer, S. (2004). *Erwerbseintritt und Berufsverlauf. Westdeutschland, Italien und Großbritannien im Vergleich*, Frankfurt/Main: Lang.

Shavit, Y./Blossfeld, H.-P. (eds.) (1993). *Persistent Inequality: Changing Educational Attainment in Thirteen Countries*, Boulder, Col.: Westview Press.

Shavit, Y./Müller, W. (eds.) (1998). *From School to Work: A Comparative Study of Educational Qualifications and Occupational Destinations*, Oxford: Oxford University Press.

Shavit, Y./Westerbeek, K. 1998. »Educational stratification in Italy: reforms, expansion, and equality of opportunity«, *European Sociological Review*, vol. 14, pp. 33–47.

Solon, G. (2002). »Cross-country differences in intergenerational earnings mobility«, *Journal of Economic Perspectives*, vol. 16, pp. 59–66.

Spence, M. (1973). »Job market signalling«, *Quarterly Journal of Economics*, vol. 87, pp. 355–374.

Steinmann, S. (2000). *Bildung, Ausbildung und Arbeitsmarktchancen in Deutschland. Eine Studie zum Wandel der Übergänge von der Schule in das Erwerbsleben*, Opladen: Leske + Budrich.

Stocké, V. (forthcoming). »Explaining educational decision and effects of families? Social class position. An empirical test of the Breen-Goldthorpe model of educational attainment«, *European Sociological Review*.

Sullivan, A. (2001). »Cultural capital and educational attainment«, *Sociology*, vol. 35, pp. 893–912.

Svalastoga, K. (1959). *Class, Prestige and Mobility*, Copenhagen: Gyldendal.

Treiman, D. J. (1970). »Industrialization and social stratification«, in: E. O. Laumann (ed.), *Social Stratification: Research and Theory for the 1970s*, Indianapolis: Bobbs-Merrill, pp. 207–234.

Treiman, D. J./Yip, K.-B. (1989). »Educational and occupational attainment in 21 countries«, in M. L. Kohn (ed.), *Cross-National Research in Sociology*, Newbury Park: Sage, pp. 373–394.

Vallet, L.-A. (1999). »Quarante années de mobilité sociale en France«, *Revue Française de Sociologie*, vol. 40, pp. 5–64.

Vallet, L.-A. (2004). »Change in intergenerational class mobility in France from the 1970s to the 1990s and its explanation: an analysis following the CASMIN approach«, in R. Breen (ed.), *Social Mobility in Europe*, Oxford: Oxford University Press, pp. 115–147.

Zapf, W. (ed.) (1977). *Lebensbedingungen in der Bundesrepublik. Sozialer Wandel und Wohlfahrtsentwicklung*, Frankfurt/Main: Campus.

I. Trends and mechanisms in educational inequality and social mobility

The persistence of persistent inequality[1]

Yossi Shavit, Meir Yaish, and Eyal Bar-Haim

Education in the stratification process

Sociologists view education as the pivot in the process of social stratification in economically advanced societies. While educational attainment is largely determined by the characteristics of people's social origins, it is, in turn, an important determinant of their subsequent life chances – their occupational and economic attainments as well as their health and longevity. Education can be seen as a double-edged sword in the stratification process. On the one hand, it is an important avenue for social mobility for men and women raised in the lower social strata who can not inherit privilege. On the other hand, education contributes to the transmission of inequality between generations since it is unequally distributed between strata. Which of these factors outweighs the other depends on the extent to which educational attainment is affected by social origins. Therefore, a central empirical question in the field of social stratification and mobility is the extent to which the association between social origins and education has declined or increased over time.

Scholars studying processes of educational attainment draw somewhat different conclusions regarding change in inequality of educational opportunity (IEO) over time. Some interpret the data to suggest that IEO has been rather persistent over time while others claim that it has declined. In this chapter, we review the comparative empirical literature on stability and change in IEO between individuals raised in different social strata in an attempt to identify the underpinnings of disagreements in this debate.

We begin with a very brief review of theoretical arguments concerning educational stratification between social strata. This is followed by an

1 We thank Hanna Ayalon, Louis-André Vallet, Reinhard Pollak, Gunnar Otte, Dan Scheinberg, Yariv Feniger, Limor Gabay-Egozi, Carmel Blank and Rinat Arbiv-Elyashiv for comments on an earlier draft of this paper.

equally brief discussion of theoretical arguments for and against the expectation that IEO would decline over time. We then review the main methodological approaches to the study of change in educational stratification: traditional OLS regressions; Mare's model of educational transitions; and log linear models of the association between people's social origins and their educational attainment. We conclude with a discussion of the effects of educational expansion on educational inequality, and of the present status of the hypothesis that inequality between strata in educational attainment persists over time.

Our review of the literature favours a weak version of the hypothesis of persistent inequality. Allowing for declining inequalities between social strata with respect to the odds of completing lower educational levels, and for declining inequalities in the middle of the twentieth century – which may be explained by period effects – inequality of educational opportunity is fairly resilient to change in most countries for which data is available. This is especially true if social origin is indicated by parental education rather than by father's class.

Why IEO between social strata?

Mass education is inherently unequal. Students are tested and graded, they are sorted into stratified tracks and curricular programs, and are labelled as more or less able. Educational systems stratify because it is in the interest of educational institutions to do so. Employers expect the educational system to sort, select and label because they rely on credentials to filter able and diligent workers (e.g. Thurow 1975, Bills 1992). Employers would not value credentials that did not convey these signals and so schools that want their credentials to carry value in the labour market are under pressure to sort and select (Rosenbaum et al. 1990). Professional organizations support selectivity in the educational system because it helps them maintain closure over their privileged positions (Collins 1979, Parkin 1979). Teachers and administrators of educational systems favour educational selection because it enhances their own prestige and power as gatekeepers (Apple 1990).

Given that mass education is inherently unequal, the question remains: why are there prevalent differences between social strata in the educational attainment of their children? The factors which mediate intergenerational transmission of IEO between strata are now well understood and include: economic and cultural resources, significant others' influences and the availability of educated role models. Educational inequality between strata is also affected by students' track placement and the curriculum that is offered in schools. When educational systems offer distinct tracks or curricular programs, track placement – and ultimately educational attainment – can be also affected by choice.[2] We now briefly discuss these factors in turn.

Economic resources: Clearly, high income families can afford the costs of education and can enable their children to stay in school longer. Research also shows that family income is linked to children's cognitive development. Family income in childhood has a stronger effect on educational attainment at the secondary level than does contemporaneous family income (Duncan et al. 1998). This suggests that the effect of family income on educational attainment is mediated by developmental processes rather than simply the ability to afford the costs of schooling. As Duncan and associates point out, preschool ability sets the stage for subsequent educational achievements, and children raised in poverty are less likely to develop the cognitive skills necessary for educational success.

Cultural resources: Children who are raised by educated parents internalize at home cultural codes of the dominant culture which is prevalent in schools. This provides them with an advantage in the educational attainment process over children whose parents mainly use different cultural codes (Bourdieu 1977). Recently, scholars (de Graaf et al. 2000) found that the main component of cultural resources that affects educational achievement is not high brow cultural codes, but rather children's exposure to reading and books, which are more prevalent in the upper strata.

---

2 In recent years scholars cast these factors within the theoretical framework initially proposed by Boudon (1974), and distinguished between primary and secondary effects on education (cf. Erikson and Jonsson 1996; Breen and Goldthorpe 1997). Primary effects are those that affect academic performance, while secondary effects are expressed via educational choices, given academic performance. The attraction of this approach is that it attributes to agents – through their actions – some of the inequality in education. However, it is not entirely clear how each of the determinants of educational inequality listed above can be classified into either a primary or secondary effect. For example, as we note below, economic resources exercise both a primary effect on children's cognitive development, and a secondary on students' educational choices through their evaluations of the costs of educational alternatives.

Significant others' influences: Students' social origin and their scholastic performance determine how much encouragement students receive from significant others (teachers, peers, and parents) regarding their future educational and occupational aspirations. These aspirations, in turn, affect students' ultimate educational attainment (Sewell and Hauser 1975). Significant others also constitute role models for children to emulate. Students raised in the privileged strata are more often exposed to educated role models than those raised in less affluent homes by less well educated parents.

Track placement: In all educational systems students are placed in distinct tracks or curricular programs. In some cases, curricular differentiation begins early in the educational trajectory while in others it only takes place at the level of higher education. At the secondary level, the most common distinction is between the academic tracks that prepare students for higher education and those tracks that prepare them for immediate entry into the labour force. Track placement is determined largely by the students' prior achievements (and choice, see discussion in the next section). But because student achievements are correlated with their socioeconomic origins, especially with parents' educational attainment, students from less privileged strata are more likely to proceed on non-academic tracks. Track placement, in turn, affects their subsequent educational attainment and magnifies inequality between social strata in subsequent attainments (Shavit 1984, Gamoran and Mare 1989, Kerckhoff 1993).

Incentives and educational choice: Breen and Goldthorpe (1997) argue that children's educational plans are shaped by forward looking rational calculus.[3] Accordingly, students and their families weigh the costs of alternative educational options (i.e. tracks and curricular programs), the benefits that may accrue, and the expected probability of success in each. Among the benefits, students and their families are said to put special emphasis on the maintenance of their class position. In other words, they desire to attain a class position commensurate with that of their parents. Although all social classes share this motivation, its implications differ. For middle class children it implies the choice of demanding and risky educational options, be-

---

3 Interestingly, only after Breen and Goldthorpe recognized that temporal variations in IEO are minimal did they move to develop a rational action theory of educational choice to explain why such inequality persists. Our main concern in this chapter is to ascertain whether educational inequality in fact persists over time or has declined, as Breen et al. (2005) and others now argue.

cause other routes do not lead to high status occupations. Conversely, working class children tend to choose less demanding educational options because they suffice for the attainment of working class occupations.

Should we expect IEO to decline over time?

It is important to note at the outset that most studies of change in educational stratification do not directly measure all the factors mentioned above. More relevant to our discussion on the association between social origins and education, however, is the standard practice in this field to represent social origins by measures of parental occupational status (e.g. SEI or class) and their education. The former is assumed to register the economic circumstances of a family, including their ability to bear the expected costs associated with alternative educational options, while the latter is assumed to relate to cultural capital, scholastic aptitude and significant others' influences on educational expectations, on track placement and on educational choices. Studies that adopt this practice show that the effect of parental education on educational attainment tends to be much larger than that of the father's occupation (e.g. Hout et al. 1993, de Graaf and Ganzeboom 1993, de Graaf et al. 2000, Buchmann et al. 1993, Tsai and Chiu 1993, Treiman and Yamaguchi 1993, Szelényi and Aschaffenburg 1993), and as we shall suggest, it is also more resistant to change over time.

Having made these preliminary but necessary clarifications, we can move to present arguments for and against the hypothesis that the effects of origins – economic and cultural – on education have declined over time.

Declining economic barriers to educational attainment

Theory and earlier research suggest that the economic barriers to education have declined in the post-WW II era in economically advanced societies. Economic development and the redistributive policies of the welfare state have improved the *economic condition* of the working class. This, in turn, reduced inequality between social classes in health and nutrition (Erikson and Jonsson 1996) which affect children's scholastic performance. It also enabled more working class families to bear the direct and indirect costs of education (Breen et al. 2005). Furthermore, the direct *costs of education* have declined over time as tuition fees have been reduced and scholarships for disadvantaged students have become increasingly available. The beneficial consequences of rising living conditions and the decline in the costs of education are hypothesized to be most pronounced in social-democratic welfare states where education has been decommodified to a greater extent than in liberal or conservative welfare regimes (Esping-Andersen 1999).

In addition, Breen et al. argue that, with the decline of farming and the transformation of the economy from production to services, education is perceived to be an important recruitment criterion for an increasing proportion of jobs. Many working class jobs now require secondary education. Therefore, working class children who seek to preserve their family class position must now attend a higher level of education than their parents. Thus, there is reason to expect declining effects on educational attainment of both family income and of fathers' class position.

Declining cultural and cognitive barriers to educational attainment?

There is scant research on change in the effects of cultural resources on educational attainment over time (cf. Guesthuizen et al. 2005). Most studies interested in this issue employ reduced form models in which parental education is a proxy for cultural resources. These studies found that the effects of parental education on educational attainment are fairly stable over time. De Graaf and Ganzeboom (1993), who found declining effects of social origins on educational attainment in the Netherlands, also found that the effects of father's education are more resistant to change than the effects of father's occupation. A similar result was reported for France by Vallet (2004), who found that whether social origins is represented by parental class or parental education, its association with highest degree attained declined over time but »the results strongly suggest that cultural inequalities are more resistant to change than socioeconomic inequalities.« (p. 26). More recently, Pfeffer (2006) compared educational mobility processes in 20 industrialized nations and found persistent inequality during the 20th Century.

Models and measures of educational inequality

OLS regression models

Having discussed the main factors that comprise the educational stratification process and those which may have affected change in IEO over time, we now turn to a review of the three main models of educational attainment which sociologists use in their research. During the 1960s and 1970s most students of educational attainment employed ordinary least square (OLS) regressions (Blau and Duncan 1967, Jencks et al. 1972, Sewell and Hauser 1975). They measured education as the number of years of schooling attended or completed by their respondents, and assumed that it is affected additively and linearly by various aspects of social origins (e.g. father's education and occupation, family size, etc.). Within the OLS model, IEO is operationalized as the effects of social origins on years of schooling. This measure is equivalent to the arithmetic *difference* between the mean quantities of education that are attained by any two social strata.

Earlier American studies using the OLS model found very little change during the first half of the twentieth century in the mean educational differences between social strata, indicated by father's occupation and father's education (e.g. Hauser and Featherman 1976). Smith and Cheung (1986) analyzed data for the Philippines and found declining effects of social origins on educational attainment. In their comparative analysis of thirteen countries, Shavit and Blossfeld (1993) found mixed results: the effect of father's education declined in five countries and was stable in eight, while the effect of father's occupation declined in three countries and remained stable or increased in ten. Only in two countries (Sweden and the Netherlands) did the effects of both variables decline over time.

Mare's model of educational transitions

In the early 1980s, Mare (1981) observed that levels of educational attainment in the United States had increased dramatically and that their dispersion declined. In view of these developments one would have expected that educational inequality between social strata declined across cohorts, but as noted above, previous American studies using OLS regression reported persistent effects of social origins on educational attainment over time. Mare realized that there are two distinct aspects to educational stratification which are often confounded: the dispersion of formal schooling in the population (i.e. the variance of educational attainment) and the degree to which some groups are allocated more education than others, *given* the degree of dispersion.

Mare developed a model of educational stratification which purports to estimate effects of social origins on educational attainment that are free of the effects of dispersion. The model views the educational attainment process as a sequence of transition points at which students either continue to the next level or drop out. At each transition point, social origins affect the log odds (logit) of continuing to the next level, given that the previous level had been attained. The parameters of the transitions model provide the researcher with measures of social selection in education that are free of the overall distribution of educational attainment, namely free of educational expansion.

In the empirical part of his paper, Mare employs both OLS regressions of educational attainment and logit regressions of educational transitions. Using both models, Mare showed that during the 20th Century the effects of social origins (social selection) on educational continuation *increased* somewhat, but that educational expansion which reduced the variance of education *attenuated* inequality in total educational attainment. On balance, the OLS effects on educational attainment declined somewhat over time. Thus, expansion can compensate for persistent social selection in education. It can reduce differences between strata in educational attainment even when social selection persists. This is an important theoretical and policy implication of Mare's analysis.

Since its publication in the early 1980s, Mare's model of educational transitions has been replicated in a large number of studies yielding both similar and different results. Several applications of the model (e.g. Shavit and Kraus 1990, Shavit and Westerbeek 1998, Jonsson 1993, de Graaf and Ganzeboom 1993, Vallet 2004) find declining effects of social origins on the lower educational transitions, and stable or even increasing effects of social origins at higher transition points (e.g. Smith and Cheung 1986, eleven of the thirteen studies in Shavit and Bossfeld 1993, Torche 2005, Vallet 2004).

This pattern of results is consistent with Raftery and Hout's MMI (maximally maintained inequality) hypothesis which states that inequality between strata in the odds of attaining a given level of education persists unless the advantaged stratum reaches the point of saturation. Saturation is defined as the point at which all sons and daughters with advantaged origins attain the educational level under consideration. The advantaged group is typically better equipped to take advantage of any new and attractive educational opportunities, and inequalities will persist as opportunities are expanded. Only when the privileged group reach saturation at a given level of education would further expansions reduce inequality, because the privileged cannot increase their attendance rates past 100%. The effects of social origins declined at the lower levels of education because the privileged strata had reach saturation while the lower strata could still benefit from expansion. At upper levels of education neither stratum is saturated and thus expansion does not reduce inequalities

Studies employing the transitions model typically find that the effects of father's education and several other indicators of social origins decline across *transitions*. This regularity has been labelled the *waning* effects. Müller and Karle (1993) suggested that this waning effect reflects a decline with age of students' dependence on their parents. They noted that countries differ in educational survival patterns: in some countries students are selected at early transition points, where IEO is high, while in other countries attrition gradually filters out small proportions of the cohort at each transition. Interestingly, Müller and Karle find that national differences in IEO are correlated with differences among them in survival patterns. Where attrition is concentrated at early transition points it is more strongly affected by class origins than in countries where it is more evenly spread out.

It would be tempting to extend Müller and Karle's logic from the comparative to the longitudinal dimension, and to hypothesize that IEO would be reduced by expanding primary and lower secondary education. This is because in countries where IEO is relatively high at low levels of education the upper level is characterized by a relatively low level of IEO. Tempting as this hypothesis might be, it was not corroborated by empirical research. On the contrary, educational expansion of lower levels of education resulted in an increase in inequality at subsequent levels. Rijken (1999) studied differences between countries, and change across birth cohorts, in the parameters of the educational transition model. She showed that the effect of social origins on a given educational transition is related to the cohort proportion that is eligible for the transition. She concludes that educational expansion, as indicated by increases in cohort proportions that survive a transition can enhance inequality in the subsequent level.

The causal mechanisms that produce this result as well as the cause for the waning effects phenomenon are the subject of considerable controversy in the literature on educational stratification and are discussed further in the next section.

Critiques of Mare's model

Although standard in the study of educational stratification, Mare's model has been criticized on several grounds. The most common criticism, however, concerns unmeasured heterogeneity in the model.[4] According to this critic, both the waning effect phenomenon and the finding that social origins have persistent effects over time are artefacts of model misspecification. This point was first acknowledged by Mare himself (Mare 1981, 1993) and was later echoed by Rijken (1999), Cameron and Heckman (1998) and others. Put simply, it states that the effects of the observed variables on the odds of successive educational transitions are biased by their correlation with *un*observed variables. The obvious example is the correlation between parental education and respondent's scholastic ability. In the absence of controls for the latter, the effect of the former is upwardly biased. Furthermore, as the cohort is repeatedly selected on ability, only the very able students from all social backgrounds progress to higher educational levels. As a result of this selection process, the association between parental education and ability declines and the measured effect of the former wanes across transitions.

This criticism is closely related to the issue of change over time in the effects of social origins on educational transitions. As Mare himself noted

---

4 The model was criticized on two additional grounds. First, Cameron and Heckman (1998) point out that the scale of logit parameters is unidentifiable. The implication of this critique is that the coefficients are not comparable across equations, transitions and population samples. Mare accepts this critique but points out that »... in typical binary response models, the effects of the covariates on the binary response, as measured either by derivatives (when they exist) or the differences in predicted probabilities, *are* identified...« (Mare forthcoming). Second, Cameron and Heckman also criticized the model for its assumption of myopic rather than foresighted individuals. Sociologists would find this critic rather naïve because it implies that students (and their families) plan their educational careers well in advance and are able to realize their plans regardless of structural constraints. Lucas has convincingly countered this criticism by showing that the process of educational attainment is affected by exogenous and unexpected constraints such as failure and placement in lower tracks (2001).

(1981: fn. 5), a rise in the proportion of a cohort exposed to the risk of successive transitions (i.e. educational expansion), increases the heterogeneity of the risk set and the correlation between observed and unobserved variables. In other words, with educational expansion the apparent bias due to unmeasured heterogeneity increases IEO *across time* at each transition point.

In an often ignored paper, Mare (1993) sought to assess the magnitude of the bias in the net effect of father's education that is due to unmeasured heterogeneity of family factors. He employs brothers' educational attainment as a proxy for all family factors that might affect respondents' educational attainment and shows that controlling for this variable accounts for some, but not all, of the waning effect of father's education. However, the net effects of father's education on educational transitions in the United States remain quite stable and even increased slightly for cohorts born 1907–1951. This pattern is very similar to the pattern found in his original analysis.

Our view is that the unmeasured heterogeneity critique is over-rated. Like all other models, the educational transition model should be viewed as a reduced form which does not specify all the intervening variables in the causal chain. Critics typically think of ability and motivation as the most important unmeasured variables that bias the measured effects of social origins. However, these variables are largely endogenous to the stratification process and mediate the effects of social origins (Sewell and Hauser 1975). Rather than an artefact of unmeasured heterogeneity, we believe that waning effects correspond to a substantive selection process: if social selection in education is stringent early-on in the transition process, schools and universities need not select on the same variable later on. For example, university access in Germany is open to most gymnasium graduates because stringent selection into gymnasium is performed early on (from 4th grade and on). By contrast, in the United States, little cognitive selection is performed at the primary and secondary levels of education and the SAT (Scholastic Aptitude Test) sorts and selects students in the transition to college.

Log-linear models

Although Mare's model has been very popular in studies of educational stratification, some researchers advocate the use of log linear models for the analysis of the origin – education association and of changes therein. As Vallet (2004: 6) notes, Mare's model is useful for the study of specific educational transitions but in and of itself it is not an effective tool with which to assess the *overall* degree of association between social origins and final educational attainment. While OLS models are suited to this end, their estimates confound true association between origins and educational attainment with the effects of change in the distribution of education. Log-linear models, on the other hand, provide margin-free measures of the total origin-education association, and are becoming more popular in studies of educational stratification.

With Ishida and Ridge, Walter Müller (Ishida et al. 1995) studied the association between origins, education and class of destination in ten industrial societies. Their paper is among the first to model the origin – education association in a log-linear framework. The authors find strong origin – education associations in all countries, coupled with differences between them in the pattern of the association. Their most interesting result in this regard concerns the difference (or lack thereof) between socialist and other countries. Their data refute the hypothesis that in the former (Hungary and Poland) the association between origins and education was generally weaker than in market economies.

With Jonsson and Mills, Walter Müller (Jonsson et al. 1996) studied change in the association between social origins and gender on the one hand, and educational attainment on the other hand, for Sweden, Germany and Britain. As in the previous paper, social origins are represented by father's class alone. The authors employ data for cohorts born in 1910–1959 for Sweden, in 1916–1959 for Germany and in 1885–1959 for Britain, and use a log multiplicative model (Xie 1992) in which change in the origin-education association is scaled by a single parameter across cohorts.

For Sweden and Germany, but not for Britain, they find significant secular declining trend across cohorts in the association between class and education. However, the decline is very small, accounting for about 6 percent of the educational upgrading during the 50 years covered by their data (p. 196). Unfortunately, the authors do not identify the specific educational barriers which declined in Sweden and Germany.

In a recent paper, Müller and his associates (Breen et al. 2005) revisit Blossfeld and Shavit's claim that IEO is persistent over time in most industrialized countries. These authors studied changes over time in the origin – education association for male residents of eight European countries. Using large data sets for Britain, Germany, France, Italy, Ireland, Britain, Sweden, Poland and the Netherlands, they fit log-multiplicative models to a table of education by class-of-origin, by country, by cohort, by year-of-survey, and find that for all but two countries (Italy and Ireland), the origin – education association declined significantly across cohorts. Importantly however, the decline was not linear. Rather, it has taken place only in the years immediately following World War II. For cohorts born since then, the authors find persistent inequality.

Six of the countries in the study were also compared by Blossfeld and Shavit (Sweden, the Netherlands, Germany, Italy, Britain, and Poland) and Breen et al.'s results contradict Blossfeld and Shavit's conclusion for three (Germany, Britain and Poland). Breen and his associates suspect that the discrepancy between the two studies is due to the small samples employed by some of the original studies which were compared by Blossfeld and Shavit. Testing this hypothesis they show that with samples of the same size as those employed in the earlier study, there is a reasonable chance to accept the hypothesis of persistent inequality for Germany, Britain, Italy and Poland, but not for the two cases in which it was also rejected by Blossfeld and Shavit (Sweden and the Netherlands).

In a detailed study of change of IEO in France, Vallet fits a series of log linear, log multiplicative and logit models to very large data sets spanning cohorts born between 1908–1972, and addresses three main questions: (i) Did the origin – education association decline over time? (ii) Did the effects of social origins decline only at early transition points or did it decline at other transition points as well? (iii) Do the results depend on the variable used to represent social origins (fathers' class or parental education)? As we noted earlier, Vallet's results show a significant (but modest) weakening of the association between origins and highest education completed. Consistent with the MMI hypothesis, Vallet's logit analysis shows that the weakening association was due fully to a decline in the effects of social class on the conditional odds of successfully making the early educational transitions. The effects of class on later transition remained stable and even increased over time. Vallet also finds that the association between parental education and own education is more resilient to change than the association between father's class and own education. This result is extended and corroborated by Pfeffer (2006) whose log-linear analyses of the association between parental and respondents' education revealed no significant changes in the association over time in any of the 20 countries that he studied.

It is noteworthy that in France the decline in the origin – education association is also far from linear over time. It was fairly stable (or even increased somewhat) for cohorts born between 1908 and the late 1920s, declined sharply for those born between the late-1930s and the late 1940s, and declined only weakly thereafter. Vallet notes that the sharp decline was unrelated to the educational reforms of the 1950s which were intended to reduce IEO in France. A similar result is reported for Italy by Barone (2006), who found that the origin – education association under a log multiplicative model, declined for cohorts born during the 1930s and 1940s and increased thereafter. Thus, the declining inequality that was reported for European countries by Breen et al., Vallet, and Barone, occurred immediately after WW II and one wonders whether it is related to the resumption of normalcy and the implementation of the American Marshall Plan after WW II.[5]

Educational expansion and IEO

As we have seen, the effect of educational expansion on IEO is a central theme in studies of educational stratification. It is important to comprehend the role of expansion in shaping IEO because expansion is an important policy tool that governments use in attempts to reduce IEO between social strata. Yet, as we have seen, scholars working in the field are not

---

5 Recently, researchers are abandoning both the transition model and log linear models of educational attainment in favour of ordinal logit regressions (e. g., Cameron and Heckman 1998, Hout forthcoming, Ballarino and Schadee 2005). Log-linear and ordered logit models alike produce measures of association between social origins and education that net out distributional effects. Furthermore, both methods model total (unconditional) educational attainment. Ordered logit models are more parsimonious than log linear models because they assume that education is an ordered variable and that the odds involving neighbouring categories are similar up to a scalar. These assumptions are questionable, especially in educational systems which are differentiated both horizontally and vertically, as most systems are (König et al. 1988).

agreed about educational expansion. Some treat it as a nuisance which must be controlled when searching for measures of *true* change in IEO. Indeed, much of the methodological acrobatics we discussed has been motivated by the desire to produce measures of IEO that are expansion-free. Other scholars (e.g. Arum et al. forthcoming, Raftery and Hout 1993, Rijken 1999) treat expansion as a theoretically important component of the stratification process and seek to understand its effects on IEO. Our review of the literature suggests the following conclusions regarding the effects of educational expansion on IEO.

Expansion and the dispersion of education: We have learned from Mare that inequality between strata in the average level of education (i.e. absolute inequality) is related to the variance of education, such that a reduction in the variance of education results in a reduction in inequality between strata in the average educational attainment. For educational expansion to reduce the variance of education it must be concentrated on the lower levels of schooling. For example, raising the level of compulsory education is an expansion of education »*from the bottom*«. Expansion from the bottom that raises the educational minimum in the population can thus reduce its variance. We define expansion from the bottom as a significant increase in cohort proportions that survive the lower educational transitions. Expansion at the top, in contrast, is defined as a significant increase in cohort proportions reaching the highest educational levels. Therefore, a rapid expansion of higher education can increase the variance of education by stretching out the right-hand tail of its distribution.

Expansion and saturation: Expansion from the bottom can also reduce *relative* inequality between strata in the odds of attaining a given level of education. Following the logic of Raftery and Hout's (1993) MMI hypothesis and given that attendance rates at lower educational levels are nearly universal among the upper strata, their further expansion stands to benefit the lower strata and reduce inequality in the odds of attaining those levels.

Expansion and carry-over effects: Declining inequality in the odds of completing lower levels of education can carry over to higher levels and reduce both relative and absolute inequality in the highest education attained. For example, in their analysis of Italian data, Shavit and Westerbeek (1998) found that inequality between strata in the odds of completing lower levels of education declined over time, while inequality in the odds of making subsequent *transitions* remained stable. However, the reduced inequality at the bottom of the educational hierarchy carried over to higher levels of education and reduced inequality in the (unconditional) odds of completing upper secondary education. Vallet (2004) finds similar results for France.

Expansion and postponed selection: Despite being able to reduce inequality between strata, in both the absolute and the relative sense, expansion from the bottom also has dis-equalizing effects. Expansion from the bottom increases not only the number of individuals at risk for subsequent educational transitions, but also the heterogeneity – in terms of social origins – of these individuals. This greater heterogeneity can then result in an increase in inequality between strata in the odds for their completion of subsequent educational transitions (Rijken 1999).

Expansion and differentiation: Educational expansion is closely related to educational differentiation. As systems expand and quantitative educational inequalities between strata diminish, they are replaced by qualitative differentiation. For example, Lucas (2001) has argued that once saturation has been reached with regard to a given level of education, inequalities in the odds of attainment may be replaced by inequalities in the odds of placement in the more selective track. Thus, while expansion may reduce quantitative inequalities in education, these may be replaced by qualitative ones.

The balance between the equalizing and dis-equalizing effects of educational expansion on IEO varies between countries and over time. In some instances, carry over effects are somewhat stronger than those of postponed selection, while in others they seem to cancel out one another. The reasons for these differences are still not well understood.

Where does persistent inequality stand?

We can now summarize the main points of agreement in the emerging consensus in the debate concerning the hypothesis of *Persistent Inequality*. In its strong version, *persistent inequality* is probably wrong: large data sets reveal weakening effects of origins on education since the early decades of the twentieth century. But if a weaker version of this thesis is considered, then we would argue that *persistent inequality* still persists. To begin with, even those who find a reduction over time in the origin-education association estimate this reduction to be moderate. Secondly, the reduction is accompanied by a devaluation of lower credentials over time that is due to both their bourgeoning supply and to technological changes in the economy. Evidence indicates that while IEO declined at the primary and lower secondary levels of education, it was not reduced in the transitions to the upper secondary or tertiary levels of education. Again, in an era of educational expansion it is the higher levels of education that count most for an individual's career success.

Thirdly, the few studies that revealed a decline in IEO over time (Vallet 2004, Breen et al. 2005) found that it occurred immediately after World War II. The results of these studies indicate, moreover, that before WWII and since then the origin – education association has been fairly persistent. Could this be an idiosyncratic period effect rather than a general pattern of change? One is tempted here to follow Sorokin's (1959) suggestion that inequality in the transmission of privilege tends to decline in periods of social upheaval such as war and revolution, but that in other periods it fluctuates constantly and persistently.

Fourthly, our review of the literature indicates that inequality between classes is substantially weaker than inequality between strata defined by parental education. This is an important pattern of results that would appear to strengthen the ›death of class‹ thesis (cf. Clark and Lipset 1991, Pakulski 1993). Proponents of this thesis argue that inequality in society is undergoing a process of individualization (Beck 1992, Giddens 1994), and hence class inequality, in education and otherwise, is declining.

References

Apple, M. W. (1990). *Ideology and Curriculum* (2nd edition), New York: Routledge.

Arum, R./Gamoran, A./Shavit, Y. (forthcoming). »More inclusion than diversion: expansion, differentiation, and market structure in higher education«, in Y. Shavit et al. (eds.), *Stratification in Higher Education: A Comparative Study*, Stanford, Cal.: Stanford University Press.

Ballarino, G./Schadee, H. (2005). *Really Persisting Inequalities?*, Paper presented at the meeting of the ISA Research Committee on Social Stratification and Mobility, Los Angeles (USA).

Barone, C. (2006). *A New Look at Schooling Inequalities in Italy and their Trends over Time*, Paper presented at the meeting of the ISA Research Committee on Social Stratification and Mobility, Nijmegen, the Netherlands.

Beck, U. (1992). »From industrial society to the risk society – questions of survival, social structure and ecological enlightenment«, *Theory Culture and Society*, vol. 9, no. 1, pp. 97–123.

Bills, D. B. (1992). »A survey of employers surveys: What we know about labor markets from talking with bosses?«, *Research in Social Stratification and Mobility*, vol. 11, pp. 3–31.

Blau, P./Duncan, O. D. (1967). *The American Occupational Structure*, New York: John Wiley.

Blossfeld, H.-P./Shavit, Y. (1993). »Persisting barriers: changes in educational opportunities in thirteen countries«, in Y. Shavit/H.-P. Blossfeld (eds.), *Persistent Inequality: Changing Educational Attainment in Thirteen Countries*, Boulder: Westview Press, pp. 1–24.

Boudon, R. (1974). *Education, Opportunity and Social Inequality*, New York: Wiley.

Bourdieu, P. (1977). »Cultural reproduction and social reproduction«, in J. Karabel/A. H. Halsey (eds.), *Power and Ideology in Education*, New York: Oxford University Press, pp. 487–511.

Breen, R./Goldthorpe, J. H. (1997). »Explaining educational differentials – towards a formal rational action theory«, *Rationality and Society*, vol. 9, no. 3, pp. 275–305.

Breen, R./Luijkx, R./Müller, W./Pollak, R. (2005). *Non-Persistent Inequality in Educational Attainment: Evidence from Eight European Countries*, Paper presented at the meeting of the ISA Research Committee on Social Stratification and Mobility, Los Angeles (USA).

Buchmann, M./Charles, M./Sacchi, S. (1993). »The lifelong shadow: social origins and educational opportunities in Switzerland«, in Y. Shavit/H.-P. Blossfeld (eds.), *Persistent Inequality: Changing Educational Attainment in Thirteen Countries*, Boulder: Westview Press, pp. 177–192.

Cameron, S. V./Heckman, J. J. (1998). »Life cycle schooling and dynamic selection bias: models and evidence for five cohorts of American males«, *Journal of Political Economy*, vol. 106, no. 2, pp. 262–333.

Clark, T. N./Lipset, S. M. (1991). »Are social classes dying?«, *International Sociology*, vol. 6, no. 4, pp. 397–410.

Clark, T. N./Lipset, S. M./Rempel, M. (1993). »The declining political significance of social class«, *International Sociology*, vol. 8, no. 3, pp. 293–316.

Collins, R. (1979). *The Credential Society: An Historical Sociology of Education and Stratification*, New York: Academic Press.

de Graaf, P. M. (1986). »The impact of financial and cultural resources on educational attainment in the Netherlands«, *Sociology of Education*, vol. 59, pp. 237–246.

de Graaf, P. M./Ganzeboom, H. B. G. (1993). »Family background and educational attainment in the Netherlands of 1891–1960 birth cohorts«, in Y. Shavit/H.-P. Blossfeld (eds.), *Persistent Inequality: Changing Educational Attainment in Thirteen Countries*, Boulder: Westview Press, pp. 75–99.

de Graaf, N. D./de Graaf, P. M./Kraaykamp, G. (2000). »Parental cultural capital and educational attainment in the Netherlands«, *Sociology of Education*, vol. 73, pp. 92–111.

Duncan, G. J./Yeung, W.-Y. J./Brooks-Gunn, J./Smith, J. R. (1998). »How much does childhood poverty affect the life chances of children?«, *American Sociological Review*, vol. 63, no. 3, pp. 406–423.

Erikson, R./Jonsson, J. O. (1996). »Explaining class inequality in education: the Swedish test case«, in R. Erikson/J. O. Jonsson (eds.), *Can Education Be Equalized? The Swedish Case in Comparative Perspective*, Boulder: Westview Press, pp. 95–112.

Esping-Andersen, G. (1999). *Social Foundations of Postindustrial Economies*, Oxford: Oxford University Press.

Evans, G. (ed.) (1999). *The End of Class Politics? Class Voting in Comparative Context*, Oxford: Oxford University Press.

Gamoran, A./Mare, R. D. (1989). »Secondary school tracking and educational inequality – compensation, reinforcement, or neutrality?«, *American Journal of Sociology*, vol. 94, no. 5, pp. 1146–1183.

Giddens, A. (1994). *Beyond Left and Right: the Future of Radical Politics*, Cambridge: Polity.

Guesthuizen, M./de Graaf, P. M./Kraaykamp, G. (2005). »The changing family background of the low educated in the Netherlands: socio-economic, cultural and socio-demographic resources«, *European Sociological Review*, vol. 21, no. 5, pp. 441–452.

Hauser, R. M./Featherman, D. L. (1976). »Equality of schooling: trends and prospects«, *Sociology of Education*, vol. 49, no. 2, pp. 99–120.

Hout, M. (forthcoming). »Maximally maintained inequality revisited: Irish educational mobility in comparative perspective«, in M. NicGhiolla Phadraig/E. Hilliard (eds.), *Changing Ireland, 1989–2003*, http://ucdata.berkeley.edu:7101/rsfcensus/papers/MMIrevisited.pdf

Hout, M/Raftery, A. E./Bell, E. O. (1993). »Making the grade: educational stratification in the United States, 1925–1989«, in Y. Shavit/H.-P. Blossfeld (eds.), *Persistent Inequality: Changing Educational Attainment in Thirteen Countries*, Boulder: Westview Press, pp. 25–49.

Ishida, H./Müller, W./Ridge, J. M. (1995). »Class origin, class destination, and education – a cross-national-study of ten industrial nations«, *American Journal of Sociology*, vol. 101, no. 1, pp. 145–193.

Jencks, C. (and associates) (1972). *Inequality: A Reassessment of the Effects of Family and Schooling in America*, New York: Basic Books.

Jonsson, J. O. (1993). »Persisting inequalities in Sweden?«, in Y. Shavit/H.-P. Blossfeld (eds.), *Persistent Inequality: Changing Educational Attainment in Thirteen Countries*, Boulder: Westview Press, pp. 101–132.

Jonsson, J. O./Mills, C./Müller, W. (1996). »A half century of increasing educational openness? Social class, gender and educational attainment in Sweden, Germany and Britain«, in R. Erikson/J. O. Jonsson (eds.), *Can Education Be Equalized? The Swedish Case in Comparative Perspective*, Boulder: Westview Press, pp. 183–206.

Kerckhoff, A. C. (1993). *Diverging Pathways: Social Structure and Career Deflections*, New York: Cambridge University Press.

König, W./Lüttinger, P./Müller, P. (1988). *Comparative Analysis of the Development and Structure of Educational Systems* (CASMIN Working Paper no. 12), Mannheim: University of Mannheim.

Lucas, S. R. (2001). »Effectively maintained inequality: education transitions, track mobility, and social background effects«, *American Journal of Sociology*, vol. 106, no. 6, pp. 1642–1690.

Mare, R. D. (1980). »Social background and school continuation decisions«, *Journal of the American Statistical Association*, vol. 75, no. 370, pp. 295–305.

Mare, R. D. (1981). »Change and stability in educational stratification«, *American Sociological Review*, vol. 46, no. 1, pp. 72–87.

Mare, R. D. (1993). »Educational stratification on observed and unobserved components of family background«, in Y. Shavit/H.-P. Blossfeld (eds.), *Persistent Inequality: Changing Educational Attainment in Thirteen Countries*, Boulder: Westview Press, pp. 351–376.

Mare, R. D. (forthcoming). »Statistical models of educational stratification: Hauser and Andrew's models of school transitions«, *Sociological Methodology*.

Müller, W./Karle, W. (1993). »Social selection in educational systems in Europe«, *European Sociological Review*, vol. 9, no. 1, pp. 1–23.

Pakulski, J. (1993). »The dying of class or Marxist class theory«, *International Sociology*, vol. 8, no. 3, pp. 279–292.

Parkin, F. (1979). *Marx's Theory of History: a Bourgeois Critique*, New York: Columbia University Press.

Pfeffer, F. T. (2006). *Intergenerational Educational Mobility in Comparative Perspective*, Paper presented at the meeting of ISA Research Committee on Social Stratification and Mobility, Durban (South Africa).

Raftery, A. E./Hout, M. (1993). »Maximally maintained inequality – expansion, reform, and opportunity in Irish education, 1921–75«, *Sociology of Education*, vol. 66, no. 1, pp. 41–62.

Rijken, S. R. H. (1999). *Educational Expansion and Status Attainment, a Cross-National and Over-time Comparison*, Utrecht: Doctoral dissertation at the Interuniversity Centre for Social Science Theory and Methodology.

Rosenbaum, J. E./Kariya, T./Settersten, R./Maier, T. (1990). »Market and network theories of the transition from high school to work: their application to industrialized societies«, *Annual Review of Sociology*, vol. 16, pp. 263-299.

Sewell, W. H./Hauser, R. M. (1975). *Education, Occupation, and Earnings: Achievement in the Early Career*, New York: Academic Press.

Shavit, Y. (1984). »Tracking and ethnicity in Israeli secondary education«, *American Sociological Review*, vol. 49, no. 2, pp. 210–220.

Shavit, Y./Kraus, V. (1990). »Educational transitions in Israel – a test of the industrialization and credentialism hypotheses«, *Sociology of Education*, vol. 63, no. 2, pp. 133–141.

Shavit, Y./Blossfeld, H.-P. (1993). *Persistent Inequality: Changing Educational Attainment in Thirteen Countries*, Boulder: Westview Press.

Shavit, Y./Westerbeek, K. (1998). »Educational stratification in Italy – reforms, expansion, and equality of opportunity«, *European Sociological Review*, vol. 14, no. 1, pp. 33–47.

Smith, H. L./Cheung, P. P. L. (1986). »Trends in the effects of family background on educational attainment in the Philippines«, *American Journal of Sociology*, vol. 91, no. 6, pp. 1387–1408.

Sorokin, P. A. (1959 [1927]). *Social and Cultural Mobility*, Glencoe, Ill.: Free Press.

Szelényi, S./Aschaffenburg, K. (1993). »Inequalities in educational opportunity in Hungary«, in Y. Shavit/H.-P. Blossfeld (eds.), *Persistent Inequality: Changing Educational Attainment in Thirteen Countries*, Boulder: Westview Press, pp. 273–302.

Thurow, L. C. (1975). *Generating Inequality: Mechanisms of Distribution in the US Economy*, London: Macmillan.

Torche, F. (2005). »Privatization reform and inequality of educational opportunity: the case of Chile«, *Sociology of Education*, vol. 78, no. 4, pp. 316–343.

Treiman, D. J./Yamaguchi, K. (1993). »Trends in educational attainment in Japan«, in Y. Shavit/H.-P. Blossfeld (eds.), *Persistent Inequality: Changing Educational Attainment in Thirteen Countries*, Boulder: Westview Press, pp. 229–250.

Tsai, S.-L./Chiu, H.-Y. (1993). »Changes in educational stratification in Taiwan«, in Y. Shavit/H.-P. Blossfeld (eds.), *Persistent Inequality: Changing Educational Attainment in Thirteen Countries*, Boulder: Westview Press, pp. 193–228.

Vallet, L.-A. (2004). *The Dynamics of Inequality of Educational Opportunity in France: Change in the Association between Social Background and Education in Thirteen Five-Year Birth Cohorts (1908–1972)*, Paper presented at the meeting of ISA Research Committee on Social Stratification and Mobility, Neuchâtel (Switzerland).

Xie, Y. (1992). »The log-multiplicative layer effect model for comparing mobility tables«, *American Sociological Review*, vol. 57, no. 3, pp. 380–95.

Social selection in Stockholm schools: primary and secondary effects on the transition to upper secondary education[1]

Robert Erikson

Introduction

It was observed some time ago that children from higher social classes on average perform better at school and that, *given performance*, they tend to choose academic tracks in school to a larger extent than children from lower social origins (Boalt 1947, Härnqvist 1958, Jencks and Riesman 1968). In his analysis of inequality of educational opportunity, Boudon (1974) labelled these two mechanisms primary and secondary effects. In a recent paper, Jackson et al. (2006) show that since around 1970 secondary effects account for between a quarter and half of the social selection to A-levels in Britain, and that no substantial change could be observed in this respect. In this contribution, I intend to provide a comparable study for Sweden, where inequality of educational attainment has diminished, in contrast to the development in Britain.[2]

Background

Social selection to upper secondary school decreased in Sweden during the 20th century (Erikson and Jonsson 1996), but how did this happen? Differences in material conditions between children in the salariat and the working class seem to have decreased through the century e.g. as indicated by decreasing differences in body height between adults from different social

1 This chapter has been much improved thanks to comments from Richard Breen, Johan Fritzell, John Goldthorpe, Jan O. Jonsson, Frank Kalter, and Michael Tåhlin. The Swedish Research Council supported the research reported here with a grant (no. 40345401).
2 New results suggest that the association between social origin and educational attainment has actually decreased in Britain (Breen et al. 2005), although such a decrease could not be observed in the data analysed by Jackson et al. 2006).

origins (Nyström Peck and Vågerö 1987). It seems fully possible that decreasing differences in material conditions could also be associated with a parallel diminishing of differences in cognitive development. Given that the absolute differences in schooling between parents in different social classes have diminished – the number of years in education among parents in the salariat has only increased slowly while the corresponding increase in the working class has been much faster – differences in intellectual climate in the family and in parents' capacity to help their children with school work may also have diminished.

Decreasing income inequality (Björklund 1998) up till the 1980s and low rates of unemployment could not only have improved the relative material conditions of children in the working class, but also made the choice of a theoretical education more attractive, since differences in the risks connected to continued education and the related costs decreased between classes (Erikson and Jonsson 1996, Breen and Goldthorpe 1997, Jonsson and Erikson 2000). On the other hand, decreasing income inequality has been assumed to decrease the incentives to acquire higher education and mostly so among youngsters from the working class, thereby leading to increasing inequality of educational opportunity (IEO).[3] However, Jonsson and Erikson found no such effect in the sense that when higher education tracks of equal length were compared, working class children did not show a greater tendency than others to choose tracks with greater economic returns, which puts the hypothesis in doubt (Erikson and Jonsson 1994).

In consequence, the decrease in inequality of educational opportunity could be related to primary effects as well as to secondary ones. The decrease may furthermore not have been equal over different tracks in upper secondary education, that is, children from the working class may be relatively more attracted by some tracks than by others. Inequality in educational attainment decreased more quickly among girls than among boys (Erikson and Jonsson 1996) and the two sexes differ in their choice of tracks. In this contribution I discuss how primary and secondary effects can be estimated, report on their magnitude in the transition to upper secondary school among boys and girls around 1970 and 1990, and investigate possible changes in these respects during this period.

---

3 This argument was advanced by economic advisors to the Swedish government and echoed in a Government Bill.

Primary and secondary effects

Erikson and Jonsson (1996, p. 76) suggested that the proportion continuing to further studies in social class i can be modelled as

$$P_{ii} = \int f_i(x) g_i(x) dx \qquad (1)$$

where $f_i(x)$ is the distribution of performance, labelled x, at school and $g_i(x)$ is the probability to continue from this level of education to further studies, at performance x. Performance is typically measured as Grade Point Average, but other measures can of course be envisaged. The integral can only be solved if assumptions are made about the functions f(x) and g(x). Erikson and Jonsson suggested the performance distribution to be normal and that transition propensities follow a logistic curve. These assumptions have turned out to give a good fit between observed values and those expected from the model (cf. Jackson et al. 2006).

By substituting one of the functions for class i in (1) with the corresponding function for another class j

$$P_{ij} = \int f_i(x) g_j(x) dx \qquad (2)$$

we produce a counterfactual proportion, in which the performance distribution is equal to that of class i, while the transition propensities follow the function for class j. By setting such counterfactual proportions in relation to the estimated ones we can obtain estimates of the sizes of primary and secondary effects (Erikson et al. 2005, Jackson et al. 2006).

The odds ratio for the transition propensities of class i as compared to class j can be written as

$$Q_{ii,jj} = (P_{ii}/(1-P_{ii})) / (P_{jj}/(1-P_{jj}))$$

where the Ps refer to the proportions making the transition in classes i and j, respectively. The counterfactual odds ratio, where the actual odds for class i are connected with the counterfactual odds resulting from class j having the same transition propensities as class i but its own performance distribution, is

$$Q_{ii,ji} = (P_{ii}/(1-P_{ii})) / (P_{ji}/(1-P_{ji}))$$

and we can likewise construct the counterfactual odds ratio

$$Q_{ii.ij} = (P_{ii}/(1-P_{ii}))/ (P_{ij}/1-P_{ij}))$$

where we compare the actual odds for class i with the counterfactual odds where class j has its own transition propensities but the same performance distribution as class i.

The sums of logarithms of appropriate pairs of counterfactual odds ratios can be shown to be equal to the logarithms of the estimated odds ratios (Jackson et al. 2006), which can be taken as measuring overall inequality of educational opportunity. Thus

$$L_{ii.ij} = L_{ij.jj}+L_{ii.ij} \tag{3}$$

and

$$L_{ii.ij} = L_{ii.ji}+L_{ji.ij} \tag{4}$$

where the first term on the right hand side in each case refers to situations with different performance distributions but similar transition propensities and the second term to situations with similar performance distributions but different transition propensities. That is, the first terms can be said to refer to primary effects while the second terms refer to secondary effects. Depending on the choice of functions in (1), the estimates of primary and secondary effects, respectively, in (3) and (4), will not be identical, but in most cases quite similar (Erikson et al. 2005). We will therefore use the averages as estimates of the primary and secondary effects, that is, primary effects will be estimated by[4]

$$IEO_p = (L_{ij.jj}+L_{ii.ji})/2 \tag{5}$$

and secondary effects by

$$IEO_s = (L_{ii.ij} +L_{ji.ij})/2 \tag{6}$$

---

4 As indicated above, Boudon discussed primary and secondary effects under the general heading »Inequality of Educational Opportunity (IEO)«.

Data

The empirical analyses are based on three data sets, (i) the Stockholm Birth Cohort Study (Stenberg et al. 2005); (ii) a 25 percent sample of all pupils who left elementary school in 1991 or 1992 collected by the Swedish Governmental Commission on Educational Inequality (Erikson and Jonsson 1993: ch. 4; 1996); and (iii) another data set collected by the Commission, utilised for the analysis of transitions to tertiary education.[5]

The Stockholm Birth Cohort study (SBC) started in 1963. In 1966, all pupils in the sixth grade in schools in Greater Stockholm, most of them 13 years of age, responded to an extensive questionnaire at school. Register data was added to the information thus gathered, including data on continued education and grades as well as on father's occupation and education. The number of students in the data set is 15 117. This data set is restricted to Greater Stockholm, which differs from the rest of Sweden in having a larger service class and a greater diversity of secondary and tertiary educational alternatives than are offered in most other communities. These conditions could result in slightly different patterns of change in the capital and in other parts of Sweden.

The two other data sets were both collected by the Swedish Governmental Commission on Educational Inequality (Erikson and Jonsson 1993). They are based on school records of grade point averages, enrolment, and examination. In order to facilitate comparisons with results from the Stockholm Birth Cohort Study, the analyses of persons in these data sets are restricted to those who grew up in the county of Stockholm.[6] The sample fractions were 25% for both data sets, producing a total sample size of 23 253 cases in the school leavers study. The study of transitions to university is restricted to those born 1962 to 1964, which results in a sample of 15 349 cases. For all three data sets, the active files are slightly reduced, due to missing information on some of the variables. Returns from the censuses of 1960, 1970, and 1980 on the characteristics of the parents and the household of orientation were linked to the information on each per-

---

5 These studies are referred to in Table 1 as SBC (Stockholm Birth Cohort study), SL (School Leaver survey), and SC (Stockholm County study).

6 Some parts of the county of Stockholm are not included in Greater Stockholm, but the vast majority of the population of the county live in Greater Stockholm, which makes the samples sufficiently comparable.

son with the help of the personal identification number assigned to every Swedish citizen.

Variables

In Stockholm Birth Cohort study, social origin is coded in five classes, (upper and upper middle class; employed lower middle class; self-employed lower middle class; skilled workers, and unskilled workers) while social origin in the two other data sets are coded according to the standard Swedish classification established in the mid-1970s (SCB 1989) and very similar to the internationally used class schema (EGP) proposed by Erikson and Goldthorpe (1992: ch. 2). In Table 1 the number of cases in the five origin classes in SBC are reported, as well as those with the corresponding class origins in the Stockholm county study and the School Leaver study, using the notation of EGP.

In Table 1, SBC53 refers to father's class in the year when those in the data set were born, i.e. 1953, while SBC63, refers to father's class at the start of the study in 1963. To check the comparability among the data sets, father's class is given for those in the Stockholm County study who were born in 1952–1954 (SC52-54). The corresponding class origins for those born 1962–1964 (SC62-64) are those actually used in the study of transitions to university.[7] SL90-91, refers to father's class in 1990 for the pupils in the School Leaver study. Further, to check the accuracy of the coding of social class, frequencies over the five classes are taken from the level of living surveys (LNU) 1968 and 1991 (Jonsson and Mills 2001), for men aged 36 to 56 living in Stockholm County.

The most sensitive issue here for studying change in educational social selection is the comparability of the class coding in SBC to that in the other studies. All the latter are coded according to the same class schema, while in SBC class is coded according to an earlier schema. A first observation from Table 1 is that the coding of class from register data (in SBC, SC and SL) seems to underestimate the number of self-employed men, as indi-

---

7 Reliable information on educational attainment is not available for those born 1952–1954 and many of those born after 1964 would not yet have entered university by 1990, which is the last year for which we have information on tertiary studies in the Stockholm County study.

Table 1. Distributions of social class origins in Stockholm Birth Cohort 1953 and 1963; Stockholm County study for persons born 1952–1954 and born 1962–1964; and School Leaver study 1990–1991; as well for men in the LNU level of living surveys 1968 and 1991, aged 36–56, living in Stockholm county (per cent)

	SBC53	SC52-54	SBC63	SC62-64	LNU68	SL90-91	LNU91
Class							
I: Salariat	13.9	13.5	17.6	14.9	18.7	28.6	33.9
II+IIIA: Employed middle class	32.0	41.6	35.6	42.0	28.8	36.1	20.4
IV: Self-employed middle class	6.4	7.8	7.9	8.7	12.3	6.3	14.0
VI: Skilled working class	28.4	22.0	22.5	21.1	24.7	9.9	15.6
IIIB+VII: Unskilled working class	19.4	15.1	16.4	13.3	15.5	13.7	16.1
No job						5.4	
Total	100.0	100.0	100.0	100.0	100.0	100.0	100.0
Number of cases	14,538	11,446	14,704	12,254	219	23,253	186

cated by the coding of class in the level of living surveys, where the numbers seem more accurate although obviously based on rather few cases.[8] It seems as if many self-employed are assigned to Class II, the employed lower middle class. It seems furthermore as if the number in the skilled working class is underestimated in SL90-91, although it is probable that this class has become smaller in Stockholm, as indicated by the change from LNU68 to LNU91. However, the low number of skilled workers in SL90-91 may partly be due to the high unemployment rate in the early 1990s (in the level of living surveys the unemployed are coded according to their regular occupation). Comparability to the other studies is therefore expected to increase if men without jobs are assigned to the working class. The considerable increase in the number of men belonging to Class I, indicated in Table 1, is most certainly mirroring the substantial change of the class structure of Stockholm in the latter part of the 20th century.

The comparison of the origin distributions in SBC with those in the Stockholm County studies suggests that relatively more men are coded in Class I in SBC (observe that SBC53 refers to the origin distributions at the births of the children – that is, in the early part of the careers of many fathers). Overall, however, the distributions from the connected years are similar enough to suggest that the origin coding can be compared between

---

8 In Vogel (1987: 21) – a report from Statistics Sweden – the proportion self-employed men in the workforce is estimated to 13.6 percent.

studies. This is supported by the fact that there is a clear link between the earlier class schema, applied in SBC, and that developed in the 1970s.

In the analysis here, we will compare children from Class I with those from the working class, leaving out the details for intermediate classes.[9] In the interpretation of the results it should be remembered that Class I probably includes more occupational positions in SBC than in the Stockholm county studies, while the inclusion of those with no jobs in SL90-91 could result in some fathers being wrongly included in the working class. In the first case we may underestimate social selection in the early period, while the inclusion of those with no jobs could result in an underestimation in the later period.

School performance will be estimated by grade point averages at exit from compulsory school as well as from upper secondary school. Grades are the overall measure of school performance and therefore seem to be the obvious choice. They give a signal to pupils and parents about how well the children can be expected to succeed in different lines of secondary school and are accordingly highly influential on the choice of school continuation. However, for our purpose it is problematic that they are not fully comparable, even within the same cohort. There were different tracks in the last years of primary school both in 1969 and 1990. In 1969 particularly one track was clearly meant for those who intended to continue to upper secondary school. In the late 1980s pupils should choose some additional subjects in the last years of primary school and some of those – particularly advanced mathematics and English, as well as another foreign language – were chosen by many who planned to continue to academic tracks in secondary school, although it remained possible to continue to upper secondary school also for those who had made other choices. Table 2 shows the proportions by social origin of boys and girls who had chosen the more academic tracks.

It is obvious that, as expected, there was a considerable effect of social origin on the choice of tracks already in primary school, much in accordance with the often made observation that selection by social origin is particularly strong at lower ages (cf. Mare 1980, Müller and Karle 1993). Table 2 also shows that social selection to these tracks was much stronger in 1969 than in 1990; the log odds in 1969 relating Class I to Class VI–VII was 2.5 and 2.3 for boys and girls, respectively, while the corresponding log

---

9 The grade distributions and transition rates for the intermediate classes fall between those for the salariat and the working class.

Table 2. Percentage in the ›academic tracks‹ in primary school by year, sex and social origin

		Class origin			
		Sal (I)	int (II–IV)	WC (IIIB, VI, VII)	Log odds ratio Sal-WC
Boys	1969	84	56	30	2.50
	1990	77	58	38	1.69
Girls	1969	87	62	39	2.32
	1990	78	58	39	1.67

odds in 1990 were 1.7 for both boys and girls. Whether this decrease in log odds is dependent upon decreasing social selection or upon non-comparability of the two sets of academic tracks is not possible to sort out, but there were no other obvious academic choices in 1990, which perhaps could be understood to mean that the institutional change of the primary school system did promote the equality of choice.

The difficulty in comparing grades also within years suggests that we should look at transitions both among all those who left primary school in 1969 and 1990 and in the restricted group consisting of those who had chosen the more academic options in primary school. When interpreting transitions among all pupils, the lack of full comparability of grades within the cohorts and possibly between years should be remembered. On the other hand, results for students in the academic tracks will clearly underestimate IEO, since the choice of these tracks is highly influenced by social origin.

There were four tracks in upper secondary school in 1969, when most of the pupils in SBC left compulsory school, as well as in 1990/91, when pupils in the school leaver survey left. The tracks were natural science (N), social science and humanities (S),[10] economics (E) and technology (T). The natural science and humanities tracks are what is left of the traditional higher secondary school with a *Realgymnasium* and a *Latingymnasium*. Not only were they, at least in 1969, the tracks that educated parents believed they had some knowledge of, but also the two tracks that gave most openings for tertiary studies, which especially was the case for those who took the natural science line. The economics (commerce) and the technology

---

10 This line of upper secondary school was kept together, while the study programmes were slightly different depending on whether the pupils chose the humanities or the social science programme. The track will here be designated S, as most students chose the social science programme.

Table 3. Transition to various tracks in upper secondary school and log odds ratios relating transitions in the salariat to those in the working class in greater Stockholm around 1969 (SBC69) and in Stockholm County around 1990 (SL90-91) (per cent and log odds)

| | SBC69 | SL90-91 | Log odds ratio (salariat vs. working class) | |
			SBC69	SL90-91
No gymnasium	59.2	43.2		
Natural science (N)	15.1	10.1	1.91	1.64
Social science/Humanities (S)	14.5	17.5	1.92	0.77
Economics/Commerce (E)	6.3	17.3	0.75	0.51
Technology (T)	5.0	11.8	0.37	0.91
Total	100	100		
Number of cases	13,417	22,799		

lines could be said to have had a vocational character, only giving very restricted access to tertiary education. However, they had recently, 1966, been reformed to give general access to university education, but parents and children may still have been uncertain about the value of these types of secondary education for further studies, they may still have been regarded as dead ends.

To what extent pupils went over to these four tracks is reported in Table 3. While the proportion of pupils who proceeded to any track in upper secondary school increased by over 15 percentage points from 1969 to 1990, the proportion who continued to the natural science track decreased by five percentage points. The proportions continuing in the other three tracks increased and this was particularly the case for economics and technology.

The tracks are ordered according to what could be regarded as their academic character in 1969, from natural sciences to technology. The log odds ratios relating the transitions of salariat children to those for the working class bear witness that parents and children may have valued the tracks in this way – N: 1.91; S: 1.92; E: 0.75; and T: 0.37 – as relatively many children from the salariat went to the supposedly more academic tracks, while relatively many from the working class went to the tracks of a vocational character.[11] Twenty years of experience with the new gymna-

---

11 The pattern was the same for both sexes.

sium changed this pattern substantially. The natural science track remained relatively most attractive to children from the salariat, but technology was second in this respect in 1990. The log odds ratios now were N: 1.64; S: 0.77; E: 051; and T: 0.91. This pattern seems to correspond to how the tracks by then were valued for continued academic studies, i.e. the technology track by that time may actually have opened more possibilities at the tertiary level than the humanities and social science track.

This change in how important the tracks were for the possibilities to continue to the tertiary level makes it more difficult to compare the transitions in 1969 and 1990, since we would not be comparing like with like. We will therefore distinguish the natural science track and beyond that only consider transitions to all four tracks together.

Results

Table 4 shows the percentages continuing from academic tracks and all primary school tracks to natural science and all tracks in upper secondary school among boys and girls from the salariat and the working class. The log odds ratios for the comparison of the salariat and the working class are furthermore reported.

What is perhaps most striking in Table 4 is the remarkable reduction in the percentage of boys continuing to natural science tracks. The percentage is around halved both among those from the salariat and the working class, a decrease which could be understood as an indication of the different lines of upper secondary school becoming more equally valued by the students (and the parents). Slightly more than three quarters of the boys from the salariat went to an academic track of upper secondary school both in 1969 and 1990, while the proportions choosing upper secondary studies among working class boys increased from 23 percent to 32 percent.

There was also a decrease in the proportion continuing to natural science studies among girls from the salariat although smaller than among boys. However, the increase in the proportions continuing to the other tracks led to an overall increase in the proportion of salariat girls taking upper secondary studies. The corresponding increase was even more marked among girls from the working class. The percentage continuing to natural science tracks remained unchanged, but there was a considerable

Table 4. *Percentages continuing from academic lines and all primary school to the natural science and all tracks in secondary school around 1969 and 1990–91 among boys and girls from the salariat (P$_s$) and the working class (P$_w$) and log odds ratios comparing salariat pupils with those from the working class (per cent and log odds)*

| From | To | Boys | | Girls | | IEO=Lss.ww | |
		Salariat P$_s$	W.class P$_w$	Salariat P$_s$	W.cass P$_w$	Boys	Girls
Academic track	Natural science						
	1969	48	24	28	12	1.08	1.04
	1990	25	10	24	11	1.09	0.93
	All upper secondary school						
	1969	88	63	79	50	1.48	1.32
	1990	91	67	89	73	1.54	1.15
All tracks	Natural science						
	1969	41	8	25	5	2.09	1.85
	1990	20	4	18	5	1.72	1.57
	All upper secondary school						
	1969	78	23	70	20	2.46	2.21
	1990	77	32	78	39	1.94	1.71

increase in numbers proceeding to the other three tracks, resulting in a doubling of the overall proportion in upper secondary education in this group of girls.

Regardless of whether we consider transitions to the natural science studies or to all of upper secondary school, the figures in Table 4 clearly show that inequality of educational opportunity is greater among boys than among girls and that the degree of social selection decreased considerably to all tracks and for both boys and girls. While we find the corresponding difference between men and women in transitions to university, change-over time in this case followed a clearly different pattern, as is shown in Table 5.[12]

Men with salariat origin continue to universities to a larger extent than women from this social class, while there hardly are any differences be-

---

12 While there is a twenty year span in the analysis of transitions to upper secondary school, we can only analyse a ten year span when looking at transitions to university, since otherwise too few in the younger cohort would have had the chance to continue to universities. The years for the transitions refer to the first year of entering university.

Table 5. Percentages continuing to university among those with grades from upper secondary school and from primary school and log odds ratios comparing salariat origins with working class origins among men and women (per cent and log odds)

	Men		Women		$IEO=L_{ss.ww}$ (salariat vs w.class)	
	Salariat P_s	W.class P_w	Salariat P_s	W.class P_w	Men	Women
With grades from upper secondary school						
-1973-	44	14	28	11	1.56	1.11
-1983-	56	14	50	14	2.09	1.80
All with grades from primary school						
-1973-	37	5	23	4	2.35	1.91
-1983-	50	9	44	10	2.29	1.99

tween men and women from the working class. The proportions entering universities increased considerably among men and women from the salariat, both among those who completed upper secondary school and among all (who finished compulsory school). In contrast, there was no increase among working class men who left upper secondary school and only a slight increase among women. The increasing proportions of working class children continuing to upper secondary school was followed by an overall increase in the proportions of children from this class who took up university studies. From these changing proportions, it follows that IEO increased in the transition from gymnasium to university, while overall it remained constant among all in the two cohorts. Mayer, Müller and Pollak (forthcoming) find similar results for Germany, where IEO to the *Abitur* is shown to have decreased over time, while social selection from *Abitur* to university has increased, at least for men.[13] The increasing social selection among graduates from secondary school could have been related to decreasing number of students entering tertiary education in the early 1980s (Jonsson and Erikson, forthcoming), possibly related to increasing unemployment among university graduates and decreasing education premiums

---

13 In contrast to what is reported here for Greater Stockholm, overall selection to tertiary studies in Germany decreased. However, social selection to universities has decreased in all of Sweden (Erikson and Jonsson 1996) and this is probably the case also for Stockholm, although it cannot be observed in the short period from 1973 to 1983.

in the 1970s. Under these circumstances, vocational schooling may have become a more attractive option for young people from the working class (cf. Erikson and Jonsson 1996, Breen and Goldthorpe 1997, Shavit and Müller 2000).

Changing primary and secondary effects

From Table 4 it is clear that the association between social origin and transitions to academic tracks in upper secondary school decreased from 1969 to 1990. But what were the mechanisms behind this decrease? Was it a question of decreasing primary effects, i.e. decreasing differences in performance at school between children from different social classes, or of weaker secondary effects, i.e. decreasing differences in transition rates, or perhaps of both? We have estimated the two types of effects through formulas (5) and (6). Performance distributions were assumed to be normal and transition propensities were estimated through logistic regression. Estimated and counterfactual proportions were found through numerical integration where grade point averages have been used to estimate performance at school.[14] Estimated proportions come close to the observed ones. Of 32 estimates, all but four are less than one percentage point from the observed proportions and the remaining four are less the two percentage points off. The resulting primary and secondary effects are shown in Table 6.

Table 6 shows, in accordance with Table 4,[15] that IEO is much greater among all pupils than among those who followed the academic tracks in primary school, and this is the case regardless whether we look at the different years, at transitions to natural science tracks or to all tracks in upper secondary school or IEO among boys and girls. Over time, IEO remains unchanged or decreases only slightly from academic tracks in primary school while the decrease is substantial for all primary school pupils. This

---

14 The integral can not be solved analytically, so numerical integration was used. This was done through the procedure at
http://people.hofstra.edu/faculty/Stefan_Waner/RealWorld/integral/integral.html
provided by Stefan Waner at Hofstra University.

15 In many cases the total IEO estimates in Table 6 differ in the second decimal place from the observed values in Table 4, which suggests that one should not put much emphasis on differences less than 0.1.

Table 6. Primary and secondary effects, total log odds and relative size of the secondary effects in the transition to tracks in upper secondary school in 1969 and 1990, in comparisons of boys and girls from the salariat and the working class

From	To	Boys				Girls			
		Pri-mary effect	Secon-dary effect	Total (log odds)	Prop. sec. effects	Pri-mary effect	Secon-dary effect	Total (log odds)	Prop sec. effects
Academic track	Natural science								
	1969	0.61	0.43	1.04	0.41	0.73	0.28	1.02	0.28
	1990	0.60	0.49	1.09	0.45	0.59	0.35	0.94	0.37
	All upper secondary								
	1969	0.82	0.73	1.55	0.47	0.78	0.56	1.34	0.42
	1990	0.51	1.01	1.52	0.66	0.50	0.66	1.15	0.57
All tracks	Natural science								
	1969	1.22	0.81	2.03	0.40	1.15	0.66	1.81	0.36
	1990	1.18	0.56	1.73	0.32	1.07	0.46	1.53	0.30
	All upper secondary								
	1969	1.19	1.25	2.44	0.51	1.03	1.13	2.16	0.52
	1990	1.10	0.79	1.89	0.42	0.96	0.73	1.69	0.43

is presumably an effect of the reform of primary school which increased the possibility to continue to upper secondary school for all pupils, irrespective of what subjects they chose at the end of primary school.

Primary effects on the whole decreased from 1969 to 1990 whereas secondary effects decreased for all pupils but increased slightly for boys and girls who had chosen the more advanced options in primary school. Primary effects seem to be of about the same magnitude or slightly greater among boys compared to girls. Secondary effects, on the other hand, are consistently greater among boys.

Secondary effects stand for between 30 and 65 percent of total IEO, in parallel with results found for England and Wales (Jackson et al. 2006).

Secondary effects among all pupils are clearly lower in 1990 than in 1969. However, due to the non-comparability of grades between tracks in 1969 mentioned earlier, this change can hardly be taken at face value, since a grade from the non-academic tracks of primary school in 1969 could be less indicative of intellectual ability than the same grade from the academic

Table 7. Primary and secondary effects, total log odds and relative size of the secondary effects in the transition from upper secondary school to university around 1973 and 1983, in comparisons of men and women from the salariat and the working class; performance indicated by grade point averages in upper secondary school

	Men				Women			
	Prim-ary effect	Secon-dary effect	Total (log odds)	Prop. sec. effects	Pri-mary effect	Secon-dary effect	Total (log odds)	Prop. sec. effects
University -1973-	0.52	1.07	1.59	0.67	0.36	0.75	1.11	0.68
University -1983-	0.61	1.48	2.09	0.71	0.50	1.35	1.84	0.73

academic track. We could put more confidence in the generally decreasing primary effects, since this decrease occurs in spite of the probably exaggerated decrease of secondary effects.

The obvious increase in social selection observable in Table 5 from upper secondary school to university was related to increasing primary and secondary effects, as shown in Table 7. Secondary effects accounted for around or slightly more than two thirds of the total effect among both men and women in both cohorts.

Summary of results

1. While in 1969 more boys continued to upper secondary education than girls, if anything the converse was true in 1990.
2. The proportion of boys continuing to natural science tracks in upper secondary schools decreased considerably, while the percentage continuing to all upper secondary tracks increased among those of working class origin. Among girls the percentages continuing to natural science studies decreased, although less so than among boys, while there was a noticeable increase in the number of girls continuing to all upper secondary education.
3. Social inequality in the transitions to upper secondary school was generally greater among boys than among girls in both cohorts.
4. Social inequality in the transition from elementary school to upper secondary decreased from 1969 to 1990.

5. This decrease seems to have been related to decreasing primary effects. Secondary effects probably decreased as well, but the non-comparability of school grades makes it difficult to asses the size of this decrease. The decrease of the primary effects was probably greater than estimated here, since over-estimated secondary effects mean that primary effects are under-estimated.

6. Social inequality in the transitions from upper secondary school to university increased, mostly dependent upon increasing secondary effects. The increase was countervailed by the decreasing inequality in transition to upper secondary school, resulting in no observed change in overall inequality of educational opportunity to university education.

Discussion

The character of the various tracks in upper secondary school changed in Sweden from 1970 to 1990, but even so natural science studies remained the best channel to continued academic studies. There is less social selection to the natural science tracks than to the whole upper secondary school, and secondary effects stand for less of the total selection to studies in natural sciences. Several mechanisms may be behind these differences, but the major one probably follows from the relatively high grades threshold to the natural science track. Differences in educational choices between pupils of different social origins seem to be greatest among those with medium or low grades, while being rather small among those with high grades. Only children with high grades, regardless of class origin, could enter the natural science track, with the consequence that a relatively large proportion of the social selection in this case is due to primary effects related to the more advantageous grade distribution among children from the salariat.

While social selection seems to have remained unchanged (among boys) or to have decreased (among girls) in transitions from the academic section of primary school, secondary effects seem to have increased in these transitions – where we presumably do not have any serious problem of comparing grades – and primary effects accordingly decreased, at least among girls. The increase of the secondary effects may be due to increasing numbers continuing to upper secondary school, since this implies that more pupils with less than excellent grades continue. Differences in continuation rates are particularly large in the middle range of the grade distribution, as already mentioned, so secondary effects may increase if more pupils in this range continue to upper secondary school. From 1969 to 1990 average grades became more equal between girls from the salariat and the working class, which presumably led to decreasing primary rates and thereby to decreasing social selection to secondary education.

The percentage of boys from the salariat who continued to upper secondary school did not increase, which could indicate that demand for upper secondary education was satisfied in this group already in 1969, perhaps a situation of »maximally maintained inequality« (Raftery and Hout 1993, cf. Ekman 1951), which in turn would have opened for a decrease in social selection at this level. As social selection also decreased among girls, where demand from salariat girls was apparently not satisfied by 1969, it seems that this could not have been the only mechanism in operation.

Decreasing social selection in the Swedish educational system has earlier been connected to decreasing differences in living conditions (Erikson and Jonsson 1996, Jonsson and Erikson 2000). Such an equalisation of living conditions could be expected to give rise to decreasing primary effects, which seems to be at least one mechanism behind decreasing social selection in Greater Stockholm. However, in the earlier studies we also concluded that the introduction of the comprehensive school did lead to reduced social selection to upper secondary school. The mechanism here could be reduced secondary effects.[16] The comprehensive school reform made it easier for pupils to continue to upper secondary school regardless of choice of tracks in primary school and thereby created greater opportunities for pupils with high grades in the non-academic tracks of primary school to choose to continue to upper secondary school – a continuation that may actually have been triggered by the high grades, since observing them could make the students realise that continued studies was an achievable option. Decisions by working class pupils to continue to the academic tracks of secondary school could further have been supported by another educational reform, which meant that the public financial support to children in secondary education increased considerably from 1970 to 1990 (Reuterberg and Svensson 1992).

---

16 As mentioned above, it is probable that secondary effects decreased, even if the magnitude of the decrease is unclear.

One of the motives for the introduction of the comprehensive school was to diminish social selection in the educational system. The possibility that educational reforms actually led to intended results suggests that policies do matter and this should come as an encouragement to educational policy makers.

References

Björklund, A. (1998). »Income distribution in Sweden: What is the achievement of the welfare state?«, *Swedish Economic Policy Review*, vol. 5, pp. 39–80.

Boalt, G. (1947). *Skolutbildning och skolresultat för barn ur olika samhällsgrupper i Stockholm*, Stockholm: P. A. Norstedt & Söner.

Boudon, R. (1974). *Education, Opportunity, and Social Inequality. Changing Prospects in Western Society*, New York: John Wiley & Sons.

Breen, R./Goldthorpe, J. H. (1997). »Explaining educational differentials: towards a formal rational action theory«, *Rationality and Society*, vol. 9, pp. 275–305.

Breen, R./Luijkx, R./Müller, W./Pollak, R. (2005). *Non-persistent Inequality in Educational Attainment: Evidence from eight European Countries* (unpublished manuscript).

Ekman, G. (1951). »Skolformer och begåvningsfördelning«, *Pedagogisk tidskrift*, vol. 87, pp. 15–37.

Erikson, R./Goldthorpe, J. H. (1992). *The Constant Flux. A Study of Class Mobility in Industrial Societies*, Oxford: Clarendon Press.

Erikson, R./Jonsson, J. O. (1993). *Ursprung och utbildning. Social snedrekrytering till högre studier (SOU 1993: 85)*, Stockholm: Fritzes.

Erikson, R./Goldthorpe, J. H./Jackson, M./Yaish, M./Cox, D. (2005). »On class differentials in educational attainment«, *Proceedings of the National Academy of Sciences*, vol. 102, no. 27, pp. 9730–9733.

Erikson, R./Jonsson, J. O. (1994). »Ökade löneskillnader – Ett sätt att tillvarata begåvningsreserven?« *Ekonomisk Debatt*, vol. 22, pp. 581–594.

Erikson, R./Jonsson, J. O. (1996). *Can Education be Equalized? Sweden in a Comparative Perspective*, Boulder, Col.: Westview Press.

Härnqvist, K. (1958). *Reserverna för högre utbildning. Beräkningar och metoddiskussion. 1955 års universitetsutredning III (SOU 1958: 11)*, Stockholm: Fritzes.

Jackson, M./Erikson, R./Goldthorpe, J. H./Yaish, M. (2006). *Primary and Secondary Effects in Class Differentials in Educational Attainment: the Transition to A-Level Courses in England and Wales*. Manuscript.

Jencks, C./Riesman, D. (1968). *The academic revolution*, New York: Doubleday & Co.

Jonsson, J. O./Erikson, R. (2000). »Understanding educational inequality: the Swedish experience«, *L'Année Sociologique*, vol. 50, pp. 345–382.

Jonsson, J. O./Mills, C. (eds.) (2001). *From Cradle to Grave*, Durham: Sociology Press.

Jonsson, J. O./Erikson, R. (forthcoming). »Why educational expansion is not such a great strategy for equality: theory and evidence for Sweden« in Y. Shavit et al. (eds.), *Stratification in Higher Education: A Comparative Study*, Stanford, Cal.: Stanford University Press.

Mare, R. D. (1980). »Social Background and School Continuation Decisions«, *Journal of the American Statistical Association*, vol. 75, pp. 295–305.

Mayer, K. U./Müller, W./Pollak, R. (forthcoming). »Institutional change and inequalities of access in German higher education«, in Y. Shavit et al. (eds.), *Stratification in Higher Education: A Comparative Study*, Stanford, Cal.: Stanford University Press.

Müller, W./Karle, W. (1993). »Social selection in educational systems in Europe«, *European Sociological Review*, vol. 9, pp. 1–23.

Nyström Peck, A. M./Vågerö, D. H. (1987). »Adult body height and childhood socio-economic group in the Swedish population«, *Journal of Epidemiology and Community Health*, vol. 41, pp. 333–337.

Raftery, A. E./Hout, M. (1993). »Maximally maintained inequality: expansion, reform and opportunity in Irish education, 1921–1975«, *Sociology of Education*, vol. 66, pp. 22–39.

Reuterberg, S.-E./Svensson, A. (1992). *Social bakgrund. Studiestöd och övergång till högre studier. Delbetänkande av utredningen om den sociala snedrekryteringen till högre studier (SOU 1992: 122)*, Stockholm: Fritzes.

SCB (Statistics Sweden) (1989). Yrkesklassificeringar i FoB85 enligt Nordisk yrkesklassificering (NYK) och Socioekonomisk indelning (SEI), Mis 1989:5, Stockholm: Statistics Sweden.

Shavit, Y./Müller, W (2000). »Vocational secondary education. Where diversion and where safety net?« *European Societies*, vol. 2, pp. 29–50.

Stenberg, S.-Å./Vågerö, D./Österman, R./Arvidsson, E./von Otter, C./Janson, C.-G. (2005). *Stockholm Birth Cohort Study 1953–2003 – a New Tool for Life Course Studies*. Manuscript.

Svensson A. (1971). *Relative Achievement. School Performance in Relation to Intelligence, Sex and Home Environment*, Stockholm: Almqvist & Wiksell.

Vogel, J. (1987). *Det svenska klassamhället*, Stockholm: Statistiska Centralbyrån.

»Cultural capital«: some critical observations[1]

John H. Goldthorpe

Introduction

A reviewer of a paper submitted to a scientific journal is said to have concluded his report as follows: »There is much in this paper that is original and sound: the difficulty is that what is sound is not original and what is original is not sound.« This nicely captures the essence of the critique that I wish to make of the work of Pierre Bourdieu, and of others, in which ›cultural capital‹ serves as a central concept.

I begin with some remarks on the research situation, within the sociology of education, that led Bourdieu first to develop the idea of cultural capital. My aim here is to show that the problems with which he was at least immediately concerned were at the time quite widely recognised; and, further, that the approach to these problems that Bourdieu developed was – up to a point – one followed by many other researchers similarly interested in cultural or subcultural influences on children's educational attainment. However, I next seek to bring out the more distinctive features of Bourdieu's approach. These are, I believe, closely linked to his introduction of, and insistence on, the concept of cultural *capital*, where others had spoken, in a more differentiated way, of cultural values and cultural resources. Cultural capital has been rightly described (Lareau and Weininger 2003: 568) as one of Bourdieu's »signature concepts«, and it plays a key role in the grand project that he pursued of integrating an explanation of social class inequalities in educational attainment into a much wider-ranging theory of *social reproduction*.

---

1 I am grateful to Herman van de Werfhorst and Nan Dirk de Graaf for helpful information, and especially to Elliot Weininger for a detailed critical commentary on an earlier draft. None of the foregoing do of course carry any responsibility for the views I express.

I then go on to argue that in so far as Bourdieu's work can be understood as ›normal science‹ within an established paradigm in the sociology of education, it may be subject to no more than standard forms of criticism; but that in so far as it is recognised as aiming to transcend this paradigm, it is open to criticism of a far more radical kind. The overarching theory of social reproduction can be shown to have serious inherent weaknesses and, further, to be overwhelmingly contradicted by empirical evidence. I conclude that, as a result of a failure to distinguish between these two possible perspectives on, and consequent evaluations of, Bourdieu's work, its reception in general and that of the concept of cultural capital in particular have come to display a divergence that is productive of much confusion.[2]

Bourdieu and the sociology of educational attainment

At the start of the 1960s, a broad consensus would appear to have existed regarding both the progress that had been made in research into the sociology of educational attainment and the problems that next called for attention. It was well established that inequalities in children's educational attainment, according to their social class, and also ethnic, origins, could not be explained simply in terms of individual variation in cognitive ability, as measured, say, by IQ. Leaving aside all questions of how IQ scores were to be interpreted, clear group differences in attainment were still apparent even when IQ was controlled. Moreover, there was a growing conviction that the further factors at work could not be limited to purely economic ones. The provision of secondary education on a free and universal basis

---

2 Like all others who seek to comment on Bourdieu's work, I face the problem of the recurrent obscurity of his prose (whether he is read in the original French or English translation) and of the deep and what must, I believe, be often willed ambiguities in his arguments. On this account, it is always likely that criticism of his work will be met with charges of misunderstanding and misrepresentation. I have found it of value to check my own interpretations of what Bourdieu might be trying to say against the – generally sympathetic – expositions found in Jenkins (2002), Lareau and Weininger (2003) and Weininger (2005). But these authors cannot of course be held responsible for the failures to appreciate the profundity of Bourdieu's thought of which I shall doubtless be accused. Although I have tried to read Bourdieu primarily in French, I give references to English translations (which may sometimes create an appearance of odd chronology).

had not succeeded in reducing inequalities in attainment to the extent that had been hoped for. There was thus wide agreement that what was further required was research that would go beyond simply establishing associations between the social characteristics of students and their educational performance, and that would seek »to specify the processes by which these characteristics are translated into differences in achievement« (Rossi 1961: 269). And, in this respect, the main focus of interest was clearly moving away from processes involving economic constraints and incentives to ones grounded in differing cultures and modes of socialisation.

Viewed in this context, the work in which Bourdieu engaged during the 1960s, chiefly in association with Passeron (see esp. Bourdieu and Passeron 1977, 1979), does not appear at all out of the ordinary. Statistical data are assembled in order to demonstrate persisting social class inequalities in educational attainment in France; and an explanation of these empirical regularities is put forward that, at least at one level, has evident affinities with those being concurrently developed by researchers concerned with similar inequalities in a number of other societies. The main emphasis is placed on causal processes arising out of what might be described as the *degree of congruence* between the cultures or subcultures into which children are socialised in their families and local communities and those that prevail in the schools and colleges that they attend.

For Bourdieu, one could say, the children of what he calls the »dominant class« are crucially advantaged over the children of subordinate classes in that they enter the educational system already well prepared to succeed within it. In their case, a clear continuity exists between the culture of the home and that of the school. These children will share a common mode of speech, style of social interaction and aesthetic orientation with their teachers, and neither the content of what they are taught (syllabus) nor the manner in which they are taught (pedagogy) are likely to appear strange to them. In contrast, for children from other class backgrounds, and especially for those of working-class or peasant origins, the school will represent an alien and indeed a hostile environment – a cultural and social world set apart from that of their families and communities, and one in which they are likely to feel out of place. Thus, while the children of the dominant class will progressively benefit from a positive interplay between the influences of home and school, children from less advantaged class backgrounds will find difficulties, and probably increasing difficulties, of adjustment. These latter children will then – other than in a few special cases

– fail to reach the higher levels of the educational system, either because they are excluded by inadequate performance or because they in effect exclude themselves.

Described in these terms, Bourdieu's account of how class inequalities in educational attainment are actually generated could be seen as having a good deal in common with those advanced in other well-known studies of the period. For example, from Britain one could cite Bernstein's work (1961, 1965) stressing the importance of class differences in linguistic codes – to which Bourdieu (Bourdieu and Passeron 1977: 133) in fact refer,[3] or Jackson and Marsden's study (1963) of the problems of adjustment faced by working-class children selected to attend traditional grammar schools. And indeed other, chiefly American, research in this same area could be regarded as going beyond that of Bourdieu not only in its methodology, but also in the recognition of how class subcultural differences might be cross-cut and, perhaps, either intensified or offset by ethnic ones: as, for example, in the impressive study by Strodtbeck (1958, cf. also Kluckhohn and Strodtbeck 1961) of the contrasting implications for educational achievement of the socialisation of working-class children of Jewish and of Italian parentage.

However, the objection could – rightly – be made that the statement of Bourdieu's position that I have given above is inadequate, and precisely because it expresses this position in the concepts and idiom of the mainstream sociology of the day. It thus fails to do justice to the quite innovatory treatment of the problem of class inequalities in educational attainment that Bourdieu attempts: that is, through the incorporation of this problem within his much larger concern with processes of social reproduction.

Cultural capital and social reproduction

Bourdieu's wish to speak of cultural capital, rather than of cultural values and resources, is clearly more than a matter of mere terminological preference. In this regard, the key text is his general statement (1986) on »forms of capital« and their significance for social reproduction. What is here of

---

3 Indeed, in the earlier stages of his work, Bourdieu sometimes refers to »linguistic« rather than cultural capital.

central interest for Bourdieu is not just the factual distribution within society of resources of differing kinds, but, further, the processes through which dominant classes effectively appropriate and monopolise these resources and use them to their own exclusive benefit – above all, in preserving their position of dominance in regard to subordinate classes. Economic capital is capital in the form of material wealth – »accumulated labour« – that is institutionalised in property rights and that then yields monetary returns, or profits, to its owners, allowing for further accumulation. Correspondingly, cultural capital is capital ›embodied‹ in individual dispositions and competencies that give privileged access to such capital in its ›objectified‹ form of cultural artefacts, and that is in turn institutionalised in criteria of cultural, including academic, evaluation and thus ultimately in educational qualifications that also provide returns to their holders. And Bourdieu further distinguishes, though with less elaboration, social capital as expressed in the possession of both informal and formal networks of acquaintance and recognition that give returns via ›contacts‹, support and representation.

Apart from the ways in which forms of capital are thus institutionalised so as to best serve the interests of dominant classes, Bourdieu also stresses their shared properties of being *convertible* and *transmissible*. One form of capital can always be, at least to some extent, converted into another; and all forms can be transmitted between individuals, whether through conversion or directly – as occurs most importantly between the individuals who make up the successive generations of families. Thus, for Bourdieu, it is the combination of institutional control over forms of capital together with processes of conversion and transmission that is crucial to the capacity of dominant classes to maintain their position – and therefore to social reproduction overall. The generalisation of the concept of capital provides the basis for an understanding of how dominant classes are able to extend and reinforce their power and privileges over all social domains, or ›fields‹, alike *and* over time.

Finally, as regards cultural capital specifically, there are two further – related – points that need to be recognised if the distinctiveness of Bourdieu's position is to be fully brought out.

First, Bourdieu (1973, 1986) at various points observes that the transmission of cultural capital shows not only similarities to, but also significant differences from, the transmission of economic capital. The main similarity is that in both cases alike the transmission operates – as a mechanism of social reproduction – primarily within and through the family. However, while the transmission of economic capital can be effected more or less instantaneously, as, say, by gifts or bequests, the transmission of cultural capital takes place over a relatively lengthy period – through what, in the language of mainstream sociology, would be called processes of socialisation. Further, though, while in both cases social reproduction is in general sustained, it would seem that, for Bourdieu, the transmission of cultural capital is, even if slower, yet more secure and irreversible than the transmission of economic capital. And crucial to this position is then another of Bourdieu's »signature concepts«, that of the *habitus*: that is, the system of socially constituted dispositions that the individual acquires, most effectively in early life, and that determines his or her entire orientation to the world and modes of conduct within it (Bourdieu 1990: 66–79).

The transmission of cultural capital, in its embodied expression, is a major part of the formation of the *habitus*. And, for Bourdieu, this would appear to be a generally more certain and predictable process than that of socialisation as conventionally understood and also one that is realised yet more exclusively within a family, and thus a social class, context.[4] Typically, the *habitus* is formed in its essentials by what Bourdieu calls »domestic« influences, and is then further developed only through the individual's own subsequent experience of »class conditions«. It remains profoundly resistant to other influences. In particular – and of chief importance for present purposes – the school and other educational institutions are seen as having only very limited potential in this regard. Bourdieu emphasises that the *habitus* acquired within their families by children of dominant classes is then underwritten, as it were, in the course of their education; but only in quite exceptional cases would he allow for the possibility of schools serving to radically redress or ›make over‹ *other* forms of *habitus* that children may bring to them. That is to say, there is little place in Bourdieu's approach for mainstream sociology's concept of ›*re*-socialisation‹, and certainly not as this might occur through the agency of the educational system.[5]

---

4 As Jenkins (2002: 109) notes, Bourdieu »appears to go to enormous lengths« to avoid speaking of socialisation.

5 Bourdieu derives the concept of *habitus* from Aquinas (via, it seems, Panofsky 1967). But, as Boudon has pointed out (2003: 142–3), he in effect elides the important distinction that Aquinas makes between the *habitus corporis* and the *habitus animae* – the former but *not* the latter being outside the individual's will and control. (To take a present-day example, one cannot decide to unlearn to ride a bicycle.) In consequence, the *habitus*, in

The second point to be recognised is one that carries particular significance in combination with the first. It is that the content of cultural capital
is regarded by Bourdieu as being in an important sense *arbitrary*. That is to
say, Bourdieu refuses to accept that particular forms of culture can, to
quote Jenkins (2002: 105, cf. Bourdieu and Passeron 1977: 5–13 esp.), »be
deduced or derived from any notions of appropriateness or relative value«.
Thus, the culture that dominant classes uphold and that in turn directs and
informs what is actually taught in schools and colleges cannot claim any
intrinsic superiority, nor yet is it open to any more pragmatic validation in
terms of the demands that modern societies typically impose upon their
members: for example, as regards the knowledge and skills that they have
to possess in order to engage in productive work or effective citizenship.
Rather, what is taught, as well as how it is taught, has to be understood as
being always determined by the interests of dominant classes, and indeed
as being so conceived that what counts as cultural capital is what will best
ensure the reproduction over time of the prevailing unequal distribution of
such capital and thus of social power and privilege more generally (cf.
Bourdieu 1973: 80–2, and for critical comment Kingston 2001).

It is especially important to recognise here that – again in contrast to
most mainstream sociologists of education – Bourdieu would reject any
attempt to *differentiate* between those aspects of culture in the teaching of
which class or other socially conditioned influences might readily be present, such as, say, the literary canon or national history, and those likely to
be more resistant to such influences, such as linguistic, mathematical or
scientific knowledge and skills.[6] For Bourdieu, »pedagogic action« is *in general* an expression – indeed, in modern societies perhaps the prime expression – of »symbolic violence«, undertaken in the interests of social reproduction. To suppose otherwise is simply to fall victim to the legitimatory
power that is exerted by the idea, promoted by dominant classes, that edu-

---

Bourdieu's conception of it, appears both exigent and unchangeable to an excessive degree. To quote Boudon: »Elle a pour effet de naturaliser l'individu, de le traiter comme
un objet soumis à des forces qui lui seraient extérieures. Elle permet de faire de la
culture une seconde nature; de voir l'individu comme le jouet passif de cette seconde nature; de transformer le sujet en objet et par suite de le rendre accessible au scalpel. « See
also van den Berg (1998: 212–20).

6 For example, one of the main critical emphases in Jackson and Marsden (1963) is on the
need for a greater distinction to be made in secondary school teaching between what
amounts to little more than middle-class convention or prejudice and »the culture that
really matters«.

cational systems function so as to develop individual talent and at the same time to serve the interests of society at large (cf. Bourdieu 1974: 32).

In sum, one could say that even if the transmission of cultural capital via the formation of the *habitus* of members of different classes were not so secure and permanent a process as Bourdieu supposes, the educational system would still not operate in any way as an engine of social transformation. It would remain an essentially conservative force, directed towards creating continuity rather than variation in the social positions of families across generations. For Bourdieu, social reproduction is, in effect, doubly guaranteed.

The failure of the theory of social reproduction

I have suggested that, from one – restricted – viewpoint, Bourdieu's account of the role of cultural capital in maintaining class inequalities in educational attainment might be seen as a rather typical expression of the educational sociology of the 1960s. In this perspective, Bourdieu's contribution does not appear as highly original but could be regarded as sound or, at all events, as not obviously mistaken. If, however, Bourdieu's explanation of educational inequalities is understood – as indeed it should be understood – as forming an integral part of his larger theory of social reproduction, it can surely claim originality. But, one must then ask: is it also sound? And just as surely, I would argue, it is not. It fails because the theory of social reproduction itself fails, and quite demonstrably so.

To hold, as Bourdieu in effect does, that the development and functioning of modern educational systems essentially confirm and stabilise the processes through which individuals and families maintain their social positions over time lacks *prima facie* plausibility. That such a claim can be made does indeed raise serious questions about the theoretical adequacy of both Bourdieu's macro- and micro-sociology: for example, in the former case, as regards the very shadowy role accorded to the state or, in the latter, as regards the grossly ›over-socialised‹ view of the individual that the concept of *habitus* implies. However, for present purposes at least, it is sufficient to concentrate on empirical issues.

One of the earliest and most compelling statements of the factual case against Bourdieu was that made by Halsey et al. (1980: chs. 4 and 8 esp.)

on the basis of British data – although data that would prove to be generally replicable from other advanced societies (cf. Shavit and Blossfeld 1993). What Halsey and his colleagues showed was that in the course of the twentieth-century expansion of secondary education in Britain, substantial and predominantly upward educational mobility did in fact occur between generations. Thus, as of the early 1970s, over two-thirds of the individuals surveyed who had attended a selective secondary school were >first-generation< – i.e. their parents had not received any education at this level; and while children of working-class background were underrepresented in this group, they were far from being excluded. Moreover, of these first-generation children, two-thirds had been successful in achieving some form of secondary educational qualification – a proportion only slightly smaller than that found among pupils who were *not* first-generation.[7]

In two respects, then, Bourdieu's position is powerfully controverted by these simple and straightforward findings. To begin with, they demonstrate that, as Halsey et al. put it (1980: 77), schools »were doing far more than >reproducing< cultural capital; they were creating it, too… They were not merely maintaining a >cycle of privilege< in which cultural capital is acquired by those from educated homes. They were at least offering an opportunity to acquire cultural capital to those homes that had not secured it in the past«. And, at the same time, the findings reported undermine the claim, crucial for Bourdieu, that (in his own prose) »an implicit pedagogic action, requiring initial familiarity with the dominant culture…offers information and training which can be received and acquired *only* [my emphasis]by subjects endowed with the sy stem of predispositions that is the condition for the success of the transmission and inculcation of the culture« (1973: 80). Or, one could say, the idea that the *habitus*, as initially formed by family and class, may be subject to confirmation by the school but not, other than quite exceptionally, to any kind of *reconstitution* is directly called into question.

Furthermore, it is today possible to see that essentially the same processes of intergenerational change that were earlier associated with the expansion of secondary education are being repeated, and, if anything, in an accentuated form, with the expansion of the tertiary sector (cf. Schofer and

---

7 The data and analyses presented by Halsey et al. are in fact limited to England and Wales, and to males. But various subsequent investigations show, not surprisingly, that essentially the same conclusions as theirs can be drawn for Scotland and for females.

Meyer 2005, Shavit et al. forthcoming). Upward educational mobility is again being extensively promoted, now to university level. And it thus becomes yet more evident than before that the idea of the family as the only, or even the main, locus of the transmission of cultural capital is, in the modern world at least, quite unsustainable.

It is important at this point to ensure clarity on two crucial issues. First, to thus set the basic evidence of educational expansion and its consequences in opposition to Bourdieu's theory of social reproduction in *not* to underwrite versions of ›modernisation‹ theory according to which this expansion is a key factor in the creation of a progressively more egalitarian and ›open‹ form of society. Indeed, the same authors who have documented processes of educational expansion have typically emphasised that the new educational opportunities that were created have been taken up to much the same degree by children of all social backgrounds alike, the children of dominant classes included. Thus, even though – contrary to the theory of social reproduction – steadily increasing numbers of children from more disadvantaged backgrounds have reached ever higher levels of educational attainment, the actual extent and significance of any narrowing in the *relative* chances of such attainment, according to class origins, remain much debated issues.[8]

However, the second point to be made is that it is then scarcely possible to rescue Bourdieu's theory of social reproduction by claiming that it is in fact to be understood in ›relative‹ terms – i.e. that the reproduction to which it refers *is* no more than the reproduction over time of the relative probabilities with which children of differing class origins achieve certain levels of educational success and, further, certain levels of employment and associated positions within the class structure.

---

8 My own position on the role of educational expansion in reducing class differentials in attainment and thus helping to create greater social fluidity is set out in elsewhere (Goldthorpe 2000/2007: vol. 2, chs. 11 and 16 esp.). However, one point may here be reiterated. In a Bourdeusien world in which the children of subordinate classes are alienated from the educational system and deprived of all hope or aspiration for success within it, the expansion of the system would then be disproportionately exploited by children of dominant classes, and class differentials in attainment would *widen*. But, whatever disagreements may exist on whether or how far such differentials have narrowed, no evidence of a sustained shift in the *opposite* direction has been produced for any modern society: i.e. working-class and other children from less advantaged backgrounds have in fact taken up new educational opportunities *at least at the same rate* as children from more advantaged backgrounds.

It is actually in one of the few places in his earlier work where Bourdieu does refer to relative rates of educational attainment that his overriding concern with *absolute* rates is best brought out. In an Appendix to Bourdieu and Passeron (1977), entitled »The Changing Structure of Higher Education Opportunities: Redistribution or Translation?«, it is observed that, in the context of university expansion in France between 1962 and 1964, the chances of children of working-class origin entering university did indeed rise, and rather *more* than those of the children of senior executives. But this finding is at once dismissed with the, quite correct, observation that even a doubling of the initial very low (1.5 per cent) rate of entry for working-class children still implies an almost negligible change – i.e. in absolute terms. And the further argument is then developed that these children's chances of gaining access to university remain far below the objective ›threshold‹ at which a significant upturn in their perceived chances of success, and hence in their aspirations, might be created. In other words, the aim is clearly to show that, even with educational expansion, the dynamics of the transmission of cultural capital mean that children of working-class (and likewise of peasant) background remain overwhelmingly *excluded from* higher education and are in fact resigned to this situation – despite, the authors add, the occasional experience of »the ›wonderboy‹, miraculously saved by the School« (1977: 227). Moreover, it is in turn evident that Bourdieu (e.g. 1973: 71, 86) would see upward class mobility from such disadvantaged origins, at least as mediated via education, as being also quite exceptional and in effect limited to specially selected cases that serve a primarily legitimatory purpose.

Now as of the early 1960s, such a position could still, conceivably, be defended, at all events in the French case. However, what has further to be noted is the very limited extent to which Bourdieu subsequently modified his position as the expansion of educational provision in France, as elsewhere, proceeded apace. In *Distinction* (1984: ch. 2, cf. also 1979) Bourdieu does recognise the evident facts of educational expansion at the secondary level – of what he calls the »schooling boom« – and in turn the growing importance of ›the scholastic mode of reproduction‹ which results in certain fractions of the dominant class pursuing strategies of ›re-conversion‹ of economic into cultural capital as the best means of securing their children's futures. But at the same time Bourdieu's chief concern is clearly to maintain that as regards social reproduction far less has in fact changed than might on a superficial view be supposed. For example, as the provision of secondary education has been expanded, it has, he argues, been *re-stratified*; and as formal qualifications have become more widely distributed, they have been correspondingly devalued. Moreover, the returns to such qualifications are in any event unequal in that children from families with greater economic and social capital are far better able to exploit them. And, consequently, increasing upward mobility, especially as achieved via education, is more apparent than real.

Indeed, Bourdieu concludes (see esp. 1984: 142–4, 154–6) that »first generation« participants in secondary education have been a »cheated« generation, to a large extent fobbed off with »worthless paper«. It is in fact when subordinate classes, rather than being simply debarred, are allowed access to secondary education, under the ideology of *l'école libératrice*, that the reality of *l'école conservatrice* is most fully revealed. For even if more gradually and subtly than before – through various means of elimination, retardation and diversion into inferior options *within* the secondary system – the ›great mass‹ of children from outside the dominant class are still excluded from the education that sustains the reproduction of this class.

There is thus little basis here for suggesting a new ›relativised‹ understanding of Bourdieu's theory of social reproduction. Bourdieu in effect seizes upon a number of social processes that could well be of importance in maintaining class differentials in educational attainment, even under conditions of rapid expansion, but then (mis)interprets these as confirming the continuing validity of his theory in essentially its original form, even at a time when it was in fact being manifestly undermined. For example, already among French children born into the working class in the late 1960s and early 1970s not just *Wunderkinder* but almost two-fifths of those of skilled workers and a quarter of those of unskilled workers did succeed in gaining the *baccalauréat* or equivalent or some higher qualification (Thélot and Vallet 2000: Table 1); and despite whatever devaluation of these qualifications might have occurred, this change was clearly linked to rising rates of upward mobility into professional and managerial positions (cf. Vallet 2004: Table 5.A2 esp.).

Cultural capital: Bourdieu domesticated and wild

The situation has then come about that in present-day discussion of educational, and wider, social inequalities, the concept of cultural capital is applied in the context of two, quite different understandings of Bourdieu's work. These can, I think, be appropriately labelled as Bourdieu ›domesticated‹ and Bourdieu ›wild‹. Following the domesticated understanding, Bourdieu is treated as a sociologist contributing to ›normal science‹ – or, one might say, as a fully paid-up member of ISA Research Committee 28, Social Stratification and Mobility – whose work is open, like that of all others involved, to qualification, refinement, development etc.[9] Following the wild, that is, more authentic understanding, Bourdieu is seen as aiming, through his theory of social reproduction, to forge a quite new conceptual and theoretical approach to the study of social inequality and hierarchy, and one that has then to be judged, at paradigm level, as being either a major social scientific advance or, as here, a failure. What I seek in conclusion to show is that because this situation has not in general been adequately recognised, various problems and no little confusion have arisen and persist.

In the domesticated understanding of Bourdieu, the concept of cultural capital is in effect prised away from the central role that it plays in his theory of social reproduction. Although it is rarely, if ever, explicitly argued by those following this understanding that the theory is intended to apply in only ›relative‹ terms, the concept of cultural capital is treated *as if* this were the case. That is to say, it is taken to be of potential value in the explanation of the class differentials in educational attainment that remain even as levels of attainment rise sharply among children of all class backgrounds alike. However, with such usage, quite serious, if unappreciated, divergences from the *ur*-concept regularly arise, and often lead to the true significance of the research findings that are reported being misconstrued, at least so far as the evaluation of Bourdieu's work is concerned.

As prime illustrations of this point, one may take, first, attempts, stemming mainly from the work of DiMaggio (1982, and see also 2001), to investigate the relative importance of cultural capital as against ›measured ability‹ in determining children's educational performance; and, second, attempts such as those initiated chiefly by Paul de Graaf (de Graaf 1986, de

---

9 To the best of my knowledge – and in no way surprisingly – Bourdieu was never a member of RC 28 nor attended any of its meetings.

Graaf et al. 2000, and see also Sullivan 2001) to distinguish among different kinds of cultural capital and their effects. I would see these two lines of research as having produced many results of major interest. But what has at the same time to be noted is that they do often involve quite radical misconceptions of Bourdieu's position, and that in turn the results presented often have a proper relation to Bourdieu's work significantly different to what the researchers themselves would suppose.

As Lareau and Weininger (2003) have pointed out, to seek, in the manner of DiMaggio, to distinguish between students' cultural capital and their ability – i.e. between their supposed status-giving participation in ›high‹ culture and their scores on various academic tests – as determinants of their achieved school grades is quite alien to Bourdieu's entire approach; and, in particular, when it is only the former that is seen as involving essentially arbitrary evaluation (DiMaggio 1982: 189; 2001: 544). As earlier indicated, Bourdieu would in fact extend the idea of the ›cultural arbitrary‹ to all forms of recognised knowledge, skill and competency, in that considerations of status dominance, and its preservation, necessarily enter into their social construction and legitimation. After citing several key passages from Bourdieu bearing on this point, Lareau and Weininger aptly remark (2003: 582): »…[T]hey reveal how far he stands from the interpretation that animates much of the English-language literature. Effects of ›status‹ for Bourdieu are not distinct from those of ›skill‹ (or by extension, ›ability‹). Cultural capital amounts to an irreducible amalgamation of the two.«[10]

Consequently, DiMaggio's research would be far better seen not as testing, and in some part supporting, Bourdieu's arguments on the role of cultural capital in social reproduction, but rather as starting out from a quite anti-Bourdeusien insistence on the *limits of* the ›cultural arbitrary‹, and in turn from a rejection of the associated (and truly wild) claim that *all* pedagogy amounts to ›symbolic violence‹ – a claim to which in fact DiMaggio never refers. In this context, the finding DiMaggio reports that students' cultural capital is clearly less important, relative to ability, in technical than in non-technical subjects would then take on a much larger significance

---

10 Lareau and Weininger's paper is the only previous attempt I have found to bring out in some detail the extent to which the application of the concept of cultural capital in research published in English-language journals entails serious but apparently unrecognised deviations from the concept as originally formulated by Bourdieu. What Lareau and Weininger call »the dominant approach« to the understanding of Bourdieu is more or less equivalent to my »domesticated« understanding.

than that he gives to it, as also would his further finding that students' cultural capital is in any event only rather weakly linked to parental education.[11]

The concern of de Graaf and others to separate out the effects of different forms of cultural capital on children's academic performance – or more generally, one might say, the effects of values from those of resources – could likewise be regarded as scarcely compatible with the concept of cultural capital as originally formulated by Bourdieu. And this becomes especially clear when a distinction is suggested between ›educational affinity‹ effects and ›educational skills‹ effects – with the former being seen as deriving more from family participation in *beaux arts* and the latter more from family reading behaviour (de Graaf et al. 2000). Essentially the same observations as were made in regard to DiMaggio's (mis)understanding of Bourdieu would again apply.

The main finding that does then emerge from this line of research is that family reading behaviour is more important for children's performance than *beaux arts* participation *and* less closely tied to the family's socioeconomic position. This result, it is true, leads to some criticism of Bourdieu that almost dares to be radical.[12] However, if Bourdieu had from the first been understood in wild – and more authentic – rather than in domesticated terms, then a critique of his work of a more fundamental and more illuminating kind would have been possible. Quite basic data on educational expansion and consequent educational mobility could first have sufficed to show, in the manner of Halsey et al., that Bourdieu's view of the transmission of cultural capital as a key process in social reproduction is simply wrong. And the more detailed findings of the research, as noted above, could then have been taken as helping to explain just *why* it is

---

11 DiMaggio does in fact end up by suggesting that his results lend more support to a ›cultural mobility‹ than to a ›cultural reproduction‹ model – i .e. cultural capital facilitates the academic success of any student who has it, and is not the exclusive resource of students from a particular social background. But, as Kingston (2001: 92) points out, if the cultural mobility model holds, then »Bourdieu's argument is severely undermined. The fact that nonelite students can benefit from this capital directly counters Bourdieu's claim that its acquisition is deeply embedded in elite families' socialization patterns.«

12 After first saying no more than that their results »do not particularly support Bourdieu's cultural reproduction theory«, de Graaf et al. are eventually led to conclude that the fact that parents of modest status and educational level can compensate by offering their children a favourable reading climate and associated skills is in »striking« contrast with Bourdieu's position which »implies that children from high status backgrounds do so well at school because their parents are at home in the cultural system.« (2000: 106, 108).

wrong.[13] That is, because differing class conditions do not give rise to such distinctive and abiding forms of *habitus* as Bourdieu would suppose; because even within more disadvantaged classes, with little access to high culture, values favouring education may still prevail and perhaps some relevant cultural resources exist; and because, therefore, schools and other educational institutions can function as important agencies of resocialisation – that is, can not only underwrite but also in various respects *complement, compensate for or indeed counter* family influences in the creation and transmission of ›cultural capital‹, and not just in the case of *Wunderkinder* but in fact on a mass scale.

In the case of sociologists who apply the concept of cultural capital within a domesticated understanding of Bourdieu, the problem is then one of a failure to appreciate just how radical – or extreme – are the claims that Bourdieu is in fact prepared to make in seeking to create his new paradigm, and in turn just how far their research findings are at odds with these claims. However, if one turns to the case of those sociologists who would wish to see ›cultural capital‹ retained with a meaning and function close to that found in Bourdieu wild, a quite different problem is apparent: that is, that of how the concept is to be used in research at all, given the loss of credibility of the theory in which it is embedded.

In this respect ample illustration is provided by a recent special number of the *British Journal of Sociology* devoted to the theme of »The Concept of Cultural Capital and Social Inequality«. In their editorial introduction, Savage and Bennett (2005: 1) refer to the »distant relationship between the sociology of stratification and class practised in the UK and USA and the tradition of social and cultural analysis associated with Bourdieu...«. Some neglect would seem here implied of the now quite extensive research carried out following the domesticated understanding of Bourdieu, to which I have referred; but this is attributable, perhaps, to the authors' concern to adhere to Bourdieu wild. At all events, it is notable that Savage and Bennett charge critics of Bourdieu from the side of stratification research of

---

13 That an initial step of the kind suggested was not taken may be because in earlier research (Ganzeboom et al. 1990: 83) a misconception occurs as regards the basis of the critique that Halsey et al., make of Bourdieu's theory of social reproduction. What Halsey et al. set in opposition to this theory is *not*, as these authors suppose, their finding of little change in class differentials in educational attainment but, rather, as earlier noted, their finding of substantial, and predominantly upward, intergenerational educational mobility.

having accepted »a reading of his concept of cultural capital which did not place it within his wider theoretical framework« (2005: 2).

This position is then maintained in a further contribution to the number by Savage et al. (2005) in which the authors argue that the concept of cultural capital has advantages over that of cultural resources (as used, for example, in my own work) on the grounds that, while the latter is a merely descriptive or ›commonsensical‹ concept, the former has a clear theoretical rationale as spelled out by Bourdieu in his general treatment of the forms of capital.[14] However, unresolved difficulties arise in the attempt to develop this argument.

It is not in fact easy to grasp just what *are* the specific advantages that Savage et al. (2005: 5–6) would see as being provided by the concept of cultural capital (readers may consult the relevant paragraphs), and no actual research illustrations are provided. What chiefly emerges is that these authors would wish to emphasise how the generalisation of the idea of capital removes the privilege given in other approaches to purely economic factors, and allows economic, cultural and social power and advantage to be treated on an equal and integrated basis: for example, all forms of capital can be considered in terms of the returns they provide and of the possibilities they offer for accumulation and convertibility.

However, what has then to be noted is a curious omission: Savage et al. say virtually nothing about the further shared feature of forms of capital identified by Bourdieu, that is, transmissibility. And it is of course, as I have earlier sought to bring out, precisely the – supposed – mode of transmissibility of cultural capital that gives it its crucial role within Bourdieu's theory of social reproduction. Cultural capital is seen as being primarily generated *and* transmitted within families, and in turn therefore within classes, via the formation of the *habitus* of their members. In this way, dominant classes achieve and sustain an effective intergenerational monopolisation of cultural capital which today is perhaps of more general importance for social reproduction even than the control that they exercise

---

14 What is not pointed out is that I would wish to use the concept of cultural resources along with that of cultural values, and that I have elsewhere argued (Goldthorpe 2000/2007: chs. 11, 13) that a failure to make this distinction – that the concept of cultural capital elides – flaws criticism put forward by Devine (1998) of a rational action approach to explaining class differentials in educational attainment: in brief, because while such an approach gives little weight to class differences in values regarding education, it readily accommodates class differences in the cultural – and other – resources necessary to the realisation of values that are largely shared.

over economic capital. But, as I have also sought to show, it is in just this regard that Bourdieu's theory has been most decisively undermined by empirical evidence, from the work of Halsey et al. onwards. It has become quite manifest that in modern societies the family is *not* the only locus of either the creation or transmission of cultural capital. Contrary to Bourdieu's claims, educational institutions also can, and do, play a major role in this regard, and one that has some significant degree of independence from the influences of family and class. And, one may add, it is in this regard that the analogy with economic capital, which tends not to be provided free or below cost by the state or other agencies, rather obviously breaks down.

The question that must then arise, so far as Savage and his associates are concerned, is that of whether or how far they would regard Bourdieu's theory of social reproduction – to which, as they insist, the concept of cultural capital must be tied – as still having validity. But to this question no clear answer is forthcoming. Rather, one may note a good deal of uncertainty if not equivocation.

Thus, Savage and Bennett at one point give the impression that they might wish to defend the theory: that is, by arguing that its critique by Halsey and his colleagues is unsound in that in their research they did not supplement information on parental education with information on cultural taste, practice and knowledge (2005: 2). But this objection has little force. For even if it were the case that those children who were first-generation acquirers of secondary qualifications did tend to come from families with some cultural resources on which schools could build, this would still be in contradiction with Bourdieu's ideas of the monopolisation of cultural capital by dominant classes, and especially so given the extent to which these children were also of working-class origin and then typically achieved upward class as well as educational mobility.[15]

Indeed, it is unclear if such a defence is convincing even to its proponents. For in Savage et al. (2005: 11; and cf. also Bennett 2005) one finds acknowledgement that a serious difficulty in Bourdieu is »a kind of latent functionalism« following from which »the process of reproduction seem-

---

15 More damaging to Halsey et al. would have been support for the hypothesis, suggested by Jackson and Marsden (1963), that many children of manual wage-workers who succeed in their secondary education are in fact of »sunken middle-class« background – i.e. the children of downwardly mobile parents. Halsey et al. give careful consideration to this hypothesis but find no evidence consistent with it.

ingly allows the endless reproduction of power«, with any apparent change being treated as no more than illusory. To which one can only respond that, rather than this being simply a difficulty in Bourdieu, it is of course what his theory of social reproduction is all about – and what has for long been the focus of criticism on theoretical as well as an empirical grounds (see e.g. Elster 1983: 104–6, Boudon 1989: 155–8).

At this point, however, Savage et al. muddy the waters with the suggestion that in its insistence that dominant classes »always win«, Bourdieu's theory has similarities with other theories, and notably my own (Goldthorpe 2000/2007: vol. 2), that are concerned with the degree of temporal stability of class differentials in educational attainment and of endogenous class mobility regimes. But this is simply an undercover attempt to rescue Bourdieu in the way I earlier referred to by implying that his theory of social reproduction has be understood in ›relative‹ terms – an interpretation that, as I have earlier shown, can find little textual support. The social regularities that I seek to explain, though indeed indicative of persisting class inequalities, are not those of social reproduction *à la* Bourdieu. Rather, they are entirely compatible with – *and do in fact coexist with* – a growing influx of working-class children into higher levels of education and long periods of rising rates of upward educational and class mobility.[16]

In sum, it remains for Savage and his associates, and for others who would believe that the concept of cultural capital has a valuable and distinctive part to play in research in social stratification, to provide a far clearer account than we so far have of just how much of the now rather embarrassing theoretical baggage that comes with this concept they would want to retain and how much to jettison; and further of how they would then see the concept as differing from the ›commonsensical‹ one of cultural resources, especially when complemented by, but kept separate from, that of cultural values. And it would of course also be helpful if such an

---

16 A failure to appreciate – or a determination to obscure – this fundamental point runs through an entire book by one of the authors in question (Devine 2004) who also tries the alternative tack of maintaining that Bourdieu and I have similar problems in our failure to recognise »the significant levels of absolute mobility, including long-range upward mobility, enjoyed (…) by many« (2004: 186). I can only wonder what I may have been writing about for a quarter of a century, starting with the first substantive chapter of my first book on mobility (Goldthorpe 1980/1987: ch. 2).

account could include actual examples of the concept at work in explanations of social regularities of a well-established kind.[17]

Conclusions

My main aim in this contribution has been to draw attention to problems associated with the concept of cultural capital that arise from its application in the context of two different understandings of the work of Bourdieu in course of which the concept was developed. Following the understanding that I have labelled as Bourdieu domesticated, his work is in effect treated as a contribution, deserving of serious consideration, within a long-standing paradigm of research into the sources of social inequalities in educational attainment. Following what I have labelled as Bourdieu wild, it is seen – far more appropriately – as an attempt to create a quite new paradigm for the study of social inequality and social hierarchy in general. It is further the case, I have argued, that while in its domesticated understanding Bourdieu's work might be regarded as tolerably sound, at least for its time, even if not very original, in its wild understanding it is certainly original but as regards its centrepiece, the theory of social reproduction, must by now be adjudged as quite unsound. Consequently, problems arise in two ways. On the one hand, sociologists accepting Bourdieu domesticated, who have in fact made most research use of the concept of cultural capital, have adapted it to their purposes in ways that are clearly not compatible with Bourdieu's general theoretical position and have often then misinterpreted their own findings: for example, as lending at least some qualified support for Bourdieu's position when they in fact go directly contrary to it.

---

17 Lareau and Weininger (2003) also make proposals for the further research use of the concept of cultural capital in what they would regard as something close to its original form: specifically, in the analysis of the knowledge, skills and competencies that parents and students are able to deploy in their interactions with teachers and administrators as they seek to comply with institutionalised standards of evaluation. This approach may well have potential, and Lareau and Weininger do provide some illustrative ethnographic data. But while it is no doubt true that knowledge etc. in the sense in question is intergenerationally transmitted within families, I would again see the key question as being that of how far this is the *exclusive* mode of transmission; and to the extent that it is not, then Bourdeusien social reproduction – as distinct from the creation of relative class advantages and disadvantages – is unlikely to be the consequence.

On the other hand, sociologists wishing to adhere to Bourdieu wild, and who have been critical of those who have detached the concept of cultural capital from its proper theoretical setting, have themselves found difficulty in showing just how the *ur*-concept can be kept fit for research purposes, given the failure – of which they show some uncomfortable recognition – of the theory that it directly serves.

In the interests of achieving the clarity that is needed for a resolution of these problems, I would make a modest proposal on the following lines. Those researchers who are concerned with cultural influences on children's educational attainment, and on persisting class differentials in such attainment, but who would not accept Bourdieu's theory of social reproduction, should likewise not accept the concept of cultural capital. They should abandon it in favour a theoretically more neutral and more limited one, such as that of cultural resources. (Some of the authors to whom I earlier referred as working in the context of Bourdieu domesticated do in fact use both concepts as, apparently, equivalents.) It will thus be possible for these researchers to recognise, without confusing themselves or others, distinctions that the concept of cultural capital would preclude: for example, between cultural resources and cultural values, between cultural resources and academic ability, or between different kinds of cultural resources that need not be closely correlated and that may enhance children's educational performance in quite differing ways. And in turn, then, the implications for processes of the intergenerational cultural transmission that would follow from Bourdeusien notions of the *habitus*, of the cultural arbitrary and of pedagogic action as symbolic violence, rather than being seemingly underwritten, could be made more closely subject to empirical scrutiny – and, I would expect, substantial rejection.

Correspondingly, the concept of cultural capital would be left as specific to Bourdieu wild or, that is, as exclusive to those sociologists who are still able to persuade themselves that Bourdieu's theory of social reproduction can be upheld. In this case, my expectation would be that its uses in research, as opposed to its display in merely programmatic statements, will prove extremely limited – short of the kind of radical revision of the theory that would then deprive the concept, and indeed the whole apparatus of ›forms of capital‹, of its very purpose.

References

Bennett, T. (2005). »The historical universal: the role of cultural value in the historical sociology of Pierre Bourdieu«, *British Journal of Sociology*, vol. 56, pp. 141–164.

Bernstein, B. (1961). »Social class and linguistic development: a theory of social learning«, in A. H. Halsey/J. Floud/C. A. Anderson (eds.), *Education, Economy and Society: a Reader in the Sociology of Education*, New York: Free Press, pp. 288–314.

Bernstein, B. (1965). »A socio-linguistic approach to social learning«, in J. Gould (ed.), *Penguin Survey of the Social Sciences*, Harmondsworth: Penguin, pp. 144–168.

Boudon, R. (1989). *The Analysis of Ideology*, Cambridge: Polity.

Boudon, R. (2003). *Y-a-t-il encore une sociologie?*, Paris: Odile Jacob.

Bourdieu, P. (1973). »Cultural reproduction and social reproduction«, in R. K. Brown (ed.), *Knowledge, Education and Cultural Change*, London: Tavistock, pp. 71-112.

Bourdieu, P. (1974). »The school as a conservative force: scholastic and cultural inequalities «, in J. Eggleston (ed.), *Contemporary Research in the Sociology of Education*, London: Methuen, pp. 32–46.

Bourdieu, P. (1979). »Avenir de classe et causalité du probable«, *Revue Française de Sociologie*, vol. 15, pp. 3–42.

Bourdieu, P. (1984). *Distinction*, London: Routledge.

Bourdieu, P. (1986). »The forms of capital«, in J. E. Richardson (ed.), *Handbook of Theory and Research for the Sociology of Education*, New York: Greenword, pp. 241–258.

Bourdieu, P. (1990). *The Logic of Practice*, Stanford: Stanford University Press.

Bourdieu, P./Passeron. J.-C. (1977). *Reproduction in Education, Society and Culture*, London: Sage.

Bourdieu, P./Passeron, J.-C. (1979). *The Inheritors: French Students and their Relation to Culture*, Chicago: Chicago University Press.

de Graaf, N. D./de Graaf, P. M./Kraaykamp, G. (2000). »Parental cultural capital and educational attainment in the Netherlands: a refinement of the cultural capital perspective«, *Sociology of Education*, vol. 73, pp. 92–111.

de Graaf, P. M. (1986). »The impact of financial and cultural resources on educational attainment in the Netherlands«, *Sociology of Education*, vol. 59, pp. 237–246.

Devine, F. (1998). »Class analysis and the stability of class relations«, *Sociology*, vol. 32, pp. 23–42.

Devine, F. (2004). *Class Practices*, Cambridge: Cambridge University Press.

DiMaggio, P. (1982). »Cultural capital and school success: the impact of status culture participation on the grades of U.S. high school students«, *American Sociological Review*, vol. 47, pp. 189–201.

DiMaggio, P. (2001). »Social stratification, life-style, social cognition, and social participation« in D. B. Grusky (ed.), *Social Stratification*, Boulder: Col.: Westview Press, pp. 542–552.

Elster, J. (1983). *Sour Grapes: Studies in the Subversion of Rationality*, Cambridge: Cambridge University Press.

Ganzeboom, H. G. B./de Graaf, P. M./Robert, P. (1990). »Cultural reproduction theory on socialist ground: intergenerational transmission of inequalities in Hungary«, *Research in Social Stratification and Mobility*, vol. 9, pp. 79–104.

Goldthorpe, J. H. (with C. Llewellyn and C. Payne) (1980/1987). *Social Mobility and Class Structure in Modern Britain* (2nd ed.), Oxford: Clarendon Press.

Goldthorpe, J. H. (2000/2007). *On Sociology* (2nd ed.) (2 vols.), Stanford: Stanford University Press.

Halsey, A. H./Heath, A. F./Ridge, J. M. (1980). *Origins and Destinations*, Oxford: Clarendon Press.

Jackson, B./Marsden, D. (1963). *Education and the Working Class*, London: Routledge.

Jenkins, R. (2002). *Pierre Bourdieu* (2nd ed.), London: Routledge.

Kingston, P. W. (2001). »The unfulfilled promise of cultural capital theory«, *Sociology of Education* (extra issue), pp. 88–99.

Kluckhohn, F. R./Strodtbeck, F. (1961). *Variations in Value Orientations*, Evanston, Ill.: Row Peterson.

Lareau, A./Weininger, E. B. (2003). »Cultural capital in educational research: a critical assessment«, *Theory and Society*, vol. 32, pp. 567–606.

Panofsky, E. (1967). *Architecture gothique et pensée scholastique* (trans. P. Bourdieu), Paris: Editions de Minuit.

Rossi, P. (1961). »Social factors in academic achievement: a brief review«, in A. H. Halsey/J. Floud/C. A. Anderson (eds.), *Education, Economy and Society: a Reader in the Sociology of Education*, New York: Free Press, pp. 269–273.

Savage, M./Bennett, T. (2005). »Editors' introduction: cultural capital and social inequality«, *British Journal of Sociology*, vol. 56, pp. 1–10.

Savage, M./Warde, A./Devine, F. (2005). »Capitals, assets, and resources: some critical issues«, *British Journal of Sociology*, vol. 56, pp. 31–47.

Schofer, E./Meyer, J. W. (2005). »The worldwide expansion of higher education in the twentieth century«, *American Sociological Review*, vol. 70, pp. 898–920.

Shavit, Y./Blossfeld, H.-P. (eds.) (1993). *Persistent Inequality: Changing Educational Attainment in Thirteen Countries*, Boulder: Westview Press.

Shavit, Y./Arum, R./Gamoran, A./Menahem, G. (forthcoming). *Stratification in Higher Education: A Comparative Study of 15 Countries*, Stanford, Cal.: Stanford University Press.

Strodtbeck, F. (1958). »Family interaction, values, and achievement« in D. D. McClelland (ed.), *Talent and Society*, New York: Van Nostrand, pp. 135–194.

Sullivan, A. (2001). »Cultural capital and educational attainment«, *Sociology*, vol. 35, no. 4, pp. 893–912.

Thélot, C./Vallet, L.-A. (2000). »La réduction des inégalités sociales devant l'école depuis le début du siècle«, *Economie et Statistique*, vol. 334, pp. 3–32.

Vallet, L.-A. (2004). »Change in intergenerational class mobility in France from the 1970s to the 1990s and its explanation: an analysis following the CASMIN approach«, in R. Breen (ed.), *Social Mobility in Europe*, Oxford: Oxford University Press, pp. 115–147.

van den Berg, A., (1998). »Is sociological theory too grand for social mechanisms?«, in P. Hedström/R. Swedberg (eds.), *Social Mechanisms*, Cambridge: Cambridge University Press, pp. 204–237.

Weininger, E. B. (2005). »Foundations of Pierre Bourdieu's class analysis«, in E. O. Wright (ed.), *Approaches to Class Analysis*, Cambridge: Cambridge University Press, pp. 82–118.

Social mobility and education: a comparative analysis of period and cohort trends in Britain and Germany[1]

Richard Breen and Ruud Luijkx

Most comparative analyses of intergenerational social mobility have dealt with differences between countries rather than change through time. Grusky and Hauser (1984) and Erikson and Goldthorpe (1992) are examples of relatively large scale inter-country period comparisons: there are numerous smaller scale comparisons of, typically, two or three countries. Temporal comparisons, when they have been made, have been of four main types. Straightforward period comparisons are found in, for example, Breen (2004) which contains chapters making period comparisons (over the last three decades of the twentieth century) within 11 European countries. The well-known study of Ganzeboom et al. (1989), which used 149 mobility tables for men drawn from 35 countries spanning the period 1947–86, analyzed variation between countries and over periods, as did Breen and Luijkx (2004). There are various studies which make period comparisons using a small number of tables from one or more countries (DiPrete and Grusky 1990, Hauser and Huang 1997, Hout 1988, Jones et al. 1994, Jonsson and Mills 1993, Luijkx and Ganzeboom 1989, Vallet 1999). Thirdly, cohort comparisons have been used in a small number of studies (Heath and Payne 2000, Müller and Pollak 2004). Here, repeated cross-sections are used to provide information on birth cohorts, whose mobility trajectories can be followed as they age. Even rarer are studies that draw comparisons over both cohorts and periods (Breen and Jonsson forthcoming, Gerber and Hout 2004, Müller and Pollak 2004). Here we add to the number of papers that look at change over both cohorts and periods, but we extend work in this area by also making a comparison between Germany and Great Britain.

In the analysis of social mobility, a distinction is drawn between absolute and relative mobility. Absolute mobility refers to the pattern of flows

1 Thanks to Jan O. Jonsson, Reinhard Pollak and Carlo Barone for comments on an earlier draft.

between class origins (the social class in which someone was brought up) and class destinations (the class they occupy at the time of the survey). Relative mobility, or social fluidity, is concerned with the degree to which class destinations depend on class origins, and it is based on the comparison – between people of different class origins – of their chances of being found in one destination class rather than another. The weaker the statistical association between origins and destinations, the greater social fluidity is said to be. Social fluidity is often interpreted as an index of equality in the chances of access to more or less advantageous social positions between people coming from different social origins. In this contribution we deal with social fluidity and ask if, and how, the inequalities between people originating in different classes in their chances of gaining access to one class destination rather than another have changed. Our data consist of repeated surveys carried out during the final twenty five years of the twentieth century, and we use these to examine change over both periods and cohorts. Our period analysis simply involves making comparisons between each of the surveys (or groups of temporally contiguous surveys), while our cohort analysis involves the comparison of fluidity between groups of individuals born at different times during the twentieth century (in other words, birth cohorts). So, while the period comparison covers the last part of the twentieth century, the cohort comparison covers a much longer period because the cohorts represented in our data were born between 1912 and 1977.

We address three specific questions. First, what have been the trends in social fluidity across both cohorts and periods in Britain and Germany? Secondly, what is the relationship between the cohort and period trends in each country? Thirdly, what is the role of education in explaining change, or the lack of it, over either cohorts or periods, and does education play a similar role in the two countries?

In the next part of the contribution, we review what is already known about social fluidity in Britain and Germany. Then we go on to outline the data that we use and how we went about setting up the analyses. The third, fourth and fifth sections of the contribution give our answers to the three questions we have posed, and we conclude with a discussion of our findings. We suggest that the process labelled by Breen and Jonsson (forthcoming) »the compositional effect of educational attainment« plays a fundamental role in accounting for change, or its absence, in trends in social fluidity.

Previous research on mobility in Great Britain and Germany

As part of the CASMIN (Comparative Mobility in Industrial Nations) project, Erikson and Goldthorpe (1992), using data from the mid-1970s, report that social fluidity among men in West Germany tended to be somewhat lower than in most other developed countries for which they had data. Müller and Pollak (2004), who use a data set comprising 22 surveys to analyze change in West German fluidity using both a period and cohort perspective, find that, over cohorts born between the 1930s and 1960s, fluidity increased somewhat, bringing Germany more into line with the other countries in the CASMIN data set. They attribute this change in large part to the role of the German educational system:

»We know that in Germany class inequality in education has been particularly high but decreasing. At the same time, Germany is one of the countries with the strongest links between educational attainment and class allocation, mostly due to the strong presence of occupational labour markets and their institutional linkages with credentials provided through the system of general education and vocational training. These strong credentialist job allocation principles have not changed markedly so far. In such a context, it is particularly likely that a decline in class inequality in education will lead to higher social fluidity.« (Müller and Pollak 2004: 111)

Nevertheless, these authors argue that certain features of German social fluidity have persisted, such as the pronounced tendency for class inheritance and a rather rigid barrier between manual and non-manual occupations.

In the British case, the vast bulk of research suggests little change over time in social fluidity from Glass's 1949 study to the present day (Heath and Payne 2000: 255–7). A number of studies have used data from the British General Election Study (BGES) to compare with the results of the 1972 Oxford Mobility Study (Goldthorpe 1987: ch. 9, Goldthorpe 1995, Jonsson and Mills 1993, Macdonald and Ridge 1988) and have found little or no change in fluidity. A recent analysis by Goldthorpe and Mills (2004) confirms the finding of no change over the closing decades of the 20th century, but this time using data from the General Household Survey. In contrast to these period results, a cohort study, also using BGES data, by Heath and Payne (2000) finds a steady increase in social fluidity among cohorts born between the last decades of the 19th century and the 1950s.

The Anglo-German comparison is thus an interesting one, since it brings together a society which, thirty years ago, was among the more fluid, or open, in Europe, but in which there has subsequently been virtually no change, and a society which was rather closed, but has become more open. The challenge we take on here is to find some plausible explanation of the differing trends that the two countries have exhibited – a task which is made possible, if not easy, by the availability of high quality data for both.

Data

The data that we use were originally assembled for a project on the comparative analysis of social mobility in Europe (Breen 2004). That project sought to bring together all the high quality data sets collected between 1970 and 2000 in 11 European countries that could be used for the analysis of social mobility. The data used here is identical to those employed in that project, except that we deal with only Britain and Germany and we added surveys for Germany.[2] The sources of data for these two countries are shown in Table 1. For Britain the data come from the General Household Survey (GHS) for the years 1973, 1975–6, 1979–1984, 1987–1992. Although the GHS has been fielded annually from 1971 onwards, information on the employment of the respondent's father (or head of the family) was not collected in 1977 or 1978 or after 1992, while information on the last job held by those not currently working was not gathered in 1985 and 1986. We omit the 1974 data because Goldthorpe and Mills (2004: 202), who have recently used the GHS for mobility analysis (and who kindly provided the data to us), report that »some serious problems« exist with the 1974 data.

The German data, which cover the period 1976 to 2002, come mainly from the ALLBUS survey, but are supplemented by other surveys. Müller and Pollak (2004: 85), who kindly provided us with the data, write that these surveys »all use similar questionnaires and procedures to collect the

---

2 The analysis closely follows that of Breen and Jonsson (forthcoming) who analyze period and cohort mobility in Sweden using the data employed in Breen (2004). Analyses involving cohorts, periods and education require large samples and would not, therefore, be possible for all 11 countries in the data set, some of which have much smaller sample sizes than are found in Britain, Sweden or Germany (as shown in Table 3.2 of Breen and Luijkx 2004).

Table 1. Sources of data

Country	# tables	Sources of data	Years for which data are included
Germany	30	ZUMABUS	1976–77 1979(2) 1980 1982
		ALLBUS	1980 1982 1984 1986 1988 1990–92 1994 1996 1998 2000 2002
		Politik in der BRD	1978 1980
		Wohlfahrtssurvey	1978
		German Life History Study	I (1981–1983) II (1985–1988) III (1988–1989)
		German Socio-economic Panel	1986 1999 2000
Great Britain	15	General Household Survey	1973 1975–76 1979–1984 1987– 1992

data« used in mobility analyses, and they express their confidence that »cumulating these databases does not introduce systematic inconsistencies«. To preserve comparability over time, they refer only to Germans resident in West Germany.

It is usual in mobility analysis to confine attention to the working age population. Accordingly, for Germany we deal with social fluidity among men aged 25 to 64 at each survey. Unfortunately, the British data force us to adopt a narrower age range: 25 to 49, because, for most years, respondents to the GHS aged 50 or over were not asked the occupation of their father. We do not analyze data for women from either country: the reasons for this are explained in the conclusion.

To define class origins (O, for short) and destinations (D), we use the EGP class schema (Erikson and Goldthorpe 1992: ch. 2) as follows:

I	(upper service),
II	(lower service),
IIIa	(higher grade routine non-manual),
IVab	(the self-employed and small employers),
IVc	(farmers),
V+VI	(skilled manual workers, technicians and supervisors), and
VIIab+IIIb	(semi- and unskilled manual, agricultural, and lower grade routine non-manual workers).

Unfortunately, however, the limitations of the GHS force us to use a six, rather than seven, class classification for Britain, because it is not possible to distinguish between classes I and II or between these and class IVa (that is, small employers): accordingly, the first class in Britain is I+II+Iva, while the third is IVb (the self-employed without employees).

We measure respondents' education by their highest level of educational attainment (education (E), for short) categorized using the CASMIN educational schema. We have amalgamated categories 1a, b and c, and also 2a and b of the original scheme (Müller et al. 1989), giving us five educational categories:

1abc	(compulsory education only),
2ab	(secondary intermediate education, vocational and general),
2c	(full secondary education),
3a	(lower tertiary education), and
3b	(higher tertiary).[3]

Although we have 28 surveys (i.e. 30 tables) for Germany and 15 surveys for Britain, we group these into three periods. Because the surveys were spread differently across the 1970–2002 period in the two countries, we use slightly different definitions of periods in each. For Britain, the periods are 1973–9, 1980–4 and 1987–92, while for Germany they are 1976–84, 1985–1993 and 1994–2002. Similarly, we define slightly different birth cohorts because of the different survey dates and age ranges covered in the two countries. So for Germany, we have birth cohorts 1912–21, 1922–30, 1931–39, 1940–48, 1949–57, 1958–66 and 1967–77, and for Britain 1924–27, 1928–34, 1935–41, 1942–48, 1949–55, 1956–62 and 1963–67. Thus, the German data span a slightly longer period than the British. Omitting cases with missing information on one or more variables gives us sample sizes of 18,961 for Germany and 58,125.5 for Great Britain. For Germany, we use unweighted data; for Britain we correct for the over-sampling of Scotland in the original data.

---

3 Higher tertiary education, 3b, means the successful completion (with examination) of a traditional, academically-oriented university education. Lower tertiary education, 3a, is usually characterised by a shorter length of study and more practically oriented study programs (e.g. technical college diplomas, social worker or, non-university teaching certificates).

Modelling strategy

Our initial analyses are concerned with change in the origin-destination association over periods and cohorts. For this purpose, our data set comprises the four-way origin (indexed i=1,...,I) by destination (J) by period (K) by cohort (L) table. This table is incomplete because not all cohorts are observed in all periods: in fact we have, for both Britain and Germany, 15 mobility tables and in each period we observe a mobility table for five of our seven cohorts. In the first period, we have a mobility table for each of the five oldest cohorts; in the second period, we no longer observe the oldest birth cohort and, instead, have a first observation of the second youngest cohort. In the third period, we lose the second oldest cohort and replace this with the youngest cohort in our data. This observation schema is shown in Table 2. For most cohorts we have three mobility tables, but for the oldest and youngest we have only one and for the second oldest and second youngest we have two.

Our analysis begins by testing for change in social fluidity across periods, ignoring cohorts, and across cohorts, ignoring periods. But, of course, these are simply two perspectives on the same set of data, and so we then address the question of the relationship between cohort and period trends. It is generally recognised that education is one of the major channels through which intergenerational class reproduction occurs (Ishida et al. 1995), and so the second stage of our analysis incorporates education as a possible explanation of our findings concerning the trend in fluidity across cohorts and periods. As far as the data are concerned, this simply means that for each cohort in each period, as identified in Table 2, we now have, in place of the two-way origin by destination table, a three-way table of origin by destination by education.

Because we are using four-way and five-way tables in these analyses, the cell counts are rather sparse in places. The bias in estimates using log-linear models can be reduced by adding a small constant equal to the number of parameters in the model divided by twice the number of cells in the table being analyzed (Firth 1993). For our data and the models, we fitted this constant was between 0.25 and 0.30, and so we chose to add 0.25 to all cell counts. While this is less exact than the procedure recommended by Firth, the use of an invariant adjustment has the advantage of allowing us to compare the fit of models having different numbers of parameters.

Table 2. Observations of Birth cohorts in periods, British and German data

| | Great Britain | 1973–79 | 1980–84 | 1987–92 |
| | Germany | 1976–84 | 1984–93 | 1994–2002 |
Birth Cohorts		Observations		
Great Britain	Germany			
1924–27	1912–21	Y	N	N
1928–34	1922–30	Y	Y	N
1935–41	1931–39	Y	Y	Y
1942–48	1940–48	Y	Y	Y
1949–55	1949–57	Y	Y	Y
1956–62	1958–66	N	Y	Y
1963–67 ·	1967–77	N	N	Y

Trends in social fluidity

Change over periods

We begin by testing for change in social fluidity over periods. The model that says fluidity is constant over periods (PO PD OD in the usual log-linear notation) returns a deviance of 84 on 50 degrees of freedom in the British case and 88 on 72 df in the German. Taking p ≤.05 as our criterion of whether to accept a model or reject it, we can see that constant fluidity must be rejected for Britain but not Germany (p =.10). The log-multiplicative layer effect (Xie 1992) or unidiff (Erikson and Goldthorpe 1992) model is a more powerful test of change. We write the model as PO PD ODφ_k and here the final term indicates that the origin-destination association differs over periods according to the scalar quantity φ_k.[4] For Britain this model is not an improvement on constant fluidity (the change in deviance is 4 on 2 df), while it is in Germany (14 on 2 df) where the values of φ_k are fixed at 1 for the 1976–84 period and estimated as .88 and .91 for the two later periods. In fact, there is no significant difference between the estimates for the 1984–93 and 1994–2002 periods, and so we conclude that fluidity increased in Germany between the 1976–84 and 1984–93 periods and remained constant thereafter. For Britain it seems

---

4 The stronger the association between origins and destinations, the larger is φ_k: it is therefore inversely related to social fluidity.

that fluidity has differed over periods but not according to any clear temporal trend towards greater or lesser openness.

Change over cohorts

We test for change over cohorts in the analogous way, using first the model of constant fluidity over cohorts (CO CD OD). This returns a deviance of 218 on 150 df in the British case and 332 on 216 df in Germany. In both cases, the hypothesis of constancy over cohorts must be rejected. The unidiff model, which we now write as CO CD ODφ_l, does not improve on the common fluidity model in Britain (the change in deviance is 10.2 on 6 df) but does in Germany (47.6 on 6 df). The estimated values of φ_l are 1, 1.00, 1.06, 0.98, 0.87, 0.79 and 0.79, suggesting a curvilinear trend in which fluidity declined over the oldest cohorts, then, from the 1931–39 birth cohort, steadily increased. This pattern was also observed by Müller and Pollak (2004: 100). Analyzing cohorts born in 1920–29, 30–39, and so on up to the cohort born 1960–69, they observe that, among men, fluidity in the 1930–39 cohort was lower than in the previous cohort, but thereafter steadily increased. They attribute this to the unusually high degree of fluidity found in their oldest cohort which they see as the consequence of the disruption caused by World War II and the subsequent large scale migration which, for many in this cohort, broke the link that would otherwise have existed between their class origins and destinations (Müller and Pollak 2004: 79–81).

In Germany, cohort change can be quite well captured as a trend towards greater fluidity, whereas in Britain change seems to be less systematic. Some further analysis of the British data showed that, in fact, a very good model for cohort change is one which allows temporal variation only in the interaction parameter for inheritance among the farmer class, IVc, while all the other origin-destination association parameters remain constant. This model returns a deviance of 173 on 150 df and so fits the data according to our criterion (p =.09). The trend in the parameter for farm inheritance is towards stronger association. Normalizing this to a value of 1 in the oldest cohort, we find values of 1, 1.08, 1.23, 1.39, 1.45, 1.55 and 1.68 across the seven birth cohorts.

Change over cohort and periods

As we noted earlier, tests of change across periods and across cohorts are being carried out on the same data, albeit arranged in a different way. But there is a clear relationship between cohorts and periods, as Table 2 shows. The mobility table for a particular period is an amalgamation of mobility tables for a set of cohorts, and differences between period mobility tables must therefore be due to changes in mobility within those cohorts that are observed in more than one period (within-cohort change), and/or the changing distribution of cohorts in each period, of which the most obvious and most important is the replacement of older cohorts by younger ones. This latter is known as cohort replacement (Mannheim 1952, Ryder 1965) and is potentially an important source of change. By comparing a model that allows for change over both periods and cohorts with models that allow for change over only cohorts or only periods we can try to determine whether period change is in fact being driven by cohort replacement.

Panel A of Table 3 reports the goodness of fit of four models fitted to the British and German data: model 1 is change over cohorts and periods; model 2 allows for change only over periods, model 3 only over cohorts and model 4 allows for no change at all. The important results, however, are found in panel B which compares the various models. The first comparison asks whether the change over cohorts is also present when we allow for change over periods, and the answer is yes, because the deviance statistics are highly significant. The second comparison turns the question around: is change over periods significant when we allow for cohort change? And now the answer is negative: once changes over cohorts are taken into account, change over periods becomes insignificant. For Britain the deviance of 59.58 on 50 df has $p = .17$, while for Germany a deviance of 90.53 on 72 df has $p = .07$. In the British case the same results holds if we carry out the tests replacing the full ODC interaction with the model that allows only farm inheritance to change over time. This model might be expressed as OCP DCP OD FC, where the final term means the seven parameters (using six degrees of freedom) that allow farm inheritance to change over cohorts. This model returns a deviance of 388.38 on 344 df. The comparison with model 1 in panel A of Table 1 yields a deviance of 227.9 and 194 df ($p = .048$), showing that this fits almost as well as the model with full cohort and period change.

Table 3. Testing for period and cohort change in social fluidity

A. Goodness of fit

Models		Great Britain		Germany	
		deviance	df	deviance	df
1 Change over periods and cohorts	ODP ODC	160.51	150	212.69	216
2 Change over periods	ODP	351.49	300	535.94	432
3 Change over cohorts	ODC	220.09	200	303.22	288
4 No change	OD	433.11	350	627.90	504

All models include the terms OCP DCP.

B. Model comparisons

Models	Great Britain		Germany	
	deviance	df	deviance	df
1 2 vs 1 Change over cohorts given change over periods	190.98	150	323.25	216
2 3 vs 1 Change over periods given change over cohorts	59.58	50	90.53	72
3 4 vs 1 Change over cohorts and periods	272.60	200	415.21	288

We can summarize our results thus far as follows. In Britain, variations in social fluidity across periods seem to be unsystematic, with no clear trend towards increasing or decreasing social fluidity. Across birth cohorts, social fluidity has remained constant over the course of the twentieth century, with the single exception of the tendency for farm inheritance to become more pronounced. This tendency, however, is of relatively little substantive significance because the share of the working age population in class IVc is very small in Britain and has declined during the century.[5] Indeed, this decline may be part of the explanation of the increasing strength of farm inheritance. Once this change is taken into account, however, variation across cohorts disappears. In the German case, the trend to increasing fluidity over periods also disappears when cohort change is taken into account, but here there is a clear trend towards greater fluidity which begins with the cohort born in the 1940s. In both cases, differences between periods are in fact the result of cohort replacement. Over time, earlier born cohorts drop out of the working age population and later born cohorts replace them. This leads to a compositional effect: the make-up of the work-

---

5 In our oldest cohort, just under six per cent of men originated in the farmer class; in the youngest cohort only just under two per cent. For class destinations, the comparable figures are 2.6 per cent and 0.7 per cent.

ing age population changes over periods and, because cohorts differ in their fluidity, this causes the observed period change in fluidity. In Britain, this change is very slight, being confined to change in farm inheritance, whereas in Germany there is a clear trend towards greater equality of mobility chances.[6]

The role of education

The differing trends that we have discovered in the two countries present us with an interesting problem: how can we account for the lack of change over cohorts in Britain and its presence in Germany? Our analysis at this point is facilitated by the fact that we have already found that we do not need to distinguish periods when we take cohort differences into account, and so from this point forward, we omit the period variable and carry out our analyses on the four-way table of origins by destinations by cohort by education. The question we now seek to answer is: can we explain change or stability over cohorts by taking account of education?

Table 4 shows the result of fitting seven models to the new data set and panel B shows a set of comparisons between models. The first four models reported in panel A parallel those reported in Table 3, except with the period variable replaced by education, and the purpose is analogous: to find out whether, when we control for education, cohort effects disappear. Model 1 of panel A allows social fluidity to vary both by educational level (ODE) and by cohort; model 2 allows variation only by education and model 3 only by cohort, while model 4 assumes no variation. The fifth model replaces the full interaction specification of model 1 with its log-multiplicative counterpart in which the association between origins and destinations is scaled up or down according to two scalars, one varying across cohorts, the other across levels of education. This model might be written OEC DEC OD$\varphi_c\varphi_m$, where m (m= 1,...,5) denotes educational

---

6 Despite this, the evidence that we have shown that Britain is a more fluid society than Germany (Breen and Luijkx 2004: 59, 72) is still supported, though the difference between the two has been diminishing. A similar result is found in respect of the association between class origins and educational attainment: Jonsson et al. (1996) find a stronger trend towards an equalization of class inequality in education in Germany than in Britain, but, nevertheless, the association between class origins and educational attainment continues to be stronger in Germany.

Table 4. Testing for variation in fluidity over cohorts and educational levels
A. Goodness of fit

Models		Great Britain		Germany	
		deviance	df	deviance	df
1	Variation over education and cohorts ODE ODC	481.18	600	534.65	864
2	Variation over education ODE	683.9	750	792.91	1080
3	Variation over cohorts ODC	706.45	700	713.3	1008
4	No Variation OD	902.76	850	982.59	1224
5	Log-multiplicative variation over education and cohorts $OD\varphi_i\varphi_m$	822.21	840	908.23	1214
6	Log-multiplicative variation over education $OD\varphi_m$	848.38	846	918.68	1220
7	Log-multiplicative variation over cohorts $OD\varphi_i$	885.11	844	963.19	1218

All models include the terms OCE DCE.

B. Model comparisons

Models		Great Britain		Germany	
		deviance	df	deviance	df
1	2 vs 1 Variation over cohorts given variation over education	202.72	150	258.26	216
2	3 vs 1 Variation over education given variation over cohorts	225.27	100	178.65	144
3	4 vs 1 Variation over cohorts and education	421.58	250	447.94	360
4	5 vs 1 Log-multiplicative vs. unrestricted variation over education and cohorts	341.03	240	373.58	350
5	6 vs 5 Log-multiplicative variation over cohorts given log-multiplicative variation over education	26.17	6	10.45	6
6	7 vs 5 Log-multiplicative variation over education given log-multiplicative variation over cohorts	62.9	4	54.96	4

levels. Model 6 allows the origin-destination association to be scaled only over levels of education, while model 7 allows it to be scaled only over cohorts.

In panel B we see that comparisons among the first three models are not conclusive: if variation in cohorts is omitted from the model the effect is statistically significant (comparison 1), and the same is true if variation over educational levels is omitted (comparison 2). These results suggest that fluidity in both countries varies according to both cohort and educational level. But if we replace the full interaction specifications of models 1,

2 and 3 of panel A with their log-multiplicative counterparts, models 4, 5 and 6, the picture becomes a little clearer, at least in the German case. As comparison 4 shows, the log-multiplicative model OEC DEC OD$\varphi_l\varphi_m$ is not a poorer fit to the data than the full interaction model, OEC DEC ODC ODE: the difference in deviance of 374 on 350 df has a p value of .18. If we then use model 4 of panel A as our point of comparison, we find that the omission of log-multiplicative variation over cohorts is not statistically significant (comparison 5 in panel B, p =.11) while omission of variation over educational levels is highly significant (comparison 6, p <.0001). This leads us to take model 6 as our preferred model and to conclude that, in the case of Germany, controlling for variation in social fluidity across levels of education explains the trend in social fluidity over cohorts. But for Britain, matters are not so simple because the log multiplicative model 5 in panel A is in fact a poorer fit to the data than its full interaction equivalent, model 1. The relevant comparison is 4 in panel B, which is highly significant (deviance of 341 on 240 df has a p value less than .0001). And, in any case, all of the subsequent comparisons, 5 and 6, are also statistically significant. So all the comparisons in Table 4 point to the same conclusion for Britain: there exists variation over cohorts and educational levels and this is not captured by the parsimonious log-multiplicative specifications.

However, we earlier saw that all the change that occurred over cohorts in Britain was captured by trends in farm inheritance. Accordingly, we replace the model OEC DEC ODC ODE (model 1 of panel A of Table 4) with OEC DEC ODE FC (using the same notation as earlier) and we find that this returns a deviance of 639 on 734 df which, when compared with model 1 of panel A, gives a difference in deviance of 158.06 on 134 df, p=.08, showing that this simpler model is not a poorer fit to the data. So now it seems that broadly the same conclusion applies to Britain as to Germany. In this case, except for the changes across cohorts in farm inheritance, all the variation in social fluidity exists between different educational levels and, once this is taken into account, there is no variation across cohorts or periods.

Anglo-German differences in social fluidity

It is perhaps appropriate at this point to take stock of what we have discovered about trends in social fluidity in the two countries. In Germany, fluidity increased between the 1976–84 and 1984–93 periods, but this change was entirely the result of cohort replacement, as more fluid younger cohorts, especially those born after the 1930s, replaced less fluid older ones. But we then found that this cohort trend disappeared once we took into account the distribution of educational attainment. For Britain, the picture is less straightforward. Social fluidity certainly varies over periods, but not in any way that could be described as a trend towards greater or lesser inequality, and, once we took account of differences between birth cohorts, this variation vanished. So, as in Germany, cohort replacement accounts for change over periods. But whereas in Germany there was a clear trend in fluidity across cohorts, in Britain the picture was one of considerable stability, with the exception of a steady strengthening in class inheritance among farmers. When education was introduced into the picture, it did not partial out the trend in farm inheritance which is not surprising, given that educational attainment is unlikely to play a role in the inheritance of property. Nevertheless, in Britain, social fluidity does vary according to educational level.

What is the mechanism that explains why, when we control for differences in social fluidity at different levels of education, the trend in fluidity across cohorts disappears, at least in the German case? The answer to this question is that another compositional effect is at work, which follows from the finding that fluidity is higher at higher levels of educational attainment. We can see this in the estimates of φ_m from our preferred model – namely model 6 in panel A of Table 4. Setting the value of φ_m at the lowest level of education (CASMIN level 1abc) to 1, the value for lower secondary education is estimated as 0.86, for upper secondary 0.59, for lower tertiary 0.50 and for higher tertiary 0.55. As we can see in Figure 1a, in the older German cohorts a large proportion of the population was concentrated at lower levels of educational attainment, but as we move to younger cohorts, the educational distribution shifts towards higher levels of attainment, so placing increasing shares of each cohort in those educational categories where the association between class origins and class destinations is weaker and fluidity is correspondingly higher.

Figure 1. Changing educational distributions, Great Britain and Germany
1a. Germany

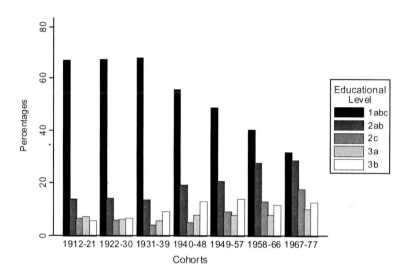

1b. Great Britain

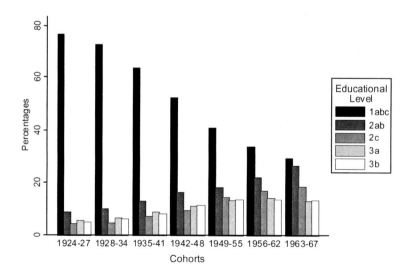

But if this is so, why do we not observe an increase in fluidity in Britain as well, given that here we also found variation in fluidity between different educational levels and that Britain has also experienced a gradual upward shift in the educational distribution of successive birth cohorts? This latter is shown in Figure 1b, which looks remarkably similar to 1a: indeed, if anything, the upward shift in the educational distribution is slightly more pronounced in Britain than in Germany. The answer appears to be that the variation in fluidity between educational levels does not display the same straightforward pattern as in Germany. If we take the model OEC DEC ODE FC, which, up to now has been our preferred model for Britain, and we replace the ODE term with its log-multiplicative counterpart, $OD\varphi_m$, we find that this leads to a much poorer fitting model (the difference is 144 on 105 df, p =.007). The estimates of the φ_m coefficients do indeed display the same kind of decline as we found in Germany (their values are 1, 0.94, 0.84, 0.67, 0.43), but the failure of the model to fit the data suggests that there is a good deal of variation around this trend.

This is evident in Figure 2. The first panel of the figure shows the trend, across levels of education, in the log odds ratios between origins and destinations in Germany. Because the best fitting model here is OEC DEC $OD\varphi_m$, all these log odds ratios follow the same downward trajectory as we move from lower to higher levels of education. The second through to the sixth panels show the estimated log odds ratios formed from adjacent class destinations for different pairs of class origins under the preferred model for Britain – namely OEC DEC ODE FC. So, panel 2 refers to the comparison between men of class origins I+II+IVa and those of III and each line represents the log odds ratios formed comparing these two in their access to particular pairs of destination classes: I+II+IVa and III; III and IVb; IVb and IVc; and so on. The shape of each line shows how that particular log odds ratio differs as one moves from considering men with low levels of education to those with higher. Panel 3 reports the same thing, but now comparing men of class III and class IVb origins, and similarly for the other panels. The clear impression from these figures is that there is no simple trend in the British data: some log odds ratios are indeed lower at higher levels of education, but some are higher, while others are roughly the same over the whole educational range. The contrast with the German case, where all inequalities are less at the higher levels of education, could hardly be more striking.

Figure 2. Log odds ratios over educational attainment

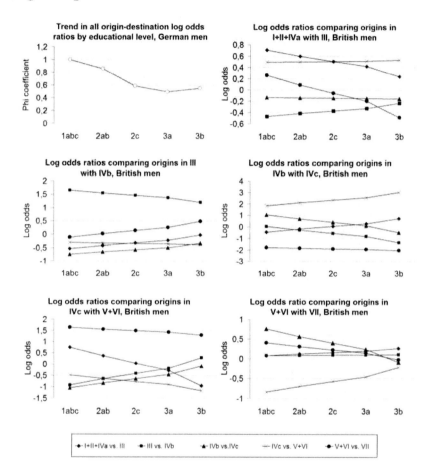

Discussion and conclusions

In a recent paper, Breen and Jonsson (forthcoming) have argued that change in social fluidity is, under normal circumstances, unlikely to be driven by period effects (that is, changes that affect all, or a large share of, the working age population at a particular point in time) and more likely to be the result of changes that affect particular birth cohorts. As a result, observed changes in social fluidity between periods are likely to be the product of cohort replacement. The results that we have obtained here support their arguments. The strongest reason for expecting change to be driven by cohort replacement is that, for most people, educational attainment is the most important single determinant of their class position, and education is attained during childhood, youth and early adulthood (or, as Müller and Pollak 2004: 110 succinctly state, »Educational participation and class inequality in education is a cohort phenomenon«). Thus, changes in the distribution of educational attainment affect specific birth cohorts and not the entire population. As Breen and Jonsson point out, one corollary of this result is that comparisons of fluidity based on two surveys which are reasonably close in time are unlikely to find change simply because they will both comprise samples from substantially the same birth cohorts.

Under what circumstances might we, nevertheless, find differences in fluidity over periods that are not the result of cohort replacement? Certainly, the kind of exceptional upheavals like that associated with the fall of state socialism in Europe is one possibility, and both Gerber and Hout (2004) and Róbert and Bukodi (2004) have found period change in social fluidity under these circumstances. But period change may also be artefactual. When we compare samples drawn from the same birth cohort in different periods, social fluidity may differ between them for reasons that have nothing to do with the true underlying inequality in mobility chances. The samples could differ because of changes in the way the defined population is sampled in different surveys (due to different sampling frames or different patterns and levels of response) or because of differences in the population itself, arising from mortality, migration or changes in labour force participation. And it is the latter that led us to exclude women from our analyses. In analyses involving class position, it is, we believe, important to confine attention only to women who are currently participating in the labour force: failure to do this will mean the inclusion of some women whose class position is one that they occupied in the distant past or which is derived from that of their spouse, depending on the conventions followed in the particular survey. But if we do indeed define our population as women in the labour force, then temporal comparisons are compromised if rates of women's labour force participation change within birth cohorts. In Britain and Germany this is the case: in both countries not only is there a historical trend towards greater female labour force participation, but there are also pronounced life-cycle patterns of participation and nonparticipation. In Sweden, this is much less of a problem because here the pattern of women's labour force participation varies less over the life course and is much more similar to men's.

Hout (1988) was the first to point to the existence of the three-way interaction between class origins, class destinations and educational attainment, and he suggested its potential to account for changing fluidity in the US when considered together with the upward trend in the US educational distribution. Vallet (2004) reported the same effect for France. Breen and Jonsson (forthcoming) found that period change in late twentieth century Sweden was wholly due to cohort replacement and that the trend of increasing social fluidity among cohorts born during the first two-thirds of the century was the result of the same process. Social fluidity in Sweden is greater at higher levels of education, and over the course of the twentieth century, an increasing share of each birth cohort has come to attain higher levels of education. We have now found that exactly the same results hold for Germany.

It may not be too fanciful to suggest that this mechanism, referred to by Breen and Jonsson as the compositional effect of educational expansion, is fundamental to understanding why social fluidity changes and, equally, why it remains unchanged (as in the British case). For this mechanism to operate, two things are required: first, the association between class origins and destinations should be weaker at higher levels of education, and, second, the distribution of educational attainment should shift upwards over time. The latter condition has been met by very many countries during the 20th century. In some cases this came about through a policy of expanding educational provision for all young people (as in the USA) while elsewhere it was the result of a policy of equalization: that is, to reduce inequalities in educational attainment between students from different class backgrounds (as in Sweden). Such equalization inevitably leads to expansion of the higher levels of the educational system because equalization can only occur in practice through increasing the share of working class children at higher levels and not through decreasing the share of middle class children. In both Britain and Germany, as Figure 1 shows, there was a marked upward shift in the educational distribution over the 20th century, which, in the German case at least, was associated with a reduction in class inequalities in attainment (Müller and Pollak 2004).

If we want to explain the difference in the trend in social fluidity between our two countries, we must therefore focus on the first condition, and here it seems that while it is met in Germany, it is not met in Britain, as Figure 2 showed. That is to say, in Britain there is considerable variation in the strength of the association between origins and destination both within as well as between levels of educational attainment. Compared with Germany, there is much more within-educational level heterogeneity in the impact of class origins on class destinations. This must arise from one or both of two sources: non-educational factors that are related to class background must play a greater role in Britain, particularly at higher levels of education, than in Germany; and there must exist in Britain more educational distinctions within educational levels and which are also linked to class background.[7] Both of these suggestions seem plausible. At higher levels of the British educational system, there are important distinctions of prestige between different institutions. At secondary level, the difference between fee paying and state secondary schools is an obvious example, while at the tertiary level British universities differ greatly in their general standing and reputation. Neither of these is a feature of the German (or Swedish) educational systems. As far as non-educational factors are concerned, it seems at least plausible that these operate more strongly in Britain than in Germany, given the much tighter relationship between educational qualifications and occupations in the latter. It may be that the weaker link between education and jobs in Britain gives more freedom to employers to base their decisions about hiring and promotion on other factors – or indeed such a weaker link may necessitate the use of additional criteria. If educational qualifications have only tenuous connections to the demands of particular jobs, then employers will be obliged to seek other criteria that might provide signals as to applicants' suitability for them. These are, of course, speculations, whose accuracy or otherwise could only be determined on the basis of studies of the detailed functioning of the British and German recruitment and promotion processes.

---

7 But we must also keep in mind the different definitions of class origins used in the two countries. In the British case, the most advantaged class origin is much more heterogeneous than in Germany because it includes classes I, II and IVa.

References

Breen, R. (2004). *Social Mobility in Europe*, Oxford: Oxford University Press.

Breen, R./Jonsson, J. O. (forthcoming). »Explaining change in social fluidity: educational equalization and educational expansion in twentieth century Sweden«, *American Journal of Sociology*.

Breen, R./Luijkx, R. (2004). »Social mobility in Europe between 1970 and 2000«, in R. Breen (ed.), *Social Mobility in Europe*, Oxford: Oxford University Press, pp. 37–75.

DiPrete, T. A./Grusky, D. B. (1990). »Structure and trend in the process of stratification for American men and women«, *American Journal of Sociology*, vol. 96, pp. 107–143.

Erikson, R./Goldthorpe, J. H. (1992). *The Constant Flux: a Study of Class Mobility in Industrial Societies*, Oxford: Oxford University Press.

Firth, D. (1993). »Bias reduction of maximum likelihood estimates«, *Biometrika*, vol. 80, no. 1, pp. 27–38.

Ganzeboom, H. B. G./Luijkx, R./Treiman, D. J. (1989). »Intergenerational class mobility in comparative perspective«, *Research in Social Stratification and Mobility*, vol. 8, pp. 3–84.

Gerber, T. P./Hout, M. (2004). »Tightening up: declining class mobility during Russia's market transition«, *American Sociological Review*, vol. 69, pp. 677–703.

Goldthorpe, J. H. (1987). *Social Mobility and Class Structure in Modern Britain* (2nd edition), Oxford: Clarendon Press.

Goldthorpe, J. H. (1995). »Le ›noyau dur‹: fluidité sociale en Angleterre et en France dans les années 70 et 80«, *Revue française de sociologie*, vol. 36, pp. 61–79.

Goldthorpe, J. H./Mills, C. (2004). »Trends in intergenerational class mobility in Britain in the late twentieth century«, in R. Breen (ed.), *Social Mobility in Europe*, Oxford: Oxford University Press, pp. 195–224.

Grusky, D. B./Hauser, R. M. (1984). »Comparative social mobility revisited: models of convergence and divergence in 16 countries«, *American Sociological Review*, vol. 49, pp. 19–38.

Hauser, R. M./Huang, M.-H. (1997). »Verbal ability and socioeconomic success: a trend analysis«, *Social Science Research*, vol. 26, pp. 331–376.

Heath, A. F./Payne, C. (2000). »Social mobility«, in A. H. Halsey (ed.), *Twentieth Century British Social Trends*, London: MacMillan, pp. 254–281.

Hout, M. (1988). »More universalism, less structural mobility: the American occupational structure in the 1980s«, *American Journal of Sociology*, vol. 93, pp. 1358–1400.

Ishida, H./Müller, W./Ridge, J. M. (1995). »Class origin, class destination, and education: a cross-national study of ten industrial nations«, *American Journal of Sociology*, vol. 101, pp. 145–193.

Jones, F. L./Kojima, H./Marks, G. (1994). »Comparative social fluidity: trends over time in father-to-son mobility in Japan and Australia, 1965–1985«, *Social Forces*, vol. 72, pp. 775–798.

Jonsson, J. O./Mills, C. (1993). »Social mobility in the 1970s and 1980s: a study of men and momen in England and Sweden«, *European Sociological Review*, vol. 9, pp. 229–248.

Jonsson, J. O./Mills, C./Müller, W. (1996). »A half century of increasing educational openness? Social class, gender and educational attainment in Sweden, Germany and Britain«, in R. Erikson/J. O. Jonsson (eds.), *Can Education be Equalized? The Swedish Case in Comparative Perspective*, Boulder, Col.: Westview Press, pp. 183–206.

Luijkx, R./Ganzeboom, H. B. G. (1989). »Intergenerational class mobility in the Netherlands between 1970 and 1985: structural composition, structurcal differences, and relative mobility«, in W. Jansen/J. Dronkers/K. Verrips (ed.), *Similar or different? Continuities in Dutch research on social stratification and social mobility*, Amsterdam: SISWO, pp. 5–30.

Macdonald, K./Ridge, J. M. (1988). »Social mobility«, in A. H. Halsey (ed.), *British Social Trends since 1900*, London: MacMillan, pp. 202–225.

Mannheim, K. (1952). »The problem of generations«, in P. Kecskeméti (ed.), *Essays on the Sociology of Knowledge*, London: Routledge and Kegan Paul, pp. 276–322.

Müller, W./Lüttinger, P./König, W./Karle, W. (1989). »Class and education in industrial nations«, *International Journal of Sociology*, vol. 19, pp. 3–39.

Müller, W./Pollak, R. (2004). »Social mobility in West Germany: the long arms of history discovered?« in: R. Breen (ed.), *Social Mobility in Europe*, Oxford: Oxford University Press, pp. 77–113.

Róbert, P./Bukodi, E. (2004). »Changes in intergenerational class mobility in Hungary, 1973–2000«, in R. Breen (ed.), *Social Mobility in Europe*, Oxford: Oxford University Press, pp. 287–314.

Ryder, N. B. (1965). »The cohort as a concept in the study of social change«, *American Sociological Review*, vol. 30, pp. 843–861.

Vallet, L.-A. (1999). »Quarante années de mobilité sociale en France«, *Revue Française de Sociologie*, vol. 40, pp. 5–64.

Vallet, L.-A. (2004). »Change in intergenerational class mobility in France from the 1970s to the 1990s and its explanation: an analysis following the CASMIN approach«, in Richard Breen *(ed.)*, *Social Mobility in Europe*, Oxford: Oxford University Press, pp. 115–147.

Xie, Y. (1992). »The log-multiplicative layer effect model for comparing mobility tables«, *American Sociological Review*, vol. 57, pp. 380–395.

Variations on a theme: trends in social mobility in (West) Germany for cohorts born between 1919 and 1971[1]

Karl Ulrich Mayer and Silke Aisenbrey

Introduction

Walter Müller has devoted an academic lifetime of almost 40 years to un-ravelling, among other things, the patterns and changes of social mobility in Germany (Mayer and Müller 1971b, Müller 1975). The first author of this chapter had the great pleasure and privilege of being an academic and personal companion on part of this highly successful journey, and in fact our first and joint publication already addressed the issue of trends in social mobility (Mayer and Müller 1971a). Walter Müller has also been the major protagonist of developing the databases and calibrating the measures and models to include Germany in large-scale international and historical com-parisons (Shavit and Müller 1998, Breen 2004a, Müller and Gangl 2004). By an extraordinary combination of tenacity and diligence he has demon-strated the innovative powers of cumulative *normal science*.

The major findings on German social structure which have emerged from this comprehensive research programme relate, on the one hand, to the similarities and dissimilarities between Germany and other advanced societies and, on the other hand, to the changes in structures of opportuni-ties across historical time. The German stratification order experienced re-peated transformations in the 20th century in the aftermath of the defeats in World Wars I and II, economic depression and the breakdown of the Weimar Republic as well the major relocation of millions of expellees and refugees and educational expansion (Lepsius 1990). But despite these

1 Data collection of the German Life History Study was generously supported by the Max Planck Association for the Advancement of Science and the Deutsche Forschungsge-meinschaft. We also thank Karola Rockmann and Ralf Künster for assistance in data or-ganization, and Yale University and its Center for Research on Inequalities and the Life Course for supporting this research. Florencia Torche shared with us her expertise on the modelling of social fluidity. We also thank Richard Breen, Daniel Oesch, Gunnar Otte and Carlo Barone for their critical comments.

shake-ups and in contrast to contrary predictions and analyses (Schelsky 1965), Germany still tops most European countries in terms of degree of social closure (Müller and Pollak 2004, Breen and Luijkx 2004). This seems not at least due to the rigidities of a selective educational system, the barriers maintained by vocational training and academic certification as well as persisting distinctions between manual and non-manual, private and public employment.

However, this high degree of social closure at the beginning of the 21st century coexists with long-term trends of decreasing inequalities of opportunities in access to education and social class by social origin. In this respect, Germany appears to be rather similar to other European societies (Breen 2004a). Among the multitude of empirical findings, Müller and Pollak (2004) conclude in their most recent studies that:

– Social fluidity, i.e. relative social mobility, has increased for the cohorts born after 1930, and social fluidity for women seems to be greater than for men.
– For men, absolute rates of intergenerational class mobility have hardly changed, although there have been some recent increases in downward mobility.
– For women, downward mobility declined while upward mobility increased.
– Strong credentialist job allocation principles have not yet changed markedly, therefore »... it is ... likely that a decline in class inequality in education will lead to higher social fluidity« (Müller and Pollak 2004: 111).

Employing a cohort perspective, Müller and Pollak (2004) find increasing social fluidity for cohorts born after 1939. Breen and Luijkx (in this volume) demonstrate the same trend, but with a halt for the last observed cohort born 1967–1977 – a cohort that was not included in previous research. Including cohort and period effects, Breen and Luijkx conclude that »differences between periods are in fact the result of cohort replacement« (in this volume). With this finding that cohort replacement is the driving force behind the increasing social fluidity in Germany, Breen and Luijkx confirm the results of Müller and Pollak.

Previous research also demonstrates a significant role of education in changes in social mobility over the last century. By including education, Müller and Pollak (2004: 108) show »declining hierarchy effects due to declining educational inequality in social mobility«. Breen and Lujikx (in this volume) ask whether taking account of education explains change or stability over cohorts. They demonstrate that the answer for Germany is yes: »Controlling for variation in social fluidity across levels of education explains the trend in social fluidity over cohorts« (in this volume). With these results, Breen and Lujixk follow earlier research by Müller and Pollak (2004) on Germany, Hout (1988) on the US, Vallet (2004) on France, and Breen and Jonsson (forthcoming) on Sweden. In addition, Müller and Pollak (2004: 99), find hardly any systematic differences in social fluidity trends for different age groups.

In this chapter, we build on the foundations laid by the secondary analyses of Müller and his associates and use our own data from the German Life History Study (GLHS) to take another look at historical trends of social mobility in (West) Germany. Our purpose in this analysis is to bring the topic of social mobility into a more comprehensive study of cohort change based on the GLHS (for other aspects of this study, see Pollmann-Schult and Mayer 2004, Brückner and Mayer 2005, Aisenbrey and Brückner 2005). We also vary some of the conceptual and methodological tools to test the robustness of prior findings. Firstly, by using data from the German Life History Study (GLHS) we draw on a comparison of fairly narrowly defined birth cohorts rather than cross-sections or broadly defined cohort groups. Secondly, we employ a different schema of social class than the EGP, arguing deficits of the latter for the German case. Thirdly, we make use of our longitudinal data. By standardizing and comparing the age at which class of destination is observed, we can analyze mobility processes of the same individuals at different points in their life courses. In addition, the age groups at which we look at social mobility are smaller than those in prior studies on social mobility. By using smaller age groups than previous studies we are able to show different tendencies in mobility trends, depending on the age group we are looking at. With these variations on Walter Müller's major theme, we wish to honour his remarkable contribution to sociological research over the last four decades.

Data and methods

The data used for the analysis is derived from the German Life History Study (GLHS) (Mayer forthcoming). The West German part of the GLHS comprises life histories of 8,500 individuals from seven cohorts of Germans born between 1919 and 1971 and living in West Germany at the time of the surveys.[2] With the longitudinal information in the GLHS one can integrate aspects of life course dynamics into the intergenerational study of social mobility. Here we do this by measuring social mobility at several points in an individual's life. The GLHS provides occupational information at age 26–28 for the cohorts of 1919–21, 1929–31, 1939–41, 1949–51, 1954–56, 1959–61, 1964 and 1971 and occupational information at age 33–36 is available for the six cohorts born in or around 1920, 1930, 1940, 1955, 1964, and 1971.[3] Following the 1971 cohort up to 2005 by a panel study, our analyses also are distinctive in presenting the most recent evidence on mobility trends. Another advantage of the GLHS data is the »narrow« cohort design. Using cohorts across only three birth-years makes it possible to discover even minor changes between cohorts. This is in contrast to prior uses of birth cohorts in social mobility research (Müller and Pollak 2004, Breen and Luijkx in this volume), which aggregate up to ten years of birth.

The disadvantage of using the GLHS data for answering questions about social mobility is the relatively small sample size for given cohorts. This is one reason why our analysis is limited to modelling social fluidity without including further factors such as education in the model for mobility trends.

As Breen and Luijkx point out in this volume, a key point is whether women are included in the analyses of social mobility. This is not only because occupational scales and class schemas are primarily constructed on the basis of male employment and earning patterns; there are also different labour market participation patterns for men, and changes in women's la-

---

2 For a documentation of the surveys see Mayer and Brückner (1989), Brückner (1993), Brückner and Mayer (1995), Hillmert and Mayer (2004). Mayer (forthcoming) provides an overview also addressing issues of retrospective measurement. A public-use version of these datasets and English-language codebooks for most cohorts are available through the Center for Research on Inequalities and the Life Course at Yale University (www.yale.edu/ciqle).

3 For convenience, the cohort groups are indicated by their midpoint in the remainder of the text.

bour market participation over cohorts. We included women in our analysis, but estimated separate models throughout. It is well known from previous research that women have higher rates of dropping out of the labour force – mostly for family related reasons – and, therefore, our sample of women at the age of 35 is significantly smaller than at the age of 27. At age 35, only 51 percent of all women in the sample were still employed (at age 27, 96 percent were employed). However, most results are not significantly different when models at age 27 are estimated using only the population of women who are employed at age 35. Any differences between the two populations are noted separately. In prior studies on social mobility, filling occupational gaps with the last occupation recorded has often solved this problem. However, since one of our emphases is on small age groups and, therefore, age specific mobility, we decided against this approach.

Modelling

The *log-multiplicative layer effect* model (Xie 1992) – or, as Erikson and Goldthorpe (1992) refer to it, the *unidiff* model – compares different tables without specifying an association pattern of the common fluidity model. Under the assumption that the pattern of association is the same across tables, the unidiff model compares the strength of this association across tables, therefore allowing very parsimonious modelling of variation (Breen 2004b). Estimating different models at two points in the life course, at around age 27 (26–28) as an early stage in a career and at around age 35 (33–36) for a more mature class position, allows capturing age specific results and changes. A third model estimates changes in social fluidity from an intragenerational perspective, looking at mobility over the individual life course between an early class position (age 27) and a more mature one (35). The cohorts present the different layers in the models and the scale parameter for the 1930 table is set to unity (1). The reported patterns of upward, downward and total mobility over the cohorts complement the picture drawn by modelling social fluidity.

The second set of models presented in this chapter are logit models, including indicators for education, social class, education of father and social origin. All of these models are estimated at two points in the life course, at ages 27 and 35.[4]

The GEC class schema

The class schema used relies on detailed categories of employment status (Table 1). We, therefore, call it the German Employment Status Class Schema (GEC). It has four vertical categories and three horizontal categories. Of these twelve possible class categories, only ten are empirically filled. The three horizontal categories distinguish workers from civil servants and employees, and from the self-employed including farmers. These categories are divided into four hierarchical (vertical) categories. The four hierarchical categories are referred to as »working«, »lower middle«, »middle middle« and »upper middle« (Table 1). In comparison, the CASMIN version of the EGP class schema which is widely used in studies of social mobility (Erikson and Goldthorpe 1992, Breen 2004a) is composed of seven classes that are grouped into three hierarchical categories. The seven class CASMIN version summarizes the service class in the first category (I+II), routine and non-manual employees in the second (III), non-farm employers in the third (IVab), farmers and other self-employed workers in primary production in the fourth (IVc), technicians, supervisors and skilled manual worker in the fifth (V+VI), semi- and unskilled manual workers in the sixth (VIIa) and semi- and unskilled manual workers in the seventh category (VIIb).

The main difference between the EGP seven group CASMIN schema and the ten group class schema used here is that in the latter a category aggregates fewer positions from different hierarchical levels, and aggregates more positions that are hierarchically equal, e.g. grouping lower status civil servants with lower status routine non-manual employers. Our class schema relies on socio-legal distinctions specific to Germany such as detailed categories of employment status and levels of training and, on the other hand, it relies on prior analyses of social distance in mobility patterns

---

4 Because of the relatively small numbers, we do not include interaction effects in these models.

Table 1. The German employment status class schema – GEC

Employment status/social class*	Workers	White collar employees	Civil servants	Self-employed	Farmers (hectares of land)
Working	Unskilled Semi-skilled	Routine non-manual	*Einfacher Dienst*	Helping family members	10
Occ. code	20, 60, 61, 68, 69	51, 58, 59	40	30	10
Lower middle	Skilled foremen			Self-employed 0–1 employees	10–20 20–50
Occ. code	62, 63			21	11, 12
Middle middle	Artisanal masters	Qualified non-manuals, *Volontäre*, Industrial masters	*Mittlerer Dienst*	Self-employed 2–9 employees	50+
Occ. code	64	50, 52, 74	41, 47, 48, 49	22	13
Upper middle		Managers, Professionals	*Gehobener Dienst*, *Höherer Dienst*	Self-employed 10–49 employees 50+ employees	
				Academic free professions	
Occ. code		53, 54	42, 43	14, 23, 24, 29, 15, 16, 17	

* Employment status categories are grouped together on the basis of their proximity in regard to intergenerational social mobility.
Source for occupational codes: Brückner and Mayer (1995).

for combining lower level categories.[5] Thus, conceptually it follows Max Weber's concept of a »social class«. At the end of our results section, we discuss differences between the two schemas.

---

5 We thank Vered Kraus (University of Haifa) for her analyses with GLHS data of social distance matrices of mobility patterns using detailed categories of employment status. For a very similar derivation of a class schema for Germany, see Mayer (1977a).

Table 2. CASMIN educational schema

1a	Inadequately completed general education	
1b	General elementary education	1abc
1c	Basic vocational qualification/General elementary education and vocational qualification	
2a	Intermediate vocational qualification/Intermediate general qualification and vocational qualification	2ab
2b	Intermediate general qualification	
2c_gen	General maturity certificate	2c
2c_voc	Vocational maturity certificate/General maturity certificate and vocational qualification	
3a	Lower tertiary education	3ab
3b	Higher tertiary education	

Based on Brauns and Steinmann (1999).

The educational schema

We use a rudimentary form of the CASMIN schema (Müller 2000) as an indicator of educational attainment. The internationally comparative CASMIN schema, developed by Müller, Karle, König and Lüttinger (1989), is widely used. Originally, it has three categories with further sub-categories. Braun and Müller (1997) demonstrate that the CASMIN schema is superior to alternative measurements of education, such as years of attainment. Brauns and Steinmann (1999) modified the CASMIN schema to capture the changes that took place in national education systems after the 1970s. Because our cohorts stretch over the period before and after relevant educational reforms, a modification is necessary. We summarize the CASMIN schema into four distinct educational groups, with a focus on schooling at the upper and lower end of the distribution (Table 2).

Gross patterns of social mobility and cohort differences in aspirations

Before analyzing social fluidity in the next section, we first present some descriptive results on changes in mobility rate over the past century. In previous research, mobility rates are mainly shown across broadly defined age, cohort and period groups. Our approach focuses on narrowly defined cohorts and age groups. What proportions are in a different class category than their father at ages 27 and at 35, and how do these rates change over cohorts? Are there changes in mobility rates between a premature class position (at 27) and a mature one (at 35) (Table 3)?

Similar to Müller and Pollak's finding for period effects, we do not find much change and certainly no trend over the cohorts when we look at total intergenerational mobility between father's class and own class at the ages of 27 or 35. This is true for men and women. The 1930 cohort has the lowest total mobility rates, and the highest mobility rates can be found in the cohort born in 1955.[6] However, the picture gets much more complicated if we also look at downward and upward mobility.

1930 and 1955 cohorts

Total mobility rates can be separated into horizontal, vertical, upward and downward mobility. All of these rates react differently to structural changes and they react differently for different groups – men and women in different cohorts at different stages of their career.

Our results suggest that, for women, the rate of upward mobility is more sensitive than the rate of downward mobility. For men, the variation in these two rates is fairly similar. Overall, women's rates of upward and downward mobility show much more variation than men's rates. What does this imply? Women born around 1930 had the least opportunities for personal upward mobility in comparison with their fathers. Men of the 1930 cohort, in comparison to other male cohorts, also had the lowest upward mobility rates. Still, in the 1930 cohort the drop in opportunities for upward mobility for men is marginal compared to the drop women en-

---

6 This is true for all age groups except for women at 35. Here the cohort born in 1920 has a marginally higher total mobility rate than the cohort born in 1955.

Table 3. Gross mobility rates for the ten GEC classes, in percentages[7]

Cohort	Mobility	Origin: father Destination: at age 27		Origin: father Destination: at age 35		Origin: age 27 Destination: age 35	
		Men	Women	Men	Women	Men	Women
1920	total	75	79	74	80	47	47
	upward	27	17	37	21	33	20
	downward	37	50	24	46	10	11
1930	total	67	71	68	70	28	23
	upward	26	08	34	16	19	08
	downward	31	53	24	44	05	04
1940	total	69	78	72	76	26	25
	upward	34	20	41	26	18	13
	downward	26	48	21	41	03	07
1950	total	74	79				
	upward	42	27				
	downward	25	38				
1955	total	77	82	78	79	34	27
	upward	39	47	52	47	28	15
	downward	29	28	17	23	04	09
1960	total	76	78				
	upward	36	36				
	downward	34	31				
1964	total	71	74	70	76	32	25
	upward	31	33	39	39	22	14
	downward	31	30	23	26	05	08
1971	total	71	71	72	75	44	39
	upward	31	36	44	38	31	20
	downward	31	26	19	28	08	15

encountered. The same is true for downward mobility rates: women's risk of downward mobility is the highest for the 1930 cohort and it is distinctly higher than for men. The circumstances of the 1930 cohort were exceptional. This group was born shortly before the National Socialist regime came to power in Germany and they were at school during the Second World War, with the result that they have lower educational attainment than other cohorts. The cohort then entered the labour market during a period of economic and political reorganisation. Most significantly, their chances for vocational training just after WWII were drastically reduced. For women's and men's life courses, these exceptional starting conditions led to fewer chances for employment in an employment class higher than

---

7 Total mobility is the sum of upward, downward and vertical mobility. For n in the different categories, see Table 10.

their father's (lower upward mobility) and, at the same time, drastically increased their risks of ending up in classes lower than their class of origin (higher downward mobility). Both risks are much higher for women. (For the earlier cohort, these effects were first demonstrated by Mayer 1977b and Müller 1978). The findings hold for both the age of 27 and 35.

On the other hand, women of the 1955 cohort have the highest rate of upward mobility compared to all other groups at age 27. However, this advantage lasts only briefly. Eight years later, men have overtaken women in their upward mobility and, at the same time, have the lowest downward mobility rates. Nevertheless, besides these gender differences in the peculiarity of the rate, overall the 1955 cohort at age 35 has the highest upward and lowest downward mobility rates. In retrospect, the 1970s and 1980s were a period of exceptional opportunities for these cohorts.

The 1960–1971 cohorts

For the cohorts born around 1960 and in 1964, the upward and downward mobility rates for men and women seem to be very similar – more similar than for the earlier cohorts. These points of observation fall in the period between 1987–1999, a time of two recessions and a short interim boom due to German unification. (Hillmert and Mayer 2004). This is still the case for the 1971 cohort at the age of 27 in the year 1998; at age 35 in 2005 this equality seems to have faded. At age 35, women born in 1971, again have considerably higher downward and lower upward mobility rates than men – a pattern we are familiar with from earlier cohorts. The same is true looking at intragenerational mobility between age 27 and 35 for this cohort.

Overall, the rates of upward and downward mobility for men and women follow the same pattern over the cohorts. The upward mobility rates overtake the rates of downward mobility. For women these changes show some delay: The first male cohort with higher upward than downward mobility is born in 1940, whereas for women this change does not take place until the 1955 cohort.

Aspirations

Women of the 1930 cohort who had the lowest opportunity for upward mobility also had hardly any chance for working in the occupation they aspired to after school (Table 4). Occupational aspiration is measured retrospectively, by capturing the aspired occupation after school. We compared the aspired occupation to the occupation reached at age 27. Only the women of the 1920 cohort have a marginal lower chance of realizing their occupational aspirations. Men overall have higher levels of realizing their occupational aspirations than women but, hand in hand with low rates of upward mobility in the 1920 and 1930 cohort, we also find low rates of realizing their occupational aspirations for these cohorts. The rates for realizing occupational aspirations rose for subsequent cohorts through the 1950 cohort and then started dropping again for men of the 1955 cohort and for women of the 1960 cohort (Aisenbrey and Brückner 2005). Except for the youngest cohorts born between 1964 and 1971, both for men and women, the upward mobility rate seems to be closely related with the possibility of realizing occupational aspirations. For men, the highest upward mobility and the highest rate of realizing occupational aspirations is in the 1950 cohort; for women, this is the case for the cohort born in 1955.

Gross social mobility: summary

Up to the 1950 cohort, women have higher rates of downward mobility and lower rates of upward mobility in all three scenarios: at age 27, age 35, and between 27 and 35. Even though there is a trend towards equality up to the 1964 cohort, especially earlier in the life course, this trend is less visible in more mature class positions and turns around again for the 1971 cohort toward less gender equality. These results underscore earlier research which shows that men and women are more equal in earlier career stages than later on in their life courses. Women's labour force participation drops after the age of 25 and careers of women become more unstable (Maier 1993, also see Brückner 2004, Huinink 1992). This is mainly due to family related career interruptions and a tentative re-entry process into the labour market (Bertram et al. 2005). Often women re-enter the labour market in lower status and/or part time positions, which might show up in our analysis as no upward mobility or even downward mobility.

Table 4. Realized occupational aspirations across birth cohorts by the age of 27, based on 2-digit occupational classification

Cohort	Men	Women
1920	21%	13%
1930	23%	14%
1940	26%	26%
1950	31%	25%
1955	23%	26%
1960	19%	22%
1964	27%	27%
1971	34%	26%

Source: Aisenbrey and Brückner (2005).

These findings confirm prior research on social mobility. Müller and Pollak (2004) show for their last period under study an equal upward mobility rate for women and men, we corroborate such a change toward gender similarities, but in addition we find tendencies for a subsequent trend toward more divergence between men and women.

It is evident that the information we get from very small cohorts provides us with valuable information that we would not get from more aggregated cohorts. For example, the high rate of upward mobility for women of the 1955 cohort would not be visible if this cohort were aggregated with the 1960 cohort.

Is there a trend in social fluidity?

In recent research, social fluidity in Germany is described as a trend toward a more open society (Müller and Pollak 2004) (Breen and Luijkx in this volume). Müller and Pollak (2004) show the trend towards more openness, starting for the cohorts born after 1939 up to cohorts born in 1969. Breen and Luijkx (in this volume) confirm and expand this finding by demonstrating that this linear development comes to a halt for the 1967–77 cohorts. Mayer (2006) presents a similar finding with the GLHS data. The process toward a more open society comes to a halt for the 1964 cohort,

Table 5. Social Fluidity, Layer Scores for Unidiff Model Based On the GEC

	Origin: father Destination: at age 27 Scaled*		Origin: father Destination: at age 35 Scaled*		Origin: age 27 Destination: age 35 Scaled*	
Cohort	Men	Women	Men	Women	Men	Women
1920			86	0.72		
1930	1.00	1.15	1.00	1.07	1.00	0.91
1940	1.07	1.01	0.95	1.03	1.01	0.95
1950	0.84	0.97				
1955	0.51	0.47	0.58	0.37	0.83	0.79
1960	0.35	0.46				
1964	0.87	0.73	0.95	0.62	0.90	0.87
1971	0.84	0.87	0.91	0.52	0.67	0.54

* Reference category male 1930.

the German baby boomers. This latter research, which uses the GLHS, is based on the last recorded occupation – as is the case with most of the cohort-designed research on social mobility. The occupation of younger cohorts is measured at a much younger age than older cohorts where the mature (or a declining) job status is measured. This proxy for occupational status often leads to vague results for groups in different structural phases of their life course. Therefore, results that point to a halt or a linear trend have to be re-examined. By focusing on narrow age groups we attempt to draw a more straightforward picture of the development of social fluidity over the cohorts born from 1920 to 1971 at the ages of 27 and 35. With this design we want to tackle the question about the halt of a further opening of the society for the youngest German generations.

Modelling narrow cohorts also makes the analysis more sensitive to historical events that influence social developments. In Germany, during and after World War II, there was hardly a social structure in place that was not disrupted during or after the war. Our first result, which pointed in this direction, forced us to exclude the 1920 cohort from the social fluidity analysis. The unidiff model (Table 5) shows no significant improvement over the constant fluidity model if the 1920 cohort at age 27 is included. Excluding this cohort, however, increases the improvement to a significant fit.[8] Considering the historical context, this finding is not surprising. Given that the 1920 cohort was 27 in 1947, during the turbulent post-war period,

---

8 The table with the fit statistics for the unidiff model is available from the authors.

we should not be surprised by a lack of structure. For a moment in German history the social forces steering the process of intergenerational inheritance of social class were in disarray. Looking at the development eight years later, or more specifically at the 1920 cohort at age 35, shows that this disorder was only true for a brief moment. The unidiff model for age 35 is significant, even with the 1920 cohort included, which demonstrates that the social forces steering the process of social mobility resumed by 1953 – only eight years after the end of World War II. Still, the development toward a more open society does not start until the mid-1960s (age 27 and born after 1940). Nevertheless, a significant unidiff model demonstrates that the patterns are already back in place and similar enough.

The unidiff models demonstrate an increasing social fluidity between social origin and class of destination at both ages under observation over the cohorts born between 1930 and 1960. Looking at men aged 27, this trend only starts with the 1940 cohort. Before this turning point, social fluidity first decreases for cohorts 1930 to 1940. At age 35 this opening already took place for the cohort born around 1930. This decrease in the early 20th century is due to »the especially unfavourable opportunities in education and in early labour market integration encountered by the cohorts born around 1930« (Müller and Pollak 2004: 80). In addition, another interpretation points to a positive period effect. Taking these two »turning« points together – 1965, when the 1930 cohort was 35, and 1967, when the 1940 cohort was 27 – places the start of the opening process in the 1960s. This was a time with enormous labour market opportunities, also referred to as the »economic miracle« or phase of »full employment« when the highest unemployment rate was 2.1 percent (Hradil 2001). To illustrate this result, we focus on the men of the 1940 cohort. At the age of 27 in 1967, this cohort still faces a relatively closed society but at age 35 in 1977 is the first cohort to experience the start of increasing social fluidity, a trend that continues for cohorts born before the early 1960s. Women at age 35 and 27 start out with less social fluidity in the 1930 cohort than men and, equal to men, social fluidity rises through the cohort of 1960.[9]

This trend toward a more open society supports prior research on social mobility in Germany. In the next step we follow findings from Breen

---

9 By including men and women in one unidiff model, we forced men and women to follow the same pattern over the cohorts. For validation of this procedure we also computed two separate models for men and women (not presented here) and the outcome confirmed our findings from the combined model.

and Luijkx (in this volume), showing an interruption of the linear development toward an increasingly open society for cohorts born between 1967 and 1977. In the GLHS this interruption can be shown for the 1964 cohort for men and women at the age of 27 and 35: social fluidity for these groups decreased significantly. In addition, our results show a further trend pointing in the direction of a diminished rate of increasing fluidity for the 1971 cohort. For women of this cohort at age 35, a reopening of the society is observable. Even though this adds a positive trend to previous research, it is noteworthy that the optimistic conclusion of a linear trend toward a more open society no longer holds. Earlier research shows that change in social fluidity is connected to educational expansion (Müller and Pollak 2004, Breen and Luijkx in this volume) and therefore related to structural changes in educational participation. We are unable to control for this with our data, but we can show how the trend in social fluidity »breaks« for later cohorts. Although we did not include education in these models, it is obvious that educational expansion in Germany did not continue to weaken the social forces of class inheritance.

Overall we were also able to show that social fluidity tends to be more similar between men and women earlier in the life course than later on, which confirms our earlier findings of less equal mobility rates at a more mature class position.

Looking at social fluidity between 27 and 35 (Table 5), we see that the pattern of a first opening of society in the later first half of the century, followed by a tendency toward closure in the second half and another phase of opening in the later second half of the century, is also evident from the intergenerational perspective. In all cohorts women show somewhat higher intragenerational fluidity levels than men. This result should not be misunderstood as a female advantage. Rather, it should be interpreted in connection with women also being exposed to lower upward and higher downward mobility rates over nearly all cohorts between age 27 and 35. Therefore, the result can also be seen as further evidence for women having less steady careers than men. These findings are also interesting because they underline the fact that intragenerational mobility can serve as a further indicator of the openness of a society.

Destination upper middle class

In this section, we want to focus on the question: Who gets to place his children best? How does this change over the cohorts? We focus on highest class-placement at the ages of 27 and 35, depending on social origin and education. Our analysis uses logit models and estimates the odds-ratios for placement in the upper middle class (Table 6). As independent variables we include four CASMIN categories for education (reference category: CASMIN 1abc), the ten GEC classes (reference category: working class – worker) and six cohorts (reference cohort: 1971). One might expect that the effects of social origin and education weaken across working lives because endogenous effects of labour markets come into play. In contrast, social class might be less consolidated in the early stage of careers and effects of education and social origin might act in a process of cumulative advantage or disadvantage, and prove to be stronger with age. For placement in the upper middle class, men's education is as much of a driving force as social origin. Compared to having the lowest level of schooling, having a university degree raises by a factor of 19 the chance of being in the upper middle class at age 27 – and or by a factor of 39 at the age of 35. Nevertheless, men with origins in the upper middle self-employed class have, at the age of 27, a five-fold higher chance to be in the upper middle class themselves compared to men whose origin is in the working class. For women, originating in the upper middle self-employed class provides no significant advantage in reaching the same status. Social origin in the category of middle middle and upper middle employees and civil servants has a significant positive effect on the class destination for men and women at the age of 27.

It is noteworthy that, at the age of 35, the class effects for women mainly disappear, while the class effects for men become stronger.[10] This corroborates our findings from modelling social mobility where we demonstrated that the processes for men and women at the age of 27 are more equal than at the age of 35. Further, the effects of education on upper middle class destination develop roughly the same for men and women between age 27 and 35. This demonstrates that social origin has a larger influence on the life courses of men than of women. Thirdly, at the age of 35, women have to rely more on their own education, while men may still

---

10 One might argue that the disappearance of significance is due to the smaller n at age 35 for women. Still, the effects are not only less significant, but also effect sizes decrease.

Table 6. Destination upper middle class, logit model

	Upper middle class at age 27		Upper middle class at age 35	
	Men	Women	Men	Women
Education (reference: Casmin 1abc)				
Casmin 2ab	2.285*	2.303*	3.209*	2.392*
	(4.62)	(5.06)	(7.95)	(4.48)
Casmin 2c	3.434*	2.944*	8.545*	4.346*
	(6.04)	(4.97)	(12.61)	(5.87)
Casmin 3ab	19.500*	25.761*	39.206*	30.692*
	(16.19)	(15.32)	(20.03)	(13.03)
Social origin (fathers class)				
(reference: working class – worker)				
Working				
Employee/civil servant	1.917+	1.765	1.741+	0.879
	(1.94)	(1.57)	(1.95)	(0.28)
Self-employed/farmer	0.496	1.410	0.642	1.428
	(0.91)	(0.71)	(0.76)	(0.69)
Lower middle				
Worker	1.382	1.574+	1.848*	1.183
	(1.31)	(1.79)	(3.03)	(0.61)
Self-employed/farmer	1.888**	1.722+	1.617**	1.334
	(2.25)	(1.81)	(1.99)	(0.87)
Middle middle				
Worker	1.706	1.916	1.641	0.858
	(1.19)	(1.23)	(1.27)	(0.22)
Employee/civil servant	1.533+	2.380*	2.231*	1.603+
	(1.68)	(3.48)	(3.79)	(1.76)
Self-employed/farmer	2.249*	1.797**	2.164*	1.506
	(2.82)	(1.97)	(3.08)	(1.24)
Upper middle				
Employee/civil servant	2.860*	2.516*	3.043*	1.679+
	(4.18)	(3.69)	(5.05)	(1.93)
Self-employed/farmer	4.591*	1.690	3.513*	1.664
	(4.61)	(1.46)	(3.95)	(1.31)
Cohort (reference: cohort 1971)				
Cohort 1920	1.355	1.822*	1.905*	1.273
	(1.41)	(2.95)	(3.26)	(0.96)
Cohort 1930	0.898	0.982	1.383	0.893
	(0.39)	(0.06)	(1.35)	(0.29)
Cohort 1940	2.046*	1.181	2.025*	1.090
	(3.15)	(0.59)	(3.15)	(0.26)
Cohort 1955	1.465**	4.865*	1.842*	3.636*
	(2.05)	(8.07)	(3.21)	(5.41)
Cohort 1964	1.081	0.815	0.934	0.731
	(0.43)	(1.00)	(0.37)	(1.38)
Pseudo R² (Mc Fadden's Rho-Sq.)	0.220	0.219	0.287	0.237
Correctly Classified	86%	88%	82%	83%
Observations	2816	2855	2596	1529

Absolute value of z statistics in parentheses.

* significant at 1%, ** significant at 5%, + significant at 10%

benefit from their social origin. Finally, the most advantaged social origin for men, the upper employer class, has no effect on women's destination, neither at age 27 nor at 35. One could argue that these results are biased due to the fact that these discrepancies apply only to women who still are in the workforce at age 35. Taking only the sub-group of those women still in the workforce at 35 in the model for women at age 27 actually supports this logic: the effects in the models for men and women are more similar. We, however, argue that our interpretation still holds. One possible explanation for the stronger class effects for women who are still in the workforce at age 35 could be that women who take advantage of their class of origin for building careers tend not to stay in the workforce, compared to women who build their career on their own credentials, i.e. their own education.[11]

The effects shown for women confirm our expectations that education comes to the fore across the life course, while at the same time advantages of social origin are mitigated. These expectations are not confirmed for the effects of social origin for men: advantageous effects for placement in the upper class become more pervasive over the life course. At the same time, the influence of higher education also rises.

Social mobility between 27 and 35

Our next question follows from these results: What are the driving forces for social mobility between 27 and 35? We restricted this analysis to individuals who have not already reached the upper middle class at age 27 (ceiling restraint). The dependent variable is defined as one if an individual experienced any kind of upward mobility between age 27 and 35. We would expect that educational credentials are the driving force for upward mobility between this early stage in one's career and the next stage. Similar to the results presented above, our expectations for the positive effects of educational credentials are confirmed, more so for men than for women (Table 7). The same is true for class effects: A higher-class origin seems to enable men to reach the upper middle class between 27 and 35. For women,

---

11 To validate our results we also checked for differences in the distribution of some relevant variables in the two groups, women still in the labour force at age 35, and women no longer in the labour force at 35: There are no differences in these two groups of women when considering class of origin, class of destination, cohort or education.

Table 7. Logit model, dependent variable: upward mobility between 27 and 35

	Men	Women
Education (reference: Casmin 1abc)		
Casmin 2ab	2.007*	1.398+
	(5.06)	(1.70)
Casmin 2c	5.039*	2.385*
	(9.05)	(3.20)
Casmin 3ab	11.139*	11.870*
	(10.46)	(7.34)
Social origin (fathers class)		
(reference: working class – worker)		
Working		
Employee/civil servant	1.557+	1.233
	(1.76)	(0.53)
Self-employed/farmer	1.133	0.745
	(0.34)	(0.59)
Lower middle		
Worker	1.379+	0.770
	(1.90)	(0.93)
Self-employed/farmer	2.503*	1.355
	(4.71)	(0.99)
Middle middle		
Worker	2.272**	0.564
	(2.47)	(0.74)
Employee/civil servant	1.668*	1.166
	(2.72)	(0.56)
Self-employed/farmer	1.423	1.839+
	(1.51)	(1.92)
Upper middle		
Employee/civil servant	2.023*	1.581
	(3.30)	(1.63)
Self-employed/farmer	2.492**	2.032+
	(2.38)	(1.75)
Cohort (reference: cohort 1971)		
Cohort 1920	1.780*	1.606+
	(3.04)	(1.86)
Cohort 1930	0.863	0.653
	(0.68)	(1.11)
Cohort 1940	0.857	1.017
	(0.70)	(0.05)
Cohort 1955	0.986	1.079
	(0.07)	(0.26)
Cohort 1964	0.677**	0.687
	(2.16)	(1.53)
Pseudo R^2 (Mc Fadden's Rho-Sq.)	0.12	0.11
Correctly Classified	75%	82%
Observations	2088	1216

Absolute value of z statistics in parentheses.

Persons were excluded if upper middle class was already reached at age 27.

* significant at 1%, ** significant at 5%, + significant at 10%

class origin hardly affects their chances for upward mobility over the same period.[12]

Comparing social mobility according to different class schemas: EGP and GEC

In the analyses above we have employed a class schema which heavily relies on specifics of the German socio-legal groupings based on detailed categories of employment status and qualification (German Employment Status Class Schema – GEC). Although the EGP in its theoretical conception is based on the idea of groups with homogeneous employment relationships, as an international comparative scale it heavily relies on occupations. We have shown earlier, however, that occupations in Germany spread widely across categories of employment status (Mayer 1979). We would therefore expect that our class schema should be more sensitive to aggregating similar mobility chances and to changes over time. To the extent to which the findings for the two class schemata coincide, this could be taken as a test of robustness for the major findings established by Müller, Breen and their associates as well as for our own, since they prove to be »classification invariant«. It should be noted, however, that this comparison between the two class schemata cannot be wholly conclusive, since the former rely on much larger sample sizes.

In Table 8, we compare our class schema to the EGP with regard to the mobility rates for all cohorts at age 27. Overall, the trends over the cohorts for men and women are very much the same. The total mobility rates are also very similar for all cohorts, even though our schema has ten classes compared to only seven of the EGP. For men and women of all cohorts our class schema shows more downward mobility than the EGP. This is not surprising since the GEC consists of four hierarchical classes, while the EGP consists only of three. But this is not just a statistical artefact, but a difference based on a substantive classification decision. For men, using the EGP results in lower upward mobility rates in comparison to the GEC. For women, upward mobility rates for all cohorts are very

---

12 See footnote 9 above concerning the small n.

Table 8. Gross mobility rates: GEC compared to EGP[13]

| Cohort | Mobility | GEC Origin: father Destination: at age 27 | | EGP Origin: father Destination: at age 27 | |
		Men	Women	Men	Women
1920	total	75	79	72	78
	upward	27	17	21	16
	downward	37	50	27	37
1930	total	67	71	65	76
	upward	26	08	17	10
	downward	31	53	27	44
1940	total	69	78	64	76
	upward	34	20	25	17
	downward	26	48	18	31
1950	total	74	79	69	80
	upward	42	27	35	28
	downward	25	38	16	· 18
1955	total	77	82	70	81
	upward	39	47	36	41
	downward	29	28	16	14
1960	total	76	78	67	77
	upward	36	36	33	35
	downward	34	31	18	20
1964	total	71	74	64	77
	upward	31	33	26	32
	downward	31	30	18	18
1971	total	71	71	69	76
	upward	31	36	29	32
	downward	31	26	21	18

much the same regardless of which class schema is used. The differences revealed using the two class schemata present a picture of smaller disparities between men and women with respect to upward mobility rates for early cohorts, if the EGP is used. Overall, comparing the two schemas, the mobility rates are more similar for women than for men.

In the unidiff model for all cohorts (Table 9) at the age of 27 carried out, first, with the EGP scale and, second, with our class schema, the main differences in trends emerge for women. For men, the overall trend in the two cases stays basically the same. With GEC, we see a monotonous trend for women from the 1930 cohort to the 1960 cohort. With EGP, we see a

13 For EGP classification see Breen (2004a).

Table 9. Unidiff model, GEC compared to EGP

	GEC Origin: father Destination: at age 27 Scaled*		EGP Origin: father Destination: at age 27 Scaled*	
Cohort	Men	Women	Men	Women
1930	1.00	1.15	1.00	0.92
1940	1.07	1.01	1.13	0.84
1950	0.84	0.97	0.98	0.98
1955	0.51	0.47	0.55	0.58
1960	0.35	0.46	0.60	0.52
1964	0.87	0.73	1.00	0.66
1971	0.84	0.87	0.63	0.71

* Reference category male 1930.

Table 10. GLHS, cases in different categories

	Origin: father Destination: at age 27 Scaled*		Origin: father Destination: at age 35 Scaled*	
Cohort	Men	Women	Men	Women
1920	508	811	551	420
1930	339	325 ·	343	144
1940	362	332	373	145
1950	328	344	(54)	(28)
1955	488	447	474	283
1960	472	462	(0)	(0)
1964	699	665	723	432
1971	686	598	345	267

* Reference category male 1930.

similar trend for women at 27, with a curious outlier for the 1950 cohort. For the 1930 cohort, women analyzed with our class schema start at a higher level of social closure than men, whereas the EGP results suggest even superior opportunities for women.

Conclusions

In these concluding remarks we want to address the following five questions:

1) Are there persistent trends in intergenerational social mobility in West Germany?
2) What are major differences in mobility between men and women?
3) What is the advantage of using a research design based on narrowly defined cohorts?
4) What do we learn from measuring mobility at specific ages and across the life course?
5) What do we learn from using a social class schema other than the EGP?

1) Trends. West German society, as measured by relative mobility rates, became markedly more open between the 1940s and the 1980s. The overall level of association declined by almost two-thirds for men and almost as much for women between the cohorts born around 1930 and born around 1960 but then, in the 1990s and after, social closure again became tighter. Men and women born in the mid-1960s face a much less open society than cohorts born earlier. Although this is true for men and women at ages 27 and 35, nevertheless men seem to be hit harder by this renewed closure, especially at later stages in their career. For women at age 35, this trend reversal is not only much less pronounced, but even reversed again for the 1971 cohort. For men at 27 and 35 there is only a marginal increase in social fluidity from the 1964 cohort to the 1971 cohort. Although these changes in trends are too small for substantive interpretation, they pose a puzzle for future research on social fluidity. Does this constitute a temporary interruption or a reversal of a long-term trend? The differences documented between men and women should not, however, be misunderstood as showing that women gain mobility advantages over men. Increased closure can also mean that men stay in the same high social class that their fathers were in and women don't manage to keep the same status. These results have to be seen in the context of women of a mature class status in the youngest cohort still having lower upward and higher downward mobility than men do. Looking at fluidity between 27 and 35 suggests a possible reason for this tightening closure: more looseness across the career in the youngest cohort. In interpreting these results, one must keep in mind

the historically specific highly disadvantaged position of the cohorts born around 1930 and 1940. But even discounting this, social closure appears now to be up to the level where post WWII Germany started for the »normal« 1950 cohort. These changes are mirrored if we are looking at gross mobility rates. While overall levels of total mobility stayed about the same, with some fluctuation, opportunities for upward mobility first increased for cohorts born between 1930 and 1950 for men and then decreased.

The trend toward greater openness and increasing opportunities and its reversal poses a true puzzle. What has often been interpreted as a universal secular trend now appears much more as a transition between two high closure equilibria. One then needs to ask: Has greater openness sparked by educational expansion been transitory and has prior class closure been replaced by meritocratic closure via educational credentials? Most recent evidence (Mayer et al. forthcoming, Mayer 2006) does not bear this out – yet.

2) Men and Women. In these analyses, we have treated women in a similar manner to men; i.e. we compared their own class destination with those of their fathers. On this basis, one can observe the huge progress West German women made. Those women who were working at 35 experienced a greater change in the opening of social opportunities in comparison to men, and also retained that advantage up to 2005. This is also reflected in mobility rates, where the 1955 cohorts, i.e. in the 1980s, show with 47% the highest rate of upward mobility across gender and cohorts. On the other hand, for the youngest cohort, we can show evidence for diminishing advantages over the life course of women: starting out at 27 with higher upward and lower downward mobility risks than men, at age 35 women end up with substantially lower upward and higher downward mobility rates than men. This is more evidence for the need to disentangle the gender puzzle piecewise.

The extraordinary opportunities of women in the 1980s are also born out in our logit models predicting access to the upper middle class. In the latter model, women differ from men remarkably in that at age 35 there are no social origin effects net of education.

3) Advantages of a design with narrowly defined birth cohorts. Analyzing social mobility with highly disaggregated birth cohorts not only reveals more variance across time, it also makes it possible to locate the start and reversal of trends more succinctly. While the disadvantaged position of the cohorts born around 1930 was well-known, we could also show here the

highly advantaged opportunities for persons born around 1955 and around 1960 and that the 1940 cohort experienced similar disadvantages as the 1930 cohorts for men up to age 27, only benefiting from the economic miracle in their later career stage, while for women these disadvantages extend well into the 1950 cohorts. What is more controversial in the literature is whether the baby boom cohort born 1964 experienced special hardships due to crowding effects and whether the 1971 cohort stays as worse or has recuperated. While the 1964 cohort seems to do worst in regard to relative mobility, the differences to the 1971 cohort seem slight except for women at age 35 who actually continued to better. Gross mobility upward and downward rates also point to some improvements in comparison with the 1964 cohort in regard to upward and downward mobility, while for women no change can be detected.[14]

4) Age-specific observations. What is new about our findings is that we could demonstrate how sensitive mobility analyses are with regard to age or career stage at which class destinations are being measured. Previous research, based on more aggregated age groups, showed hardly any differences. Our research, focusing on very small age groups, shows evidence that strongly points in the direction of different stories about mobility trends, depending on age. Age groups differ both with regard to how successfully careers are launched and how they progress. Aggregating observations of class destinations over a wide range of ages might easily overlook mobility hurdles that change over the life course. Even though using smaller cohorts and age groups gives us the opportunity to uncover rather small changes in trends that might only affect cohorts of certain birth years and/or individuals at a certain age, these advantages don't come without a price. The smaller number of individuals in each group limits our modelling possibilities and makes our results more tentative. Each of these two approaches – more vs. less aggregated groups – provides us with valuable insights into the trends of social mobility.

5) EGP vs. GEC. The development and application of the EGP class schema has been a breakthrough in the comparative study of intergenerational social mobility, although, as we demonstrate here, this comes with a price. Our class schema, with specific consideration of the German social structure, captures less mobility within and more mobility between the

---

14 Problems of panel selectivity might have affected the most recent data. However, since panel attrition should if at all show a bias in favour of the more successful respondents, we should have in fact a conservative estimate of the trend reversal.

categories. Moreover, it has not only proven to be more sensitive in catching the relative size effects of trends in fluidity (see also Mayer 2006) as well as in gross rates – at least in one instance it also leads to a different conclusion. Based on the EGP classification (Table 6) one would conclude that the men of the 1964 cohort experienced a severe restriction of their opportunities, while this peak does not show for the GEC classification. The task of tracking trends of intergenerational mobility is neverending. In the past two decades a predominant interpretation of largely stable patterns of social fluidity has given way to an image of long term trends of increasing openness. For Germany, the work of Walter Müller and his associates has been pathbreaking in bringing about this change of perspective. However, our findings indicate that this might, in fact, not be the end of the story. If our findings (for men) of again increasing rigidities prove to be robust in further research, a new explanatory puzzle arises that challenges many of our assumptions about advanced societies: What are the tendencies within modern societies which work towards more social closure?

References

Aisenbrey, S./Brückner, H. (2005). *Occupational Aspirations, Gender Segregation, and the Gender Gap in Wages*, Paper presented at the Social Science History Conference, Portland, Oregon, November 2005.

Bertram H./Rösler, W./Ehlert, N. (2005). »Zeit, Infrastruktur und Geld: Familienpolitik als Zukunftspolitik«, *Aus Politik und Zeitgeschichte*, vol. 23–24, pp. 6–15.

Braun, M./Müller, W. (1997). »Measurement of education in comparative research«, *Comparative Social Research*, vol. 16, pp. 163–201.

Brauns, H./Steinmann, S. (1999). »Educational reform in France, West-Germany, the United Kingdom and Hungary. Updating the CASMIN educational classification«, *ZUMA-Nachrichten*, vol. 23, pp. 7–44.

Breen, R. (2004a). »The comparative study of social mobility«, in R. Breen (ed.), *Social Mobility in Europe*, Oxford: Oxford University Press, pp.1–16.

Breen, R. (2004b). »Statistical methods of mobility research«, in R. Breen (ed.), *Social Mobility in Europe*, Oxford: Oxford University Press, pp.16–35.

Breen, R./Jonsson, J. O. (forthcoming). »Explaining change in social fluidity: educational equalization and educational expansion in twentieth century Sweden«, *American Journal of Sociology*.

Breen, R./Luijkx, R. (2004). »Social mobility in Europe between 1970 and 2000«, in R. Breen (ed.), *Social Mobility in Europe*, Oxford: Oxford University Press, pp. 37–75.

Brückner, E. (1993). *Lebensverläufe und gesellschaftlicher Wandel. Konzeption, Design und Methodik der Erhebung von Lebensverläufen der Geburtsjahrgänge 1919–1921* (Materialien aus der Bildungsforschung 44), Berlin: Max Planck Institute for Human Development.

Brückner, H. (2004). *Gender Inequality in the Life Course: Social Change and Stability in West Germany, 1975–1995*, New York: Aldine De Gruyter.

Brückner, H./Mayer, K. U. (1995). *Lebensverläufe und Gesellschaftlicher Wandel. Konzeption, Design und Methodik der Erhebung von Lebensverläufen der Geburtsjahrgänge 1954–1956 und 1959–1961*, (Materialien aus der Bildungsforschung 48), Berlin: Max Planck Institute for Human Development.

Brückner, H./Mayer, K. U. (2005). »The de-standardization of the life course: What it might mean and if it means anything whether it actually took place«, *Advances in Life Course Research*, vol. 9, pp. 27–54.

Erikson, R./Goldthorpe, J. H. (1992). *The Constant Flux: A Study of Class Mobility in Industrial Societies*, Oxford: Oxford University Press.

Hillmert, S./Mayer, K. U. (2004). *Geboren 1964 und 1971*, Wiesbaden: Verlag für Sozialwissenschaften.

Hout, M. (1988). »More universalism, less structural mobility: the American occupational structure in the 1980s«, *American Journal of Sociology*, vol. 93, pp. 1358–1400.

Hradil, S. (2001). *Soziale Ungleichheit in Deutschland* (8th edition), Opladen: Leske und Budrich.

Huinink, J. (1992). »Die Analyse interdependenter Lebensverlaufsprozesse: Zum Zusammenhang von Familienbildung und Erwerbstätigkeit bei Frauen«, in H.-J. Andreß et al. (eds.), *Theorie, Daten, Methoden: Neue Modelle und Verfahrensweisen in den Sozialwissenschaften*, Munich: Oldenbourg, pp. 343–366.

Lepsius M. R. (1990). »Soziale Ungleichheit und Klassenstrukturen in der Bundesrepublik Deutschland«, in M. R. Lepsius (ed.), *Interessen, Ideen und Institutionen*, Wiesbaden: Westdeutscher Verlag, pp. 117–152.

Maier, F. (1993). »Zwischen Arbeitsmarkt und Familie-Frauenarbeit in den alten Bundesländern«, in G. Helwig/H. M. Nickel (eds.), *Frauen in Deutschland 1945–1992*, Berlin: Akademie Verlag, pp. 257–279.

Mayer, K. U. (1977a). »Statushierarchie und Heiratsmarkt«, in J. Handl et al. (eds.), *Klassenlagen und Sozialstruktur*, Frankfurt/Main: Campus, pp.152–232.

Mayer, K. U. (1977b). Recent Developments in the Opportunity Structure of (West) German Society 1935–1971, Johann Wolfgang Goethe University of Frankfurt/Main: SPES-Working Paper Nr. 67.

Mayer, K. U. (1979). »Berufliche Tätigkeit, berufliche Stellung und beruflicher Status: Empirische Vergleiche zum Klassifikationsproblem«, in F.-U. Pappi (ed.), *Sozialstrukturanalyse mit Umfragdaten*, Königstein/Taunus: Athenäum, pp. 79–123.

Mayer, K. U. (2006). »Sinn und Wirklichkeit – Beobachtungen zur Entwicklungen sozialer Ungleichheiten in (West-)Deutschland nach dem Zweiten Weltkrieg«, in K.-S. Rehberg (ed.), *Soziale Ungleichheit, kulturelle Unterschiede. Verhandlungen des 32. Kongresses der Deutschen Gesellschaft für Soziologie in München 2004*, Frankfurt/Main: Campus, pp. 1329–1355.

Mayer, K. U. (forthcoming). »Retrospective longitudinal research: the German life history study«, in S. Menard (ed.), *Handbook of Longitudinal Research: Design, Measurement and Analysis*, San Diego, CA: Elsevier.

Mayer, K. U./Brückner, E. (1989). *Lebensverläufe und Wohlfahrtsentwicklung: Konzeption, Design und Methodik der Erhebung von Lebensverläufen der Geburtsjahrgänge 1929–1931, 1939–1941, 1949–1951* (Materialien aus der Bildungsforschung 35), Berlin: Max Planck Institute for Human Development.

Mayer, K. U./Müller, W. (1971a). »Trendanalysen in der Mobilitätsforschung – Eine Replik auf Gerhard Kleinings ›Struktur und Prestigemobilität in der Bundesrepublik Deutschland‹«, *Kölner Zeitschrift für Soziologie und Sozialpsychologie*, vol. 23, no. 4, pp. 761–788.

Mayer, K. U./Müller, W. (1971b). »Progress in social mobility research? Some comments on mobility analysis and new data on intergenerational mobility in West-Germany«, *Quality and Quantity*, vol. 5, no. 1, pp. 141–178.

Mayer, K. U./Müller, W./Pollak, R. (forthcoming). »Institutional change and inequalities of access in German higher education«, in Y. Shavit et al. (eds.), *Stratification in Higher Education: A Comparative Study*, Stanford, Cal.: Stanford University Press.

Müller, W. (1975). *Familie, Schule, Beruf: Analysen zur sozialen Mobilität und Statuszuweisung in der Bundesrepublik*, Opladen: Westdeutscher Verlag.

Müller, W. (1978). *Klassenlage und Lebenslauf: Untersuchung zu Prozessen sozialstrukturellen Wandels in der Bundesrepublik Deutschland* (Habilitationsschrift), Mannheim: University of Mannheim, Faculty of Social Sciences.

Müller, W. (2000). *CASMIN educational classification*, http://www.nuff.ox.ac.uk/Users/Yaish/NPSM/Casmin%20Educ.pdf (last accessed on October 25, 2006).

Müller, W./Gangl, M. (2004). *Transitions from Education to Work in Europe. The Interpretation of Youth into EU Labour Markets*, Oxford: Oxford University Press.

Müller, W./Karle, W./König, W./Lüttinger, P (1989). »Class and education in industrial nations«, *International Journal of Sociology*, vol. 19, no. 3, pp. 3–39.

Müller, W./Pollak, R. (2004). »Social mobility in West Germany: the long arms of history discovered?«, in R. Breen (ed.), *Social Mobility in Europe*, Oxford: Oxford University Press, pp. 77–113.

Pollmann-Schult, M./Mayer, K. U. (2004). »Returns to skills: vocational training in Germany 1935–2000«, *Yale Journal of Sociology*, vol. 4, pp. 73–98.

Schelsky, H. (1965 [1953]). »Die Bedeutung des Schichtungsbegriffes für die Analyse der gegenwärtigen deutschen Gesellschaft«, in H. Schelsky (ed.), *Auf der Suche nach Wirklichkeit. Gesammelte Aufsätze*, Düsseldorf: Diederichs, pp. 331–336.

Shavit, Y./Müller, W. (1998). *From School to Work. A Comparative Study of Educational Qualifications and Occupational Destinations*, Oxford: Oxford University Press.

Xie, Y. (1992). »The log multiplicative layer effect model for comparing mobility tables«, *American Sociological Review*, vol. 57, pp. 380–395.

Vallet, L.-A. (2004). »Change in intergenerational class mobility in France from 1970s to the 1990s and its explanation: an analysis following the CASMIN approach«, in R. Breen (ed.), *Social Mobility in Europe*, Oxford: Oxford University Press, pp. 115–147.

Wagner, M. (1996). »Lebensverläufe und Gesellschaftlicher Wandel. Die Westdeutschen Teilstudie«, *ZA-Information*, vol. 38, pp. 20–27.

II. Special issues in current stratification research

Self-employment and social stratification[1]

Richard Arum

Self-employment has been conceptualized by Walter Müller and others as involving an individual's decision to engage in such activity »under conditions of bounded rationality« that »consider existing and potential resources, opportunities and constraints« (Müller and Arum 2004: 12). Educational attainment, labour market experience and family context are resources that have been demonstrated to serve as determinants of self-employment activity. Self-employment has varied cross-nationally and ebbed and flowed historically given changes in the opportunity structure that have defined the range of potential rewards and costs of engaging in self-employment relative to alternative labour market activities.

Social scientists have begun to pay increasing attention to self-employment in recent decades given its persistence and resurgence. A recent analysis of data on twenty-eight Organization for Economic Cooperation and Development (OECD) countries suggests that self-employment increased its share of non-agricultural economic activity in most advanced economies over recent decades (OECD 2000). The increase in self-employment activity in the United States occurred concurrent with the ascendancy of neo-liberal economic policies and a concurrent growth in economic inequality. Since 1975, the gini-coefficient measuring inequality in individual incomes in the United States rose from 0.327 to 0.409 in 2001 (CPS 2004).

There are additional related reasons why renewed attention to self-employment is warranted. First, self-employment as an activity, although by definition an act of an individual, emerges at the complex intercises of family, state and market. Second, the re-emergence of self-employment has involved not just an increase in its prevalence in the non-agricultural sector of the economy, but a transformation of the character of the phenomenon.

---

1 The author would like to thank Paolo Barbieri for comments improving this manuscript.

This transformation, in a manner corresponding to the larger societal trends surrounding it, has involved a rise in heterogeneity of self-employment forms. In particular, changes in self-employment have corresponded with growing inequality of individuals involved in the activity. Simultaneous increases have occurred in both the number of well compensated free-lancing professionals and entrepreneurs as well as those in the most unstable, marginal unskilled activities, who receive neither significant financial returns for their work nor even the assurance of access to health care in the United States (Arum 1997). Thirdly, self-employment and entrepreneurship are essential to study both due to their role in economic growth as well as the political consequences of this phenomenon. The self-employed, after all, are different from the rest of society. They have been argued to »support fascist and other extreme middle class extremist ideologies« (Lipset 1981: 105); sociologists have identified how proprietors in the United States have increasingly voted conservatively (Hout et al. 1995).

The recognition of the heterogeneous nature of self-employment is necessary for accurate and informative investigation of the phenomenon. Arum (1997) demonstrated the importance of distinguishing self-employment broadly into professional and non-professional occupations as these forms of self-employment have dramatically different individual-level determinants as well as economic consequences. In subsequent research, self-employment has been further investigated through distinguishing between non-professional skilled and unskilled self-employment as well as through classification schemas that vary in their handling of proprietors (see e.g., Arum and Müller 2004, Shavit and Yuchtman-Yaar 2001, Laferrère 2001, McManus 2000). Conflating professional, skilled and unskilled types of self-employment obscures whether increases in self-employment have occurred in desirable or undesirable positions as well as the extent to which traditional forms of self-employment have persisted or been replaced by new forms.

Variation in the Opportunity Structure

Müller's work on self-employment follows his broader interest in examining how variation in institutional characteristics across nation-states structures the influence which social background and educational attainment have on individuals' labour market destinations. Müller's broader contributions to this literature are well known. As a necessary precursor to conducting systematic comparative cross-national research, Müller and his colleagues worked to develop, refine and apply a comparative educational scale: CASMIN (see König et al. 1988, Müller et al. 1989, Braun and Müller 1997). The CASMIN classification schema is based on both educational level (e.g., elementary, secondary, tertiary) and the extent to which the curriculum is academically or vocationally focused. The CASMIN classification system allowed Müller to explore systematically how institutional characteristics of society affected school-to-work transitions (Shavit and Müller 1998, Müller and Gangl 2003) as well as the character of the relationship between educational attainment and various forms of self-employment (Luber et al. 2000, Arum and Müller 2004). Müller's work on institutional variation in educational systems focused specific attention not simply on overall educational attainment levels, but on the extent to which occupational training was specialized and differentiated.

The comparative project on self-employment organized by the Mannheimer Zentrum für Europäische Sozialforschung (Müller et al. 1999, 2000) grew out of a distinct research tradition that Müller had been at the forefront of developing over the past two decades. This research tradition has been labelled by Ganzeboom and his colleagues as constituting a »fourth generation« of social stratification research: one that is focused on the extent to which organizational variation across countries affects both intergenerational mobility and associations between social class and educational attainment (Treiman and Ganzeboom 2000, see also Ganzeboom et al. 1991). By focusing on self-employment, Müller and his associates attempted to identify causes for the dramatic variation across societies in the character, level, determinants and historical trajectory of this labour market activity. What were the factors that led self-employment rates in Italy, Japan and Taiwan to occur at levels more than double those in neo-liberal societies such as the United States, the United Kingdom and Australia? How did the determinants of entry into and exit from self-employment vary across societies?

In our comparative analysis (Arum and Müller 2004), we distinguished broadly between four categories of societies based on two dimensions that produced variation in the resources, opportunities and relative advantages of self-employment and thus were related to variation in the structure and determinants of self-employment. These system-level characteristics were the extent of labour market regulation in a society and the degree to which family-based social capital was prevalent as a socio-economic organizing principle. The effect of labour market regulation on entrepreneurial activity has long been a focus of social scientific analysis (see e.g. Arum et al. 2000, Blau 1987, Piore and Sabel 1984); as too has the exploration of the role of family dynamics in promoting self-employment (see e.g., Aldrich and Zimmer 1986). Broader economic structural shifts have also been explored in terms of associations with changes in self-employment (see e.g., Blanchflower 2000, Steinmetz and Wright 1989).

While the family unit remains a central feature of all advanced societies, Müller and Arum (2004) argued that groups varied on the strength of extended kin networks and the degree to which intergenerational obligations extended throughout the life-course. Our schema identified a set of *corporatist states* (i.e., Germany, France and the Netherlands) that had relatively high levels of labour market regulation and lower levels of family-based social capital. *Neo-liberal economies* (such as the United States, Australia and the United Kingdom) had low levels of both labour market regulation and family-based social capital. The *post-socialist societies* in our comparative project – Russia and Hungary – had moderate, but declining levels of labour market regulation and low to moderate levels of family-based social capital. A final set of countries in the project had high levels of family-based social capital, but varied on the extent to which their economies faced labour market regulation: Japan and Italy with high levels of regulation; Taiwan with lower levels.[2]

The comparative project identified growing heterogeneity in the form of self-employment cross-nationally. While traditional forms of self-employment – i.e., craft-based activity or small proprietorship – persisted in all the countries examined in our project, in the vast majority of advanced economies, self-employment now occurs primarily in professional activities and unskilled marginal pursuits. Labour market regulation exhibited a curvilinear relationship to self-employment with the highest levels of self-employment, particularly in its professional forms, occurring in economies with either the highest or lowest levels of government control over labour markets. In these societies the relative advantages of self-employment were argued to increase: given the entrepreneurial opportuni-

---

2 It is worth noting that the comparative project measured labour market regulation based on Organization for Economic Cooperation and Development EPL scores that have been subsequently revised, affecting classification for some countries such as Italy.

ties produced by stringent labour market regulation leading to higher employer costs to hierarchical economic organization; or when the relative returns to dependent employment decreased for individuals when labour market regulation was particularly weak. In countries with greater family-based social capital, self-employment rates were uniformly higher, particularly in traditional inherited petty bourgeois and unskilled self-employment forms.

The Reemergence of Self-Employment: A Comparative Study of Self-Employment Dynamics and Social Inequality volume (Arum and Müller 2004) attempted to extend Müller's interest in identifying variation in labour market outcomes across societies, but also to explore how the effects of social background and educational attainment – understood as individual resources – varied in relationship to societal-level differences in social organization. While Müller's work on self-employment was distinguished by an explicitly comparative focus, it built on earlier sociological research that sought to identify the influences of educational attainment, labour market experience and family context on paths into and out of self-employment. I will briefly discuss the contributions Müller and others have made to identifying changes in the composition of self-employment as well as exploration of the relationship between individual resources and self-employment activity, before presenting original analysis of historic and contemporary U.S. data to illustrate how changes in self-employment and individual-level determinants of involvement in such enterprises correspond to the analytical propositions advanced by Müller in his cross-national work.

Individual Determinants of Self-Employment

Human capital has repeatedly been demonstrated to affect the likelihood of self-employment activity (Arum 1997, Evans and Leighton 1989, Fuchs 1982). In most societies, education has a positive association with self-employment, although the form of the association can either be quasi-linear as in the case of Germany and post-socialist Russia (Gerber 2001, Luber et al. 2000) or curvilinear as in the United Kingdom and Israel (Shavit and Yuchtman-Yaar 2001, Luber et al. 2000, Meager et al. 1992). In societies with greater prevalence of self-employment, negative associations between education and self-employment have been observed (Blanchflower 2000). Most of these differences in effects of education on self-employment are produced by variation in differences in the respective occupational composition of self-employment across societies (Arum and Müller 2004).

Prior research has argued that immigrants in the United States vary widely in their proclivity to engage in self-employment. Self-employment is particularly prevalent amongst Korean, Chinese, Japanese, Russian and Middle-Eastern immigrants in the United States. The extent to which self-employment is concentrated in specific immigrant groups, rather than dispersed uniformly regardless of immigrant origins, is not shared in all other advanced economies (see e.g., Shavit and Yuchtman-Yaar 2001). Social networks, familial relations, educational attainment and entrepreneurial experience have all been shown as factors influencing the proclivity of specific immigrant groups to engage in self-employment activity (Aldrich and Waldinger 1990, Portes and Rumbaut 1990, Kim and Hurh 1985, Min 1984). In addition, variation in self-employment success across different racial and ethnic groups has been linked to liquidity constraints and discrimination (Evans and Jovanovic 1989, Blanchflower and Oswald 1990, Borjas and Bronars 1989).

Self-employment also varies strongly with respect to gender. Prior research has demonstrated that while men have higher rates of self-employment overall, female self-employment is increasing more dramatically than male self-employment (Arum 1997).

While women increasingly are engaging in self-employment, female self-employment is characterized by higher risks of entrepreneurial failure and a higher rate of involvement in non-desirable and less rewarding occupations (Arum 1997, Kalleberg and Leicht 1991, Wharton 1989). Women's self-employment success has also been shown to be hampered by family commitments (Loscocco and Leicht 1993, Hisrich and Brush 1986). Wharton (1989) has demonstrated that occupational sex segregation is as prevalent in self-employment as patterns found in waged and salaried employment.

Data and Methods

This chapter utilizes census data to provide historical perspective on self-employment and data from the General Social Survey (GSS) to identify contemporary patterns in the United States. Census data was taken from IPUMS samples drawn from the 1920, 1940, 1960, 1980 and 2000 censuses. The General Social Survey was conducted approximately every two years from 1972 to 2004; this project utilizes pooled data from these surveys. Analysis was restricted for this project to white individuals, aged 20–60, who were employed or self-employed in the non-agricultural labour force. Results are thus conditional on active labour market participation (outside agriculture). The analyses were conducted separately by gender on 65,306 men and 33,208 women in the pooled sample of U.S. census data and 11,690 men and 10,192 women in GSS data. Descriptive statistics on variables drawn from these two datatsets are found in Table A1.

Self-employment is measured overall as well as with respect to the classification scheme employed in the Arum and Müller volume (2004). Specifically, the analysis distinguishes amongst three types of self-employment: professional self-employment, skilled self-employment and traditional forms of proprietorship, and unskilled self-employment. Self-employment is defined as non-agricultural self-employment and is differentiated through the application of a three category schema that extends the earlier professional and non-professional distinction advanced by Arum (1997) and further elaborated by Müller, Lohmann and Luber (1999, 2000) to identify as distinct categories skilled and unskilled non-professional self-employment occupations. Professional self-employment in this schema includes all individuals who based on their occupations would ordinarily be classified in E.G.P. categories I or II, with the notable exception of self-identified proprietors of restaurants, hotels and small retail shops who have been assigned to a skilled and traditional bourgeois self-employment category. Skilled self-employment is the category assigned to proprietors or individuals whose occupations would fall into E.G.P. categories IIIa, V and VI. Unskilled self-employment is the category for occupational codes associated with E.G.P. categories IIIb or VII (Erikson and Goldthorpe 1993). Note that this classification schema assigns individuals based on their occupational self-identification, rather than on whether they employ others. In census analysis, the study relies on the IPUMS recoding of occupation into a 1950 U.S. census occupational metric for classification purposes; in

GSS analysis recoding of 1970 U.S. Census occupation codes are utilized for data prior to 1990, 1980 codes are relied on for GSS data after 1990.

Given limitations in the measurement of education in these datasets, only four categories of educational attainment are identified. The analysis distinguishes among primary education (CASMIN 1ab, omitted as the reference category in regressions), secondary education (CASMIN 2abc) and two forms of post-secondary education (CASMIN 3a for individuals with post-secondary educational attainments greater than high school attainment, but lower than the baccalaureate level; and CASMIN 3b for individuals with a baccalaureate level or higher). There are slightly more women than men with CASMIN 3a attainments, while the opposite is the case for CASMIN 3b in the datasets.

Social background is measured along multiple dimensions in the analysis of GSS data. Variables identify whether an individual's father was self-employed as well as the category of the class of father's occupational position (measured in the Erikson-Goldthorpe-Portocarero 1979 schema as EGP I/II for professional and managerial occupations, EGP III for routine non-manual occupations, EGP V/VI for skilled occupations, with EGP IV/VII employed by others omitted as a reference category). Social background is also measured by father's educational attainment (measured in a comparable manner as respondents' education identified above). Parental status as an immigrant and the number of respondent's siblings is also considered in GSS analysis. Social background measures, other than immigrant status, are not available in U.S. Census data.

A respondent's family context is also considered in this analysis. Given interest in family-based social capital, a measure of parental presence in the adult household is included. In GSS and Census datasets, this variable is measured in different ways. The GSS identifies whether parent of adult household head is present with a much lower prevalence than the broader census definition of parent of adult respondent in household. Although these operationalizations yield considerably different frequencies, they are each considered in the respective analyses. In both datasets identification of marital status and number of children exist (although the latter is again measured somewhat differently in the two datasets with census data providing lower estimates). An interaction for marriage*children is also included in the analysis.

Age and age-square are utilized in the analysis as proxies for work-experience. The analysis also controls for rural residence as well as time period. In analysis of U.S. census data, dummy variables for 1940, 1960, 1980 and 2000 (with 1920 omitted) are included to capture period effects as self-employment recedes and then rises during this observation window. Since GSS data begins in 1972, the multivariate analysis relies on a simple linear operationalization of time-period.

Self-employment rates over time are presented first to identify trends in the level and form of this activity over time. The chapter then presents logistic regressions predicting the likelihood of self-employment in U.S. Census (1920–2000) and GSS (1972–2004) data as well as multinomial logistic regressions that consider as distinct outcomes: professional self-employment, skilled and traditional petty bourgeois self-employment and unskilled self-employment. Because of the cross-sectional character of the data, dynamic event history modelling of self-employment entry and exit is not possible. All analyses are conducted separately for men and women.

Findings

Tables 1a and 1b present the percentage of men and women, aged 20–60 in the non-agricultural economic sector engaged in various forms of self-employment activities in the U.S. Census (1920–2000) and GSS (1972–2004) data respectively. Inspecting the U.S. Census data in Table 1a, one observes a steady decline in male and female self-employment from 1920 through 1960. Male non-agricultural self-employment falls from 15.4% in 1920 to 10.8% in 1980, before increasing to 12.1% in 2000. Female non-agricultural self-employment declines from 9.7% in 1920 to 4.8% in 1960, before increasing to 7.5% in 2000.[3] Although male self-employment historically occurs at a rate significantly higher than that of female self-employment, the prevalence of self-employment regardless of gender drops to rates lower than one-third of the original level from the second to the eight decade in the twentieth century. In the last quarter of the century, the self-employment rate rises for both men and women. Consistent with

---

3 Total male self-employment, inclusive of the agricultural sector, falls from 29.7% to 15.4% in 1960, then declines again slightly to 12.6% in 1980 and 13.4% in 2000. Total female self-employment (inclusive of agriculture) declines from 12.6% in 1920 to 5.2% in 1960, before rising to 5.4% in 1980 and 7.9% in 2000.

Table 1a. Self-employment rate by time-period and gender (U.S. Census data)

	Professional	Skilled	Unskilled	All S.E.	N of row
Males					
1920	2.4%	11.8%	1.2%	15.4%	13,827
1940	1.8%	10.1%	0.7%	12.7%	13,864
1960	1.7%	8.8%	0.8%	11.3%	14,122
1980	2.4%	7.7%	0.7%	10.8%	12,529
2000	2.6%	8.5%	1.0%	12.1%	10,964
Females					
1920	1.8%	4.5%	3.4%	9.7%	3,745
1940	1.0%	3.6%	1.8%	6.4%	4,809
1960	0.9%	2.8%	1.1%	4.8%	6,641
1980	1.0%	2.9%	1.2%	5.0%	8,682
2000	1.8%	3.3%	2.5%	7.5%	9,331

Table 1b. Self-employment rate by time-period and gender (G.S.S data)

	Professional	Skilled	Unskilled	All S.E.	N of row
Males					
1972–1983	7.5%	3.2%	1.2%	11.9%	4,074
1984–1994	8.8%	4.4%	1.2%	14.5%	4,157
1995–2004	8.6%	4.5%	1.7%	14.8%	3,466
Females					
1972–1983	4.1%	2.5%	1.3%	7.9%	2,916
1984–1994	5.5%	3.3%	2.3%	11.0%	3,903
1995–2004	5.7%	2.0%	2.7%	10.4%	3,379

prior research (Arum 1997), the observed increase is particularly pronounced for women.

Distinguishing between types of self-employment is informative in understanding the character of recent changes. Comparing the 1960 to 2000 rates of male self-employment in the three categories, one notes that self-employment rates have increased in both professional as well as unskilled forms of self-employment, but traditional skilled craft and petty bourgeois forms of self-employment have slightly declined. Male self-employment is becoming increasingly heterogeneous with its most advantageous and disadvantageous forms growing. Examining rates of female self-employment across categories, one observes a similar pattern. From 1960 to 2000, there is pronounced growth in both professional and unskilled self-employment (i.e., more than a doubling of the rate in both these categories), but only modest growth in traditional skilled and petty bourgeois forms of entrepreneurship.

The occupations most prevalent within these categories of self-employment activity also shifted over time as larger changes in the economy occurred. Popular occupations for male professional self-employment in 1920 were lawyers (20.4 percent of men in that category), doctors (25.2 percent) and dentists (12.4 percent); by 2000, these respective occupations declined to 17.2%, 10.2% and 6.3% respectively, while new occupations became more prevalent (such as accounting at 7.4%). Female professional self-employment changed its composition even more dramatically. In 1920, the two leading female professional self-employment occupations were musicians and music teachers (41.8 percent) and other self-employed teachers (17.9 percent); by 2000, those two occupations declined to 7.2% and 3.0% of female professional self-employment respectively. In 2000, the most popular self-employed professional occupations for women were designers (10.2%) and accountants (7.8%).

Male skilled and traditional petty bourgeois self-employment was relatively stable in terms of occupational composition. In 1920, 57% of male self-employment in this category occurred in the census occupational code »managers, officials and proprietors (not elsewhere classified)«; no other occupational code in this category had more than 4 percent of skilled male self-employment concentrated in it. In 2000, the greatest change in the male occupational distribution was in a decline in the proprietor category to 33.9 percent and the concurrent growth of a variety of craft enterprises (such as carpentry from 3.1 percent in 1920 to 9.1 percent). Female skilled and traditional petty bourgeois self-employment experienced even more profound changes in occupational composition. In 1920, the most common female skilled self-employment occupational category was (non-factory based) dressmaking and seamstressing, 53.3 percent; proprietors comprised 25.4 percent of this category. In 2000, the percentage of female skilled self-employment comprised of seamstresses and dressmakers was only 1.6 percent; female proprietors increased slightly to 32.6 percent and several new clerical occupations appeared as common self-employment activities (bookkeepers, 6.5%; stenographers, typists and secretaries, 7.8%; and clerical and kindred workers not elsewhere classified, 9.8%).

Supporting claims that one dimension of the increase in self-employment is the increasing marginalization of the work force, the most pronounced change in male unskilled self-employment is the growth of the labourers not elsewhere classified category from 12.0 percent in 1920 to 38.5 percent in 2000. Janitors have also become increasingly engaged through self-employed sub-contracting arrangements – often without job benefits such as health insurance, job security or paid vacations – with their presence increasing from 0.6 percent in 1920 to 8.3 percent of this category in 2000. Female unskilled self-employment has also changed with a shift away from the unskilled self-employment activity of boarding and lodging house keepers (39.4% in 1920 to no observations in that category in 2000); on a related note the 2000 occupation of non-household professional and personal service attendants not elsewhere classified (40.2 percent) was not utilized as a code for any of the 1920 census observations.

Table 1b presents GSS data that focuses attention on the last several decades of self-employment growth (1972–2004). The incidence of self-employment activity is slightly higher in this non-governmental data source than in the census data, as individuals were potentially more likely to report entrepreneurial activity to non-government sources where any perceived fear of potential legal liabilities associated with such revelations were diminished. Over this time-period self-employment increased from 11.9% to 14.8% for men and from 7.9% to 10.4% for women. The growth appears particularly pronounced in the late 1970s and 1980s. Again, the data indicates a higher rate of self-employment growth for women than men.

Examining changes in the prevalence of different types of self-employment over time, one observes a similar pattern of growth in all three categories for men. Female self-employment, however, again demonstrates a pattern of growth concentrated in the two extremes: professional and unskilled categories of self-employment.

Table 2a analyses U.S. census data to identify individual determinants of self-employment overall and by occupational type for men and women over the course of the twentieth century. Controlling for changes in individual-level characteristics, the likelihood of overall male self-employment

Table 2a. Logistic regression of self-employment by gender (U.S. Census data)

| | Male self-employment | | | | Female self-employment | | | |
	All S.E.	Profes-sional	Skilled	Unskilled	All S.E.	Profes-sional	Skilled	Unskilled
Intercept	-6.042**	-8.843**	-6.402**	-6.571**	-5.844**	-6.947**	-8.089**	-5.702**
	(0.199)	(0.505)	(0.225)	(0.639)	(0.361)	(0.768)	(0.540)	(0.618)
Time period								
1940 census	-0.367**	-1.831**	-0.255**	-0.296*	-0.673**	-1.917**	-0.504**	-0.623**
	(0.037)	(0.133)	(0.041)	(0.130)	(0.088)	(0.280)	(0.119)	(0.149)
1960 census	-0.598**	-2.420**	-0.461**	-0.125	-1.405**	-2.502**	-1.300**	-1.424**
	(0.041)	(0.144)	(0.046)	(0.136)	(0.095)	(0.292)	(0.127)	(0.167)
1980 census	-0.654**	-2.577**	-0.506**	0.099	-1.322**	-2.731**	-1.194**	-1.174**
	(0.047)	(0.149)	(0.053)	(0.155)	(0.098)	(0.300)	(0.132)	(0.168)
2000 census	-0.666**	-2.911**	-0.464**	0.747**	-1.084**	-2.676**	-1.240**	-0.224
	(0.051)	(0.153)	(0.058)	(0.166)	(0.102)	(0.300)	(0.140)	(0.168)
Education								
CASMIN 2abc	0.130**	0.824**	0.123**	-0.513**	0.010	0.909**	0.013	-0.261*
	(0.039)	(0.161)	(0.042)	(0.130)	(0.073)	(0.271)	(0.096)	(0.123)
CASMIN 3a	0.324**	1.965**	0.232**	-0.849**	0.398**	2.048**	0.448**	-0.352*
	(0.046)	(0.149)	(0.051)	(0.177)	(0.081)	(0.264)	(0.106)	(0.145)
CASMIN 3b	0.655**	3.623**	-0.038	-1.746**	0.321**	2.851**	0.098	-1.635**
	(0.042)	(0.128)	(0.053)	(0.241)	(0.084)	(0.254)	(0.119)	(0.220)
Social background								
Immigrant	0.160**	-0.441**	0.250**	0.292*	0.119	-0.242	0.178t	0.183
	(0.035)	(0.100)	(0.039)	(0.118)	(0.077)	(0.201)	(0.102)	(0.131)
Family context								
Parent in home	0.147**	0.185	0.163**	-0.121	-0.192*	0.027	-0.117	-0.514**
	(0.049)	(0.114)	(0.056)	(0.172)	(0.084)	(0.165)	(0.120)	(0.159)
Married	0.336**	0.231**	0.400**	0.007	0.492**	0.187	0.765**	0.288*
	(0.039)	(0.085)	(0.044)	(0.129)	(0.063)	(0.134)	(0.089)	(0.114)
Children	0.041	-0.170	0.064	0.016	0.187**	-0.059	0.201**	0.269**
	(0.039)	(0.132)	(0.042)	(0.123)	(0.041)	(0.118)	(0.058)	(0.061)
Married*children	-0.054	0.091	-0.071t	0.020	-0.112t	0.110	-0.146*	-0.145*
	(0.040)	(0.134)	(0.043)	(0.126)	(0.046)	(0.127)	(0.064)	(0.070)
Age and residence								
Age	0.163**	0.229**	0.162**	0.074*	0.142**	0.145**	0.195**	0.092**
	(0.010)	(0.025)	(0.011)	(0.032)	(0.018)	(0.040)	(0.027)	(0.032)
Age-squared (multiplied by 100)	-0.150**	-0.222**	-0.146**	-0.057	-0.124**	-0.144**	-0.167**	-0.077*
	(0.012)	(0.029)	(0.013)	(0.039)	(0.022)	(0.049)	(0.032)	(0.039)
Rural	0.290**	0.037	0.318**	0.528**	0.209**	-0.341*	0.246**	0.410**
	(0.028)	(0.070)	(0.031)	(0.095)	(0.057)	(0.146)	(0.076)	(0.100)

N = 65,306 (men) and 33,208 (women)

**p<.01, *p <.05, t p<.10

is lowest in the 2000 census; the nadir of female self-employment is the 1960 census. Examining the time-period coefficients for the distinct types of self-employment, however, one notices that unskilled self-employment has become increasingly pronounced in recent decades net of individual-level determinants.

In terms of education, college graduates (CASMIN 3b), particularly male, are more likely than those with primary and secondary education to be self-employed. When one examines the results for distinct types of self-employment, the positive association between CASMIN 3b and self-employment is found to be solely the product of professional forms of self-employment; CASMIN 3b is not related to skilled and traditional petty bourgeois self-employment and is actually negatively related to unskilled self-employment. The effects of CASMIN 3a on men and women are largely similar across gender. While post-secondary experience less than baccalaureate attainment is positively related to both professional and skilled self-employment, it is negatively associated with unskilled self-employment. The effects on female skilled and traditional petty bourgeois forms of self-employment are particularly pronounced for women. In the U.S., women often attain post-secondary certificates and associate level degrees in areas that can facilitate paths into self-employment. Such areas include degrees in business, management, marketing and related services, as well as health professions and related clinical sciences. Men are more likely than women to earn associate (A.A.) degrees in engineering and computer science (NCES 2003).

Profound gender differences exist in the effects of family context on self-employment likelihood. Having a parent living in the same household as the adult respondent increased male self-employment, but decreased female self-employment. The positive effect of parents in the household on men is found in the skilled and traditional petty bourgeois category (as well as the professional category). For women, the negative effect is due primarily to the association with unskilled self-employment. For men, parents in the household apparently can serve as a resource facilitating self-employment entry; while similar situations for women create barriers to self-employment. Gender differences extended into other variables measuring family context. While the results suggest that marriage is an institutional and inter-personal resource that is drawn on to support the increased likelihood of self-employment for both men and women; this familial resource is associated with professional and skilled self-employment for men, but not unskilled self-employment. For women, the effect of marriage is particularly pronounced on skilled and traditional bourgeois self-employment forms.

On the other hand, the presence of children has no significant effects on self-employment for men, but has effects on female self-employment, conditional on marriage. Unmarried women with children have a pronounced increased likelihood of self-employment, concentrated in non-professional occupations. This effect is possibly the result of the flexibility in work schedules inherent to some forms of self-employment. The effect of children on married women is significantly greater than for non-married women with children (0.187 children, -0.112 married*children).

In terms of age, which is being used in this analysis as an imperfect proxy for work experience, men and women's likelihood of self-employment generally increases over the life course until the early or mid fifties at which time its prevalence begins to decrease slightly. The effects of rural residence on self-employment likelihood are more pronounced for men than women. In general, rural residence is associated with higher rates of non-professional self-employment for both men and women.

Table 2b presents results from logistic regressions predicting the likelihood of male and female self-employment using the more contemporary General Social Survey data. The effects of time-period in this analysis are measured by a simple linear term (year). GSS 1972–2004 data suggests that female self-employment has been increasing, net of effects of individual-level determinants, over recent decades; male self-employment follows a fairly similar upward trend (the coefficient for year in the analysis of men is significant at the $p<.10$ level and is not statistically different than the coefficient for year in the analysis of women). Inspecting the coefficient for year in the multinomial logistic regression results with distinct forms of self-employment modelled as outcomes, one observes that the overall increase in self-employment net of individual determinants is largely being driven by an increase in unskilled self-employment.

The effects of education on overall self-employment likelihood are not particularly pronounced in this set of analyses when extensive controls for social background are included. CASMIN 3a and CASMIN 3b are associated with increased likelihood of professional forms of self-employment, but this effect is counterbalanced by a negative association between post-secondary education and non-professional self-employment. In supplementary analyses, where father's employment, occupation and education

Table 2b. Logistic regression of self-employment by gender (GSS data)

	Male Self-employment				Female Self-employment			
	All S.E.	Profes-sional	Skilled	Unskilled	All S.E.	Profes-sional	Skilled	Unskilled
Intercept	-26.071*	-7.934	-42.155*	-77.891*	-32.453*	-17.145	-5.532	-96.591**
	(11.008)	(14.133)	(18.569)	(31.958)	(13.296)	(18.471)	(25.292)	(25.872)
Time period								
Year	0.010t	0.000	0.018t	0.037*	0.014*	0.005	-0.001	0.047**
	(0.006)	(0.007)	(0.009)	(0.016)	(0.007)	(0.009)	(0.013)	(0.013)
Education								
CASMIN 2abc	-0.026	0.253t	-0.157	-0.445*	-0.160	-0.114	0.222	-0.467*
	(0.098)	(0.153)	(0.141)	(0.219)	(0.126)	(0.213)	(0.233)	(0.195)
CASMIN 3a	0.135	0.754**	-0.289t	-0.707**	-0.141	0.415t	0.127	-1.208**
	(0.103)	(0.153)	(0.156)	(0.253)	(0.135)	(0.216)	(0.253)	(0.242)
CASMIN 3b	0.143	1.112**	-1.345**	-1.904**	-0.216	0.668**	-1.228**	-1.482**
	(0.105)	(0.152)	(0.197)	(0.348)	(0.143)	(0.219)	(0.317)	(0.287)
Social background								
Father	0.685**	0.716**	0.672**	0.596**	0.446**	0.497**	0.546**	0.147
self-employed	(0.064)	(0.079)	(0.113)	(0.186)	(0.079)	(0.105)	(0.144)	(0.179)
Father	0.408**	0.526**	0.227	-0.325	-0.080	0.195	-0.454t	-0.486
EGP I/II	(0.107)	(0.133)	(0.211)	(0.313)	(0.133)	(0.184)	(0.235)	(0.336)
Father	0.255	0.314	0.494	-0.935	0.101	0.313	-0.131	-0.127
EGP III	(0.178)	(0.217)	(0.323)	(0.738)	(0.205)	(0.277)	(0.359)	(0.494)
Father	0.171	0.018	0.702**	-0.746*	-0.131	-0.174	-0.129	-0.097
EGP V/VI	(0.109)	(0.147)	(0.180)	(0.322)	(0.135)	(0.213)	(0.209)	(0.274)
Father	0.119	0.072	0.185	0.150	0.115	0.077	0.172	0.134
CASMIN 2abc	(0.080)	(0.103)	(0.133)	(0.228)	(0.094)	(0.133)	(0.166)	(0.191)
Father	0.190t	0.364**	-0.223	-0.271	0.111	0.147	0.160	-0.073
CASMIN 3a	(0.111)	(0.130)	(0.239)	(0.421)	(0.134)	(0.174)	(0.256)	(0.314)
Father	0.362**	0.371**	0.366t	0.556t	0.346**	0.376*	0.521*	0.082
CASMIN 3b	(0.097)	(0.116)	(0.187)	(0.306)	(0.120)	(0.153)	(0.240)	(0.297)
Parent immigrant	0.262**	0.369**	0.087	0.096	-0.190t	-0.225	-0.484*	0.115
	(0.082)	(0.100)	(0.150)	(0.254)	(0.108)	(0.145)	(0.236)	(0.203)
Family context								
Parent of head in	0.330	0.583*	0.086	-0.739	-0.114	-0.703	0.601	-0.330
home	(0.231)	(0.275)	(0.406)	(1.011)	(0.299)	(0.519)	(0.403)	(0.723)
Siblings	-0.035**	-0.033*	-0.049*	0.005	-0.042**	-0.076**	-0.045t	0.022
	(0.011)	(0.015)	(0.019)	(0.028)	(0.014)	(0.021)	(0.026)	(0.024)
Married	-0.050	-0.077	-0.164	0.395	0.533**	0.407**	0.749**	0.593**
	(0.085)	(0.109)	(0.148)	(0.247)	(0.108)	(0.144)	(0.214)	(0.229)
Children	0.094**	0.039	0.130*	0.146	-0.011	-0.111t	-0.008	0.174*
	(0.035)	(0.049)	(0.053)	(0.095)	(0.041)	(0.059)	(0.080)	(0.076)
Married*children	-0.036	0.051	-0.104	-0.211t	0.034	0.099	-0.031	-0.015
	(0.040)	(0.054)	(0.064)	(0.111)	(0.047)	(0.069)	(0.092)	(0.087)

Table 2b. Logistic regression of self-employment by gender (GSS data) (continued)

	Male Self-employment				Female Self-employment			
	All S.E.	Profes-sional	Skilled	Unskilled	All S.E.	Profes-sional	Skilled	Unskilled
Age and residence								
Age	0.151**	0.215**	0.113**	0.029	0.124**	0.187**	0.173**	0.009
	(0.022)	(0.030)	(0.036)	(0.059)	(0.027)	(0.039)	(0.051)	(0.051)
Age-squared								
(multiplied by	-0.140**	-0.204**	-0.103*	-0.018	-0.122**	-0.168**	-0.185**	-0.038
100)	(0.026)	(0.035)	(0.043)	(0.071)	(0.032)	(0.046)	(0.061)	(0.064)
Rural	0.162t	0.053	0.299*	0.236	-0.006	-0.129	0.072	0.085
	(0.084)	(0.115)	(0.132)	(0.219)	(0.105)	(0.158)	(0.177)	(0.201)

N =11,690 (men) and 10,192 (women)
**p<.01, *p <.05, t p<.10

are not included as controls, higher educational attainment is associated with an increased likelihood of male self-employment – coefficients (and standard errors) were: CASMIN 3a, 0.182 (0.089); CASMIN 3b, 0.259 (0.089). Female self-employment in the analysis of contemporary GSS data was not significantly related to educational attainment, even when controls for social background are omitted. In the regression with the full set of controls, however, women with baccalaureate degrees (CASMIN 3b) are more likely than other women to be engaged in professional self-employment and less likely involved in non-professional forms of self-employment. In additional supplementary analyses men with tertiary education (CASMIN 3ab) were more likely than other men (CASMIN 1ab and CASMIN 2abc combined) to engage in self-employment activity.

In terms of social background, the type of occupation the father attained has significant effects on male self-employment. Men with fathers who were in professional occupations (EGP I/II) have an increased likelihood of self-employment, particularly in professional self-employment. Father's occupation was not clearly associated with female self-employment. Father's education and self-employment, however, were significant predictors of self-employment for both men and women. The higher the father's educational attainment, the greater the likelihood of self-employment predicted regardless of gender. Interestingly, this effect held fairly constant across all forms of self-employment for both men and women. The effects of father's self-employment in the GSS analysis replicates findings identified in our earlier comparative work (Arum and Müller 2004). Men are 2.0

times, and women are 1.6 times, more likely self-employed if their fathers were self-employed than otherwise. Male self-employment was also predicted by father's immigrant status as a result of its strong association with professional forms of this activity. Female self-employment, particularly in skilled and traditional petty bourgeois forms, was slightly dampened by parental immigrant status.

While family context affected the likelihood of self-employment overall, particular aspects varied in their influence by gender. Consistent with the census analysis, men with parents in their household were significantly more likely to engage in professional self-employment activity. Siblings were negatively associated with professional as well as skilled and traditional petty bourgeois forms of self-employment. Marriage was a predictor of female, but not male, self-employment activity. Children were positively associated with male, particularly skilled self-employment, but had mixed effects on female self-employment (negatively associated with professional self-employment, but positively associated with female unskilled self-employment). Older individuals were more likely self-employed, although in the early to mid-fifties a slight decline in self-employment likelihood is observed. Rural residence was associated with male self-employment, particularly in skilled and traditional petty bourgeois endeavours.

Conclusion

Although the research in this chapter was not able to model the dynamic character of self-employment entry and exit with event history analysis and did not have a comparative cross-national design, the U.S. findings in this contribution lend support to many of the empirical propositions advanced by Müller and Arum in the *Reemergence of Self-Employment*. These propositions focused on self-employment heterogeneity and the extent to which self-employment was related to education, prior work-experience, family embeddedness and gender.

In terms of self-employment heterogeneity, Arum and Müller (2004) argued that »self-employment has developed into a more heterogeneous employment type with increases prevalent in professional-managerial and unskilled occupations, but declines in traditional forms of petty bourgeois and skilled self-employment.« (p. 430) A similar pattern was found here.

Evidence of unskilled self-employment growth was particularly pronounced, especially in the multivariate analyses that provide estimates controlling for individual-level educational attainments and other factors that are historically changing in their overall distributions. Emerging self-employment occupations in the United States include today such marginal and precarious activities as labourers and janitors for men and personal service attendants for women.

The effects of human capital in this chapter are also consistent with Arum and Müller's earlier findings. Specifically, tertiary education was argued to have strong effects on professional self-employment entry and persistence as it provided human capital skills facilitating this activity as well likely as a taste for professional autonomy (p. 439). CASMIN 3b was strongly and consistently associated with professional self-employment activity in both the GSS and census analysis. Prior work experience, proxied imperfectly by age, was also demonstrated to increase self-employment well into an individual's fifties.

Self-employment has also been argued to be embedded in family contexts. Arum and Müller (2004) argued that: »Family support, provided in terms of either direct inheritance of parental self-employment position, other parental support, or spousal assistance and involvement in the enterprises, are significant individual-level resources that encourage an individual's decision both to become and remain self-employed« (p. 444) Although spousal self-employment is not included as a determinant of self-employment in this analysis, strong evidence existed on the other dimensions of self-employment's family embeddedness. In the GSS analysis, men were 2.0 times more likely and women were 1.6 times more likely self-employed if their fathers had been self-employed than otherwise. Father's tertiary education was related to individual self-employment, particularly in professional enterprises, as was father's professional occupation background in the case of male self-employment. There was also evidence that self-employment was related to marriage and the presence of parents in the adult respondent's household.

Finally, the study identified profound gender differences in self-employment, given that »women – since they differ from men in their relative resources, opportunities, and constraints – have distinctly different patterns and determinants of self-employment.« (p. 446) Female self-employment, particularly in unskilled occupations, is increasing at a rate greater than male self-employment.[4] The effects of family context in particular varied by gender: parents and children in the household can either be a resource or obstacle to self-employment. The effect of baccalaureate attainment (CASMIN 3b) on self-employment is stronger for men than women.

These findings in general contribute additional empirical evidence of changes in self-employment over time as well as identification of the determinants of this activity. As such it follows in the tradition of Müller's work on self-employment and is thus itself a part of a larger intellectual agenda to identify how opportunity structures vary across societies and over time periods, and how institutional factors affect the process whereby social origins, education and other factors contribute to shaping an individual's social destinations. Müller's attention to empirical rigor, methodological sophistication and analytical specification of the process whereby individuals considered resources, opportunities and constraints in their educational and occupational decision making advanced not just our understanding of self-employment, but more broadly how systems of social stratification varied.

---

4 Calculated as $(t2-t1)/t1$.

Appendix

Table A1. Descriptive statistics on General Social Survey 1972–2004 and U.S. Census, 1920/1940/1960/1980/2000 IPUMS data

	Census sample		GSS	
	Men	Women	Men	Women
Time period				
			1988.100	1989.460
Year			(9.768)	(9.363)
1940 census	0.212	0.145		
1960 census	0.216	0.200		
1980 census	0.192	0.261		
2000 census	0.168	0.281		
Education				
CASMIN 2abc	0.234	0.333	0.320	0.360
CASMIN 3a	0.118	0.179	0.265	0.281
CASMIN 3b	0.132	0.157	0.275	0.260
Social background				
Father self-employed			0.228	0.229
Father EGP I/II			0.149	0.146
Father EGP III			0.035	0.034
Father EGP V/VI			0.158	0.130
Father CASMIN 2abc			0.239	0.256
Father CASMIN 3a			0.089	0.096
Father CASMIN 3b			0.140	0.142
Immigrant	0.128	0.083		
Parent immigrant			0.109	0.119
Family context				
Parent of head in home			0.011	0.012
Parent in home	0.127	0.172		
Siblings			3.357	3.389
			(2.740)	(2.700)
Married	0.738	0.564	0.638	0.564
	1.222	0.824	1.600	1.656
Children	(1.512)	(1.162)	(1.579)	(1.543)
	1.190	0.673	1.338	1.114
Married*children	(1.509)	(1.118)	(1.582)	(1.482)
Age and residence				
Age	38.340	37.668	38.314	38.417
	(11.064)	(11.393)	(10.895)	(10.839)
Age-squared	1592.370	1548.670	1586.580	1593.250
	(877.983)	(891.233)	(868.680)	(861.976)
Rural	0.264	0.213	0.129	0.118
N	65,306	33,208	11,690	10,192

References

Aldrich, H./Waldinger, R. (1990). »Ethnicity and entrepreneurship«, *Annual Review of Sociology*, vol. 16, pp. 111–135.

Aldrich, H./Zimmer, C. (1986). »Entrepreneurship through social networks«, in H. Aldrich (ed.), *Population Perspectives on Organizations* (Studia Oeco-nomiae Negotiorum 25), Uppsala: Acta Universitatis Upsaliensis, pp. 13–28.

Arum, R./Müller, W. (eds.) (2004). *The Reemergence of Self-Employment: A Comparative Study of Self-Employment Dynamics and Social Inequality*, Princeton, N.J.: Princeton University Press.

Arum, R. (2004). »Entrepreneurs and marginal laborers: two sides of self-employment in the United States«, in R. Arum/W. Müller (eds.), *The Reemergence of Self-Employment: A Comparative Study of Self-Employment Dynamics and Social Inequality*, Princeton, N.J.: Princeton University Press, pp. 170–202.

Arum, R./Budig, M./Grant, D. (2000). »Labour market regulation and the growth of self-employment«, *International Journal of Sociology*, vol. 30, no. 4, pp. 1–26.

Arum, R. (1997). »Trends in male and female self-employment: growth in a new middle class or increasing marginalization of the labor force?«, *Research in Social Stratification and Mobility*, vol. 15, pp. 209–238.

Blanchflower, D. (2000). »Self-employment in OECD countries«, *Labour Economics*, vol. 7, pp. 471–505.

Blanchflower, D./Oswald, A. J. (1990). *What Makes a Young Entrepreneur? Evidence on inheritance and capital constraints* (NBER Working Paper No. 3252), Cambridge, Mass.: National Bureau of Economic Research.

Blau, D. (1987). »A time-series analysis of self-employment in the United States«, *Journal of Political Economy*, vol. 95, no. 3, pp. 445–467.

Borjas, G./Bronars, S. (1989). »Consumer discrimination and self-employment«, *Journal of Political Economy*, vol. 97, no. 3, pp. 581–605.

Braun, M./Müller, W. (1997). »Measurement of education in comparative research«, *Comparative Social Research*, vol. 16, pp. 163–201.

Brock, W./Evans, D. (1986). *The Economics of Small Businesses: Their Role and Regulation in the U.S. Economy*, New York: Holmes and Meier.

Current Population Studies (CPS) (2004). *Measures of Individual Earnings Inequality for Full-Time Year-Round Workers by Sex: 1967–2001*, Annual Demographic Supplements, Table IE-2.

Erikson, R./Goldthorpe, J. H. (1993). *The Constant Flux: A Study of Class Mobility in Industrial Societies*, Oxford: Oxford University Press.

Erikson, R./Goldthorpe, J. H./Portocarero, L. (1979). »International class mobility in three Western European Societies«, *British Journal of Sociology*, vol. 30, pp. 415–441.

Evans, D./Jovanovic, B. (1989). »An estimated model of entrepreneurial choice under liquidity constraints«, *Journal of Political Economy*, vol. 97, no. 4, pp. 808–827.

Evans, D./Leighton, L. (1989). »Some empirical aspects of entrepreneurship«, *The American Economic Review*, vol. 79, no. 3, pp. 519-535.

Fuchs, V. R. (1982). »Self-employment and labor force participation of older males«, *Journal of Human Resources*, vol. 17, pp. 339–357.

Ganzeboom, H./Treiman, D./Ultee, W. (1991). »Comparative intergenerational stratification research: three generations and beyond«, *Annual Review of Sociology*, vol. 17, pp. 277–302.

Gerber, T. (2001). »Paths to success: individual and regional determinants of self-employment entry in post-communist Russia«, *International Journal of Sociology*, vol. 31, no. 2, pp. 3–37.

Hisrich, R./Brush, C. (1986). *The Woman Entrepreneur*, Lexington, Mass.: Lexington Books.

Hout, M./Brooks, C./Manza, J. (1995). »The democratic class struggle in the United States, 1948–1992«, *American Sociological Review*, vol. 60, no. 6, pp. 805–828.

Kalleberg, A./Leicht, K. (1991). »Gender and organizational performance: determinants of small business survival and success«, *Academy of Management Journal*, vol. 34, pp. 136–161.

Kim, K. C./Hurh, W. M. (1985). »Ethnic resources utilization of Korean immigrant entrepreneurs in the Chicago minority area«, *International Migration Review*, vol. 19, pp. 82–111.

König, W./Lüttinger, P/Müller, W. (1988). *A Comparative Analysis of the Development and Structure of Educational Systems: Methodological Foundations and the Construction of a Comparative Educational Scale* (CASMIN Working Paper No. 12), Mannheim: University of Mannheim.

Laferrère, A. (2001). »Self-employment and intergenerational transfers: liquidity constraints and family environment«, *International Journal of Sociology*, vol. 31, no. 1, pp. 3–26.

Lipset, S. (1981). *Political Man: The Social Basis of Politics*, Baltimore: Johns Hopkins Press.

Loscocco, K./Leicht, K. (1993). »Gender, work-family linkages and economic success among small business owners«, *Journal of Marriage and the Family*, vol. 55, pp. 875–887.

Luber, S./Lohmann, H./Müller, W./Barbieri, P. (2000). »Male self-employment in four European countries: the relevance of education and experience across industries«, *International Journal of Sociology*, vol. 30, no. 3, pp. 5–44.

McManus, P. (2000). »Market, state, and the quality of new self-employment jobs among men in the U.S. and Western Germany«, *Social Forces*, vol. 78, no. 3, pp. 865–905.

Meager, N./Kaiser, M./Dietrich, H. (1992). *Self-Employment in the United Kingdom and Germany,* London: Anglo-German Foundation for the Study of Industrial Society.

Min, P. G. (1984). »From white-collar occupations to small business: Korean immigrants' occupational adjustment«, *Sociological Quarterly*, vol. 25, pp. 333–352.

Müller, W./Arum, R. (2004). »Self-employment dynamics in advanced economies«, in R. Arum/W. Müller (eds.), *The Reemergence of Self-Employment: A Comparative Study of Self-Employment Dynamics and Social Inequality*, Princeton, N.J.: Princeton University Press, pp. 1–35.

Müller, W./Gangl, M. (eds.) (2003). *Transitions from Education to Work in Europe: the Integration of Youth into EU Labour Markets*, Oxford: Oxford University Press.

Müller, W./Lohmann, H./Luber, S. (2000). *Minutes from First Workshop on Self-Employment in Advanced Economies*, Libourne (France), 10 May.

Müller, W./Lohmann, H./Luber, S. (1999). *Self-Employment in Advanced Economies: Project Summary*, Mannheim: Mannheimer Zentrum für Europäische Sozialforschung.

Müller, W./Karle, W./König, W./Lüttinger, P. (1989). »Class and education in industrial nations«, *International Journal of Sociology*, vol. 19, no. 3, pp. 3–39.

National Center for Educational Statistics (NCES) (2003). *Associate's Degrees Conferred for First Majors by Title IV Degree Granting Institutions, by Race/Ethnicity, Field of Study, and Gender: United States, Academic Year 2002–03*, Integrated Postsecondary Education Data System.

Organization for Economic Cooperation and Development (OECD) (2000). *The Partial Renaissance of Self-Employment* (OECD Employment Outlook), Paris: OECD.

Piore, M./Sabel, C. (1984). *The Second Industrial Divide: Possibilities for Prosperity*, New York: Basic Books.

Portes, A./Rumbaut, R. G. (1990). *Immigrant America: A Portrait*, Berkeley: University of California Press.

Shavit, Y./Arum, R./Gamoran, A./Menahem, G. (eds.) (forthcoming). *Stratification in Higher Education: A Comparative Study*, Stanford, Cal.: Stanford University Press.

Shavit, Y./Müller, W. (eds.) (1998). *From School to Work: A Comparative Study of Educational Qualifications and Occupational Destinations*, Oxford: Oxford University Press.

Shavit, Y./Yuchtman-Yaar, E. (2001). »Ethnicity, education and other determinants of self-employment in Israel«, *International Journal of Sociology*, vol. 31, no. 1, pp. 59–91.

Steinmetz, G./Wright, E. O. (1989). »The fall and rise of the petty bourgeoisie: changing patterns of self-employment in the postwar United States«, *American Journal of Sociology*, vol. 94, no. 5, pp. 973–1018.

Treiman, D./Ganzeboom, H. (2000). »The fourth generation of comparative stratification research«, in S. R. Quah/A. Sales (eds.), *The International Handbook of Sociology*, London: Sage, pp. 122–150.

Wharton, A. S. (1989). »Gender segregation in private sector, public sector, and self-employed occupations, 1950–1981«, *Social Science Quarterly*, vol. 70, no. 4, pp. 923–940.

Youth unemployment in the enlarged European Union

Irena Kogan, Marge Unt, and Ellu Saar

Introduction

In 2004 the European Union experienced the largest expansion in its history having accepted ten new member states of which eight were Central and Eastern European (CEE) countries. Two further Eastern European countries (Bulgaria and Romania) joined the European Union in 2007. The enlargement has finally put an end to a painful division of the European continent and enhanced prospects of sharing Europe's rich cultural heritage in peace. At the same time it has increased the cultural heterogeneity, social disparities and economic imbalances within the EU, exemplified for instance in the lower living standards and higher unemployment in some of the new member states. Unsurprisingly, turbulent school-to-work transitions and soaring youth unemployment are on top of the agenda for both researchers and policy makers in many CEE countries. Most existing studies remain, however, single-case analyses or comparisons of only a small number of countries (e.g. Cedefop 2001, Gerber 2003, Toomse 2003, Kogan and Unt 2005, Róbert and Bukodi 2005, Saar 2005). Despite the importance of the above-mentioned research, educational and labour market stratification and school-to-work transitions in post-socialist CEE countries have not yet been studied systematically, as has been accomplished for Western industrialized countries (e.g. Allmendinger 1989, Kerckhoff 1996, 2000; Hannan et al. 2001, Garonna and Ryan 1991, Müller and Gangl 2003a, Shavit and Müller 1998). Moreover, hardly any comparative research able to elaborate an integrated picture of the structural and regional inequalities in the enlarged European Union has been undertaken thus far. This study aims to bridge this gap in two ways. First, it will compare CEE countries and the EU-15 with respect to the organisation of their educational systems and labour market regulation. Secondly, it will identify distinct country-clusters of youth unemployment incidence and duration in the late 1990s-early 2000s.

Institutions and labour market entry

Two factors have been identified as being of central importance for young school leavers' labour market entry patterns: the structure of the education system and the degree of labour market regulation (Müller 2005). Education endowes individuals with productive capacities and potential employers with signals of those capabilities (Spence 1973, Becker 1993, Polachek and Siebert 1993, Breen et al. 1995). Two of the most crucial features of an education system identified by potential employers are the absolute level to which students are educated and the extent of the education system's vocational specificity (Shavit and Müller 1998, Brauns et al. 1999).[1] The more successful education systems are in providing standardised and specific vocational qualifications of immediate and clear labour market value to prospective employers, the more these employers will use educational signals (rather than, for example, experience) in labour market allocation decision-making.[2]

Scholars have traditionally contrasted internal labour markets (ILM) with occupational labour markets (OLM) (Marsden 1990), or »organisational« and »qualificational« spaces (Maurice et al. 1986, Müller and Shavit 1998). In qualificational spaces (or OLM), labour markets are structured predominantly along occupational segments related to corresponding tracks of vocational training in the education and training system. In countries that cannot rely on employment related training systems, (i.e. in or-

---

1 The level of education is commonly understood to be an indicator of general ability and cognitive capabilities, while vocational specialization is regarded as a set of transferable specific skills related to particular occupations and industries (Gangl 2003a).

2 Employers have to make their decisions under conditions of uncertainty, since the match between job applicants' capabilities and the skills required by the job is not something that can be readily determined. In other words, employers face a screening problem (Spence 1973, Arrow 1973). Educational credentials play a particularly important role during the screening process of recent school leavers, who unlike more experienced workers normally do not possess productivity signals other than their education (Gangl 2003a).

ganisational spaces or ILM), training of the workforce is tied to the specific needs of individual firms and their internal labour markets.

Research shows that, as a rule, different dimensions of education and training systems as well as their linkages to the labour market are correlated at the national level, so that different national models of labour market integration can be distinguished (e.g. Hannan et al. 2001, Kerckhoff 2000, Garonna and Ryan 1991, Estevez-Abe et al. 2001). The authors of »Comparative Analysis of Transitions from Education to Work in Europe« (CATEWE) (Smyth et al. 2001) suggest that national transition systems could be represented as a single continuum. At one end of this continuum are countries such as Germany, having strong occupational labour markets, standardised and track-differentiated education systems, and strong links between education and the labour market. At the other end of the continuum are countries dominated by internal labour markets, with less standardised and less differentiated education systems, weaker links between education and the labour market, and little formal work-based training, e.g. America or Ireland. Gangl (2003b) distinguishes between three clusters of EU-15 countries with regard to patterns of labour market entry. A first group comprises a set of countries with extensive vocational systems at the upper secondary level and occupational labour markets (Austria, Germany, Denmark and the Netherlands). A second group encompasses the rest of Western and Northern EU countries, including Spain, with a more pronounced internal labour market organisation, where labour market allocation predominantly relies on experience. Finally, Gangl proposes treating Italy, Portugal, and Greece as a separate Southern European cluster, in which both strong qualification and strong experience effects occur in conjunction with very high unemployment risks in early careers, but relatively little volatility once initial employment has been secured.

Above and beyond the role of the education system it has been argued that the degree of labour market regulation influences an employer's decision-making when hiring workers. Labour market regulation ténds to dampen the dynamics of the labour market and hence affects the job-finding rates amongst job seekers in general (Bertola and Rogerson 1997, Gregg and Manning 1997, Gangl 2003c, 2003d). This is particularly relevant for the employment entry chances of first-time job seekers. Research suggests that when employers have higher firing costs they may set higher productivity expectations for potential employees. This arguably may pose particular problems for young people as both their need for additional training as well as the higher level of uncertainty inherent in recruiting inexperienced school leavers work to their disadvantage (Müller and Gangl 2003b). However, stricter labour regulation, such as a strong union presence, a centralised system of collective bargaining or co-operative relationships between corporate partners, can generate economically viable institutional structures of youth labour market integration (Soskice 1994, Estevez-Abe et al. 2001, Ryan 2001).[3]

Empirical evidence regarding the effect of labour market regulation on school-leavers' labour market outcomes is still inconclusive. According to Van der Velden and Wolbers (2003), the level of employment protection legislation appears to effect youth unemployment chances, but the effect is not stable once the structure of training systems is taken into account. Bertola et al. (2002) argue that the rigidities created by various labour market institutions have a negative effect on youth employment, but only in some countries. Using macro-level data, Breen (2005), on the other hand, finds a clear effect of employment protection on the extent to which youth unemployment exceeds adult unemployment, but only in the interaction with the structure and organisation of the education system. Systems of vocational training that teach specific skills and incorporate a strong work-based element provide a preventative to youth unemployment by offsetting the negative effects of extensive employment protection.

Garonna and Ryan (1991) take labour market legislation into account when trying to distinguish ideal types of youth labour market entry – regulated inclusion, selective exclusion and competitive regulation. Regulated inclusion occurs most often in occupational labour markets which require training through apprenticeships, e.g. Germany, Austria, Denmark (Marsden and Ryan 1991). Selective exclusion arises in countries with internal labour markets, high employment protection and little provision of specialised training, e.g. Greece, Italy. In competitive regulation settings, employers look for short-term profitability. This may occur in cases of high unemployment, weak employment protection and weak union power. Employers take maximum advantage of the competition between experi-

---

3 An example of corporate efforts might be a wage moderation policy designed to enhance youth labour market integration both at the level of particular firms or industries and also across the whole economy. Other forms include efforts to establish common training standards for certain occupations or industries or to involve corporate bodies in the formulation and implementation of training curricula (Hannan et al. 1999).

Table 1. Typology of institutional arrangements and youth unemployment patterns

Educational signalling	Labour market regulation	
	High	Low
High	Germany, Austria, Netherlands, Slovenia	Denmark
	Hungary Czech Republic Poland Slovak Republic **?**	
Low	France, Belgium, Luxembourg, Sweden, Finland, Italy, Spain, Portugal, Greece Estonia, Latvia, Lithuania	UK Ireland

Note: Based on Breen (2005). Signalling refers to the percentage of persons enrolled in upper secondary education who are in vocational or technical programmes that combine school and workplace training. Labour market regulation refers to employment protection legislation of regular employment.

enced workers and new entrants. According to Couppié and Mansuy (2003) a more realistic model is a mixture of selective exclusion and competitive regulation, which occurs in the context of internal labour markets when deregulation and flexibility policies are introduced under economic pressure e.g. France, Sweden, Finland. In addition, the classification distinguished a so-called »composite« group comprised of the rest of the EU-15 countries: Belgium, the Netherlands, Portugal, Spain, UK, and Ireland.

Despite the consensus on the importance of labour market regulation and the signalling capability of the education system in explaining variation in employment entry patterns and above all rates of youth unemployment in different countries, indicators of labour market flexibility have not been used thus far to distinguish empirically between various patterns of labour market entry among young people. The current study will use a model proposed by Breen (2005) and cluster 8 »new« and 15 »old« EU countries with respect to youth unemployment using indicators related to a) the education system and b) the extent of labour market regulation (see Table 1).

While the location of EU-15 countries in the educational signalling/labour market regulation typology has been more or less established (Breen 2005, Gangl 2003a, Scherer 2005), there is far less consensus on where CEE countries are placed in the above-mentioned nexus. Hence before discussing the methodological aspects of the empirical analyses, the following section sheds light on the arrangements of the education systems and labour market regulation in post-transformation CEE countries, and predicts possible locations for these countries within the typology.

Education systems and labour market regulation in CEE countries

As a result of their Socialist histories, practically all CEE countries inherited a highly centralised and state-controlled education system with pronounced tracking and smooth school-to-work transitions (e.g. Roberts and Szumlicz 1995, Titma and Saar 1995, Saar 1997, Helemäe and Saar 2000, Gerber 2003, Róbert and Bukodi 2005). The transformation years brought about the restructuring of education and training systems, as well as the dismantling of established links between education providers and enterprises. Five of the main reforms undertaken in the 1990s should be mentioned. First, curricula of general education were revised, while the curricula of vocational education and training courses were broadened. Second, the introduction of new post-secondary vocational programmes and the emergence of private institutions diversified the structure of post-secondary education. Third, vocational education has increasingly come under the auspices of schools (in particular in the Baltic states), as enterprises, particularly with the onset of the privatisation and restructuring processes, were unable to maintain the infrastructure for training or afford the financing of apprentices. Fourth, with the initiation of market reforms the earlier well-established link between schools and enterprises was dismantled and started to re-emerge in a modified form only in a few CEE countries. In particular, elements of partial, enterprise-based apprentice training were preserved but continued to shrink in the Czech Republic, Slovakia and Poland. The dual system of apprenticeship training was, on the other hand, re-introduced in Hungary and Slovenia (Strietska-Ilina 2001). Fifth, tertiary education participation has substantially increased, not least due to the emergence of private institutions of higher education and the expansion of short, practically oriented programmes (e.g. Roberts 1998, Mickelwright 1999, Matějů and Simonová 2003). The demand for higher education could be attributed, at least partially, to the larger proportion of young people opting to extend of their studies in order to escape increasing youth unemployment and postpone their labour market entry (ILO 1999, Helemäe and Saar 2000, Róbert 2003).

Strietska-Ilina (2001) argues that most countries with traditionally high participation in vocational education compared to general education (the Czech Republic, Hungary, Poland, Slovakia and Slovenia) had substantially higher enrolments in vocational education and training in the late 1990s. The education systems of the Baltic countries, on the other hand, have become characterised by a stronger emphasis on general education at the upper secondary level[4] (Helemäe and Saar 2000, Kogan and Unt 2005). Even though the organisation of education systems in CEE countries into different tracks largely resembles the highly stratified arrangement of German-speaking countries, weak links between the education system and labour market in some CEE countries, particularly in the Baltic states, make such systems more similar to the moderately stratified systems, found in France and the UK (Toomse 2003, Saar 2005). This means that the vocational qualifications obtained in the education system do not necessarily guarantee smooth and quick school-to-work transitions.

Alongside the restructuring of the education system, CCE countries' economic reforms in the 1990s created labour relations common to market-based systems. One of the most important changes occurred in employment regulation laws; the average index of employment protection legislation (EPL) in CEE countries was found to be similar to the EU-15 average, meaning that the majority of transition countries settle in the middle of the labour market flexibility scale[5] (Riboud et al. 2002, Wallace 2003, Cazes and Nesporova 2003). Nevertheless, as in the old EU countries, there is variation within CEE states with respect to employment protection. Hungary has the most flexible labour legislation, with an EPL index[6] value of 1.7, closely followed by the Czech Republic and Slovakia (1.9), and Poland (2.1). The Baltic countries occupy the middle ground, with an index

---

4 It seems that in CEE countries geographically and historically closer to Germany, vocationally oriented secondary education has maintained its dominance over more general curricula. An opposite trend has been observed further to the East (Roberts 1998).

5 This implies that the labour markets of CEE countries are less flexible than those of the United Kingdom, but certainly not as rigid as those in Southern Europe.

6 Employment Protection Legislation indexes (version 2) consider legislation on permanent and temporary employment as well as legislation on collective dismissals (see Riboud et al. 2002).

value of 2.5 to 2.7. Finally, Slovenia has the most restrictive labour regulation (2.9).

A problem of the legal regulation of labour market activity in the CEE countries is that employers do not always adhere to rules; in the private sector and in small firms, violations are particularly common (see Eamets and Masso 2004 for the Baltic countries). The low coverage of trade unions (see Saar et al. 2006) means that violations are often not investigated and workers' representatives cannot protect workers. In addition, in a climate of high unemployment, employees do not initiate individual claims against employers for fear of losing their jobs. Eamets and Masso (2004) conclude that for CEE countries the estimated labour market strictness or flexibility needs to be determined not only by reference to formal legislation but also by its enforcement and the degree of violations.

In addition it should be mentioned that at the start of the transition period, most workers were employed on permanent contracts. By the early 2000s fixed-term work had become a widespread form of employment and is being increasingly used as an important source of flexibility, especially in Poland and Slovenia (European Commission 2004, see also Table 2). In the Baltic states about 5% of the work force labours without any written contract; their employment and working conditions are settled verbally with the employer. All in all, it might appear that labour markets in CEE countries are somewhat more flexible than EPL indices suggest. While in the EU-15 countries flexibility (reflected in the EPL indices) is attained by using flexible employment contracts (temporary contracts, temporary work agency employment etc.), in CEE countries (especially in the Baltic states) employers often attain flexibility by simply not following the regulations.

Some attempts have been made to identify the position of CEE countries within typologies of labour market entry patterns. According to Cedefop (2001), the majority of CEE countries have been moving away from the model of regulated inclusion, characteristic of occupational labour markets (e.g. Germany), to the model of competitive regulation, characteristic of the flexible labour markets of the USA. Róbert and Bukodi (2005) assert that in Hungary mobility space, typically qualificational in nature, started to change slowly in the direction of an organisational mobility space, where the curriculum of the educational institutions is more general and where the match between the type of qualification and the type of job is not strong anymore. Saar (2005) argues that in Estonia the transition from school to work resembles the competitive pattern.

Previous analysis has shown that the CCE countries are moving in different directions adopting various employment protection models and changing their education systems (see for example Helemäe and Saar 2002, Hampalová 2003). Thus a uniform classification of post-socialist transition countries with regard to youth unemployment hardly seems feasible. We expect youth unemployment patterns in Slovenia, a country characterized by relatively strong employment protection coupled with vocational specificity of the education system, to resemble those found in the group of more rigid OLM countries (see Table 1). The Baltic states, known for their less flexible labour markets and for their lack of meaningful vocational training, should cluster with the rest of Europe since they have similar education systems and labour market regulations. Predictions for Poland, Slovakia, the Czech Republic and Hungary are less straightforward. On the one hand, Poland, Hungary and the Czech Republic are somewhat more flexible than the rest of continental Europe, but their economies are certainly less liberalized than in the UK, Ireland or Denmark. On the other hand, vocational education remains rather strong in these countries, particularly in the Czech Republic and Hungary, but it looks as though an effective link between educational providers and enterprises has been lost during the transformation years.

Data and statistical methodology

To assess the patterns of youth unemployment in the enlarged European Union using indicators related to the signalling character of the education system and the degree of labour marker regulation the following descriptive and cluster analyses draw upon data from the European Union Labour Force Surveys (EULFS) conducted between 1998 and 2004 in 15 old and 8 new EU countries (see Eurostat 1998 for details). A primary objective is to include as many observations for each country as possible, but due to data deficiencies the number of observations per country had to be limited.[7]

---

7 The data for the second quarter (if not specified otherwise) for the following country-years have been included: Austria, years 2002, 2003 (first quarter); Belgium, years 1999, 2000, 2004; the Czech republic, years 2002, 2003; Germany, years 2000, 2001 of the micro census; Denmark, years 2001, 2002; Estonia, years 1999, 2000, 2001, 2002; Spain, years 1999, 2000, 2001, 2002, 2003; Finland, years 2000, 2001, 2002; France, years 2003,

The basic idea is thus to use the available data on labour market entrants, to compare them to more experienced workers, and to generate a set of macro-level indicators describing youth unemployment patterns in the CEE countries in the backdrop of other European countries. *Labour market entrants* are defined here as individuals in the labour force, aged 15 to 34, who attained their highest educational level five years prior to the survey. Such a definition is certainly not ideal, but unfortunately the EULFS does not collect the starting date of first (significant) employment. As a result an approximation has to be made and in this regard Couppié and Mansuy's (2003) approach was adopted. *Experienced workers* are defined as economically active individuals, 35–54 years old, who entered the labour market more than five years prior to the survey.

The choice of indicators has been related to the two theoretical axes described above – the signalling power of the education system and the degree of labour market regulation. Indicators of educational signalling pertain to the gradients of low-secondary, upper-secondary vocational and tertiary education as compared to the upper-secondary general education on youth unemployment incidence. Indicators for the flexibility of the labour market include rates of long-term (longer than one year) unemployment and rates of fixed-term employment for labour market entrants as well as the differentials between labour market entrants and experienced workers in these indicators. We also tried to include indicators of unemployment exit and entry in the year of survey compared to the preceding year, but this information is unavailable for the Netherlands, France and Ireland, which therefore reduces the sample of the analysed countries.[8] Finally, youth unemployment rates and the relative advantage/disadvantage of labour market entrants as compared to more experienced workers are also subjected to cluster analysis (exact definitions of all indicators included in the cluster analyses can be found in Table A in the appendix).

2004; Greece, years 2001, 2002, 2003, 2004, Hungary, years 2001, 2002, 2003, 2004; Ireland, years 2002, 2003, 2004; Italy, years 1998, 1999, 2000, 2001, 2002, 2003; Lithuania, years 2001, 2002, 2003; Luxembourg, years 1999, 2000 and 2001 have been pooled into one dataset due to small sample sizes; Latvia, years 2002, 2003, 2004; the Netherlands, years 2003, 2004; Poland, years 2001, 2002, 2003, 2004; Portugal, years 1998, 1999, 2000, 2001, 2002; Slovenia, years 2000, 2001, 2002; Slovakia, years 2002, 2003, 2004; and finally, in the UK the labour force survey for year 2000 was used. Sweden has been excluded from the analysis due to unavailable information of vocational education.

8 Once including the whole set of indicators results remained quite robust.

Alongside a number of simple rate indicators, such as the youth unemployment rate or rate of fixed-term contracts, measures of the association between individual education and unemployment incidence are included. These measures, as well as gradients for labour market entrants (compared to experienced workers) in unemployment incidence and duration, and fixed-term employment are estimated from a set of auxiliary logistic regressions fitted for each of the 67 country-year cases. These regressions control for the composition of the sample in terms of gender, marital status and the interaction between the two. The paper first focuses on the differences in the unemployment incidence between labour market entrants and experienced workers in the CEE countries as well as in the EU-15 countries. Further evidence on other labour market outcomes is subsequently included in the cluster analyses. Finally, based on the macro-level data the analysis then attempts to identify empirically distinct country clusters. The cluster analysis is conducted in two steps. First, indicators pertaining to the educational signalling hypothesis are included and the resulting cluster patterns are discussed and compared with those produced by Gangl (2003b), whose analyses distinguished three groups of countries: OLM, ILM and a mixed Southern European type. Secondly, indicators of labour market flexibility are further included in the clustering procedure and the results are subsequently interpreted in light of theoretical expectations.

The cluster analysis is carried out by the Ward algorithm, using a squared Euclidean distance matrix based on the z-standardized transformations of labour market indicators summarised in Table A in the appendix. The Ward algorithm belongs to the broad class of hierarchical clustering algorithms and has been selected due to its property of producing a small number of rather homogeneous clusters, which is achieved via a sequential fusion of least-deviant cases (Bacher 1996, Gordon 1999). Results of the cluster analyses reported below appear to be fairly robust for appropriate alternative clustering algorithms and largely coincide with analyses based on country cases only (see Saar et al. 2006). The cluster analysis is conducted using the SPSS 14 program.

Findings

Labour market entry patterns in the new and old EU member states

Before providing details of the cluster analysis, we offer a brief descriptive overview of the situation of labour market entrants in new and old member states, as measured by the set of indicators chosen for the analysis. The overview starts by analysing the cross-national differences in the unemployment rates of labour market entrants compared to experienced workers. An illustration of these differences can be found in Figure 1, where eight CEE countries (Hungary, the Czech Republic, three Baltic states, Slovenia, Slovakia and Poland) are compared to the old European Union member countries grouped into a set of OLM countries (the Netherlands, Denmark, Austria and Germany), two groups of ILM countries – one characterized by more rigid labour markets, i.e. Sweden, Finland, Belgium, France and Luxembourg, and the other with more flexible ones, i.e. Ireland and the UK, and, finally, a group of southern European countries (Portugal, Spain, Italy, Greece).

A variation in unemployment patterns both across and within the groups of countries is evident from the figure. The lowest unemployment rates for labour market entrants and the smallest gaps between entrants and more experienced workers are observed in countries with occupational labour markets, a finding that is not surprising. Similarly, one finds small to moderate unemployment rates among young people and relatively small unemployment gaps between recent school leavers and more experienced workers in the most liberal economies of the UK and Ireland. Youth unemployment incidence rates are much higher in the continental ILM countries (except for Luxembourg and Sweden) and Southern European countries (except for Portugal). Moreover, the gap between labour market entrants and more experienced workers is large in Southern Europe (a finding confirmed by net regression coefficients presented in column 2 of Table 2). The unemployment disadvantages of recent school leavers are also quite pronounced in the Nordic and continental countries, being somewhat in-between what have been found for Southern European and liberal countries.

How do CEE countries fare with regard to the employment situation of recent labour market entrants? The patterns observed for Hungary, the Czech Republic and Slovenia resemble those found in the UK or Sweden. These are countries with low to medium unemployment levels; youth

Figure 1. Unemployment rates of labour market entrants and experienced workers

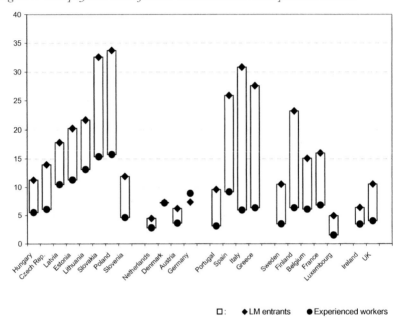

□:   ◆ LM entrants   ● Experienced workers

Source: EULFS 1998–2004 (selected years), country averages.

chances in finding employment differ moderately from those of experienced workers. In the Baltic states, the unemployment level of labour market entrants is relatively high but the differences between entrants and experienced workers are of average level and are quite similar to those observed in Hungary, the Czech Republic and Slovenia. The youth unemployment rate is very high in Slovakia and Poland, being even higher than in Italy and Greece, Southern European countries that for years have been struggling with the labour market insertion of young school leavers. Moreover, the differences between labour market entrants and experienced workers are high in Poland and Slovakia and are comparable to those observed in Southern Europe.

Not only is the unemployment incidence rate high in Poland and Slovakia, the rate of long-term youth unemployment, i.e. unemployment longer than one year, is quite high in these, as well as in other CEE countries, and is comparable to the rates observed in Southern Europe, as well as Belgium, France and Germany (see column 6 in Table 2). The net gaps between labour market entrants and older persons who are unemployed

Table 2. Indicators of labour market entry in Europe

| Country | Unemployment incidence | | | | | Long-term unemployment | | Fixed-term employment | |
	% entrants	β entrants	β low educ.	β tert. educ.	β voc. educ.	% entrants	β entrants	% entrants	β entrants
Hungary	11.39	0.14	0.29	-0.56	-0.04	31.28	-0.33	13.70	0.22
Czech Rep.	14.00	0.09	0.44	-0.35	0.19	26.19	-0.70	15.40	0.36
Latvia	17.97	0.15	0.34	-0.73	-0.02	20.97	-0.72	15.75	0.17
Estonia	20.08	0.10	0.29	-0.65	-0.24	23.84	-0.63	6.96	0.29
Lithuania	22.13	0.07	0.11	-0.53	-0.29	39.72	-0.42	11.13	0.11
Slovakia	32.44	0.18	0.38	-0.44	0.22	49.17	-0.52	10.52	0.34
Poland	33.78	0.24	-0.08	-0.45	0.16	41.70	-0.39	39.92	0.58
Slovenia	11.92	0.21	0.10	-0.44	-0.13	45.48	-0.62	44.28	0.94
Netherlands	4.43	0.01	0.21	-0.25	0.01	13.70	-0.69	29.13	0.66
Denmark	7.33	-0.15	0.07	0.01	0.01	10.07	-0.82	22.05	0.42
Austria	6.06	0.01	0.01	-0.25	-0.13	11.82	-0.53	33.01	1.16
Germany	7.55	-0.18	0.25	-0.13	0.05	23.76	-0.46	38.88	0.71
Portugal	9.58	0.37	0.11	-0.16	-0.03	25.77	-0.51	45.46	0.64
Spain	25.25	0.33	0.07	-0.15	-0.02	27.11	-0.39	66.78	0.68
Italy	30.76	0.53	0.04	-0.22	-0.18	52.42	-0.23	31.89	0.55
Greece	27.55	0.44	-0.06	-0.23	-0.08	46.73	-0.26	27.29	0.42
Sweden	10.54	0.39	0.36	-0.37	-	4.34	-0.97	44.46	0.89
Finland	23.17	0.48	0.54	-0.49	-0.04	5.21	-1.20	45.83	0.86
Belgium	15.12	0.21	0.17	-0.53	-0.03	29.71	-0.72	29.76	0.68
France	16.00	0.24	0.22	-0.39	-0.07	25.79	-0.54	39.81	0.73
Luxembourg	4.93	0.28	0.23	-0.41	-0.18	16.87	-0.75	14.20	0.61
Ireland	6.73	0.08	0.19	-0.34	-0.02	15.54	-0.64	13.05	0.65
UK	10.56	0.16	0.38	-0.53	0.03	16.42	-0.63	11.83	0.34

Note: β parameters are from auxiliary regressions, controlling for gender, marital status und an interaction between the two. Educational effects contrast low secondary education (ISCED 0–2), tertiary education (ISCED 5–6) and upper-secondary (or post secondary non-tertiary) vocational education (ISCED 3–4 with vocational training) against upper-secondary (or post secondary non-tertiary) (ISCED 3–4) without vocational training.
Source: EULFS 1998–2004 (selected years), country averages.

for longer than one year vary across Europe being particularly high in the Nordic countries, Finland, Sweden and Denmark (known for their activation policies), and lower in Italy and Greece (their family safety nets allowing young people to »wait« longer for agreeable employment). It should be noted in this regard that negative β-coefficients signify that recent school leavers have lower chances to stay long-term unemployed compared to

their older counterparts. Larger negative coefficients hence signal that labour market entrants have much lower risks of long-term unemployment.

Another informative indicator of the flexibility of youth labour markets
is the extent to which fixed-term employment has been used to encourage
young school leavers into work. While column 8 in Table 2 reports the
overall level of youth fixed-term employment, the last column assesses the
degree to which young people are over-represented in this type of contract
(in all countries they are over-represented as the β-coefficients are positive.) Research suggests that the country with the highest proportion of
young people employed in fixed-term contracts is Spain, and this well-
established finding is also corroborated by the data presented in Table 2.
Among CEE countries only Poland and Slovenia decisively adopted fixed-
term employment as a strategy to include young people in the labour market. Lower levels of youth fixed-term employment are observed in the rest
of the CEE countries (above all in Estonia), Ireland, the UK and Luxembourg. Column 9 provides interesting insights into the question of whether
these are young people who bear the »burden of flexibility«, being over-
represented in fixed-term employment. Interestingly, Austria, Slovenia,
Sweden, Finland, France and Germany are countries in which fixed-term
employment is particularly wide-spread among young labour market entrants, while in other CEE countries (except for Poland) and the UK, the
youth are less disproportionately covered by fixed-term contracts.

Finally, columns 3–5 present gradients for various educational attainment levels (compared to upper-secondary general education) on the unemployment incidence risk. The overall trend is that lower levels of secondary education are associated with higher unemployment risks among labour market entrants compared to upper-secondary general education
whilst tertiary education is associated with a lower risk of unemployment.
Vocational education in the upper-secondary and post-secondary non-
tertiary level protects from unemployment compared to general education
in the majority of countries. In a few countries there are virtually no differences between leavers from general or vocational education in their unemployment propensity. In the Czech Republic, Slovakia and Poland vocational education, however, is valued negatively by potential employers; the
risk of unemployment for a young person holding a vocational qualification is substantially higher than for graduates from non-vocational education tracks. Overall, the gradients for low-secondary and tertiary education

in the CEE countries (except Poland) are similar to the patterns observed in the continental ILM countries, as well as Ireland and the UK.

Patterns of labour market entry in the enlarged EU

The analysis presented in this section focuses on distinguishing patterns of labour market entry in Europe, especially for CEE countries. To this end, detailed annual measures of indicators, summarized in Table 2 (discussed above), have been used as an input into a 2-step cluster analysis. In the first step, indicators pertaining to the effects of educational attainment on unemployment incidence together with unemployment rates and net unemployment differentials for labour market entrants (indicators shown in columns 1–5, Table 2) have been subjected to cluster analysis with the aim of establishing the relevance of educational signalling for patterns of youth unemployment. The cluster dendrogram is presented in Figure A.1 in the appendix. Three clusters are clearly identifiable from the dendrogram according to the Mojena I criterion. These results seem to be comparable to the previous classification by Gangl (2003b), established for Western and Southern European countries using a somewhat broader set of labour market indicators.

The results show that the following three country clusters can be distinguished. The first cluster is comprised of OLM countries Austria, Germany, Denmark and the Netherlands. In addition, surprisingly, it appears that the Irish pattern for years 2002–3 was also clustered with this set of countries. The second cluster includes ILM countries Belgium, France, Luxembourg, the UK and Ireland (year 2004) as well as seven CEE countries (Estonia, Latvia, Lithuania, the Czech Republic, Slovakia, Hungary and Slovenia). Finally the third cluster consists of the Southern European countries, Spain, Greece, Italy and Portugal, plus one CEE country – Poland (see Table 3).

When one also includes indicators of labour market flexibility (see columns 6–9 in Table 2) in addition to the rest of the measures, a three-cluster solution is preferred according to the Mojena I criterion and the cluster dendrogram (see Figure A.2 in the appendix). At the same time, according to the Bayesian classification modelling estimates (Myllymäki et al. 2002), the classification accuracy of a three-cluster model and of a four-cluster model are approximately the same, 20.9% and 19.4% respectively.

Table 3. Results of the cluster analysis

Youth unemployment	Cluster 1		Cluster 2	Cluster 3
1 plus indicators for educational signalling	Austria Germany Denmark Netherlands Ireland (2002–3)		Belgium France Luxembourg UK Ireland (2004) Finland **Estonia** **Latvia** **Lithuania** **Czech Republic** **Slovakia** **Hungary** **Slovenia**	Spain Greece Italy Portugal **Poland**
2 plus indicators for labour market flexibility (a three-cluster solution)	Austria Germany Denmark Netherlands Belgium France Luxembourg Finland Portugal Spain Ireland **Slovenia**	.	UK **Estonia** **Latvia** **Lithuania** **Czech Republic** **Slovakia** **Hungary**	Greece Italy **Poland**
3 plus indicators for labour market flexibility (a four-cluster solution)	Austria Germany Denmark Netherlands Ireland Luxembourg	Belgium France Finland Spain Portugal **Slovenia**	UK **Estonia** **Latvia** **Lithuania** **Czech Republic** **Slovakia** **Hungary**	Greece Italy **Poland**

Note: Clustering is carried out by the Ward algorithm using a squared Euclidean distance matrix based on z-standardized transformations of labour market indicators (see Table 2).
Source: EULFS 1998–2004 (selected years).

The difference between a three and a four-cluster solution is that typical OLM countries, Austria, Germany, Denmark, the Netherlands, together with Luxembourg and Ireland at a certain stage of the fusion process are accompanied by Belgium, France, Spain, Portugal and Slovenia, as well as Finland in a single cluster. The second cluster of countries (in a three-cluster solution) is comprised of the UK as well as the Baltic states, the Czech and Slovak Republics and Hungary. Finally, the third cluster consists of Greece and Italy (notice that Spain and Portugal are no longer clustered with their less-flexible Southern European neighbours), as well as Poland.[9]

The results of the cluster analyses have a number of implications for the classification of CEE countries. One of the most important inferences of the analysis is that there are clear differences within the group of CEE countries in terms of youth unemployment. Slovenia clearly contrasts with the other CEE countries, clustering with Western EU countries. As expected from the descriptive results, youth labour market entry patterns in Poland resemble those observed in Southern European countries: labour market entrants are strongly disadvantaged and exhibit high rates of unemployment and long-term unemployment. Finally, Hungary, the Czech Republic, Slovakia and the Baltic states are clustered together, but do not form a uniform cluster of CEE countries, sharing a number of the features of their youth labour markets with the UK.

To assess the substantive differences between the four country clusters (from step 2 of the cluster analysis) in more detail Table 4 compares the averages of various rate indicators among young school leavers (including the means of their differentials (β-coefficients)) to those of experienced workers. (Standard deviations are found in brackets).

Countries in cluster 1 are marked by the lowest, while countries in cluster 4 by the highest, rates of youth unemployment and long-term unemployment. Clusters 2 and 3 are in-between, with unemployment and long-term unemployment rates for school leavers being higher in the latter. Differentiating between cluster 1 and 2 (as is done if a four-cluster solution is accepted) seems to be meaningful with regard to unemployment incidence and unemployment duration rates, as the two clusters vary substantially in these two indicators.

The gap between labour market entrants and more experienced workers in unemployment incidence is the lowest in countries represented in

---

9 It should be mentioned that the cluster solution depends heavily on the choice of indicators as well as on the presence of influential indicators, rather than on the sheer number of indicators. When some indicators are removed from the second step of the analysis, variation in the clustering of some countries could be observed. The divide between Southern European countries plus Poland on the one hand, and the rest of Europe on the other hand remains pronounced irrespective of the choice of indicators.

Table 4. Labour market entry patters within clusters, a four-cluster solution

	Cluster 1	Cluster 2	Cluster 3	Cluster 4
Unemployment rate	6.32	16.60	19.70	30.70
of LM entrants	(1.26)	(6.08)	(8.04)	(3.64)
Unemployment differential	-0.01	0.32	0.14	0.42
	(0.14)	(0.10)	(0.07)	(0.13)
Long-term unemployment (rate)	15.18	26.22	30.64	47.73
of LM entrants	(4.86)	(11.49)	(10.48)	(5.16)
Long-term unemployment	-0.64	-0.63	-0.54	-0.28
(differential)	(0.16)	(0.27)	(0.18)	(0.10)
Fixed term employment (rate)	24.96	47.40	14.91	32.87
among LM entrants	(10.26)	(12.20)	(13.83)	(6.63)
Fixed term employment	0.70	0.73	0.28	0.52
(differential)	(0.24)	(0.12)	(0.17)	(0.07)
Effect of low-secondary education	0.16	0.19	0.30	-0.02
among LM entrants	(0.10)	(0.16)	(0.14)	(0.07)
Effect of tertiary education	-0.22	-0.32	-0.54	-0.29
among LM entrants	(0.15)	(0.18)	(0.20)	(0.11)
Effect of vocational education	-0.03	-0.05	-0.04	-0.05
among LM entrants	(0.09)	(0.10)	(0.20)	(0.16)

Note: Clustering is carried out by the Ward algorithm using a squared Euclidean distance matrix based on z-standardized transformations of labour market indicators (see Table 2). Standard deviations are in parentheses.
Source: EULFS 1998–2004 (selected years).

cluster 1 and the highest in the fourth cluster. Here, again, clusters 1 and 2 differ substantially: while in the first cluster there is virtually no difference between labour market entrants and more experienced workers in unemployment incidence in the late 1990s-early 2000s, young job seekers seem to be particularly disadvantaged in countries constituting the second cluster. With regard to the long-term unemployment incidence, the differences between the first three clusters are minimal – young school leavers are much less likely to be long-term unemployed than more experienced workers. The same is true for cluster 4, but the difference between young and older job seekers in their chances of remaining unemployed after a year of search is half as large as in the rest of Europe. This finding could also be related to a comparatively higher (when compared to the rest of Europe) risk of long-term unemployment among older people in countries in cluster 4, i.e. Italy, Greece and Poland.

Countries forming cluster 2 are marked by an extensive use of fixed-term contracts among young people; almost half of all recent school leavers are employed temporarily. Moreover, in cluster 2 countries, the youth bear the heaviest burden of flexibility, being disproportionately channelled into fixed-term employment. A similar burden rests on young shoulders in countries forming the first cluster, but the absolute rate of fixed-term employment among young people in these countries is half as large as in countries of the second cluster. In sharp contrast, the lowest rate of fixed-term employment is found in the UK and the CEE countries (except Slovenia and Poland), both in terms of the absolute rates among school leavers, as well as the difference between young and more experienced workers. It appears that flexibility is achieved in these countries through means other than fixed-term employment. In Italy, Greece and Poland (countries of the fourth cluster) fixed-term employment levels among young people are slightly higher, while youth over-representation in these type of contracts is somewhat lower than in cluster 1 countries.

Finally, with regard to the unemployment effects of education, differences between country-clusters are also apparent. The strongest educational gradients are observed in cluster 3 countries, while the weakest are found in cluster 4 countries. In the cluster formed by the majority of CEE countries and the UK (cluster 3) the least educated have the highest risks of unemployment, while those who have a tertiary education are mostly protected from unemployment. In countries comprising the fourth cluster (Italy, Greece and Poland) the least-skilled are, on the other hand, better off, as their relative unemployment risks are the lowest in Europe. The effects of tertiary education are quite similar in clusters 1 and 2, albeit being somewhat stronger in the second cluster. Finally, the effects of vocational education are in the expected direction in all countries but seem to be of a somewhat low magnitude.[10] It should also be mentioned that the results show substantial within-cluster variation with regard to the effects of vocational training, as signified by large standard deviations. All in all, the effects of vocational education are also somewhat higher in clusters 2 and 4, implying that school leavers with vocational training in these countries

---

10 This might be related to the problems with the data concerning the vocational training in the EULFS, so this issue should be further explored in the future.

(compared to the rest of Europe) have slightly better chances of avoiding unemployment.

Conclusions

Summarising the empirical results of the study, we found substantial support for distinct patterns of youth unemployment and labour market entry in terms of features such as the stratification of labour market exclusion (unemployment) among labour market entrants in different CEE countries. A joint clustering of all CEE countries proved to be unrealistic, since the levels of vulnerability among labour market entrants differ in these countries.

In Poland the situation for school leavers is the worst among CEE countries and resembles a malaise for which Southern European countries are known. There are indeed some indicators for the formation of an insider-outsider division in the Polish labour market. Due to high general unemployment young school leavers have persistent difficulties in entering the labour market. They have a higher unemployment incidence compared with experienced workers and experience longer unemployment. Vocational qualifications hardly seem to be meaningful for protecting young people from employment exclusion in Poland.

Slovenia differs remarkably from the rest of the CEE countries. It has stronger labour market legislation, higher trade union presence, and more effective programs of vocational training (in the form of apprenticeships). But despite its formally rigid labour market youth employment is governed by larger flexibility in this country, expressed by an extensive use of fixed-term contracts for recent school leavers. Although, the overall labour market entry process in this country rather resembles the patterns observed in Western countries than in other CEE countries, Slovenian patterns have not clustered together with those observed in typical OLM countries – neither in the first step of the analysis (when we included the indicators of educational signalling only) nor in the second step (upon including indicators of labour market flexibility).

In Hungary, the Baltic states, the Czech Republic and Slovakia youth employment patterns resemble, to some extent, the UK as far as large educational differentials in outcomes and low representation in precarious forms of employment are concerned. But these countries also exhibit their own peculiarities: medium to high levels of long-term unemployment and a smaller difference between job entrants and more experienced workers in unemployment incidence. Whilst the Baltic states are known for their shift towards more general education, the Czech Republic has maintained its levels of vocational training. However, the effects of vocational qualifications on unemployment seem to work in an unexpected direction in the Czech Republic. Our finding that Czech youth with vocational qualifications do not fare as well compared to Lithuanian and Estonian leavers of vocational schools has to be corroborated with the national data, since some problems with the coding of vocational training in the EULFS have been reported.

The results of our cluster analyses using indicators related solely to the signalling character of the education system confirm the European pattern of labour market entry proposed by Gangl (2003b) for the EU-15 in the 1990s. We discovered a group of traditional OLM countries (Germany, Austria, Denmark and the Netherlands), Western countries with more pronounced ILM structures, joined by the bulk of CEE countries, and finally Southern European countries (this time with Spain) together with Poland. In the late 1990s-early 2000s the annual variation in the chosen indicators appears to be stronger for the countries analysed here as compared to the 1990s-data subjected to the cluster analysis by Gangl (2003b). Indeed, the fusion process clearly singled out the youth unemployment pattern in Ireland for 2002–3 from the situation observed in 2004. Whether this differential clustering is a result of substantial change in youth employment patterns or rather an artefact of the Irish data remains to be further explored.

Beyond the extension of existing research on a larger set of European countries, we also attempted, in this study, to reflect the increasing precariousness of European youth labour markets by including indicators of unemployment duration and fixed-term employment into the clustering procedure. This exercise proved to be fruitful. We found some evidence indicative of convergence in youth unemployment patterns in Western Europe, a trend shared by Slovenia. It is to be noted though that OLM countries still cluster together in the early stages of the fusion process even when indicators of labour market flexibility are included. Only later are they grouped together with other Western EU countries which show their unique standing within the cluster of continental Europe. The labour market outcomes of young people in OLM countries differ to some degree from those observed in the rest of Western Europe, Spain and Portugal. This is particularly evident by the lower unemployment incidence and lower rates of long-term and fixed-term employment in the OLM countries.

It should be stressed here that the general labour market rigidities for which Western European countries have often been criticized seem to be less pronounced in youth labour markets. Results of the descriptive analyses showed that in all EU countries school leavers are more dynamic with regard to employment, being found less among the long-term unemployed, and are over-represented in the fixed-term contracts. It should not be forgotten, though, that European countries differ with regard to the indicators mentioned above; we observe variation in youth employment patterns across Europe. Southern European countries with the exception of more flexible Portugal and Spain, accompanied by Poland, share similar problems of youth labour market inclusion. These include markedly high unemployment incidence rates, higher rates of long-term unemployment, and use of flexible forms of employment contracts. Finally, the Baltic countries, Hungary, Slovakia and the Czech Republic together with the UK have a lower proportion of youth employed fixed-term and smaller differences between labour market entrants and more experienced workers employed without a permanent contract. This group of countries has medium unemployment disadvantages among young school leavers, as well as stronger education gradients for employment inclusion chances.

One should, however, be cautious about implying a direct causal effect of a particular institution using indicators measured at the individual level. Our measures for unemployment duration and fixed-term employment (both absolute and relative) were selected to pick up the role of labour market regulation for youth unemployment. Alternative driving forces behind the observed patterns in the above-mentioned indicators cannot be discarded. The length of unemployment might be influenced by the extent of unemployment protection, either formal, i.e. via unemployment benefits or active labour market policies, or informal ones, e.g. via familial networks often associated with Southern European countries. Moreover, despite our attempt to include net differentials for young people (compared to more experienced workers) as indicators in the cluster analyses, it remains unclear what role structural factors, e.g. cross-national differences in macroeconomic conditions, might have played in generating the observed patterns. We agree with Gangl (2003b) that by using macro-level country classifications one can encounter problems with disentangling the relative power of rival explanations. Finally, the analyses focused on a single aspect of school-leavers' labour market entry – youth unemployment. Other aspects of youth labour market integration like occupation, earnings and job mobility, were ignored here not least due to their less elaborated connection to educational signalling and labour market flexibility (for attempts to establish and test such connections see Gangl 2003c, Scherer 2004, 2005). Despite its limitations, it is fair to conclude that this study elucidates the variety of youth employment patterns in the enlarged European Union more systematically than has been achieved thus far.

Appendix

Table A. Indicators used for the cluster analysis

Indicator	Description
Unemployment rate of labour marker (LM) entrants (1)	Out of the total labour force, in percent
Unemployment differential of LM entrants (2)	A standardized coefficient (β) from auxiliary regressions (controlling for gender, marital status und an interaction between the two; experienced workers are a reference group)
Effect of low-secondary education on unemployment rate for LM entrants (3)	A standardized coefficient (β) from auxiliary regressions (controlling for gender, marital status und an interaction between the two; upper-secondary non-vocational education is a reference category)
Effect of tertiary education on unemployment rate for LM entrants (4)	A standardized coefficient (β) from auxiliary regressions (controlling for gender, marital status und an interaction between the two; upper-secondary non-vocational education is a reference category)
Effect of upper-secondary vocational education on unemployment rate for LM entrants (5)	A standardized coefficient (β) from auxiliary regressions (controlling for gender, marital status und an interaction between the two; upper-secondary non-vocational education is a reference category)
Long-term unemployment rate of LM entrants (6)	Unemployment of more than one year out of total unemployment, in percent
Differential for LM entrants in long-term unemployment (7)	A standardized coefficient (β) from auxiliary regressions (controlling for gender, marital status und an interaction between the two; experienced workers are a reference group)
Rate of LM entrants with fixed-term contracts (8)	Out of total employment, in percent
Differential for LM entrants in fixed-term employment (9)	A standardized coefficient (β) from auxiliary regressions (controlling for gender, marital status und an interaction between the two; experienced workers are a reference group)

Figure A.1. Cluster dendrogram from the reduced set of indicators for employment entry

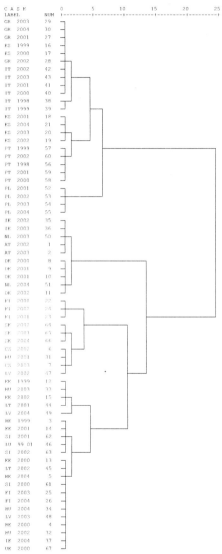

Note: Clustering is carried out by the Ward algorithm using a squared Euclidean distance matrix based on z-standardized transformations of labour market indicators (see Table 2).
Source: EULFS 1998–2004 (selected years).

Figure A.2. Cluster dendrogram from the full set of indicators for employment entry

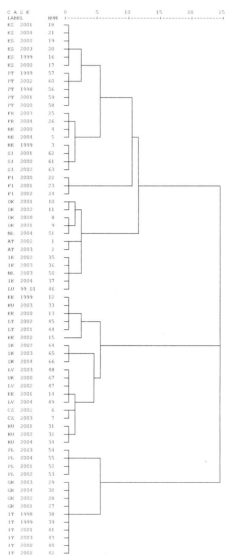

Note: Clustering is carried out by the Ward algorithm using a squared Euclidean distance matrix based on z-standardized transformations of labour market indicators (see Table 2).
Source: EULFS 1998–2004 (selected years).

References

Allmendinger, J. (1989). »Educational systems and labour market outcomes«, *European Sociological Review*, vol. 5, no.3, pp. 231–250.

Arrow, Kenneth J. (1973). »Higher education as a filter«, *Journal of Public Economics*, vol. 2, no. 3, pp. 193–216.

Bacher, J. (1996). *Clusteranalyse*, Munich and Vienna: Oldenbourg.

Becker, G. S. (1993). *Human Capital. A Theoretical and Empirical Analysis with Special References to Education* (3rd edition), Chicago: University of Chicago press.

Bertola, M. G./Blau, F. D./Kahn. L. M. (2001). »Comparative analysis of labour market outcomes: lessons for the United States from international long-run evidence«, in A. B. Krueger/R. Solow (eds.), *The Roaring Nineties: Can Full Employment be Sustained?*, New York: Russell Sage Foundation, pp. 159–218.

Bertola, M. G./Rogerson R. (1997). »Institutions and labour reallocation«, *European Economic Review*, vol. 41, no. 6, pp. 1147–1171.

Brauns, H./Steinmann, S./Kieffer, A./Marry C. (1999). »Does education matter? France and Germany in comparative perspective«, *European Sociological Review*, vol. 15, no. 1, pp. 61–89.

Breen, R. (2005). »Explaining cross-national variation in youth unemployment: market and institutional factors«, *European Sociological Review*, vol. 21, no. 2, pp. 125–134.

Breen, R./Hannan, D. F./O'Leary, R. (1995). »Returns to education: taking account of the employers' perception and use of educational credits«, *European Sociological Review*, vol. 11, no. 1, pp. 59–73.

Cazes, S./Nesporova, A. (2003). *Labour Markets in Transition: Balancing Flexibility and Security in Central and Eastern Europe,* Geneva: International Labour Organisation.

CEDEFOP (European Centre for the Development of Vocational Training) (ed.) (2001). *The Transition from Education to Working Life. Key Data on Vocational Training in the European Union* (Cedefop Reference series), Luxembourg: Office for Official Publications of the European Communities.

Couppié, T./Mansuy M. (2003). »Young people and new entrants in European labour markets: the timing of gradual integration«, in W. Müller/M. Gangl (eds.), *Transitions from education to work in Europe. The Integration of Youth into EU Labour Markets*, Oxford: Oxford University Press, pp. 63–106.

Eamets, R./Masso J. (2004). *Labour Market Flexibility and Employment Protection Regulation in the Baltic States* (IZA Working Paper No. 1147).

Estevez-Abe, M./Iversen, T./Soskice, D. (2001). »Social protection and the formation of skills: a reinterpretation of the welfare state«, in P. A. Hall/D. Soskice (eds.), *Varieties of Capitalism. The Institutional Foundations of Comparative Advantage*, Oxford: Oxford University Press, pp. 145–183.

European Commission (2004). *Industrial Relations in Europe*, Brussels: EU.

Eurostat (1998). *Labour force survey: Methods and Definition,* Luxembourg: Eurostat.

Gangl, M. (2003a). »Returns to education in context: individual education and transition outcomes in European labour markets«, in W. Müller/M. Gangl (eds.), *Transition from Education to Work in Europe. The Integration of Youth into EU Labour Markets*, Oxford: Oxford University Press, pp.156–185.

Gangl, M. (2003b). »The structure of labour market entry in Europe: a typological analysis«, in W. Müller/M. Gangl (eds.), *Transition from Education to Work in Europe. The Integration of Youth into EU Labour Markets*, Oxford: Oxford University Press, pp. 107–128.

Gangl, M. (2003c). »The only way is up? Employment protection and job mobility among recent entrants to European labour market«, *European Sociological Review*, vol. 19, no. 5, pp. 429–449.

Gangl, M. (2003d). *Unemployment Dynamics in the United States and West Germany: Economic Restructuring, Institutions, and Labour Market Processes,* Heidelberg: Physica-Verlag.

Garonna, P./Ryan P. (1991). »The regulation and deregulation of youth economic activity«, in P. Ryan et al. (eds.), *The Problem of Youth: The Regulation of Youth Employment and Training in Advanced Economies*, Houdmills: Macmillan, pp. 35–81.

Gerber, T. P. (2003). »Loosening links? School-to-work transitions and institutional change in Russia since 1970«, *Social Forces*, vol. 82, no. 1, pp. 241–276.

Gordon, A. D. (1999). *Classification* (2nd edition), London and New York: Chapman and Hall.

Gregg, P./Manning A. (1997). »Labour market regulation and unemployment«, in D. J. Snower/G. de la Dehesa (eds.), *Unemployment Policy: Government Options for the Labour Market*, Cambridge: Cambridge University Press, pp. 395–429.

Hampalová, D. (2003). *Women and the Labour Market in the Czech Republic: Transition from Socialist to Social Democratic Regime* (GLOBALIFE Project Working Paper No. 46), University of Bamberg, Faculty of Sociology: Globalife project.

Hannan, D. F. et al. (1999). *A Comparative Analysis of Transition from Education to Work in Europe (CATEWE)* (vol. 2), Dublin: ESRI.

Hannan, D. F. et al. (2001). »The effect of national institutional difference on education/training to work transition in Europe: a comparative research project (CATEWE) under the TSER programme«, in P. Descy/M. Tessaring (eds.), *Training in Europe. Second Report on Vocational Training Research in Europe 2000: Background Report* (vol. 3) (Cedefop Reference series), Luxembourg: Office for Official Publications of the European Communities, pp. 43–90.

Helemäe, J./Saar E. (2000). »Linkages between the education system and labour market: Estonia against the backdrop of EU countries«, in *Estonian Human Development Report,* Tallinn: TPU RASI, pp. 85–99.

Helemäe, J./Saar E. (2002). *Employment careers of men in Estonia* (GLOBALIFE Project Working Paper No. 39), University of Bamberg, Faculty of Sociology: Globalife project.

ILO (1999). *Employment and Labour Market Policies in Transition Economy,* Geneva: International Labour Office.

Kerckhoff, A. C. (1996). »Building conceptual and empirical bridges between studies of educational and labour force careers«, in A. C. Kerckhoff (ed.), *Generating Social Stratification: Toward a New Research Agenda*, Boulder: Westview Press, pp. 37–56.

Kerckhoff, A. C. (2000). »Transition from school to work in comparative perspective«, in P. A. Hallinan (ed.), *Handbook of the Sociology of Education*, New York/Boston: Kluwer Academic/Plenum Publishers, pp. 543–574.

Kogan, I./Unt, M. (2005). »Transition from school to work in transition economies«, *European Societies*, vol. 7, no. 2, pp. 219–253.

Marsden, D. (1990). »Institutions and labour mobility: occupational and internal labour markets in Britain, France, Italy and West Germany«, in R. Brunetta/C. Dell'Aringa (eds.), *Labour Relations and Economic Performance*, Houndmills: Macmillan, pp. 414–438.

Marsden, D./Ryan P. (1991). »Initial Training, Labour Market Structure and Public Policy: Intermediate Skills in British and German Industry«, in P. Ryan (ed.), *International Comparisons of Vocational Education and Training for Intermediate Skills*, London: Falmer Press, pp. 251–285.

Matějů, P./Simonová, N. (2003). »Czech higher education still at the crossroads«, *Czech Sociological Review*, vol. 39, no. 3, pp. 393–410.

Maurice, M./Sellier, F./Silvestre, J.-J. (1986). *The Social Foundations of Industrial Power: A Comparison of France and Germany*, Cambridge, Mass.: MIT Press.

Mickelwright, J. (1999). »Education, inequality and transition«, *Economics of Transition*, vol. 7, pp. 343–376.

Müller, W. (2005). »Education and youth integration into European labour market«, *International Journal of Comparative Sociology*, vol. 46, no. 5–6, pp. 461–485.

Müller, W./Gangl M. (2003a). *Transition from Education to Work in Europe. The Integration of Youth into EU Labour Markets*, Oxford: Oxford University Press.

Müller, W./Gangl M. (2003b). »The transition from school to work: a European perspective«, in W. Müller/M. Gangl (eds.), *Transition from Education to Work in Europe. The Integration of Youth into EU Labour Markets*, Oxford: Oxford University Press, pp.1-22.

Müller, W./Shavit, Y. (1998). »The institutional embeddedness of the stratification process: a comparative study of qualifications and occupations in thirteen countries«, in Y. Shavit/W. Müller (eds.), *From School to Work. A Comparative Study of Educational Qualifications and Occupational Destinations*, Oxford: Clarendon Press, pp. 1–48.

Myllymäki, P./Silander, T./Tirri, H./Uronen, P. (2002). »B-course: a web-based tool for Bayesian and causal data analysis«, *International Journal on Artificial Intelligence Tools*, vol. 11, no. 3, pp. 369–387.

Riboud, M./Sánchez-Páramo, D./Silva-Jauregui, C. (2002). »Does eurosclerosis matter? Institutional reform and labour market performance in Central and Eastern Europe countries«, in B. Funck/L. Pizzati (eds.), *Labor, Employment, and Social Policies in the EU Enlargement Process*, Washington D. C.: World Bank, pp. 243–311.

Polachek, S. W./Siebert, W. S. (1993). *The Economics of Earnings,* Cambridge: Cambridge University Press.

Róbert, P. (2003). »Self-selection and selection. Transition from secondary to tertiary education in Hungary«, *Czech Sociological Review*, vol. 39, no. 3, pp. 325–349.

Róbert, P./Bukodi, E. (2005). »The effects of the globalization process on the transition to adulthood in Hungary.« in H.-P. Blossfeld et al. (eds.), *Globalization, Uncertainty and Youth in Society*, London/New York: Routledge, pp. 177–214.

Roberts, K. (1998). »School-to-work transitions in former communist countries«, *Journal of Education and Work*, vol. 111, no. 3, pp. 221–238.

Roberts, K./Szumlicz, T. (1995). »Education and school-to-work transitions in post-communist Poland«, *British Journal of Education and Work*, vol. 8, pp. 54–74.

Ryan, P. (2001). »The school-to-work transition: a cross-national perspective«, *Journal of Economic Literature*, vol. 39, no. 1, pp. 34–92.

Saar, E. (1997). »Transitions to tertiary education in Belarus and the Baltic countries«, *European Sociological Review,* vol 13, no. 2, pp. 139–158.

Saar, E. (2005). »New entrants on the Estonian labour market: a comparison with the EU countries«, *European Societies*, vol. 7, no. 4, pp. 547–580.

Saar, E./Unt, M./Kogan I. (2006). *Transition from Educational System to Labour Market in the European Union: A Comparison between New and Old Members,* Paper presented at the meeting of ISA Research Committee on Social Stratification and Mobility, Nijmegen, the Netherlands.

Scherer, S. (2004). »Stepping-stones or traps? The consequences of labour market entry positions on future careers in West Germany, Great Britain and Italy«, *Work Employment and Society*, vol. 18, no. 2, pp. 369–394.

Scherer, S. (2005). »Patterns of Labour Market Entry – Long Wait or Career Instability? An Empirical Comparison of Italy, Great Britain and West Germany«, *European Sociological Review*, vol. 21, no. 5, pp. 427–440.

Smyth, E. et al. (2001). *A Comparative Analysis of Transition from Education to Work in Europe (CATEWE)* (vol. 1), Dublin: ESRI.

Shavit, Y./Müller, W. (eds.) (1998). *From School to Work: A Comparative Study of Educational Qualifications and Occupational Destinations*, Oxford: Clarendon Press.

Soskice, D. (1994). »Reconciling markets and institutions: the German apprenticeship system«, in L. Lynch (ed.), *Training and the Private Sector – International Comparisons*, Chicago: University of Chicago Press, pp. 25–60.

Spence, M. (1973). »Job market signalling«, *Quarterly Journal of Economics*, vol. 87, no. 3, pp. 355–374.

Strietska-Ilina, O. (2001). »Research on vocational education and training at the crossroads of transition in Central and Eastern Europe«, in P. Descy/M. Tessaring (eds.), *Training in Europe. Second Report on Vocational Training Research in Europe 2000: Background Report* (vol. 3) (Cedefop Reference series), Luxembourg: Office for Official Publications of the European Communities, pp. 209–311.

Titma, M./Saar, E. (1995). »Regional differences in the secondary education of the former Soviet Union«, *European Sociological Review*, vol. 11, no. 1, pp. 37–58.

Toomse, M. (2003). »Youth labour market outcomes in Estonia: What kind of jobs do recent school leavers hold?«, *Trames*, vol. 7, no. 4, pp. 269–294.

Van der Velden, R. K. W./Wolbers M. H. J. (2003). »The integration of young people into the labour market: the role of training systems and labour market regulation«, in W. Müller/M. Gangl (eds.), *Transition from Education to Work in Europe. The Integration of Youth into EU Labour Markets*, Oxford: Oxford University Press, pp. 186–211.

Wallace, C. 2003. »Work flexibility in eight European countries: a cross-national comparison«, *Czech Sociological Review*, vol. 39, no. 6, pp. 773–794.

Disentangling recent trends of the second generation's structural assimilation in Germany[1]

Frank Kalter, Nadia Granato, and Cornelia Kristen

Introduction

In Germany, like in many other European countries, there is a growing concern that ethnic stratification and accompanying segmentation might become a permanent and problematic characteristic of the society. Looking at labour market integration, which for several reasons is the most crucial dimension of integration (Esser 2000: 304, Kalter and Granato 2002), the common finding is that the descendants of the labour migrants from Italy, Greece, former Yugoslavia, Portugal, Spain, and above all Turkey suffer severe disadvantages. Although the members of the second generation clearly do better than those of the first generation, they are far from reaching outcomes that can be compared to Germans with no migration background. This has been confirmed in a series of studies (e.g. Seifert 1992, Szydlik 1996, Granato and Kalter 2001, Granato 2003).

Still, however, it is hard to tell whether there is indeed evidence for a consolidation of ethnic disadvantages or whether there is a trend towards structural assimilation, albeit at a modest rate. This is mainly due to a lack of adequate data. While the availability of surveys to analyse integration processes of the second generation is generally restricted (Kalter 2005: 314f), the situation is even worse when searching for large-scale information over time. Recently, however, scientific use files have become available from the German Microcensus (GMC) which now make it possible to follow patterns of ethnic disadvantage between 1989 and 2004 in a repeated cross-sectional design. Building on prior GMC-analyses using single

---

1 Large parts of the chapter were written during a visit of the first author at Nuffield College, University of Oxford. We are grateful to Nuffield's sociology group, especially to Anthony Heath, for this opportunity. We would like to thank Clemens Kroneberg, Gunnar Otte, Reinhard Pollak, and Stefani Scherer for helpful comments on an earlier draft.

Figure 1. Integration research and the OED triangle

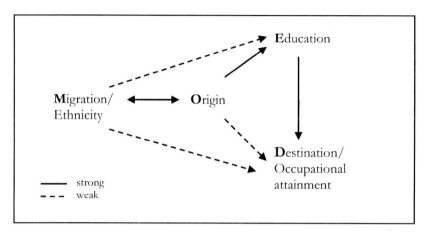

or only a few years (Granato and Kalter 2001, Granato 2003, Kalter and Granato 2007), the basic aim of this contribution is to employ these data in order to sketch recent trends of structural assimilation and thus to give an appropriate empirical answer to one of the most basic questions of integration research.

This chapter does not, however, have purely descriptive aims. Further to determining the gross trends of labour market integration we also try to identify the basic mechanisms which are responsible for either continuity or change. This is where general social stratification research comes in. Studies on the structural integration of the second generation have so far not only shown that ethnic stratification is still severe in the second generation, but also that this seems to be due to a large degree to general mechanisms of social inequality. Lower labour market success is mainly a matter of education (Granato and Kalter 2001, Granato 2003, Seibert and Solga 2005, Kalter and Granato 2007, Konietzka and Seibert 2003), but lower educational attainment seems to follow primarily from class origin rather than from genuine ethnic traits (Alba et al. 1994, Baumert and Schümer 2002, Kristen and Granato 2004). This fits with well-known results of comparative research on social stratification showing that in Germany the link between the educational system and the labour market is particularly close (Müller et al. 1998) and that the impact of social class origin on educational attainment is particularly strong (Erikson and Goldthorpe 1992, Müller et al. 1989). By and large, the story of second generation inequalities in Germany is about former strongly negative selective in-migration (Heckmann 1992) with peculiarities of the German institutional structure leading to general inter-generational transmission of disadvantages.

The basic relation of integration research and social stratification research and its importance for understanding the situation of the second generation in Germany can be sketched (Figure 1) by an extension of what has been called the OED triangle (Breen and Luijkx 2004). In social stratification research, the most basic questions centre on: How is one's class destination (D) influenced by one's class origin (O) and to what degree is this mediated by education (E)? As noted above in Germany OE and ED have proven to be rather strong. In integration research one of the main interests is in the total effect MD of migration background or ethnicity (M) on labour market outcomes (D). And here, results so far suggest that the partial MD relation as well as the partial ME relation are rather weak, while OM is strong because the former recruitment of foreign labour was strongly negatively selective. That means that the OED triangle plays a major part in understanding the persistence of ethnic stratification with respect to the second generation in Germany.

At the same time social stratification research reminds us that the components of the OED triangle are themselves subject to change (Breen and Luijkx 2004). These changes are crucial for understanding the development of ethnic disadvantages as they may speed up or slow down potential assimilation trends. So, further to describing the gross trends the chapter also deals with respective trends in the individual components. For each of the paths in Figure 1 we outline the basic underlying mechanisms, the theoretical expectations that can be derived for potential change, as well as the available empirical evidence. We will then use the GMC data to analyse the trends over the last 15 years empirically, which is possible for most of the components (except for OD). We will proceed as follows: First, we will deal with occupational attainment as the dependent variable, and study the gross trends of structural assimilation as well as trends in the strength of the paths leading directly to D. We will then go on to analyse the educational attainment, again outlining the gross trends and the trends in the strength of the paths leading directly to E. In the concluding part we will bring all the pieces together in order to give a summarizing picture on the trends of the second generation's occupational assimilation and the particular structural changes that account for them.

Trends in the second generation's occupational attainment (D as a dependent variable)

This part of the contribution analyses the occupational attainment of the second generation, or more precisely the trends in relative disadvantages as compared to the reference group of Germans. In the first subsection we briefly describe the data and look at the gross trends, meaning the total relationship between migration background (M) and destination (D) in terms of Figure 1. Then, we start disentangling the respective trends by breaking them down into two major components. The first are influences of migration background on occupational attainment which are not mediated by education, usually referred to as ›ethnic penalties‹ (next subsection).[2] The second component is the general impact of education on occupational attainment and possible changes (last subsection). While the first subsection is purely descriptive – in a certain sense it outlines the explananda – the following subsections discuss the most basic mechanisms underlying the variable relationship and try to derive expectations about trends given the empirical evidence for the background conditions in the German case.

Data and gross trends in occupational attainment (MD total)

Analysing and decomposing trends of the second generation's occupational attainment empirically places high demands on the data. What is needed is individual-based information, comprising, amongst other things, ethnic group membership, occupational attainment, and educational attainment. These variables should be based on measures that are identically observed over a certain time span. Samples should deliver an unbiased picture of the immigrant population and be large enough to contain a sufficient number of its members. Fortunately, data from the German Microcensus (GMC) have become available which can in principle fulfil all these needs. The GMC is an annual 1-percent household survey of the population in Germany (Lüttinger and Riede 1997). In the meantime scientific use files exist for several years, each consisting of a 70%-subsample. Beginning in 1989 it is possible to identify the classic labour migrant groups. The

---

2 As social origin cannot be controlled for, the data do not allow a distinction between influences which are mediated by social origin (the MO-OD path) or not (the direct MD path).

most recent file is the GMC of 2004. For the analyses in this part we combined all files available (n = 13) between these two time points, i.e. the years 1989, 1991, 1993, and each year from 1995 to 2004.[3] This provides us with large numbers of cases in a trend design and thus with a unique possibility to study the integration of immigrants' children over time.[4]

It has to be mentioned, however, that the cumulated GMC still has some drawbacks when assessing trends of immigrants' structural assimilation. Above all, migration status or ethnic group membership must rely on citizenship, as there is no information on parents' countries of birth.[5] Thus processes of naturalization interfere with the trends over time. On the one hand, this has an impact on the reference population and may lead to an overestimation of assimilation, e.g. when taking into account that considerable numbers of ›Aussiedler‹ from Eastern Europe who entered the reference population in the late 1990s. On the other hand, it seems reasonable to assume that former labour migrants and their descendents who become naturalized are somehow positively selected with respect to structural integration (Diehl and Blohm 2003) thus underestimating somewhat the trend towards assimilation when looking only at those with foreign citizenship. These minor biases might arise and should be kept in mind in the following.

In order to describe and decompose the trends of structural assimilation we basically follow the analyses of Granato and Kalter (2001) using a very simple indicator of labour market positioning: the odds of attaining a salaried employee position (*Angestellte*) vs. being a worker (*Arbeiter*).[6] Surely, this is a somewhat restricted indicator of occupational attainment, but many possible alternatives (Granato 2003: 59–68) cannot be used because they cannot be constructed for all the GMC scientific use files. In contrast, the characteristic of being a salaried employee or a worker is directly measured in the same way over all of the years under consideration. Moreover,

---

3 To avoid complications arising from the German reunification and the special features of the economy in East Germany we restrict all analyses to respondents living in the West. This seems appropriate also because classic labour migrants still are highly restricted to this area.

4 When looking at people aged 18–65 and being either a worker or salaried employee for each year we can draw on average on 1.363 members of the second generation and more than 110.000 respondents of the reference group.

5 This has changed only recently with the GMC 2005.

6 Other kinds of occupational status, e.g. self-employed, and public servants (›Beamte‹), are treated as missing values.

Figure 2. Gross trends of structural assimilation

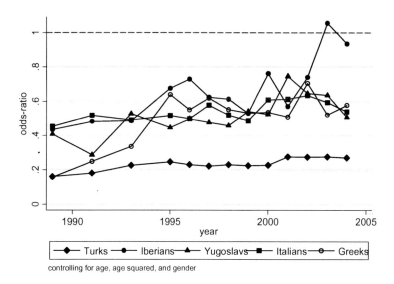

controlling for age, age squared, and gender

the dichotomy turns out to be quite telling regarding many important labour market outcomes (income, prestige, job security) and is historically
deeply rooted in the German occupational structure (Müller and Pollak
2004: 78). It should also be noted that in the meantime for several single
years similar analyses like the following have been conducted using alternative indicators (Granato 2003, Kalter and Granato 2007) delivering by and
large the same results.

With the dichotomy (salaried employee vs. worker) as the dependent
variable, the odds-ratios of attaining a salaried employee position for
members of the second generation as compared to the reference group of
Germans serve as the basic indicator of ethnic disadvantage. Figure 2
shows the development of these disadvantages for five important labour
migrant groups over time. The odds-ratios are derived from logistic regression models in which age, age squared, and gender are also controlled for.[7]
As noted above, group membership is defined by formal citizenship, and

---

7 A brief description of all models underlying the Figures 2 to 5 can be found in Table A1
in the appendix.

thus we can differentiate between Italians, Ex-Yugoslavs, Greeks, and Turks. Portuguese and Spaniards were combined to a group called ›Iberians‹ because of the small number of cases in each group. The second generation is defined as those non-Germans who were born in Germany or immigrated at age 6 or younger.

Figure 2 shows that in 1989 the situation in the labour market is far from structural assimilation, which would be indicated by a value of 1 for the reference group (horizontal line). Italians, Iberians, and Yugoslavs show odds-ratios only slightly above .4 while those for the remaining two groups (Turks and Greeks) are even below .2. However, one can clearly see that in the following 15 years occupational attainment has improved relative to the reference group of Germans. All odds-ratios have tended to rise over time, the trends being highly significant (p < .001) for all of the groups.[8] Lately, second generation Iberians have even reached an odds-ratio of nearly 1 which signals ›perfect‹ assimilation. This is not true, however, for the remaining four groups. Although the trend is significantly positive, the odds-ratios rise only slightly over time bouncing around a value of .6 in the latest years for Italians, Greeks, and Yugoslavs. Very obviously, Turks are the most disadvantaged group even staying below an odds-ratio of .3 in recent years.

It is worth noting that the trends observed could either stem from period effects or cohort replacement. Recently it has been re-stressed in social mobility research that the latter might often be more important for social change because many mechanisms assumed to account for change – most obviously those connected to educational attainment – turn out to affect specific age groups only (Müller and Pollak 2004: 96ff). This holds true especially for our dependent variable of occupational attainment, as intrapersonal vertical mobility is known to be rare at older ages (Erikson and Goldthorpe 1992: 72). The importance of analyzing cohorts has also been emphasized by migration researchers (Waters and Jiménez 2005: 121). However, given that we do not have longitudinal information on an individual basis it is not possible to separate period effects from cohort effects convincingly.

---

8 Table A1 in the appendix also contains a description of the models underlying the significance assessment of time trends.

Ethnic penalties in the labour market (MD partial, including MO-OD)

In this section we deal with ethnic disadvantages which might be observed even if we control for educational qualifications. Following Heath and Ridge (1983) we use the term ›ethnic penalties‹ to refer to them. How might they arise? In principle, one can find two different starting points to explain them, the first being some form of discrimination. In a narrower sense of the word this means differential treatment which is not mediated by other factors, but directly related to an ascribed characteristic (Arrow 1973a), in this case ethnicity. Following neo-classical economic theory closely, discrimination is unlikely to exist in perfect markets. Rather some kind of market failure is a necessary condition for it to exist: Monopsonistic discrimination theory (Madden 1973) emphasizes the lack of competition on the demand side for labour, the theory of taste discrimination (Becker 1971) builds up on the existence of personal preferences, while theories of statistical discrimination (Phelps 1972, Arrow 1972, Aigner and Cain 1977) or error discrimination (England 1992: 60) trace discriminative behaviour back to incomplete or ›false‹ information.

A second branch of explanations relates ethnic penalties to the lack of skills and resources besides education. To start with, formal qualifications are only a proxy for human capital, and ethnic differences may be due to unmeasured aspects of this. This holds true especially as some of these aspects are specific for the receiving society, like language proficiency or other kinds of cultural knowledge. Actually, this aspect offers the most obvious explanation why residual effects of ethnicity (controlling for education) may be observed for the first generation (Chiswick 1978, 1991; Friedberg 2000). However, although immigrants' children will probably do much better than their parents with respect to such culturally specific skills, there might still be a considerable gap to the indigenous youth. Furthermore, there might be a direct impact of parental resources on children's success (OD) which is not mediated by children's educational attainment. If, as in the case of former labour migration to Germany, incomers are negatively selected (MO) this may also account for ethnic disadvantages (MO-OD). Finally, besides parental resources young job seekers might also draw upon the resources of others, i.e. they might utilize their social capital. It is well known in the economic literature that social networks play an important part in the labour market (Granovetter 1995, Montgomery 1991: 1408 f., Lin 1999) and the networks of immigrant groups often turn out to

Figure 3. Trends of ethnic penalties

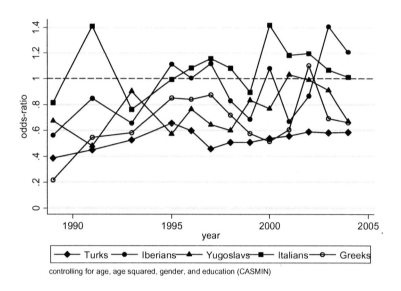

controlling for age, age squared, gender, and education (CASMIN)

be less helpful than those of the indigenous population (Portes and Rumbaut 2001: 48, Petersen et al. 2000).

Roughly, both branches of explanations in principle give rise to the expectation that ethnic penalties of the second generation in the German labour market should diminish over time. As regards discrimination, it is a well-known argument against the concept of taste discrimination and also error discrimination that these forms of behaviour will not persist in the medium or long term (e.g. Arrow 1972: 192, Arrow 1998). As regards the lack of resources specific for the receiving country, time should also be on the side of the children of immigrants. The longer the exposure of an individual or its ethnic group to the host society the higher the probability of attaining host country specific instead of sending country specific resources.[9]

---

9 Note again that the datasets used here are not longitudinal data for individuals but are based on a trend design. Therefore, re-migration and replenishment will be interfering to a certain degree (Waters and Jiménez 2005).

Looking at Figure 3 one finds that ethnic penalties for the second generation do exist, even if only on a relatively modest level.[10] Like Figure 2 the graph shows the odds-ratios of the five second generation groups, now controlling for educational qualifications as measured by the CASMIN-scheme (Brauns et al. 2003). Ethnic penalties are thus represented by the distance to the horizontal line through 1 on the y-axis. While the odds-ratio for the group of Italians bounces around the value of 1, signalling no severe disadvantages net of education, the group of Turks suffers the strongest penalties in nearly all of the years. All other groups are somewhere in between, ethnic penalties showing up in at least some of the years. Most importantly, however, the figure demonstrates that the odds-ratios net of education have tended to increase over the last 15 years. The trend is significantly positive for all of the groups, meaning that ethnic penalties indeed have been decreasing over time. In recent years the odds-ratios of four of the groups have more or less approached the 1-line, while the Turks still suffer severe penalties. But also for this group the odds-ratios net of education have risen from .4 to nearly .6.

The impact of education on occupational attainment (ED)

Comparing the ›gross‹ effects of group membership in Figure 2 to the effects net of education in Figure 3 re-confirms the introductory notion that educational qualifications play a dominant role in explaining labour market disadvantages of the second generation in Germany. Lately, except for the group of Turks they seem to account for almost all of the difficulties: While in most recent years considerable gross disadvantages are still observable in Figure 2 (except for the Iberians), controlling for qualifications, disadvantages have nearly vanished in Figure 3 for all groups except the Turks. But how has the strength of the ED relation developed over time? As this might also have influenced the gross trends of assimilation, we will now address this question.

---

10 While we are not able to disentangle the ethnic penalties according to the different branches of explanations with the GMC data, in a recent study based on data from the German Socio-economic Panel it could be shown that they are mostly due to language proficiency and ethnic composition of friendship networks rather than to discrimination (Kalter 2006). The direct impact of social origin (the MO-OD path) turned out to be of minor, albeit significant importance.

The fact that education is the most decisive factor in explaining occupational destination might seem obvious without further elucidation. In order to account for potential change in the strength of the relationship over time, however, it is helpful to recall the basic mechanism behind this: According to micro-economic theory, employees will try to maximize their labour market outcomes given their productivity, and employers will try to maximize the productivity of an employee in their hiring decisions given a job vacancy. So, in a perfect market the best jobs will match with the most productive employees. However, information is incomplete and employers are not able to observe productivity directly. Rather they must rely on available indicators of productivity and formal qualifications serve as the best among them. That is the core idea of the so-called signalling theory (Arrow 1973b, Spence 1973).

The strength of the signalling power is determined, above all, by institutional arrangements which vary between countries and might also vary over time within countries. It is argued that the signalling power is stronger the higher the degree of standardization of educational credentials and the more stratified the educational system (Allmendinger 1989, Müller and Shavit 1998). There is no doubt that Germany ranks high on both dimensions, making the relatively strong link between the educational system and the labour market plausible (Müller et al. 1998: 144–151). At the same time, it is argued that no severe institutional changes have taken place in recent decades which could give rise to expectations of severe changes in the link's strength (Müller et al. 1998: 153). Further to institutional changes the impact of education on labour market attainment could also be influenced by the general educational expansion. It is a widespread view that rising proportions of the population with higher education might lead to an inflation of credentials, blurring their significance for the labour market (Blossfeld 1985, Handl 1996). However, there is no straight-forward reasoning of how pure shifts in the marginal distribution of education translate into relative chances. Contingent on assumptions about the skills connected to educational qualifications, the demand in the labour market, and the concrete values in the margins, an expansion of higher education could algebraically lead to an increase or a decrease in specific odds-ratios.

The empirical evidence so far is ambiguous. While Handl (1996) finds that the returns to education have declined at least for certain groups since the 1980s, Müller and his collaborators (Müller et al. 1998, Brauns et al. 1997) report mixed results: On the one hand, the impact of secondary

Figure 4. Trends in the impact of education (on attaining salaried employee positions)

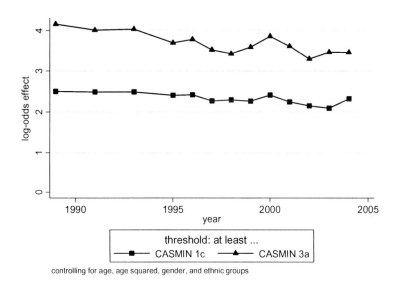

threshold: at least …
—■— CASMIN 1c   —▲— CASMIN 3a

controlling for age, age squared, gender, and ethnic groups

education on prestige of the first job has decreased, on the other hand, the respective returns to tertiary education have increased. Moreover, results depend on the variables chosen (Müller et al. 1998: 178f).

So what is the empirical situation with regard to the dependent variable and the time span analysed in this contribution? Figure 4 shows the log-odds effects[11] for two selected dichotomies constructed according to different thresholds in the full CASMIN scheme. The threshold ›at least CASMIN 1c‹ means more than just compulsory education while the threshold ›at least CASMIN 3a‹ means some kind of tertiary education. For both dummies we find a slight but highly significant decline over time meaning that access to salaried employee positions has indeed become less dependent on educational qualifications. Considering that according to prior research (Granato and Kalter 2001, Granato 2003, Seibert and Solga 2005, Kalter and Granato 2007, Konietzka and Seibert 2003) lower educa-

---

11 Here, log-odds effects rather than odds-ratios are shown because the latter are very high in this case and thus lead to difficulties in graphic representation. E.g. a log-odds value of 4 reflects an odds-ratio of more than 54.

tional qualifications are playing the main part in explaining labour market disadvantages of the second generation, the structural change in the ED relation could thus potentially also have worked in favour of structural assimilation. In order to draw that conclusion one has to assume, however, that the part not explained by education is not related to ethnicity (an assumption that is supported by the trends of ethnic penalties shown in Figure 3).

Trends in the second generation's educational attainment

In this part we will analyse how assimilation with respect to education has developed and how this has been influenced by the paths of the MOD sub-triangle in Figure 1. In order to disentangle these components we have to rely on a specific subset of the GMC data which will be described together with the gross trends of educational attainment (ME, total) in the first subsection. The second subsection will then address ethnic penalties and their development in the educational system (ME, partial), while the third subsection will focus on the general influence of social origin on educational success (OE). Finally, we will address the remaining path (OM), which deals with the question how the gap in parental background between native born Germans and the second generation has developed in recent years. It turns out that this path is not fixed either, which might become clear only at second glance.

Data and gross trends in educational attainment (ME, total)

Between 1989 and 2004 not only the impact of education on occupational attainment changed, but also the marginal distributions in educational qualifications. Using the GMC data one finds that some ethnic groups tended to close the gap to the reference group at least to a certain degree. Figure 5 shows the odds-ratios stemming from an ordered logit model (e.g. Long 1997: 40–47, 116–122) using the full CASMIN scheme as the dependent variable. Although the assumption of parallel regressions is violated (Long 1997: 138ff) for most of the ethnic effects in most of the years, the ordinal logit model is used here for convenience. The figure shows that

Figure 5. Ethnic disadvantages in educational attainment over time

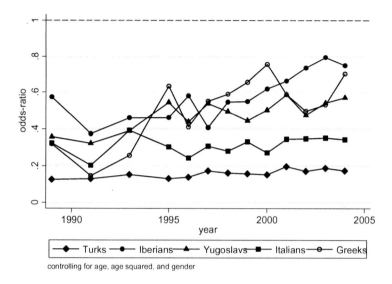

controlling for age, age squared, and gender

in the most recent years two groups (Iberians and Greeks) were doing increasingly well, even if they did not fully catch up with the reference group of Germans (odds-ratios above .7). Next come the Ex-Yugoslavs (odds-ratio below .6), followed by the Italians (odds-ratio below .4). Very clearly, the Turks still face the biggest problems in the educational system (odds-ratio around .2). Most importantly, while the trends over the years turn out to be significantly positive for the other three groups, this does not hold for second generation Turks and Italians. Additional logit models using different threshold-dummies as dependent variables (analyses not shown here) indicate that Turks tend to make better relative progress with respect to higher thresholds (e.g. at least CASMIN 3a vs. not) than to lower ones (e.g. at least CASMIN 1c vs. not) whereas the result for Italians (lacking progress) is more stable.

Unfortunately, it is not possible to use the data in a straight-forward way to determine the impact of social origin on the process of educational attainment, as parental occupation and education are not regular variables in the GMC data. However, being basically a household survey, the GMC does offer data on each household member and allows the identification of familial relationships. Thus information on social origin, including parental educational and occupational attainment, is available for the subset of those individuals who still live with their parents. For this subset, however, we cannot use the CASMIN classification as an indicator for educational attainment like we did above, because in most cases respondents are still in vocational training or in tertiary education. Therefore we focus only on respondents who are 18 years old and look at the final school qualification, (*Abitur*), which qualifies for admission to tertiary education.[12] More precisely, the new dependent variable used in the following distinguishes between those who have already obtained the *Abitur* or are preparing for it (i.e. those who are in the last three years of a track leading to the *Abitur*) and those who have only elementary or intermediate general education and are not preparing for the *Abitur*.[13] Following the analyses above we use all available files between 1991 and 2004.[14]

Figure 6 shows the development of ethnic disadvantages for this subset of data and the new dependent variable.[15] It shows the odds-ratios resulting from logistic regression models controlling also for gender. Due to the small number of cases, all ethnic groups other than Turks have to be combined. Again, Turks of the second generation are clearly disadvantaged and no perceptible changes have occurred in recent years. The trend in the odds-ratios is slightly positive, but not significant. In contrast to Figure 5, the same holds true for the group of all other labour migrants.[16] Note, however, that the non-significance partly results from the smaller number of cases and partly from the fact that the residual group is an amalgam of all remaining nationalities, including the Italians, who clearly perform poorest within this group and for whom no progress is visible in Figure 5

---

12 A more comprehensive and much better way to capture educational attainment would be to distinguish between the three secondary educational levels (general elementary education, intermediate general qualification and the maturity certificate of general education). Unfortunately, the GMC does not provide information on the type of track attended for those who have not yet completed general education.

13 A detailed description of the German educational system is given by Brauns and Steinmann (1999).

14 The 1989 GMC file has to be excluded because the information on which the dependent variable is based is not available.

15 A sketch of the models underlying the Figures 6 to 9 is given in Table A2 in the appendix. Like Table A1, Table A2 also describes the models used to assess the significance of trends over time.

16 We have no explanation for the obvious outlier in 1998 but checked the data very carefully.

Figure 6. Ethnic disadvantages in educational attainment over time – reconsidered

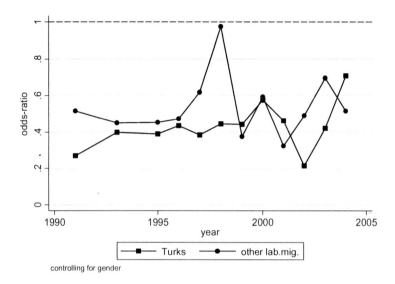

controlling for gender

either. If one excluded the Italians, there would be a significant positive trend.

One might object that the results might be biased because respondents at age 18 who still live with their parents may aspire to or may have attained the *Abitur* more often than those not living with their parents. This turns out to be true, but it does not seem to question our findings with respect to the relative disadvantages of immigrants. Given that 93 percent of respondents at age 18 still live with their parents, *both* Germans and second generation immigrants are positively selected in this respect. Including all respondents at age 18 in the analysis (not shown here) does not affect the gross ethnic disadvantages in Figure 6 severely.[17]

---

17 Technically speaking there is only a main effect of the dummy variable »still living with parents«, but no significant interactions with ethnic group membership.

Ethnic penalties in the educational system (ME, partial)

Usually, the term ethnic penalties has been used to describe the relative disadvantages that immigrants and their children experience in the labour market net of educational qualifications. When we address ethnic penalties in the educational system, we use the term analogously for all those disadvantages which are not due to social origin. In other words we ask why for the same level of parental educational qualification (and the same social class position) we may observe ethnic differences in educational performance.

Roughly, we can apply the same two general sets of answers as for the labour market. The first pertains to discrimination: In the school context, discrimination may occur if teachers pursue tastes for discrimination or lack relevant information such as that on student's ability and in this case discriminate statistically. With respect to tastes, the situation is somewhat different from that for the labour market because treating the educational system as a market system may be less adequate. Therefore a prediction of development over time is less straight-forward than in the case of the labour market. Also with respect to statistical discrimination, the school offers a specific setting. Statistical discrimination is likely to occur in situations in which teachers do not yet have information about their students, for example, at the beginning of a new school year or when schools are entitled to choose among future students (Kristen 2006). However, throughout the school year teachers have access to very detailed information about individual performance making persistent statistical discrimination unlikely.

The second branch of answers, again, refers to a lack of resources, now especially to those which are required for successful progress through the school system. Obviously, immigrant parents could not acquire the same resources specific to the German educational system as native born parents. At the same time, the resources they have may not prove as instrumental in the school system of the receiving society. A prime example is educational knowledge, that is, profound knowledge of the functioning of the school system which is not only indispensable for effectively supporting a child's academic development but which may be particularly relevant at central transition points in the school career (Kristen 2005). Besides parental resources, students may further encounter differential learning conditions in their environment which may be related to their networks' ethnic composition as well as to segregation in schools (Stanat 2006, Portes and

Hao 2004). Especially language acquisition, a key competence for educational success, is probably a more difficult task in contexts in which large numbers of non-native speakers, often of low socioeconomic status, concentrate together (Caldas and Bankston 1998: 554). Finally, it has been argued that educational aspirations in immigrant families may differ from those of the indigenous population (Kao and Tienda 1995).[18] By and large, as for the labour market we expect that with a longer exposure to the new educational system individuals and ethnic groups acquire more host country specific capital and that throughout intergenerational transmission processes capital specific to the country of origin becomes less important.

Looking at the GMC data we find that ethnic penalties do not play an important role for explaining relative educational disadvantages of the second generation, at least not when looking at the dependent variable used here. Figure 7 shows the odds-ratios for the Turks and the combined group of other second generation youth now controlling for social origin in terms of parental education.[19] A significant net Turkish disadvantage is only found in 1991. All other odds-ratios turn out not to be significantly different from 1 (except for the positive outlier in 1998), many of them are even slightly above 1. When pooling the data and adding an interaction with time (metric), a negative main effect (indicating the disadvantage in 1991) arises for Turks while the interaction effect is significantly positive then. Neither the main effect nor the interaction effect are significant for the group of others. So the picture seems very clear: The ethnic disadvantages in aspiring or achieving the *Abitur* are almost completely due to social origin while ethnic penalties are not relevant. Turks seem to have suffered from them on a modest level in earlier years, however, they have been vanishing over time.

---

18 However, rather than referring to penalties mostly this issue has been addressed to account for exceptional educational success such as that of the Greeks in the German school system (Hopf 1987).

19 Parental educational qualifications measured by the full CASMIN scheme turn out to be the best predictor among all available indicators of social origin, the others being parental occupational status and income. Although including these other indicators leads to further (significant) increases of the likelihood, we only consider education to keep the models and the reasoning simple. As Figure 7 shows, this alone could account for ethnic differences. Parental means that father's education is used if available and mother's only if not.

Figure 7. Trends of ethnic penalties in educational attainment

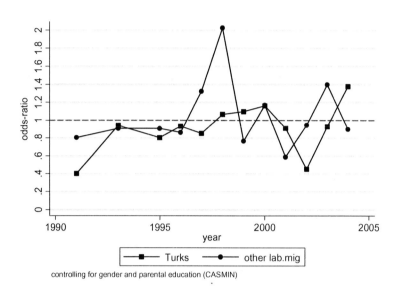

controlling for gender and parental education (CASMIN)

The impact of social origin (OE)

Comparing Figure 7 to Figure 6 shows that ethnic differences in the completion of the highest schooling qualification are primarily a matter of differences in parental socio-economic background. This central result has been established in various studies of immigrants and their children's educational attainment in the German school system (Alba et al. 1994, Müller and Stanat 2006). Our interest now shifts to the mechanisms by which social origin affects educational outcomes and thus to one of the core questions of stratification research: In which ways are educational disadvantages transmitted across generations? And how has this relationship developed over time?

In general, educational outcomes can be conceived as the result of a continuous process of developing and accumulating school-relevant skills, stretching from birth through the different stages of the pre-school and school career. Specific conditions associated with an individual's social and educational background not only shape this process (primary effects), but they may also influence the educational decisions individuals make at different transition points in their educational careers (secondary effects; Boudon 1974). Several arguments have been advanced to account for both primary and secondary effects. First, and above all, childhood conditions systematically vary with the financial, cultural, and social resources available within the family and the immediate environment and so do the means for educational investments. These family-based differences may be further reinforced by contextual conditions such as differential learning environments in schools due to social (and ethnic) segregation (Stanat 2006, Portes and Hao 2004). A second argument concerns class differences in educational aspirations with the higher social classes pursuing the more demanding and prestigious degrees (Boudon 1974, Breen and Goldthorpe 1997, Erikson and Jonsson 1996).[20]

In addition, institutional arrangements might shape the degree to which educational and class disadvantages are transmitted across generations. In Germany, the very early first educational transition from primary to secondary schooling has been frequently associated with a relatively high degree of social inequality in education (Allmendinger 1989, Müller and Karle 1993). Also temporal variation in the OE relationship has been frequently associated with institutional reforms. Although in comparison to other countries the German school system has undergone relatively few educational reforms and has conserved its rather rigid tracking system, some arguments have been raised which may account for at least slight changes. For example, the gradual increase in the length of compulsory education to nine years in the 1970s is assumed to have reduced social inequality in education because the costs associated with the attendance of the different tracks have become more similar (Müller and Haun 1994: 6–7, Müller and Pollak 2004: 83). Moreover, with the establishment of the socially less selective universities of applied sciences (Fachhochschule), as an alternative to traditional university education, inequalities in tertiary education might also have been decreasing (Müller and Pollak 2004: 83). Empirical evidence indicates that there has indeed been a substantial decline in social inequality in education, although the results for the development of the OE relationship have not been unequivocal (Blossfeld 1993, Henz and Maas 1995, Müller and Haun 1994).

---

20 Educational inequalities have also been attributed to genetic factors or to middle class norms pervading the school system (Erikson and Jonsson 1996: 10–11). However, these answers have not been central to mobility research.

Figure 8. Impact of parental education on educational attainment over time

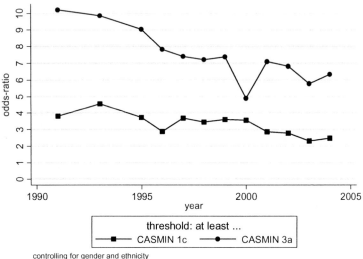

The GMC datasets used here also confirm that the impact of social origin has weakened over time. Figure 8 shows the odds-ratios referring to two different thresholds in the CASMIN classification. The dependent variable of the underlying logistic regression models is again the dummy variable for aspiring or passing the *Abitur*. Whether the father has tertiary education (at least CASMIN 3a) or not has become clearly less important for the odds of attaining the *Abitur* over time, the trend being highly significant. The same holds true when looking at whether the father has more than only compulsory education (at least CASMIN 1c). It is worth noting, nevertheless, that educational inequality with respect to social class continues to be especially pronounced, as is shown by the high absolute level of the odds-ratios. In spite of the declining impact, it is still a very important factor mediating ethnic inequalities.

The selectivity of migration (OM)

The last aspect of the structural assimilation process analyzed here is the OM link, i.e. the possible disadvantages with respect to socio-economic background arising from the selectivity of migration. It might seem less obvious why this link could be important when analysing trends over time, but we will see that neglecting it would mean missing an interesting piece of the puzzle.

There is no doubt that labour migration in the 1960s and early 1970s from Greece, Italy, Ex-Yugoslavia, Portugal, Spain, and Turkey to Germany was highly negatively selective with respect to human capital as compared to the native born Germans. Immigrants were explicitly recruited to provide unskilled labour in a few industrial sectors, with unfavourable working conditions (Hoffmann-Nowotny 1973, Heckmann 1992: 81). Although the subsequent phase of family reunification did change the demographic composition considerably, it did not fundamentally alter the negative selection of human capital. In the GMC data the fathers of the 18-year-olds are on average 48 years old (within all groups considered) and only a small proportion of them belong to the second generation (5% of the Turkish fathers and 3% of the others), giving no reason to expect pronounced changes in family background conditions of the 18-year-olds over time. The parents in the German reference group, however, have benefited from the educational expansion. This leads to a very important aspect when talking about the likelihood of the second generation's structural assimilation: There is reason to believe that socioeconomic background conditions have even worsened *in relative terms* over time.

Figure 9 shows that this seems to hold for the specific sub-sample of the GMC used here. The graph illustrates the development of odds-ratios over time, which stem from an ordered logit model using parental education (full CASMIN) as the dependent variable. Not only are these odds-ratios very small (note the scale of the y-axis) but they also decrease highly significantly over time for both groups. This means that the enormous socio-economic background gap between the second generation and their German peers has actually widened in recent years.

Figure 9. Labour migrant parents' educational attainment relative to German parents over time

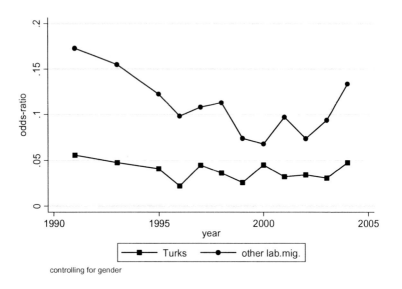

controlling for gender

Conclusions

Summarizing the results it seems suitable to start with an answer to the most basic question of migration research: Yes, there is a trend towards assimilation when looking at the structural situation of the second generation in Germany. Despite the fact that labour market disadvantages of the classic labour migrant descendants are still severe, the second generation is nevertheless moving towards the reference group. While many studies have shown that this holds very clearly in an intergenerational sense, i.e. when comparing the second generation to the first, the analyses in this contribution demonstrate that a trend towards assimilation is also evident within the second generation over time (Figure 2).

Disentangling this process into several components according to the extended OED Scheme and generalizing roughly over all the ethnic groups considered the trend towards structural assimilation is a combined result of

Figure 10. Summary of trends in the MOED diagram

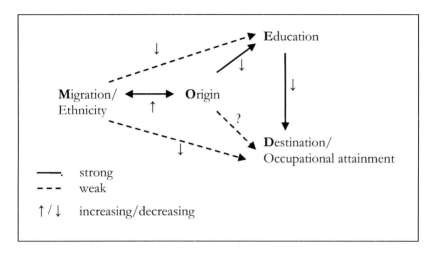

several distinct processes (see now Figure 10). First of all, the specific *ethnic* parts in the explanation of disadvantages, i.e. the direct negative impacts of having a migration background (ME and MD) – in a certain sense the genuine contributions of research on migration and integration – have further weakened. In accordance with economic discrimination theory and resource-based explanations of integration processes, so-called ethnic penalties seem to have declined over the past 15 years both in the labour market (Figure 3) and the educational system (Figure 7). However, as noted in the introduction, these paths are known to be of minor importance for the reproduction of ethnic inequalities, at least in Germany. Therefore it is important to see that structural changes in the genuine contributions of stratification research, expressed by the OED triangle, have worked in the same direction and thus speeded up the assimilation process. The impact of level of educational qualifications on occupational attainment has decreased (Figure 4), and as ethnic penalties did not increase simultaneously, this has worked in favour of the second generation, which is considerably less well-educated than the reference group. Whether the second generation has also moved towards gross assimilation in education is less clear. In general, we find only slightly positive trends (Figure 5 and 6) with varying significance for specific groups and specific dependent variables. Again, we find that a classic component of stratification research has supported the assimilation of the second generation: The impact of social origin on educational outcomes, the most decisive factor in explaining ethnic disadvantages in the German educational system, has weakened in recent years (Figure 8). However, its impact is still extremely pronounced and at the same time the gap in socio-economic background has widened between the second generation and native Germans (Figure 9). To understand the current difficulties of the second generation it is important to see that their parents still represent a population strongly negatively selected with respect to human capital while the corresponding German parents have already benefited from educational expansion. Another variant of the »long arms of history« (Müller and Pollak 2004) thus constitutes the only component that has slowed down assimilation.

To get the full picture it is necessary to illustrate not only why structural assimilation is taking place in principle, but also why it moves only at a low pace and why there is still a long way to go, at least for some of the groups. With the genuine ethnic elements in the explanation scheme being of minor (and diminishing) importance, the speed of assimilation mainly depends on how fast the general mechanisms of social inequality will change. And with respect to this it is worth noting again, that in spite of all gradual tendencies, the absolute strength of OE (Figure 8) is still more than remarkable, not to mention OM (Figure 9).

While this story of the second generation's structural assimilation seems rather stable in many of its parts, it has already been implied that in other parts the detected trends might be dependent on the specific choice of variables. The latter is especially true for trends in the ED link and for the general strength of the direct ME path. So, obviously, analyses using alternative indicators would be very helpful to either confirm or differentiate the picture. The cumulated GMC surely offers many opportunities with respect to ED, however, the data situation with respect to trends in ME seems much less promising. Further to that, the separation of birth cohort, life-cycle, and period effects needs much more attention for understanding the mechanisms of changing or perpetuating ethnic inequalities. So in many respects further research is needed in order to better understand the trends in the mechanisms of structural assimilation. In any case, the general lesson from this contribution is that marrying migration research more explicitly to general social stratification research is an extremely promising route to follow.

Appendix

Table A1. Details on the models in Figures 2 to 5

	Fig. 2 Assessing significance of trends over time		Fig. 3 Assessing significance of trends over time		Fig. 4 Assessing significance of trends over time		Fig. 5 Assessing significance of trends over time	
Dependent variable	Salaried employee vs. worker		Salaried employee vs. worker		Salaried employee vs. worker		Education	
Age	X	X	X	X	X	X	X	X
Age squared	X	X	X	X	X	X	X	X
Gender	X	X	X	X	X	X	X	X
Ethnic group	X	X	X	X	X	X	X	X
Year of survey discrete)		X		X		X		X
Education (full CASMIN)			X	X				
Education (thresholds)					X	X		
Year (metric) × ethnic group		X		X				X
Year (metric) × education				X		X		
GMC (years)	sepa-rate	pooled	sepa-rate	pooled	sepa-rate	pooled	sepa-rate	pooled
Type of model	logistic regression		logistic regression		logistic regression		ordered logit	

Population in the Dataset: second generation and German workers and salaried employees aged 18–65.

Time span: 1989–2004.

When pooling the data one has to remember that the GMC is a rotating panel. More precisely, every year only one quarter of the households is renewed so that a respondent may stay in the survey for four consecutive years. In order to correct for this fact a design weight for years is used in the analyses. This leads to a conservative estimate of standard errors.

Table A2. Details on the models in Figures 6 to 9

	Fig. 6 Assessing significance of trends over time		Fig. 7 Assessing significance of trends over time		Fig. 8 Assessing significance of trends over time		Fig. 9 Assessing significance of trends over time	
Dependent variable	*Abitur*		*Abitur*		*Abitur*		Parental education	
Gender	X	X	X	X	X	X	X	X
Ethnic group	X	X	X	X	X	X	X	X
Year of survey (discrete)		X		X		X		X
Parental education (full CASMIN)			X	X				
Parental education (thresholds)					X	X		
Year (metric) × ethnic group		X		X				X
Year (metric) × parental education						X		
GMC (years)	sepa-rate	pooled	sepa-rate	pooled	sepa-rate	pooled	sepa-rate	pooled
Type of model	logistic regression		logistic regression		logistic regression		ordered logit	

Population in the Dataset: second generation and Germans, age 18, living with parents.
Time span: 1991–2004.

References

Aigner, D. J./Cain, G. G. (1977). »Statistical theories of discrimination in labor markets«, *Industrial and Labor Relations Review*, vol. 30, pp. 175–187.

Alba, R. D./Handl, J./Müller, W. (1994). »Ethnische Ungleichheit im deutschen Bildungssystem«, *Kölner Zeitschrift für Soziologie und Sozialpsychologie,* vol. 46, no. 2, pp. 209–237.

Allmendinger, J. (1989). »Educational systems and labour market outcomes«, *European Sociological Review*, vol. 5, no. 3, pp. 231–250.

Arrow, K. J. (1972). »Some Mathematical Models of Race Discrimination in the Labor Market«, in A. H. Pascal (ed.), *Racial Discrimination in Economic Life*, Lexington, Mass.: D.C. Heath, pp. 187–203.

Arrow, K. J. (1973a). »The theory of discrimination«, in O. Ashenfelter/A. Rees (eds.), *Discrimination in Labor Markets*, Princeton: Princeton University Press, pp. 3–33.

Arrow, K. J. (1973b). »Higher education as a filter«, *Journal of Public Economics*, vol. 2, pp. 193–216.

Arrow, K. J. (1998). »What has economics to say about racial discrimination?«, *Journal of Economic Perspectives*, vol. 12, pp. 91–100.

Baumert, J./Schümer, G. (2002). »Familiäre Lebensverhältnisse, Bildungsbeteiligung und Kompetenzerwerb im nationalen Vergleich«, in J. Baumert et al. (eds.), *PISA 2000. Die Länder der Bundesrepublik Deutschland im Vergleich*, Opladen: Leske + Budrich, pp. 159–202.

Becker, G. S. (1971 [1957]). *The Economics of Discrimination* (2nd edition), Chicago: University Press.

Blossfeld, H.-P. (1985). *Bildungsexpansion und Berufschancen: Empirische Analysen zur Lage der Berufsanfänger in der Bundesrepublik*, Frankfurt/New York: Campus.

Blossfeld, H.-P. (1993). »Changes in educational opportunities in the Federal Republic of Germany«, in Y. Shavit/H.-P. Blossfeld (eds.), *Persistent Inequality. Changing Educational Attainment in Thirteen Countries*, Boulder: Westview Press, pp. 51–74.

Boudon, R. (1974). *Education, Opportunity, and Social Inequality*, New York: Wiley & Sons.

Brauns, H./Steinmann, S. (1999). »Educational reform in France, West-Germany and the United Kingdom: updating the CASMIN educational classification«, *ZUMA-Nachrichten*, vol. 44, pp. 7–44.

Brauns, H./Müller, W./Steinmann, S. (1997). *Educational expansion and returns to education. A comparative study on Germany, France, the UK, and Hungary* (Working Paper Arbeitsbereich I No. 23), Mannheim: Mannheimer Zentrum für Europäische Sozialforschung.

Brauns, H./Scherer, S./Steinmann, S. (2003). »The CASMIN educational classification in international comparative research«, in J. H. P. Hoffmeyer-Zlotnik/C. Wolf (eds.), *Advances in Cross-National Comparison. A European Working Book for Demographic and Socio-Economic Variables*, New York: Kluwer Academic/Plenum Publishers, pp. 196–221.

Breen, R./Goldthorpe, J. H. (1997). »Explaining educational differentials. Towards a formal rational action theory«, *Rationality and Society*, vol. 9, no. 3, pp. 275–305.

Breen, R./Luijkx, R. (2004). »Conclusions«, in R. Breen (ed.), *Social Mobility in Europe*, Oxford: Oxford University Press, pp. 383–410.

Caldas, S. J./Bankston III, C. (1998). »The inequality of separation: racial composition of schools and academic achievement«, *Educational Administrative Quarterly*, vol. 34, no. 4, pp. 533–557.

Chiswick, B. R. (1978). »The effect of americanization on the earnings of foreign-born men«, *Journal of Political Economy*, vol. 86, pp. 897–921.

Chiswick, B. R. (1991). »Speaking, reading, and earnings among low-skilled immigrants«, *Journal of Labor Economics*, vol. 9, pp. 149–170.

Diehl, C./Blohm, M. (2003). »Rights or identity? Naturalization processes among labor migrants in Germany«, *International Migration Review*, vol. 37, pp. 133–162.

England, P. (1992). *Comparable Worth. Theories and Evidence*, New York: de Gruyter.

Erikson, R./Goldthorpe, J. H. (1992). *The Constant Flux: A Study of Class Mobility in Industrial Countries*, Oxford: Clarendon Press.

Erikson, R./Jonsson, J. O. (1996). »Explaining class inequality in education. The Swedish test case«, in R. Erikson/J. O. Jonsson (eds.), *Can Education Be Equalized? The Swedish Case in Comparative Perspective*, Stockholm: Westview Press, pp. 1–63.

Esser, H. (2000). *Soziologie. Spezielle Grundlagen. Band 2: Die Konstruktion der Gesellschaft*, Frankfurt/Main: Campus.

Friedberg, R. M. (2000). »You can't take it with you? Immigrant assimilation and the portability of human capital«, *Journal of Labor Economics*, vol. 18, pp. 221–251.

Granato, N. (2003). *Ethnische Ungleichheit auf dem deutschen Arbeitsmarkt* (Band 33 der Schriftenreihe des Bundesinstituts für Bevölkerungsforschung), Opladen: Leske + Budrich.

Granato, N./Kalter, F. (2001). »Die Persistenz ethnischer Ungleichheit auf dem deutschen Arbeitsmarkt. Diskriminierung oder Unterinvestition in Humankapital?«, *Kölner Zeitschrift für Soziologie und Sozialpsychologie*, vol. 53, no. 3, pp. 497–520.

Granovetter, M. (1995). *Getting a Job. A Study of Contacts and Careers* (2nd edition), Chicago and London: University of Chicago Press.

Handl, J. (1996). »Hat sich die berufliche Wertigkeit der Bildungsabschlüsse in den achtziger Jahren verringert? Eine Analyse der abhängig erwerbstätigen, deutschen Berufsanfänger auf der Basis von Mikrozensusergebnissen«, *Kölner Zeitschrift für Soziologie und Sozialpsychologie*, vol. 48, no. 2, pp. 249–273.

Heath, A./Ridge, J. (1983). »Social mobility of ethnic minorities«, *Journal of Biosocial Science Supplement*, vol. 8, pp. 169–184.

Heckmann, F. (1992). *Ethnische Minderheiten, Volk und Nation. Soziologie interethnischer Beziehungen*, Stuttgart: Enke.

Henz, U./Maas, I. (1995). »Chancengleichheit durch die Bildungsexpansion?«, *Kölner Zeitschrift für Soziologie und Sozialpsychologie*, vol. 47, no. 4, pp. 605–633.

Hoffmann-Nowotny, H.-J. (1973). *Soziologie des Fremdarbeiterproblems. Eine theoretische und empirische Analyse am Beispiel der Schweiz*, Stuttgart: Enke.

Hopf, D. (1987). *Herkunft und Schulbesuch ausländischer Kinder. Eine Untersuchung am Beispiel griechischer Schüler*, Berlin: Max Planck Institute for Human Development.

Kalter, F. (2005). »Ethnische Ungleichheit auf dem Arbeitsmarkt«, in M. Abraham/T. Hinz (eds.), *Arbeitsmarktsoziologie. Probleme, Theorien, empirische Befunde*, Opladen: VS Verlag für Sozialwissenschaften, pp. 303–332.

Kalter, F. (2006). »Auf der Suche nach einer Erklärung für die spezifischen Arbeitsmarktnachteile von Jugendlichen türkischer Herkunft. Zugleich eine Replik auf den Beitrag von Holger Seibert und Heike Solga: ›Gleiche Chancen dank einer abgeschlossenen Ausbildung?‹ (ZfS 5/2005)«, *Zeitschrift für Soziologie*, vol. 35, pp. 144–160.

Kalter, F./Granato, N. (2002). »Demographic change, educational expansion, and structural assimilation of immigrants: the case of Germany«, *European Sociological Review*, vol. 18, pp. 199–226.

Kalter, F./Granato, N. (2007). »Educational hurdles on the way to structural assimilation in Germany«, forthcoming in A. F. Heath/S. Y. Cheung (eds.), *Unequal Chances: Ethnic Minorities in Western Labour Markets*, Oxford: Oxford University Press for the British Academy.

Kao, G./Tienda, M. (1995). »Optimism and achievement. The educational performance of immigrant youth«, *Social Science Quarterly*, vol. 76, no. 1, pp. 1–19.

Konietzka, D./Seibert, H. (2003). »Deutsche und Ausländer an der ›zweiten Schwelle‹. Eine vergleichende Analyse der Berufseinstiegskohorten 1976–1995 in Westdeutschland«, *Zeitschrift für Pädagogik*, vol. 49, no. 4, pp. 567–590.

Kristen, C. (2005). *School Choice and Ethnic School Segregation. Primary School Selection in Germany*, Münster: Waxmann.

Kristen, C. (2006). »Ethnische Diskriminierung in der Grundschule? Die Vergabe von Noten und Bildungsempfehlungen«, *Kölner Zeitschrift für Soziologie und Sozialpsychologie*, vol. 58, no. 1, pp. 79–97.

Kristen, C./Granato, N. (2004). »Bildungsinvestitionen in Migrantenfamilien«, in K. Bade/M. Bommes (eds.), *Migration – Integration – Bildung* (IMIS-Beiträge No. 23), Osnabrück: Institute for Migration Research and Intercultural Studies, pp. 123–141.

Lin, N. (1999). »Social networks and status attainment«, *Annual Review of Sociology*, vol. 25, pp. 467–487.

Long, S. J. (1997). *Regression Models for Categorical and Limited Dependent Variables. Advanced Quantitative Techniques in the Social Sciences Series*, Thousand Oaks: Sage.

Lüttinger, P./Riede, T. (1997). »Der Mikrozensus: amtliche Daten für die Sozialforschung«, *ZUMA-Nachrichten*, vol. 41, pp. 19–43.

Madden, J. F. (1973). *The Economics of Sex Discrimination*, Lexington, Mass.: Lexington Books.

Montgomery, J. D. (1991). »Social networks and labor market outcomes: toward an economic analysis«, *The American Economic Review*, vol. 81, pp. 1408–1418.

Müller, A. G./Stanat, P. (2006). »Schulischer Erfolg von Schülerinnen und Schülern mit Migrationshintergrund. Analysen zur Situation von Zuwanderern aus der ehemaligen Sowjetunion und aus der Türkei«, in J. Baumert et al. (eds.), *Herkunftsbedingte Disparitäten im Bildungswesen. Differenzielle Bildungsprozesse und Probleme der Verteilungsgerechtigkeit*, Wiesbaden: VS Verlag für Sozialwissenschaften, pp. 221–255.

Müller, W./Haun, D. (1994). »Bildungsungleichheit im sozialen Wandel«, *Kölner Zeitschrift für Soziologie und Sozialpsychologie*, vol. 6, no. 1, pp. 1–42.

Müller, W./Karle, W. (1993). »Social selection in educational systems in Europe«, *European Sociological Review*, vol. 9, no. 1, pp. 1–23.

Müller, W./Shavit, Y. (1998). »The institutional embeddedness of the stratification process. A comparative study of qualifications and occupations in thirteen countries«, in Y. Shavit/W. Müller (eds.), *From School to Work. A Comparative Study of Educational Qualification and Occupational Destinations*, Oxford: Clarendon Press, pp. 1–48.

Müller, W./Pollak, R. (2004). »Social mobility in West Germany: the long arms of history discovered?«, in R. Breen (ed.), *Social Mobility in Europe*, Oxford: Oxford University Press, pp. 77–113.

Müller, W./Lüttinger, P./König, W./Karle, W. (1989). »Class and education in industrial nations«, *International Journal of Sociology*, vol. 19, pp. 3–39.

Müller, W./Steinmann, S./Ell, R. (1998). »Education and labour-market entry in Germany«, in W. Müller/Y. Shavit (eds.), *From School to Work. A Comparative Study of Educational Qualification and Occupational Destinations*, Oxford: Clarendon Press, pp. 143–187.

Petersen, T./Saporta, I./ Seidel, M.-D. L. (2000). »Offering a job: meritocracy and social networks«, *American Journal of Sociology*, vol. 106, pp. 763–816.

Phelps, E. S. (1972). »The statistical theory of racism and sexism«, *The American Economic Review*, vol. 62, pp. 659–661.

Portes, A./Hao, L. (2004). »The schooling of children of immigrants. Contextual effects on the educational attainment of the second generation«, *Proceeding of National Academy of Science*, vol. 101, no. 33, pp. 11920–11927.

Portes, A./Rumbaut, R. G. (2001). *Legacies. The Story of the Immigrant Second Generation*, New York: Russell Sage Foundation.

Seibert, H./Solga, H. (2005). »Gleiche Chancen dank einer abgeschlossenen Ausbildung? Zum Signalwert von Ausbildungsabschlüssen bei ausländischen und deutschen jungen Erwachsenen«, *Zeitschrift für Soziologie*, vol. 34, pp. 364–382.

Seifert, W. (1992). »Die zweite Ausländergeneration in der Bundesrepublik. Längsschnittbeobachtungen in der Berufseinstiegsphase«, *Kölner Zeitschrift für Soziologie und Sozialpsychologie*, vol. 44, no. 4, pp. 677–696.

Spence, M. (1973). »Job market signaling«, *The Quarterly Journal of Economics*, vol. 87, no. 3, pp. 355–374.

Stanat, P. (2006). »Schulleistungen von Jugendlichen mit Migrationshintergrund. Die Rolle der Zusammensetzung der Schülerschaft«, in J. Baumert et al. (eds.), *Herkunftsbedingte Disparitäten im Bildungswesen. Differenzielle Bildungsprozesse und Probleme der Verteilungsgerechtigkeit*, Wiesbaden: VS Verlag für Sozialwissenschaften, pp. 189–219.

Szydlik, M. (1996). »Ethnische Ungleichheit auf dem deutschen Arbeitsmarkt«, *Kölner Zeitschrift für Soziologie und Sozialpsychologie*, vol. 48, pp. 658–676.

Waters, M. C./Jiménez, T. R. (2005). »Assessing immigrant assimilation: new empirical and theoretical challenges«, *Annual Review of Sociology*, vol. 3, pp. 105–125.

Lessons from social mobility research: could the index discussion in occupational sex segregation benefit?

Johann Handl and Stephanie Steinmetz

Introduction

Modern societies are affected by various processes of social change – such as the increase in formal education, the shift of demographic structures and the structural change of work. In particular, the latter phenomenon is often discussed as a crucial part of the social modernisation of societies in the course of their transition from an industrial to a service-orientated economy. It implies a shift in the distribution of occupations and jobs that, in various ways, determine the life chances of working people and their families. This also includes the reshaping of gender relations on the labour market, which evolve in a complex interplay of changing economic structures, state policies and cultural ideas and traditions.

One facet of these ongoing processes is the increasing involvement of women in paid employment in all European Members States over the last decades. Participation rates have soared in some countries (such as the Netherlands and Spain) and exceeded a level of 70% in most Northern European countries. The rising female labour force participation is strongly related to an increase in the formal education of girls and the feminist movement in the 70s. Nowadays, it is also considered a response to the increasing demand for qualified labour and a necessary protection of women and their children against the increasing risks of poverty and instability in family life. In general, women's participation in the labour market is therefore no longer regarded as ›temporary‹, and women more frequently continue to work when they get married or give birth to a child.

Despite this progress regarding the participation of women in the labour market, some concerns remain that these remarkable changes have not increased equal opportunities between women and men in society and in the labour market at all. Even though women have gained access to occupations and positions from which they have been excluded in the past, they are still concentrated in the service sector and rarely hold jobs at the top. Moreover, they tend to be found in ›precarious‹ and ›highly flexible‹ jobs and they are often disadvantaged in respect of social security and income.

These negative peculiarities of female employment are components of a phenomenon which has been labelled as ›sex-specific occupational segregation‹. Generally, the concept refers to the fact that women and men work in different occupations and sectors, are assigned to different hierarchical levels, and, very often, work under different terms and conditions (Hakim 1979, 1993).[1]

Occupational sex segregation is a phenomenon that can be observed throughout the world. It is often described as an important source of labour market rigidity, as it indicates exclusion as well as wasteful use of human resources. Political and scientific interest in this issue has increased over the last decades. From a political point of view, the request of the European Union to further gender equality in the labour market as well the role of gender equality as an indicator of societal and economical progress makes it indispensable to describe and analyse occupational sex segregation. The scientific interest in sex segregation is motivated by its theoretically unexpected persistence, its tight connection to other forms of sex-specific inequalities, such as the status or the wage gap (Beller 1982), and by the methodological question of adequate measurement (Blackburn et al. 1993).

Against this background, the next section starts with a short evaluation of sex-specific occupational segregation in the context of equal opportunity policies of the EU. This is followed by a discussion of milestones in the scientific area, concentrating on methodological aspects. Here, in particular, the issue of how sex-specific occupational segregation can be measured adequately from a comparative perspective is discussed. In the following section, arguments are presented for the central thesis of the chapter: that the methodological discussion in segregation research could strongly benefit from solutions applied in social mobility research, where similar problems have occurred. Finally, in order to demonstrate the usefulness of the perspective introduced on this subject, some empirical findings are pre-

---

1 In segregation research two dimensions are distinguished: horizontal segregation refers to the fact that women and men work in different occupations. In contrast, the vertical dimension looks at the unequal distribution of women and men across hierarchical levels.

sented on patterns and changes in occupational sex-specific segregation in the EU for the 1990s.

Occupational sex segregation and European gender policies

As pointed out above, institutional contexts and cultural traditions play a crucial role in enabling women to combine employment with family responsibilities. Although the EU Member States show a wide variety of institutional and cultural settings, various efforts have been made by the EU to harmonise these different social arrangements and to create a common basis for the equal treatment of men and women. Generally, the EU equality law defines the principle of equal treatment as a prohibition of discrimination on grounds of sex and marital status (Council Directive76/207/EEC, European Communities 1976). The ultimate goal of equal opportunities is material equality, e.g. an equal distribution of work, care tasks and income between men and women, implying a change in the life of both.

In this context, Rubery (1998: 17) has provided three main arguments for the close relation between employment and gender issues: The first one underlines that employment policy is critical to gender equality, because there is little evidence that women will achieve greater power without first improving their position in the labour market. The second argument is connected with the goal of high employment in Europe that will not be achieved without further and major expansion of women's involvement in the labour market. The last argument arises from the fact that employment does not only have a productive but also a social reproductive role. In this respect, it is essential that social structures are in flux and that employment policies need to be integrated into a broader agenda, involving a more articulated development of employment, family and welfare policy.

With respect to occupational sex segregation it is not surprising that the observed time stability increases the importance of ›closing gender gaps‹[2] in the EU. Particularly, ›desegregation‹ of the labour market has become one of the main objectives of the European Action Programme for Equal Op-

---

2 Defined as gaps in employment and unemployment, gender segregation or unequal payment.

portunities and the European Employment Strategy.[3] With this strategy a new procedure for the annual adoption of a series of employment guidelines was established which created an unexpected window of opportunity to strengthen equality between women and men as the fourth pillar of the employment guidelines. In 1999, the Commission additionally introduced the term ›gender mainstreaming‹[4] as a central element of employment which provided a further impetus to the integration of equal opportunities into the employment framework. In the guideline the Commission called for ›positive‹ action in three areas: first, tackling gender gaps through active state support for an increased employment of women. Second, improving the reconciliation of work and family life (most notably by raising levels of child care provision), and, third, making it easier for women to re-enter the labour market after an absence (by improving their access to vocational training). At the Lisbon summit 2000, the Council re-emphasised the gender dimension to employment, by calling on the one hand for a national target to increase the availability of childcare facilities and, on the other hand, for a specific overall target to increase women's employment from 51% in 2000 to 60% by 2010 (European Commission 2001: 15). In this context, the issue of equal opportunities in employment is not only a normative goal on which the EU has focused over many decades. Political actors have also supported various studies to visualise the existing ›gender gaps‹ and to make the Member States and their citizens more sensitive to this issue.

Nevertheless, statements regarding the European efforts towards an improvement of gender equality, particularly on the labour market, are diverse. Critical voices underline that, as far as the substance of policy is concerned, the operation of the EU did not intend to reduce unemployment or improve the equality between the sexes. In particular, the actual aim of raising the female employment rate up to 60% by the year 2010 is seen as at once ambitious and problematic. It is ambitious, because reach-

---

3 With this strategy, set out in 1997 by the Council, a four-pillar structure (employability, entrepreneurship, adaptability and equal opportunities) has been introduced for employment policy guidelines.

4 This term refers to the systematic integration of respective situations, priorities and needs of women and men in all policies. The aim is to promote gender equality by taking into account the effects of all general policies and measures on the respective situations of women and men. It has been implemented during the fourth action programme of the European Commission (European Commission (1996), COM (96) 67 final, 21.2.1996).

ing it would take female employment in the EU to a level never seen before. It is also problematic, because it can be doubted whether a higher participation rate alone will really lead to more equality between the sexes in the labour market.

Summarising these arguments, ›equality in employment‹ is obviously a vague term that has more facets than the mere increase of the female employment rate. It is questionable whether or not ›marginally employed‹ women and the so-called ›silent reserve‹ could be calculated adequately and should be covered by the indicator used in the discussion. On account of this problem, a high female participation rate scarcely ever guarantees that all women are active in full-time employment.

A further objection stems from the diverse dimensions and meanings of the term ›equal opportunities‹. In our opinion, this term should not be restricted to the ›level of employment‹, but should attach the same importance to aspects of ›quality‹, ›intensity‹ and ›continuity‹ of employment. The term ›quality‹ is used here as a synonym for different aspects of sex segregation, including the social standing of jobs, which women typically attain during their life course, the status and prestige they gain, and the income they receive. The kind of work and the positions available for women are often linked with the dimension of ›intensity‹ of a job, which refers to the number of hours that employees typically work. Finally, the third dimension concerns the ›continuity‹ of work and therefore the aspect of how frequently women interrupt employment over their life-course and in which way their labour-market participation is affected by familial burdens.

The interplay of these dimensions is of particular importance, because only a focus on the various aspects of inequality will guarantee the equal treatment of the future female workforce in the labour market, as envisioned by the EU. In this context, such a differentiated view could elucidate, more clearly than a single indicator, whether women and men really have equal labour market chances or if there is rather a more sophisticated division of roles. Furthermore, it would yield information about the effectiveness of the various gender policies which, first and foremost, should bring into focus the decrease of inequality in various dimensions.

Occupational sex segregation in the scientific discussion

Since the 1960s, there has been a continuous scientific interest in aspects of sex-specific occupational segregation in Europe as well as in the U.S. The growing concern on the subject culminated in numerous articles, books and studies in the 1980s and 1990s. Thereby, different research strands have been developed, which treat aspects of the phenomenon both methodologically and theoretically and comprise analyses from micro- and/or macro-sociological perspectives. Perhaps even more importantly, researchers have brought to light the social and economic cost of occupational sex segregation. First, there has been tremendous research on the relationship between segregation and the gender wage gap (Tienda et al. 1987, England et al. 1988, Blau et al. 2002); in later years, also the relationships between other conditions of work (fewer benefits etc.) have been analysed.

One core aspect of sex segregation research is related to the question why change in occupational sex segregation has been so slow and why certain occupations have remained ›hypersegregated‹ (Charles and Grusky 2004). For the U.S. labour market, Gross (1968) was the first who documented the remarkable stability of occupational sex segregation. Numerous researchers followed over the next three decades showing that occupational sex segregation has indeed declined since the 1970s, but at a modest rate. This confirms the view of sex-specific occupational segregation as a time-stable phenomenon not only in the United States but also worldwide (Blau and Hendricks 1979, England 1981, Beller 1984, Jacobs 1989, Jacobsen 1994).

Over the last decades, a number of studies have focused on explanations of country-specific patterns of occupational segregation, taking into account several social and economic factors, such as the female employment rate and the level of modernisation etc. (e.g. Oppenheimer 1970, Semyonov 1980, Cotter et al. 1998). These cross-national studies open new perspectives and tasks in the analysis of occupational sex segregation and, as underlined by Anker (1998: 10) »They help to identify the extent to which various aspects of occupational segregation by sex are universal in nature as opposed to being specific to a particular culture, country or region.«

Table 1. Constructed cross-tabulation of broad occupational groups by sex

sex	occupational groups			total
	1	2	3	
		occupational chances		
male	500	⟶ 150 ⟶	50	700
female	50	↓ sex typing 150	100	300
total	550	300	150	1000
		occupational structure		female share in employment

Nevertheless, the comparative approach of occupational sex segregation also suffers from various problems, such as the comparability of data sets and the harmonisation of the classifications used. One of the most important methodological problems has been the implementation of an adequate measurement of the concept. In this respect, numerous researchers have proposed various indices and techniques which all claim to measure ›segregation‹. As a result, a long and disparate debate has started about the construction of such an index of segregation, whereas in practice most available methods and indices have not considerably improved over the last 30 years.

To illustrate the reasons underlying the construction of different segregation indices and to support the central argument of the contribution that, besides the methodological debate, a theoretical refinement is necessary, it seems useful to have a closer look at the structure of a cross-tabulation, which is typically used in empirical segregation research.

When looking at the constructed cross-tabulation (see Table 1), showing the distribution of men and women across different occupations, a number of different research questions on which an empirical analysis of segregation could focus can be distinguished. Even though the analysis can concentrate on four topics, only the last two mentioned are of interest in segregation research:

- The share of females in all employed persons (column marginal);
- The size of occupational groups (row marginal);
- The share of females as the total number of employed persons in each occupation (›column percentages‹);

– The ›chances‹ of male and female employees to work in one of the occupational groups (›row percentages‹).

Similar tables, based on ›real observed data‹, can be quite large and complex (depending on the number of occupations). Due to this, a first extension to the cross-tabulation approach are segregation indices trying to
summarise the observable amount of segregation into one single number.

In spite of the discussion about the ›best‹ index, there is no doubt that
in most macro-sociological work the index of dissimilarity (D) – proposed
1955 by Duncan and Duncan – is most frequently used but also most frequently criticised (Gross 1968, Jonung 1984, Jacobs 1993). The index is
based on the understanding that sex segregation means a different distribution of women and men across occupational categories; the more equal the
distribution, the less the segregation. In this respect, D measures the sum
of the absolute differences in women's and men's distribution across occupations. From the mathematical formula it is evident that D equals 0 in the
case of complete equality (where women's employment is distributed similarly to men's across occupational categories) and 1 in the case of complete
dissimilarity (where women and men are in totally different occupational
groups):

$$D = \frac{1}{2} \sum_{j=1}^{J} \left| \frac{F_j}{F} - \frac{M_j}{M} \right|$$

with

F   total number of females in employment;
M   total number of males in employment;
F_j number of employed females in occupation j;
M_j number of employed males in occupation j;
J   number of occupations.

Irrespective of the widespread use of D, the index has come under criticism very soon as inappropriate for measuring occupational segregation by
sex, especially over time (Watts 1990, Siltanen et al. 1995). The common
critique is D's dependence on the size of categories of the classification
used. As a consequence, both, changes in the occupational structure of the
labour force and the extent to which occupations are feminised, influence
D. From a purely methodological perspective, however, a measure that is

only sensitive to the sex composition of occupational groups and its changes would be more favourable.

The first attempt to avoid the marginal dependence of D and, consequently, to control for changes over time in the relative size of an occupational group has been made by Gibbs (1965) who proposed the standardised index of dissimilarity (D_{st}).

$$D_{st} = \frac{1}{2} \sum_{j=1}^{J} \left| \frac{\frac{F_j}{T_j}}{\sum_{j=1}^{J} \frac{F_j}{T_j}} - \frac{\frac{M_j}{T_j}}{\sum_{j=1}^{J} \frac{M_j}{T_j}} \right|$$

with

T_j total number of males and females in the jth occupation ($T_j = M_j + F_j$);
all other parameters are defined as before.

The basic principle of D_{st} is to treat all occupations as equal in size. In this way the occupational structure is held constant, such that changes in D_{st} over time or between countries can only be due to differences in the sex composition of occupations. Unfortunately, an often undesired consequence of this procedure is that it gives the same weight to changes in the percentage of female workers in all occupations, small and large occupations alike. This means that, as Kalter (2000: 7) pointed out, »…the change of the size of D_{st} is strongly influenced by changes in the feminisation of small occupations«. Moreover, Charles and Grusky (1995) have shown that the standardisation procedure used for the construction of D_{st} is not successful in achieving the goal of ›marginal independence‹.

Due to the presented critique of D and D_{st}, several other segregation indices have been proposed in recent years. To mention only the well-known indices: there are the WE index, proposed by the OECD for a report on women and employment (OECD 1980), and the sex-ratio index (SR) developed by Hakim for the United Kingdom's Department of Employment (Hakim 1979). Both are based on D and, for this reason, they give rise to more or less the same problems. Another example of a ›new index‹ is the IP index of Karmel and MacLachlan (1988) that, as Watts (1992) has shown, could also be seen as a weighted form of D.

To sum up, it should be critically underlined that all presented measures share the dependency on the occupational structure of economy. Particularly, none of the traditional approaches provide an entirely satisfactory method of measuring sex segregation over time or between countries. Moreover, it is possible that these indices may even point in different directions for the same changes in segregation structures.

Against this background, the most promising approach to the twin problem of measuring and explaining levels of occupational sex segregation across countries or over time is based on log-linear techniques (see Handl 1984, Charles and Grusky 1995, 2004, Kalter 2000). Log-linear modelling has for a long time been a standard procedure in stratification research – like social mobility analysis (Erikson and Goldthorpe 1992, Müller 1990, Müller and Pollak 2004). The biggest advantage of the log-linear approaches is that they are, while building up on odds and odds ratios, independent of the marginal distributions of a segregation table. As a consequence, they are perspective invariant, which means that they focus on both dimensions of the cross classification.

In earlier work by Handl (1984), log-linear techniques have been used to carry out a decomposition of changes in segregation, measured by D, into two parts: namely changes caused by variations in the size of occupational structures and changes caused by a reduction or a growth of the female share in occupations. Later on, Charles (1992) and Charles and Grusky (1995) adopted ANOAS-models, originally developed for the analysis of social mobility tables, for the analysis of so-called ›segregation regimes‹. These techniques, which, in the meantime, have been applied in a series of international comparative studies (Nermo 1999, Chang 2000, Charles and Grusky 2004), allow not only for a description of patterns of segregation but also for a thorough statistical analysis of changes in occupational sex segregation. In this context, Charles and Grusky (1995) underline that the purpose of using log-linear modelling in the field of sex segregation research is clearly not to construct a scalar index. Nevertheless, due to the fact that there seems to be a demand for summary measures in this research context, they propose a scalar index (A) derived from a log-multiplicative model.

Even though the methodological weakness of single number indices seemed to be solved by indices based on log-linear methods, a central ambiguity in segregation research has, in our opinion, not been tackled. This refers to the fact that the different indices have been proposed with varying connotations, and their authors have rarely specified the term ›segregation‹ precisely. Consequently, besides the methodological improvements, a clarification of the concept of segregation, like in mobility research, is necessary to avoid further misunderstandings in the interpretation of research results. Thereafter, also the ›deviant‹ indices would probably be very helpful – especially in the context of more politically oriented research. To underline this argumentation, the next section briefly summarises the theoretical and methodological developments in social mobility research and tries to relate them to the difficulties in sex segregation research.

Learning from advances in mobility research

Social mobility and segregation research are based on data of a similar structure. In both areas very simple cross-tabulations are the starting point of a more elaborate analysis. In social mobility, it is a cross classification of the current class position (using occupations and social status as a backbone) of sons or daughters by social class origin (e.g. social class position of the father). In segregation research, a similar occupational variable (mostly based on the ISCO88) is used, but is splitted only by a dichotomous variable, namely ›sex‹ (see Table 1).

At the beginning of mobility research, the central interest has been the measurement of the ›amount of mobility‹, summing up the number of persons outside of the main diagonal of the mobility table (upward and downward mobility). Very soon it was detected that in international or historical comparisons this indicator of the ›amount of openness in a society‹ was heavily influenced by the strength of changes in the occupational distribution between father and son/daughter's generation. To solve the problem, a decomposition of ›total mobility‹ into ›structural‹ mobility, forced by changes in the social structure, and the so-called ›pure‹ or ›exchange‹ mobility has been proposed (Yasuda 1964, Ramsøy 1966). This decomposition (similarly to the differentiation between upward and downward mobility) was obviously only a very rough analysis of the huge amount of information included in a detailed mobility table. As a consequence, various attempts were made to compare mobility patterns in more detail. One strategy has been the summation of differences in the mobility chances of children with differing social origin into one single number (usually the index of dissimilarity). Due to the fact that a mobility table allows for k(k-1)/2 independent comparisons and the basis of the comparison remains arbitrary, this strategy has been seldomly used.[5] More common has been a detailed inspection of mobility patterns across the cells of the mobility table using different indices.

Also in mobility research a long lasting methodological discussion started, because it was soon realised that not only the highly aggregated mobility rates, but also the indices used for the detailed comparisons are dependent on structural changes in the marginals of a mobility table (Yasuda 1964, Tyree 1973). Particularly, the so-called ›association-index‹ (Glass 1954, Ramsøy 1953, Carlsson 1958) did not achieve the goal of marginal independence. This problem was finally solved by Goodman (1965, 1979) and Hauser (1978), who introduced log-linear modelling into mobility research, which has been subsequently expanded by the development of log-multiplicative models (Hout 1983).

However, it was only Goldthorpe (1987) and Erikson and Goldthorpe (1992), who applied this new advanced technique for intensive comparative research and introduced a clear theoretical distinction between ›social mobility‹ (absolute mobility) and ›social fluidity‹ (relative mobility). In this theoretical refinement, ›social fluidity‹ means the degree of relative inequality, according to class origins, in a person's chances of acquiring a better, rather than a poorer, class position. It is conceived as a measure of the permeability of a class system, independent of the fact how many persons are found in each of the classes. In consequence, ›social mobility‹ has been defined as the amount of directly observable mobility, resulting from ›patterns of fluidity‹ and the size of different classes.

To sum up, the advances in mobility research have two bases: one is the methodologically driven progress in statistical modelling, the other is the theoretical refinement of the term ›mobility‹, which now combines different measurement and modelling procedures with different theoretical concepts.

With respect to occupational sex segregation, in our opinion, particularly with the work of Charles and Grusky (2004) and their proposal of a marginal free A-Index as well as the application of advanced log-multiplicative modelling, the crucial methodological improvements have been done. Nevertheless, a thorough review of the literature shows that a

---

5 In the analysis of a segregation table, only one single comparison (between women and men) exhausts all the available information.

convincing conceptual clarification is still missing. This is an unsatisfactory situation at least for two reasons: First, it remains unclear for the discussion which aspects are covered by the term segregation: is it used for differences in the observed distributions between the sexes or for the description of the underlying structure of unequal treatment (which results in differences in sex typing of occupations). Second, particularly in a politically driven analysis of occupational sex segregation in different countries, not only the marginal free, but also the marginal dependent measures of changes and differences in the distribution between two groups could be of outmost importance. For example, for political recommendations it makes a difference if the share of females rises in a very small or a large occupational group. Consequently, despite the fact that scholars have called for a marginal free measure, it has to be asked whether this is always the adequate method. As Weeden (1998: 486) has underlined, it always depends on the goal of the analysis and research should be aware of the central research question and the ›best‹ measurement before preferring ›any‹ index.

As pointed out previously, the term ›segregation‹ is used with very different connotations: some authors, for example, restrict their understanding of the term to the amount of, what we would like to call, ›sex typing‹ (mostly measured with D_{st}) of occupations. This aspect identifies the gender composition of an occupation or a sector, i.e. in how far it is typically male or female. Other researchers, however, are more focused on the unequal distribution of men and women over the whole occupational structure. This aspect studies the degree of ›sex-specific occupational chances‹ (mostly measured with D) of male and female employees, taking into account the ›size‹-aspect (or the weight) of each occupational category.

Based on this examination, it becomes clear that the term ›segregation‹ is imprecise in its meaning and should therefore be kept as a generic term, covering different aspects of sex-specific differences. Furthermore, when comparing the described aspects of occupational sex segregation with the different aspects of social mobility, in our opinion, a similar theoretical distinction could be implemented. As mentioned above, the terms ›social mobility‹ and ›social fluidity‹ are reserved for different theoretical and methodological perspectives and procedures. Analogously to this, in segregation research a comparable distinction could be drawn, differentiating between ›patterns of sex typing across occupations‹ (similar to ›social fluidity‹) and ›sex-specific differences in occupational chances‹ (similar to the concept of

›social mobility‹). The measurement of these dimensions does not necessarily require the use of sophisticated log-linear procedures. The proposed perspective could also be followed by using different indices, selected according to the different dimension of segregation which they measure.

Occupational sex segregation throughout the 1990s – some empirical findings

In the following section, an attempt is made to demonstrate the usefulness of the proposed theoretical differentiation for empirical research. The results are based on the European Labour Force Survey (ELFS) covering the period 1995–2000.[6] Apart from the socio-demographic variables (e.g. sex and age-cohorts), information on the labour market position, in particular on the occupational and sector position, of employed persons for fifteen EU Member States (the ›old‹ Member States) was also available. The analysis is exclusively based on ›occupation‹ measured by the ISCO88 classification on the 3-digit level, which allows for a distinction of 116 different occupational categories. If necessary, it has been collapsed to the 1-digit level with 9 major occupational groups. The fundamental logic of this classification mainly derives from an analysis of skill requirements included in the occupational categories. This means that a ›lower‹ code implicates a higher skill in the sense of »the ability to carry out the tasks and duties of a particular job« (ILO 1988: 2). Even though, the concept of ›occupation‹ and its specific content differs between national and/or cultural contexts and the mapping of national classifications into the ISCO88 is sometimes problematic and defective, the variable is one of the most differentiated and reliable measures of labour market structures. Despite controversial opinions expressed in the literature,[7] our own studies on the dependency of the results on the use of a more or less differentiated version of the clas-

---

6 The ELFS was kindly made available to us by the FENICs research group of the University Paris X (Nanterre) in the framework of the EU funded project *Female Employment and Family Formation in National Institutional Contexts (FENICs)*. For detailed information see: http://www.warwick.ac.uk/ier/fenics/index.html.

7 While Ganzeboom and Treiman (1996: 210) suggest the use of the most detailed 4-digit level, Elias (1997: 3) pointed out that »... coding/recoding studies indicate that the submajor group [2 digit] level of ISCO-88 represents a useful level at which to undertake comparative analyses of occupational data.«

Figure 1. Patterns of sex-typing of occupations for seven selected EU countries (percentage of women in a given occupational group), in 2000 (ISCO88 1-digit)

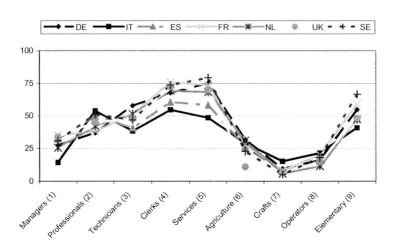

sification convinced us to use the ISCO88 on the more detailed 3-digit level, whenever possible.

Patterns of sex-typing

Starting with the question which occupations are ›typically‹ male or female, the simplest way to discover the dimension of occupational ›sex typing‹ is to look at the share of women and men employed in different occupations or sectors. Figure 1 is an example for the ›sex typing profiles‹ of seven selected EU-countries on the level of nine major occupational groups (ISCO88, 1-digit).

First of all, it is interesting that the patterns of sex typing are very similar for the countries selected. For example, clerks (4) and service-orientated (5) occupations are highly feminised, with female participation rates varying from 76% (France) to 55% (Italy) and 79% (Sweden) to 48% (Italy), respectively. Hence, it is possible to speak of a ›feminisation‹ of these occupational groups, because more than half of the employed persons are women. The mostly male-dominated occupations are those of the producing industry (crafts (7) and machine operators (8)) as well as agriculture (6). This confirms results of earlier studies indicating that feminised occupa-

Figure 2. Distribution of employed men and women (%) among occupations: Germany and Spain, in 2000 (ISCO88 1-digit); see text for details

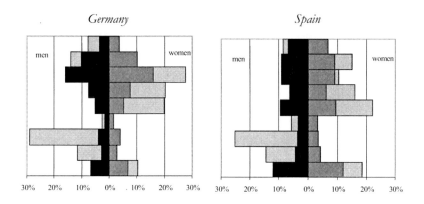

tions are often associated with attributes of ›serving‹ and ›caring‹, whereas men's occupations are associated with attributes of ›physical strength‹ and ›power‹. As Anker et al. (2003) pointed out, it is especially striking how sex stereotypes in society about appropriate roles for women and men are replicated in the labour market. They examined that in 1990 approximately 50% of all workers were in gender-dominated occupations.

Nevertheless, as the presented results reveal, there are also some occupations (like professional, technical and the elementary occupations) that can be classified as ›integrated‹ in almost all countries.

Patterns of sex-specific occupational chances

So far, the above-presented figure gives an idea of the sex composition of different occupational groups across countries. A second possibility to look at occupational sex segregation is to examine the distribution of women and men across occupations. This perspective takes the size of the each occupation into account, so that it is feasible to explore how ›evenly‹ women or men are spread across all occupational groups and in how far they are ›ghettoised‹ into specific occupational groups.

To illustrate this aspect, it is possible to apply the well-known age-pyramid used in demography. Figure 2 exemplarily presents the structure of sex-specific occupational chances for Germany and Spain in 2000 on the basis of the ISCO88 1-digit. The light grey fields mark the differences in occupational chances between the two sexes. The sum of the light grey fields on the left is equal to the sum on the right side and corresponds to the value of D. For each country, the figures yield a detailed insight into the structure of sex-specific occupational chances, showing the chances of males (black) and females (dark grey) to access the nine major occupational groups. Even though this graphical presentation is intricate and more difficult to compare across countries, a comparison between Germany and Spain shows similarities as well as country-specific patterns.

Starting with similarities, it can be observed that in both countries women have especially high chances to work in the group of technicians and associate professionals (3), clerks (4), service workers (5) and elementary occupations (9). In contrast, men are very likely to be found in occupations necessitating a ›high qualification‹[8], such as legislators, senior officials and managers (1). Furthermore, occupations for which a lower qualification is sufficient show a predominance of men like those in the major groups 7 (craft and related trades workers) and 8 (plant and machine operators and assemblers).

Nevertheless, there are also some peculiarities concerning the specific labour market structure in each country. For example, in Spain, the percentage of women who are employed in the first occupational category is higher than in Germany. Moreover, an overrepresentation of women could also be found in the group of professionals (2). On the one hand, the percentage and the overrepresentation of women in the third occupational category (technicians) are much higher in Germany than in Spain. On the other hand, there are fewer women employed and overrepresented in the last occupational category (elementary occupations).

Due to the fact that the graphical methods used above are limited, particularly on the ISCO88 3-digit level, it is obvious why it makes sense to use single number indices for comparative purposes. Thus, for an overview of segregation and its different aspects across countries, such measures are in the following calculated for the occupational chances using the index of dissimilarity (D) and for the aspect of sex typing using the standardised index of dissimilarity (D_{st}).

---

8 It is necessary to remark that the hierarchy of the ISCO88 is problematic and not quite correct. For example, the seventh group of the ISCO88 also contains highly qualified occupations, like a master craftsmen.

Figure 3. Positioning of European Member States in the »segregation space«, in 2000
(ISCO88 3-digit)[9]

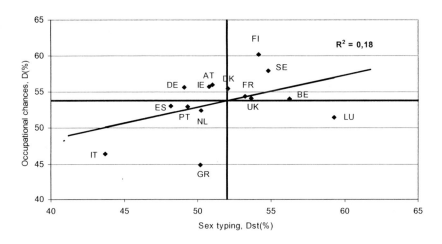

Based on these results it is possible to visualise the positioning of European Member States with respect to the different aspects of sex segregation in a scatter plot. Thereby, the vertical line in Figure 3 represents the average degree of sex typing and the horizontal line the average degree of the dissimilarity of occupational chances for all countries.

First of all, only a moderate correlation can be observed between the two distinguished aspects of segregation ($r^2=0.18$). Furthermore, the graph discovers two clusters, which compose the extreme poles: the Mediterranean countries (Italy and Greece), characterised by very low levels of sex-specific occupational chances and sex typing (at least Italy), and the Northern countries (Finland and Sweden), which are located fairly high in both dimension. Finally, a third cluster is formed by a big group of countries centred on the averages of both dimensions. In this case it is, on the one hand, possible to distinguish between countries with above-average levels of occupational chances and below average levels of sex typing (Austria, Germany, Ireland) and countries with below-average levels of dissimilarity of occupational chances, but fairly low levels of sex typing (Spain, Portugal

9 We exclude occupations with N<10 to avoid an influence of very small groups, particularly when looking at changes over time (see Table 2).

and the Netherlands). On the other hand, some countries (Denmark, France, the United Kingdom and Belgium) are characterised by above-average levels of dissimilarity of occupational chances and fairly high levels of sex-typing.

These results confirm previous findings. The Nordic, ›more gender egalitarian‹ countries (like Sweden and Finland) are characterised by very high levels of occupational sex segregation, while the more ›traditional‹ and ›familiaristic‹ countries (like Italy and Greece) have the lowest occupational sex segregation. The only exception is the Iberian Peninsula with Spain and Portugal, which seem to be more adapted to continental European segregation patterns. The high values for the Nordic countries have partly been explained by a fundamental outsourcing of house and family related services, which has created typically female occupations in the labour market (Hansen 1995, Melkas and Anker 1997). For the low values of Southern European countries, however, sufficient explanations are still missing (Molto 1992, Conduto de Sousa 2005).

In this context, it is important to recognise that differences in sex segregation in the labour market cannot be examined without including a discussion of differences between countries on the scale of women's employment. For example, researchers (Charles 1992) have shown that a high female employment rate tends to be connected with high sex segregation in the labour market. Moreover, differences between countries may also be connected with the sensitivity of indices to sectoral composition, to differences in the gender division of labour within sectors and the impact of occupational classification systems (Rubery et al. 2003: 61).[10]

Based on these results the question arises in how far the presented clustering of countries is only an artefact of the indices used. Indeed this could be possible, especially against the background of the discussion of serious deficiencies of single number indices. To check this possibility, correlations are calculated between a series of different indices. They are selected according to the principle that they sum up rather ›differences in chances‹ or ›differences in sex typing‹. To verify the measurement of D, the frequently used IP-index has been calculated. This index is not only very familiar in the scientific literature, but is also used in the statistical monitoring system

---

10 Some authors underline that agriculture should be excluded from the analysis because of its gender blindness (many women are only counting as helping family members and therefore not registered adequately in the occupational classifications).

of the EU.[11] The measurement of the standardised index of dissimilarity (D_{st}) is compared with results for the A-Index based on log-linear modelling.

As expected, the correlation coefficients for the four selected indices show a high and significant association between the values of D and IP (0.99) measuring the differences in ›occupational chances‹, as well as between D_{st} and A (0.83) measuring the amount of ›sex typing‹. All other correlations, which measure different aspects of segregation, are much lower.

These findings underline that the theoretically driven differentiation between ›sex-typing‹ and ›occupational chances‹ as distinct but correlated dimensions of segregation is justified. The distinction is not only confirmed by the traditional indices of dissimilarity, but also by the use of alternative indices of segregation. Taking this result into account, it should be possible to systematise previous and sometimes divergent findings of developments in sex segregation more adequately.

Stability and change of occupational segregation during the 1990s

As already mentioned at the beginning, the above described distribution of men and women in the labour market at a specific point in time is the result of an ongoing process of employment shifts due to the modernisation of national economies and societies in general. Thereby, the transition from industrial to more service-orientated economies opens new employment perspectives, especially for women who usually dominate the field of service occupations. But what are the implications of these processes of social change for the development of occupational segregation and its different aspects?

In order to pursue the idea that, in particular for a political evaluation of gender equality, both changes in the unequal distributions of male and female employees and changes in the amount of sex typing of occupations are important, it would be necessary to look at changes in both aspects of segregation in parallel. This could be approached in different ways: First, by using D and performing a decomposition of changes in this measure (see Blau and Hendricks 1979, Handl 1984). But this procedure cannot be

---

11 Also the European Commission (the EMCO indicator group) proposed two statistical indicators for the continuous observation and measurement of sex-specific occupational segregation.

applied in a simple way when taking more then two time-points into account. Another possibility is to look at both aspects of segregation using different indices and to compare the directions of changes for the different measures over a time period.

In the following, the latter strategy is pursued, looking at changes in the aspects of ›segregation‹ of EU Member States for the years 1995, 1998 and 2000 (see Table A1 in the appendix). As D and D_{st} are most commonly used in literature and their correlation with more complicated indices is high, further results are only presented for these simple, well-known indices. This decision also ensures the comparability of the results with prior findings.

Starting with measures for ›sex-specific chances‹, it is possible to differentiate between:

– countries where the distribution of male and female employees (i.e. the occupational chances) has become more and more similar (Denmark, Finland, Germany, the UK and Luxembourg),
– countries which show almost constant degrees in occupational chances (Italy, the Netherlands, France, Greece and Sweden), and
– countries where the occupational chances for men and women have become more and more unequal (Austria, Belgium, Ireland, Portugal and Spain).

The main trends with respect to ›sex typing‹ are less clear. In most of the countries examined, only more or less oscillating values could be found. Just in two countries (Spain and Germany), the sex typing of occupations has constantly decreased over the whole time period.

Based on these findings, it is hard to speak about a consistent trend of ›segregation patterns‹ in Europe during the 1990s. However, it is interesting that this ›inconsistency‹ in the five-year period is in many respects comparable with patterns found by Jacobs and Lim (1995) for the period 1960–1980.

So far, the development of sex typing and occupational chances has been examined separately. Now the question is raised in how far a correlation exists between changes in both aspects. The following Table 2 shows that only in five countries coherent trends took place:[12] in the case of Germany, Denmark (and Finland) a decreasing trend over the whole pe-

---

12 We speak from a change when there is approximately 1% increase or decrease in the values of the segregation indices.

Table 2. Direction of change for both aspects of sex segregation, 1995, 1998, 2000 (ISCO88 3-digit)

| | | Direction of change in differences in occupational chances | | |
		Decrease (–)	Constant (=)	Increase (+)
Direction of change in sex typing	–	DE, DK, (FI)*	IT, NL	ES
	=	UK, (LU)	FR, GR	PT
	+		(SE)*	AT, BE, IE

Notes: *Trends for the Nordic countries FI and SE are only measured between 1998 and 2000 due to missing data for the year 1995.
Source: ELFS, SFE4, own calculations, only categories with N>10 are included.

riod of time and for both aspects could be observed, while in Austria, Belgium and Ireland the values have increased. In France and Greece, however, nothing has changed more or less over the whole period.

For the rest of the countries, more or less opposed developments are found: In three countries a decrease of sex typing is accompanied by a constant level of differences in occupational chances (Italy and the Netherlands), or an increase in the differences (Spain). In Portugal, however, an increase in the differences in occupational chances goes along with a more or less constant value for the aspect of sex typing. The opposite could be observed for the United Kingdom and Luxembourg, where a constant degree of sex typing is combined with a decrease in the sex-specific differences in occupational chances.

The observed discontinuity of segregation and the divergent development in its aspects is also a well-known fact in the segregation literature (Blackburn et al. 1993). However, the results were predominantly ascribed to measurement problems linked with the indices used, and have been seen as an argument for the search of an ›ideal‹ index.

Against the background of the theoretical refinement of the concept of segregation and the careful selection of the indices applied, the argumentation that the ›inconsistency‹ is a result of measurement problems seems short-sighted. It is more convincing that it is a result of complex developments in segregation patterns. It seems logical that a reduction of sex typing does not necessarily immediately lead to an adjustment in the distribution of men and women over all occupations. It is, for example, important where the change takes place: is it predominantly in shrinking occupational areas, or does the decrease of sex typing take place in expanding areas.

Obviously, from a political point of view the ›equality effect‹ seems to be higher and more fundamental in the latter situation. However, focusing only on this aspect seems to be purely conditionally useful, because improvements could be signalled even when nothing has changed with respect to the sex typing in an occupation, but when the change is mainly caused by a shrinking number of persons employed in this occupation.

Consequently, it should be underlined that for a careful analysis of gender inequalities, both aspects should be taken into account. This avoids the drawing of false conclusions and seems to be the most adequate approach for capturing the complexity of occupational sex segregation.

Conclusion

As pointed out above, sex-based occupational segregation is one aspect of the inequality of opportunity that men and women face in society, and it negatively affects the efficiency of the labour market as a whole. Yet, political efforts to reduce such obstacles and to realise more equality, such as the guidelines of the European Commission, tackle a very complicated matter.

Against this background, the aims of this contribution have been twofold. First, attention has been devoted to the theoretical and methodological clarification of ›occupational sex segregation‹, applying ideas and developments originating from mobility research. In this respect, it has been demonstrated that social mobility and segregation research have comparable starting points: in both research strands the focus is on social inequality between different groups in society, and also from a methodological point of view parallels can be drawn. As a result, in analogy to ›social fluidity‹ and ›social mobility‹, the aspects of ›sex-typing‹ and ›occupational chances‹ have been distinguished as distinct but correlated aspects of segregation. The benefit of this theoretical clarification is that some of the disadvantages of traditional indices, particularly their marginal dependency, are no longer important. Instead, it becomes clear that the search for the ›right‹ measurement (i.e. the selection of the adequate index) is highly dependent on the focus of interest. Furthermore, in a political context, a marginal dependent approach seems to be sometimes more suitable and fruitful to evaluate improvements in gender equality. Specifically, it has been argued that, when focusing only on a comparison between the structures of ›sex-typing profiles‹ between countries, the number of persons that are privileged or suffer from the inequality relation is not taken into account

The second part of the contribution has focused on the empirical evidence of the proposed theoretical distinction. For this purpose, patterns and changes in the amount of sex typing and of sex-specific occupational chances during the 1990s have been analysed for 15 European Member states. A number of well-known and somehow surprising results are validated by the findings obtained: Nordic countries are characterised by high levels of occupational sex segregation, while in most Southern European countries the lowest levels could be found.

Due to the fact that societies and economies are not static but subject to a continuous process of social change, the development of occupational segregation and its different aspects have been examined in a further step. Interestingly, no uniform trend in occupational sex segregation has been found across the European Member States at the end of the 1990s. In most countries the values are often, at least in one aspect, more or less constant, which has also been confirmed by previous studies. In this framework, Spain, characterised by a decrease in sex typing and an increase in occupational chances, seems to be a ›deviant‹ case. The result might be explained by an atypical process of occupational change, particularly in the size of occupations. Nevertheless, a ›final‹ clarification whether this result has ›empirical‹ evidence or is an artefact of the methods used cannot be undertaken with an index-based analysis. Here, thorough in-depth case studies using advanced multivariate methods are necessary, which are better suited to examine in detail the relation between sex typing and occupational chances.

Finally, the contribution has shown that an index-based analysis of occupational sex segregation can be a useful starting point for the understanding of sex segregation patterns. However, as Charles and Grusky (2004: 73) pointed out »... it is only rarely an appropriate end point«. This is of crucial importance, particularly when policy makers classify countries, using only a single index, with respect to the ›advantaged‹ or ›disadvantaged‹ situation of women, and base recommendations on such measures which are often short-sighted.

Appendix

Table A1. Development of occupational sex segregation in 15 EU Member States (ISCO88 3-digit)

Country	Sex-typing of occupations (D_{st})				Occupational chances (D)			
	1995	1998	2000	Trend	1995	1998	2000	Trend
Austria	42.94	51.06	50.78	+	48.75	56.20	55.68	+
Belgium	53.71	53.26	56.23	+	52.84	53.30	54.05	+
Denmark	54.36	55.33	52.08	–	61.12	57.40	55.39	–
Finland	–	57.96	54.16	–	–	61.74	60.25	–
France	52.59	52.73	53.23	=	54.47	54.75	54.38	=
Germany	49.96	49.81	49.09	–	56.77	56.22	55.58	–
Greece	49.94	50.56	50.18	=	44.20	45.57	44.87	=
Ireland	45.63	–	51.01	+	53.47	–	55.94	+
Italy	45.22	43.32	43.68	–	46.74	46.26	46.36	=
Luxembourg	59.39	59.46	59.24	=	54.79	54.49	51.40	–
Netherlands	51.96	49.85	50.23	–	52.56	52.22	52.41	=
Portugal	49.49	47.21	49.31	=	49.46	50.84	52.96	+
Spain	49.76	49.68	48.16	–	52.05	52.87	53.05	+
Sweden	–	53.89	54.80	+	–	58.10	57.95	=
United Kingdom	53.81	53.41	53.65	=	55.84	55.21	54.13	–

Trend Symbols: – decrease, + increase, = constant

Notes: Particular for the Nordic countries, no data was available for the year 1995 and for Ireland 1998.

Source: ELFS, SFE4, own calculations only categories with N>10 are included.

References

Anker, R. (1998). *Gender and Jobs: Sex Segregation of Occupations in the World*, Geneva: International Labour Organization (ILO).

Anker, R./Malkas, H./Korten, A. (2003). *Gender-based Occupational Segregation in the 1990s* (ILO Working Paper 16), Geneva: ILO.

Beller, A. (1982). »Occupational segregation by sex: determinants and changes«, *Journal of Human Resources*, vol. 17, no. 3, pp. 371–392.

Beller, A. (1984). »Trends in occupational segregation by sex and race 1960–1981«, in B. Reskin (ed.), *Sex Segregation in the Workplace: Trends, Explanations, and Remedies*, Washington: National Academy Press, pp. 11–26.

Blackburn, R./Jarman, J./Siltanen, J. (1993). »The analysis of occupational gender segregation over time and place: considerations of measurement and some new evidence«, *Work, Employment and Society*, vol. 7, no. 3, pp. 335–362.

Blau, F./Ferber, M./Winkler, A. (2002). *The Economics of Women, Men and Work* (4th edition), Prentice Hall: Upper Saddle River.

Blau, F./Hendricks, W (1979). »Occupational Segregation by sex: trends and prospects«, *Journal of Human Resources*, vol. 14, no. 2, pp. 197–210.

Carlsson, G. (1958). *Social Mobility and Class Structure*, Lund: Gleerup.

Chang, M. L. (2000). »The evolution of sex segregation regime«, *American Journal of Sociology*, vol. 105, no. 6, pp. 1658–1701.

Charles, M. (1992). »Cross-national variation in occupational sex segregation«, *American Sociological Review*, vol. 57, no. 4, pp. 483–502.

Charles, M./Grusky, D. (1995). »Models for describing the underlying structure of sex segregation«, *American Journal of Sociology*, vol. 100, no. 4, pp. 931–971.

Charles, M./Grusky, D. (2004). *Occupational Ghettos: the Worldwide Segregation of Women and Men*, Stanford: Stanford University Press.

Conduto de Sousa, S. (2005). *Occupational Segregation and Female Labour Force Participation in Southern Europe*, Florence: European University Institute, Working Paper of the Department of Economics, http://www.iser.essex.ac.uk/epunet/2005/docs/pdf/papers/sousa.pdf.

Cotter, D. A./DeFiore, J./Hermsen, J. M./Kowalewski, B./Vanneman, R. (1998). »The demand for female labour«, *American Journal of Sociology*, vol. 103, no. 6, pp. 1673–1712.

Duncan, O./Duncan, B. (1955). »A methodological analysis of segregation indices«, *American Sociological Review*, vol. 20, no. 2, pp. 210–217.

Elias, P. (1997). *Occupational Classification (ISCO-88) – Concepts, Methods, Reliability, Validity and Cross-national Comparability* (Labour market and social policy occasional papers no. 20), Paris: OECD.

England, P. (1981). »Assessing trends in occupational sex segregation 1900–1976«, in I. Berg (ed.), *Sociological Perspectives on the Labor Market*, New York: Academic Press, pp. 273–295.

England, P./Farkas, G./Kilbourne, B./Dou, T. (1988). »Explaining occupational sex segregation and wages. Findings from a model with fixed effects«, *American Sociological Review*, vol. 53, pp. 544–558.

EGGE – EC's Expert Group on Gender and Employment (eds.) (no year). *Equality in the European Employment Strategy. Report of EGGE – EC's Expert Group on Gender and Employment*. Manchester: European Work and Employment Research Centre, Manchester School of Management UMIST.

Erikson, R./Goldthorpe, J. H. (1992). *The Constant Flux: a Study of Class Mobility in Industrial Societies*, Oxford: Clarendon Press.

European Commission (1996). *Égalité entre femmes et hommes*, COM(1996)67 final du 21/02/1996: http://ec.europa.eu/employment_social/equ_opp/gms_de.html.

European Commission (2001). *Chancengleichheit für Frauen und Männer in der Europäischen Union, Jahresbericht 2000*, Luxembourg.

European Communities (1976). Council Directive76/207/EEC: Official Journal L 39 of 14.02.1976: http://europa.eu/scadplus/leg/en/cha/c10906.htm.

Ganzeboom, H./Treiman, D. J. (1996). »Internationally comparable measures of occupational status for the 1988 International Standard Classification of Occupation«, *Social Science Research*, vol. 25, no. 2, pp. 201–239.

Gibbs, J. (1965). »Occupational differentiation of negroes and whites in the United States«, *Social Forces*, vol. 44, no. 2, pp. 159–165.

Glass, D. (1954). *Social Mobility in Britain*, London: Routledge and Kegan Paul.

Goldthorpe, J. H. (1987). *Social Mobility and Class Structure in Modern Britain* (2nd edition), Oxford: Clarendon Press.

Goodman, L. A. (1965). »On the statistical analysis of mobility tables«, *American Journal of Sociology*, vol. 70, no. 5, pp. 564–585.

Goodman, L. A. (1979). »Simple models for the analysis of association in cross-classifications having ordered categories«, *Journal of the American Statistical Association*, vol. 74, pp. 537–552.

Gross, E. (1968). »Plus ça change…? The sexual structure of occupations over time«, *Social Problems*, vol. 16, no. 1, pp. 198–208.

Hakim, C. (1979). *Occupational Segregation – a Study of the Separation of Men and Women's Work in Britain, the United States and Other Countries* (Research Paper No. 9), London: Department of Employment.

Hakim, C. (1993). »Segregated and integrated occupations: a new approach to analysing social change«, *European Sociological Review*, vol. 9, no. 3, pp. 289–314.

Handl, J. (1984). »Chancengleichheit und Segregation: Ein Vorschlag zur Messung ungleicher Chancenstrukturen und ihrer zeitlichen Entwicklung«, *Zeitschrift für Soziologie*, vol. 13, no. 4, pp. 328–345.

Hansen, M. (1995). *Sex Segregation and the Welfare State*, Oslo: Institute for Social Research.

Hauser, R. (1978). »A structural model of the mobility table«, *Social Forces*, vol. 56, pp. 919–953.

Hout, M. (1983). *Mobility Tables*, Beverly Hills, Cal.: Sage Publications.

ILO (1988). *International Standard Classification of Occupations – ISCO-88*, Geneva: ILO.

Jacobs, J. A. (1989). »Long-term trends in occupational segregation by sex«, *American Journal of Sociology*, vol. 95, no. 1, pp. 160–173.

Jacobs, J. A. (1993). »Theoretical and measurement issues in the study of sex segregation in the workplace: research notes«, *European Sociological Review*, vol. 9, no. 3, pp. 325–330.

Jacobs, J. A./Lim, S. (1995). »Trends in occupational and industrial sex segregation in 56 countries«, in J. A. Jacobs (ed.), *Gender Inequality at Work*, Thousand Oaks, Cal.: Sage, pp. 259–293.

Jacobsen, J. P. (1994). »Trends in work force sex segregation 1960–1990«, *Social Science Quarterly*, vol. 75, no. 1, pp. 204–211.

Jonung, C. (1984). »Patterns of occupational segregation by sex in the labor market«, in G. Schmid/R. Weitzel (eds.), *Sex Discrimination and Equal Opportunity. The Labour Market and Employment Policy*, Aldershot: Gower Publishing, pp. 44–68.

Kalter, F. (2000). *Measuring Segregation and Controlling for Independent Variables* (MZES-Working Paper No. 19), Mannheim: Mannheimer Zentrum für Europäische Sozialforschung.

Karmel, T./MacLachlan, M. (1988). »Occupational sex segregation – increasing or decreasing?«, *The Economic Record*, vol. 64, no. 3, pp. 187–195.

Melkas, H./Anker, R. (1997). »Occupational segregation by sex in Nordic countries: An empirical investigation«, *International Labour Review*, vol. 136, no. 3, pp. 341–364.

Molto, M. (1992). *Occupational Segregation in Spain: Final Report*. Report prepared for the Equal Opportunities Unit, European Commission, by the Expert Group of Gender and Employment, Valencia: Universidad de Valencia.

Müller, W. (1990). »Class mobility in industrial nations«, in J. Clark et al. (eds.), *John H. Goldthorpe: Consensus and Controversy*, Basingstoke: Falmer Press, pp. 307–318.

Müller, W./Pollak, R. (2004). »Social mobility in West Germany: the long arms of history discovered«, in R. Breen (ed.), *Social Mobility in Europe*, Oxford: Oxford University Press, pp. 77–114.

Nermo, M. (1999). *Structured by Gender: Patterns of Sex Segregation in the Swedish Labour Market. Historical and Cross-national Comparisons*, Stockholm: Swedish Institute for Social Research, (Dissertation series no. 41).

OECD (1980). *Women and Employment*, Paris: OECD.

Oppenheimer, V. K. (1970). *The Female Force in the United States*, Berkley: University of California Press.

Ramsøy, N. R. (1953). *Recent Trends in Occupational Mobility*, Glencoe, Ill.: Free Press.

Ramsøy, N. R. (1966). »Changes in rates and forms of mobility«, in N. J. Smelser/S. M. Lipset (eds.), *Social Structure and Mobility in Economic Development*, Chicago: Aldine, pp. 213–234.

Rubery, J. (1998). *Gender Mainstreaming in European Employment Policy*. A report by the European Commission's group of experts on gender and employment in the framework of the fourth action programme for equal opportunities for women and men, Manchester: Manchester School of Management UMIST.

Rubery, J./Emerek, R./Figueiredo, H./González, P./Gonäs, L. (2003). *Indicators on Gender Segregation* (Discussion Paper 2003–02), Porto: CETE – Centro de Estudos de Economia Industrial, do Trabalho e da Empresa, Faculdade de Economia, Universidade do Porto.

Semyonov, M. (1980). »The social context of women's labour force participation: a comparative analysis«, *American Journal of Sociology*, vol. 86, no. 3, pp. 534–550.

Siltanen, J./Blackburn, R./Jarman, J. (1995). »The measurement of occupational gender segregation: current problems and a new approach«, *Royal Statistical Society Series A (Statistics in Society)*, vol. 158, no. 2, pp. 319–331.

Tienda, M./Smith, S./Ortiz, V. (1987). »Industrial restructuring, gender segregation, and sex differences in earnings«, *American Sociological Review*, vol. 52, no. 2, pp. 195–210.

Tyree, A. (1973). »Mobility ratios and association in mobility tables«, *Population Studies*, vol. 27, no. 3, pp. 577–588.

Watts, M. (1990). »The sex ratio index revisited«, *Work, Employment and Society*, vol. 4, no. 4, pp. 595–603.

Watts, M. (1992). »Notes and issues: How should occupational sex segregation be measured?«, *Work, Employment and Society*, vol. 6, no. 3, pp. 475–487.

Weeden, K. (1998). »Revisiting occupational sex segregation in the United States 1910–1990: Results from a log-linear approach«, *Demography*, vol. 35, no. 4, pp. 475–487.

Yasuda, S. (1964). »A methodological inquiry into social mobility«, *American Sociological Review*, vol. 29, no. 1, pp. 16–23.

Linked lives in modern societies. The impact on social inequality of increasing educational homogamy and the shift towards dual-earner couples

Hans-Peter Blossfeld

Introduction

Theories of social inequality, whether influenced by Durkheim, Marx, or Weber, have traditionally defined social class as a market relationship, with the family as the key unit of social stratification. In this approach, conjugal families were regarded as collective entities in which family members share the rewards gained by the family head through relationships within labour markets and production units, and as primary agents of socialisation and institutions channelling social and economic inheritance, which transmitted privilege as well as power and prestige to the next generation (Coser 1973). It is therefore not surprising that until the early 1980s intra- and intergenerational social mobility studies (e.g. Goldthorpe 1980) as well as status attainment research (e.g. Blau and Duncan 1967, Sewell and Hauser 1975) regarded the variation in the social position of male family heads as the key dependent variable to be explained. Measuring the effects of the father's education and occupation on his son's education and occupational attainment dominated stratification research for many years. When these social mobility models were extended to married women, it was not women's own resources that were studied, but the education and occupation of women's fathers were compared with those of their husbands (e.g. Handl et al. 1977, Goldthorpe 1983, 1984).

As women's educational participation has increased (Erikson and Jonsson 1996, Shavit and Blossfeld 1993) and also married women's paid employment (e.g. Blossfeld and Hakim 1997) the share of family income contributed by wives has steadily risen in modern societies, and the pervasive »male bias« in the stratification literature has increasingly been criticised (e.g. Sørensen and McLanahan 1987). A growing stream of research suggested that in empirical studies women should be treated just like men, and that individuals and not families should be the units of analysis in inequality studies. Subsequently, the focus gradually shifted from traditional stratification research to labour market research and from household heads to individual women and men in the marketplace, largely ignoring their marriage patterns and their family or household contexts, their income-sharing within the family, and their social security or other benefits enjoyed through family relationships.

A fundamental drawback of this individualistic line of thought is that by ignoring marriage patterns and familial relationships, or by not explicitly taking them into account, it is implied that men and women are all alike, that there are no differences between families and households, and that employment decisions within the family are based on gender-free considerations. A major conceptual limitation of individualistic approaches to the study of social inequality seems to be their failure to acknowledge the degree to which lives of men and women are linked via marriage and family relationships. In this contribution, we will therefore consider the effects of changes in marriage patterns and the interdependencies of couples' careers on social inequality in modern societies. For this purpose, we will summarise the main findings of two cross-nationally comparative volumes published by Hans-Peter Blossfeld and Andreas Timm (2003) on educational homogamy and by Hans-Peter Blossfeld and Sonja Drobnič (2001) on careers of couples in contemporary society. This focus on changes in union formation and the division of work within the household allows us to study how unequal access to resources has been created, exacerbated, reduced, modified, or perpetuated by families.

Educational expansion and changes in educational homogamy

Educational expansion has dramatically increased the participation in higher education in recent decades, and more so for women than for men. We are therefore particularly interested in exploring the role of the educational system as a marriage market and studying the changes in marriage patterns induced by educational expansion in modern societies. Educational expansion means that there is an increasing chance to meet people of the opposite sex with the same educational level at an age when individuals typically begin to form couples. Educational expansion could therefore – quite unintentionally – increase the likelihood of educational homogamy across cohorts and, as a consequence, not only reinforce social inequality among married couples from one birth cohort to the next, but also lead to a growing divergence of social opportunities for the next generation of children.

In a study of educational homogamy (Blossfeld and Timm 2003), we presented findings of thirteen very similar longitudinal studies on assortative mating. Included in this analysis were West Germany, Belgium (Flanders), France, the Netherlands, Italy, Spain, Great Britain, Denmark, Sweden, Hungary, Slovenia, the United States of America, and Israel. We concentrate here on the results for women because the results for men are equivalent. Since homogamous, upward and downward marriage rates are not only dependent on the number of educational attainment levels in each country but also on the educational distributions of men and women and their changes across cohorts, we did not directly compare the absolute marriage rates across countries. Rather we concentrated on the differences between empirically observed and estimated rates and their trends across cohorts. The computation of the estimated rates is based on the assumption that marriage decisions in each birth cohort were taken randomly, given the distributions of educational attainment levels of men and women within each birth cohort. All country studies show that the observed homogamy rates have always been higher than the rates estimated under the assumption of a random marital matching. In other words, there has been always a certain preference for an equally educated partner in all countries. This finding supports Becker's (1981) hypothesis that men and women benefit mostly from each other if they resemble themselves as much as possible or Blau's (1994) thesis that »like likes like«.

The most important finding of this comparative study is that for all countries the gaps between observed and estimated homogamy rates have been increasing with the expansion of education. This finding can be considered as an important hint that through educational expansion the structurally increased chance of meeting a partner of equal qualification in the educational system raises the level of educational homogamy. In this sense, the educational system seems to increase its role as an important marriage market for equally qualified people in modern societies – even across ethnic groups, as shown in the Israeli case study in this volume (Stier and Shavit 2003).

If women's rates of upward marriage are considered, we find the opposite pattern. In all eight countries, the observed upward rates for women have been consistently lower than the upward rates estimated under the assumption of a random marital matching. This means that even in earlier and more gender-traditional historical periods, to a large extent women's upward marriages have been structurally forced marriages. Many women had to marry upwardly (or many men had to marry downwardly) simply because the average level of education of women was below that of men. However, in more gender-traditional historical periods 40 to 50 years ago, this downward marriage of men was economically rational because women were supposed to stay at home. Of course, this situation changed fundamentally when societies moved from male breadwinner to dual earner societies, as we will discuss below. In the course of this transition, wives' income has become a significant determinant of the economic basis and »lifestyle« of the family. Thus, educational attainment gained importance for young women, too. The country-specific analyses show that the proportion of women's upward marriage has declined sharply as women's educational attainment levels have caught up with those of men. They document that in this decline the gap between observed and estimated rates has been stable in most countries over time or has even widened, so that the proportions of women marrying upwardly declined faster than they were forced by the convergence in the average educational attainment levels of men and women.

Women's rate of downward marriage is even more interesting. In almost all countries in the study (the exception is France) women's observed downward marriage rates have always been systematically lower than the rates estimated under the model of random marriage. For earlier gender-traditional historical periods, this result is not surprising. A good education was particularly important for men, since it was the husband's income which normally determined the economic and social status of the family. Thus, women in gender-traditional societies tended to prefer men with high levels of education and good labour market opportunities and competed for them in the marriage market. In such gender-traditional societies, women who married downwardly (or men who married upwardly) deviated from the dominant pattern regarding the gender of providers and dependents (see Brines 1994). They also violated socially sanctioned arrangements offering recurrent opportunities to advance claims about the self as »naturally« male and female (Berk 1985) and they risked social accountability, negative judgments from relatives, friends, colleagues, and even a threat of their gender identities (Brines 1994). It is therefore not surprising that for women downward marriage was the exception in all countries in the past.

Based on the fact that gender roles are deeply entrenched in all social relations and interactional pressures concerning the male breadwinner role continue to be important even in dual-earner societies, we expected that the increase in women's downward marriage across cohorts should be lower than it could have been based on the increasingly balanced educational attainment levels of men and women across cohorts. And indeed, the empirical results reveal an increasing divergence between observed and estimated downward marriage rates for women in most countries. The male breadwinner norm still seems to be a significant mechanism for partner choice. This norm defines wives as secondary providers and makes it still difficult for women (and men) to marry downwardly (upwardly) in terms of educational level. The study on Israel (Stier and Shavit 2003) demonstrated that highly educated women sometimes have another option. Instead of downward marriage within the own ethnic group, they marry across ethnic lines in search for equally educated men (see also Stier and Shavit 1994). Of course, another increasingly used option is to stay single. The analysis on Germany reports the highest never-married rates for unskilled men and highly-educated women. Unskilled men are unattractive marriage partners. Highly-educated women have difficulties finding a partner with a university degree, if still a substantial proportion of these men is engaged in downward marriage.

Further, we studied the impact of the structure of the educational system on the rate of homogamous marriage in greater detail. We hypothesized that the organizational structure of educational systems in modern societies imposes a stepwise selection process and a relatively rigid age-graded logic on the life course, so that educational expansion translates into highly time-dependent homogamy rates over the life course. In each generation the less able and educationally disadvantaged leave the educational system earlier so that the stepwise selection process in the educational system creates increasingly homogeneous groups. With rising duration in school, we expected an increasing likelihood of establishing a social relationship with a similarly qualified partner – and then perhaps of later marriage. These opportunities to meet not only include the contacts made within the classroom or the educational institution itself, but also the opportunities to meet similar people in leisure and sports activities, because these are also, to a large extent, structured by the fact that young people continue to be in school. The case studies demonstrate that in most countries, there is indeed the expected statistically significant positive effect of »duration in school« on the rate of homogamous marriage for women. This results also holds for men. This means that with increasing duration in school (and increasing opportunities to meet) the rate of homogamous marriage rises. However, three countries (the United States, Sweden, and Slovenia) report no statistically significant impact of »duration in school« on the homogamous marriage rate. In these countries, duration in school does not matter for the homogamy rate at all. It seems that these are especially those countries that are characterized by an open and unstratified educational system. In these educational systems, almost all children have the opportunity to attend school until the age of about 18. In Spain there is a negative effect, which is particularly difficult to interpret. It might be a methodological artefact or an instance of an interesting difference of the Spanish society. Further in-depth research seems to be necessary here. The general picture, however, is that there is a high degree of similarity with regard to the positive effect of »duration in school« on the rate of homogamy in very different societies. The longer men and women stay in school the higher the homogamy rate.

We assumed that in most modern countries attaining an education makes it difficult to adopt family roles and educational participation is connected to a high degree of economic dependence on parents or the state. Most young men and women participating in the educational system are therefore »not ready« to start a family. Completing education is thus a socially significant precondition for entering into marriage. The empirical results show that in all countries the time-dependent variable »in school« has the expected delaying effect on the homogamy rate. This means that the transition from school to work has a cross-nationally consistent impact on (homogamous) marriage (see also Blossfeld and Huinink 1991 who studied the impact of education on the general marriage rate). In all twelve countries, varying widely in important characteristics, the transition from school to work is therefore an important step in the normative (and economic) conception for entering into (homogamous) marriage.

Finally, since young people participating in the educational system are »not ready« for marriage, they not only postpone family formation, but often transform their partnerships into marital unions after leaving school. Thus, we expected that after leaving the educational system, the tendency to marry homogamously should at first increase steeply because many school leavers transform partnerships formed in school into marital ones, and then, with increasing exposure to a more heterogeneous environment outside the educational system, decrease again. The country-specific estimates show that for most countries the rate of homogamous marriage at first increases and then decreases after people have left school. In some cases (Flanders, Great Britain, and Hungary) the rate jumps up immediately after the transition from school to work, and afterwards declines. The general pattern is therefore that with increasing duration in more heterogeneous environments after leaving school, the educational homogamy rate declines.

In summary, it seems that in most modern societies a combination of at least three factors tends to increase educational homogamy: (1) people often prefer to associate with equally educated partners; (2) educational expansion increases contact opportunities for equally educated men and women at an age when young people start to look for partners and form couples; and (3) women's changing economic role in dual-earner societies increases the importance of women's education and labour force attachment. Thus, the increasing role of the educational system as a marriage market in the course of educational expansion and the fact that wives' employment and income have become a significant determinant of the »lifestyle« of the family are the main driving forces behind this development. Since rising rates of homogamy reflect the degree to which individuals with the same characteristics such as education marry each other, they also indicate the degree of exclusion through the social structure and the extent to which social networks are closed to outsiders (Simmel 1917 [1970], Laumann 1973).

The rise of cohabitation and the increase in separation and divorce rates do not seem to change this result. An international comparative study on the impact of assortative partnership selection, division of work in the household and union separation shows that educational heterogeneity of partners in cohabiting couples does indeed increase the rate of separation (Blossfeld and Müller 2002–3). Thus, in modern societies cohabitation seems to function as an additional social inequality filter in the process of family formation. In addition, this research shows that the divorce rate is higher for marriages where the partners have different educational attainment levels, in particular, if women have married downwardly in terms of education.

From male breadwinner to dual-earner regime

An implication of higher (educational) marriage homogamy is that more couples are emerging where there is a high similarity in earnings, at least at the beginning of the marriage. Also, the situation where women have higher earnings potential than their partner has become slightly more common. This development questions the view that the male partner should automatically be regarded as the breadwinner and should influence the decision-making process on the allocation of time and effort to paid and unpaid work between the partners. In other words, an increasing symmetry in educational resources, occupational chances and earnings potential should also lead to a more symmetric allocation of time by husbands and wives, at least within the neoclassical household production framework, as exemplified by Gary Becker's work (1965, 1993).

The neoclassical model of the family assumes that the family behaves as if it were trying to allocate the time of its members to satisfy a common set of ›family‹ preferences or a joint utility function. Under the gender neutral assumptions of this model, the comparative advantage of one partner over the other drives the decisions to allocate time to market or household production. Also, the spouse-specific sources of non-earned income must exert the same effects on family allocative behaviour. However, the challenge to the neoclassical model arises if non-earned income of different family members is observed to affect differently the household's allocation of resources (Schultz 1990). When examining the allocation of time to market work and household production within couples, this restriction of the neoclassical model of family behaviour has not been supported in any of the countries studied in the volume by Blossfeld and Drobnič (2001). Specialisation in unpaid work – scheduling work and family roles sequentially over the life course – is so uncommon among men that no parallel dynamic analysis for men and women was even feasible. Therefore, in the Blossfeld and Drobnič study the longitudinal empirical analyses of transitions between paid and unpaid work were limited to women. Twelve countries were analyzed and five welfare state regimes were compared: conservative (Germany, The Netherlands, and Belgium/Flanders), the Mediterranean (Italy and Spain), liberal (Great Britain and the U.S.), social democratic (Denmark and Sweden), and (former) state socialist countries (Hungary, Poland and China).

We used the more general term ›couples‹ instead of ›spouses‹ because in some of the countries studied the process of family formation and the structure of households have changed to such an extent that the distinction between marital and cohabitational unions has become blurred (e.g. Sweden). The focus of the research, however, was on husbands' and wives' coupled transitions between full-time or part-time work and unpaid housework over the life course, beginning with the time of entry into the marital union. The distinction between full-time and part-time jobs in this study makes it possible to evaluate the relationship of primary and secondary earners over time. The applied life-course approach explicitly recognizes the dynamic nature of family roles and circumstances as partners move through their life paths, the interdependence of lives and life choices among family members, the situational imperatives confronting families in different countries, and the accumulation of advantages and disadvantages experienced by individual members of the family.

The country-specific studies demonstrate that the linked life courses of husbands and wives exhibit similarities and differences in various societies. In all countries, we find a clear division between paid and unpaid work along gender lines in families and households. This result is reflected in labour market research, which still shows a gender-based earnings gap and (even increasing) occupational segregation (Hakim 1998) in modern societies. In particular, housework and childcare seem to remain primarily »women's work« despite substantial changes in women's employment patterns and in attitudes once thought to underpin the sexual division of labour (e.g. Schulz and Blossfeld 2006). Husbands do not increase their housework and childcare participation more substantially when their wives work and earn money (e.g. Brines 1994, Schulz and Blossfeld 2006). They seem to insist on the provider role, even when their wife's income potential is substantial.

From the point of view of the economic theory of the family, the resource-bargaining model, and the marital dependency model, the division of labour in modern couples therefore remains a puzzle (England and Farkas 1986, Brines 1993, 1994). These theories adhere to the view that the relations underlying the division of labour in the household are fundamentally gender neutral and governed by symmetric processes of change for husbands and wives. However, the results in our comparative study and recent empirical studies on housework (Brines 1993, 1994; Schulz and Blossfeld 2006) suggest that married women and men still respond quite differently to increased wives' employment. Wives respond in ways consistent with the logic of the three gender-neutral theoretical approaches: they do less housework and spend less time on childcare when they do more paid work. But the same is not true for husbands: their participation in housework has hardly changed. Thus, gender role change has been generally asymmetric, with a greater movement of women into the traditional male sphere than vice versa. This means that in most countries, whether capitalist or socialist, liberal, conservative, or social democratic, the role performance of women has changed considerably, while the dimensions of role specialisation in dual-earner couples have not transformed to the same extent (Crompton and Harris 1999, Mintz 1998).

In sum, the findings clearly support »doing gender« approaches or a gender-specific identity formation model. These theories locate gender itself at the heart of the division of labour between women and men and also predict asymmetrical processes of change for husbands and wives. They suggest that the equalisation of gender roles is a much slower process than assumed by economic and bargaining approaches and – at least in the initial stages – leads only to a modest reduction of sex segregation in the workplace and even less change in the household division of labour.

The country-specific studies show that women with higher educational resources have a higher participation rate in the labour market. Their risk of employment exit tends to be considerably lower and the re-entry rate higher. Or, in the case of Flanders and Sweden, women with higher occupational resources tend to move from full-time to part-time jobs instead of leaving the labour market. Furthermore, the country-specific analyses show that the family cycle – in particular the age of the youngest child – and the historic periods have a strong impact on the participation of women in paid employment.

However, when the impact of partners' resources on women's work careers is examined, a significant diversity across countries can be detected. In countries associated with the conservative and Mediterranean welfare state regime, the career paths over the course of the marriage are clearly gendered, leading to an increasing division of labour within couples, specialisation of spheres, economic dependency of wives on their partners, and the prevalence of a breadwinner family model. Women's paid employment is negatively correlated with the occupational position of their husbands. In the social democratic welfare state regime and generally in (former) socialist countries, this relationship is reversed. There is a symmetry in couples' careers; high occupational resources cumulate in couples and are translated into more symmetric employment career paths over the life course and the dual-earner family model. Finally, there are countries where no impact of husbands' resources is detected, such as Great Britain, or where other studies indicate that a country rapidly moved from a typical breadwinner to a modern dual-earner family type, such as the United States.

Summary and conclusions

A great problem of individualistic social inequality studies is that they do not consider marriage patterns and familial relationships. It is often implied that men and women are all alike, that there are no differences between households, and that job decisions within the family are based on gender-free considerations. In this contribution, we looked at the impact of changes in union formation and the division of work within the household context on social inequality in modern societies.

Rising educational homogamy and the shift from male-breadwinner to dual-earner families have changed the structure of inequality in modern societies. Educational expansion has – quite unintentionally – increased the degree of educational homogamy across cohorts and, as a consequence, has not only reinforced social inequality among households, but also engendered a growing divergence of economic and educational resources across families for the next generation of children. Increasing educational marriage homogamy therefore means an increasing degree of exclusion through social networks. This accumulation of resources within couples over the life course through marriage would not be visible in individualistic mobility or labour market studies.

Another implication of higher (educational) marriage homogamy is that there are more and more couples where husband and wife have a similar earnings potential, at least at the beginning of the marriage. Based on gender-symmetric theories, this increasing symmetry in educational and job resources should lead to a more egalitarian division of work between husbands and wives. However, this hypothesis was not supported. Housework and childcare is quite uncommon among men.

In all modern countries, there has been a shift from a male breadwinner to a dual-earner model but the strength and the pace of this shift is contingent on broader structural, political, and ideological country »packages«.

Gender role specialisation as predicted by the economic theory of the family seems to work well in conservative and Mediterranean welfare states where the middle-class male breadwinner is still able to earn a family wage and husbands' resources have a negative impact on their wives' labour force participation. This can particularly be seen in Germany, where the tax system directly penalises wives' full-time employment and protects the male breadwinner family (Dingeldey 2000). This of course dampens the speed of diffusion of dual-earner families in these countries. However, also in conservative and Mediterranean welfare state regimes, role specialisation in the household means that the small nuclear family is particularly vulnerable to the temporary or permanent loss of a unique individual who provides an essential function at home or in the labour market. Hence, specialisation involves a potentially serious loss of flexibility and wives' employment becomes a highly adaptive family strategy. At the same time there is an asymmetrical development of gender roles.

The increasing influx of women into the work force diminishes the role of men as sole breadwinners and leads to a point where the whole system shifts from a family wage economy to an individual wage economy. In the individual wage economy, the socio-economic status of the family is increasingly determined by two income sources. The combined income of the two-earner family comes to form the social standard; thus, the wife's employment and income is also in the interests of the husband. This can be seen in the positive effects of husbands' resources on their wives' labour force participation, particularly in social democratic and (former) socialist countries. In countries associated with the social democratic welfare state regime, the spread of the dual-earner model was particularly fast because of their steeply progressive individualised tax system and public-sector provision of family services. Also in (former) socialist countries, the dual-earner family was a social norm, supported by the official gender equality ideology and economic necessity. In the liberal welfare state regimes, no clear effect of husbands' resources on their wives' labour force participation could be detected. It seems that these countries, particularly the United States, have experienced a very fast transition from the family wage economy into the individual wage economy, accompanied by the stagnation or actual decline of real male wages and the increase of job instability (Mintz 1998).

Our results highlight the way in which gender inequality within couples affects the process of socio-economic stratification and material inequality generated in the stratification process. Research on the development of inequalities in the distribution of household income indicates that after the early 1980s, in many countries the tendency towards declining inequalities was halted and even reversed, most dramatically so in the United States and Great Britain (Atkinson et al. 1995, Gottschalk and Smeeding 1997, Gustafsson and Johansson 1999, Karoly and Burtless 1995).

Changing family structure and patterns of income receipt contribute directly to the level of income inequality. Single-headed families, for example, only have half as many potential adult earners as families headed by a married couple. An increase in the proportion of single-headed families will probably increase income inequalities between households. In husband-wife families, marriage homogamy and the division of labour between husbands and wives also bears broader societal relevance. The level of women's participation in the labour force is not only likely to affect the distribution of resources within the couples, their interaction patterns and bargaining positions within the family, but also has an impact on the inter-household distribution of economic well-being and class status. Thus, an interesting but under-researched aspect of the diffusion of dual-earner couples in male breadwinner societies is that it will probably enhance social inequality – at least during a transition period. Since in most modern societies, couples tend to marry homogamously with regard to traits determining earnings capacity, husbands and wives with high wages and influential social networks pool their resources and reinforce social differences between families.

As long as wives are secondary earners, their earnings have a generally equalising effect on inter-household income. Wives most likely to be employed in such a situation are those married to low income husbands. The wife's pay-cheque can considerably raise the total family income and in this way reduce inter-household inequalities. But this effect would be reversed if there were a major increase in the proportion of wives entering the labour force, particularly with the influx of well-educated, high earning women who are also more often married to men with high earnings. As working women become more ubiquitous, other household members' income becomes less and less of a predictor of who works and who does not. The working and non-working groups encompass more socio-economic diversity and resemble one another more in terms of other income (Treas 1987). This can double the advantage of couples at the upper end of the income scale. So, when women married to men with high earnings enter the labour force, this can increase the inequality between spouses and households.

These developments again have important consequences for the distribution of male breadwinner families and dual-earner families across social classes in a society, as well as for the systems of social inequalities: First, male breadwinner families lose ground in relative terms in the pyramid of social inequality of a society. Especially at the lower end, low-income male breadwinner families are likely to fall below a (relative) poverty line. Thus, the advantage of dual-earner families compared to traditional male breadwinner families is likely to stimulate the further diffusion of dual-earner families. Secondly, because working-class families traditionally already had a higher proportion of dual-earner couples after World War II (Esping-Andersen 1999), they become relatively poorer with the increase of dual-earner couples in the middle and upper-middle classes. Thus, part of the increasing inequality observed in many contemporary societies might in fact be attributed to a changing composition of male breadwinner and dual-earner families across social classes.

Of course, the implication is not that the integration of women into paid employment and an increasing gender equality in this respect is undesirable because it can increase income inequality and poverty in underprivileged classes. Indeed, such an outcome is not unavoidable, as demonstrated by the countries associated with the social democratic welfare state regime. The extent to which the equalisation of the position of women in the labour market and the diffusion of dual-earner families affect class inequalities, with lower-income families as losers, depends largely on the redistributive role of the welfare state through a broad spectrum of mechanisms, particularly the tax system, insurance institutions, and family-related policies.

In countries where the tax-system penalises wives' employment and the state provision of welfare services is meagre, such as Germany, male breadwinner families are to some extent protected, and the speed of the diffusion of dual-earner families is dampened. Also the conservative and Mediterranean welfare state regimes still provide a shelter for the traditional breadwinner family model and at the same time some protection against rising income inequalities. But the trend towards a dual-earner family model can also be detected in these countries and will continue in the future. In market-oriented societies, it is to be expected that the trend towards a dual-earner family model will have a strong and direct impact on social stratification and increasing income inequalities, particularly in the United States with a comparatively unprogressive tax system and few government transfers to the families. In the social democratic welfare state regime, however, the prevalence of the dual-earner family model does not have the same strong impact on class inequalities due to the equalising effects of state policies. In Sweden, for example, in spite of a recent increase in income inequality (Gottschalk and Smeeding 1997), the tax system with steeply progressive taxes produces considerably less inter-household inequality than in countries associated with the liberal welfare state regime. Finally, we expect that in the (former) socialist countries the dual-earner family model will continue to remain a prevailing societal norm. However, our results also show that these countries might develop in disparate directions, generating a diversity of outcomes, as is already the case in Western capitalist countries. Results for Hungary and Poland support Deacon's (1992) projections of disparate evolution of welfare policy in Central and Eastern Europe. However, because of the underdevelopment of a comprehensive system of insurance institutions and the erosion of state legitimacy, the medium-term outcome in these countries will probably be increasing inter-household inequality.

References

Atkinson, A. B./L. Rainwater/Smeeding, T. M. (1995). *Income distribution in OECD countries: Evidence from the Luxembourg Income Study* (Social Policy Studies No. 18), Paris: Organisation for Economic Co-operation and Development.

Becker, G. S. (1965). »A theory of the allocation of time«, *Economic Journal*, vol. 75, pp. 493–519.

Becker, G. S. (1981). *A Treatise on the Family*, Cambridge, Mass.: Harvard University Press.

Becker, G. S. (1993 [1981]). *A Treatise on the Family* (enlarged edition), Cambridge, Mass.: Harvard University Press.

Berk, S. F. (1985). *The Gender Factory: the Apportionment of Work in American Households*, New York: Plenum Press.

Blau, P. M. (1994). *Structural Contexts of Opportunities*, Chicago and London: University of Chicago Press.

Blau, P. M./Duncan, O. D. (1967). *The American Occupational Structure*, New York: Wiley.

Blossfeld, H.-P./Drobnič, S. (2001). *Careers of Couples in Contemporary Society*, Oxford: Oxford University Press.

Blossfeld, H.-P./Hakim, C. (eds.) (1997). *Between Equalization and Marginalization. Women Working Part-time in Europe and the United States of America*, Oxford: Oxford University Press.

Blossfeld, H.-P./Huinink, J. (1991). »Human capital investments or norms of role transition? How women's schooling and career affect the process of family formation«, *American Journal of Sociology*, vol. 97, pp. 143–168.

Blossfeld, H.-P./Müller, R. (2002–3): *Assortative Partnership Selection, Division of Work in the Household, and Union Separation*, Armonk, N. Y.: Sharpe (Issues 31 (2002):3, 32 (2003):1 and 32 (2003):2 of *International Journal of Sociology*).

Blossfeld, H.-P./Timm, A. (eds.) (2003). *Who Marries Whom? Educational Systems as Marriage Markets in Modern Societies*, Dordrecht: Kluwer Academic Publisher.

Brines, J. (1993). »The exchange value of housework«, *Rationality and Society*, vol. 5, pp. 302–340.

Brines, J. (1994). »Economic dependency, gender, and division of labor at home«, *American Journal of Sociology*, vol. 100, pp. 652–688.

Coser, L. (1973): *Greedy Institutions: Patterns of Undivided Commitments*, New York: The Free Press.

Crompton, R./Harris, F. (1999). »Attitudes, women's employment, and the changing domestic division of labour: A cross-national analysis«, in: R. Crompton (ed.), *Restructuring Gender relations and Employment. The Decline of the Male Breadwinner*, Oxford: Oxford University Press, pp. 105–127.

Deacon, B. (1992). »The future of social policy in Eastern Europe«, in B. Deacon et al. (eds.), *The New Eastern Europe: Social Policy Past Present and Future*, Newbury Park, Cal.: Sage, pp. 167–191.

Dingeldey, I. (ed.) (2000). *Erwerbstätigkeit und Familie in Steuer- und Sozialversicherungssystemen*, Opladen: Leske + Budrich.

England, P./Farkas, G. (1986). *Households, Employment, and Gender: a Social, Economic, and Demographic view*, New York: Aldine.

Erikson, R./Jonsson, J. O. (eds.) (1996). *Can Education be Equalized?*, Boulder, Col.: Westview Press.

Esping-Andersen, G. (1999). *Social Foundations of Post-industrial Economies*, Oxford: Oxford University Press.

Goldthorpe, J. H. (1980). *Social Mobility and Class Structure in Modern Britain*, Oxford: Clarendon Press.

Goldthorpe, J. H. (1983). »Women and class analysis: in defence of the conventional view«, *Sociology*, vol. 17, pp. 465–488.

Goldthorpe, J. H. (1984). »Women and class analysis: a reply to the replies«, *Sociology*, vol. 18, pp. 491–499.

Gottschalk, P./Smeeding, T. M. (1997). »Cross-national comparisons of earnings and income inequality«, *Journal of Economic Literature*, vol. 35, pp. 633–687.

Gustafsson, B./Johansson, M. (1999). »In search of smoking guns: What makes income inequality vary over time in different countries?«, *American Sociological Review*, vol. 64, pp. 585–605.

Hakim, C. (1998). *Social Change and Innovation in the Labour Market: Evidence from the Census SARs on Occupational Segregation and Labour Mobility, Part-time Work and Student Jobs, Homework and Self-employment*, Oxford: Oxford Univ. Press.

Handl, J./Mayer, K. U./Müller, W. (1977). *Klassenlagen und Sozialstruktur*, Frankfurt/Main and New York: Campus.

Karoly, L. A./Burtless, G. (1995). »Demographic change, rising earnings inequality, and the distribution of personal well-being, 1959–1989«, *Demography*, vol. 32, no. 3, pp. 379–405.

Laumann, E. O. (1973). *Bonds of pluralism. The form and substance of urban social networks*, New York: Wiley.

Mintz, S. (1998). »From patriarchy to androgyny and other myths: placing men's family roles in historical perspective«, in A. Booth/A. C. Crouter (eds.), *Men in Families. When do they Get Involved? What Difference does it Make?*, Mahwah, N. J.: Erlbaum, pp. 3–30.

Schultz, T. P. (1990). »Testing the neoclassical model of family labor supply and fertility«, *Journal of Human Resources*, vol. 25, pp. 599–634.

Schulz, F./Blossfeld, H.-P. (2006). »Wie verändert sich die häusliche Arbeitsteilung im Eheverlauf? Eine Längsschnittstudie der ersten 14 Ehejahre in Westdeutschland«, *Kölner Zeitschrift für Soziologie und Sozialpsychologie*, vol. 58, pp. 23–49.

Simmel, G. (1917 [1970]). *Grundfragen der Soziologie*, Berlin: De Gruyter.

Sewell, W. H./Hauser, R. M. (1975). *Education, Occupation and Earnings*, New York: Academic Press.

Shavit, Y./Blossfeld, H.-P. (1993). *Persistent Inequality: Changing Educational Attainment in Thirteen Countries*, Boulder, Col.: Westview Press.

Sørensen, A./McLanahan, S. (1987). »Married women's economic dependency, 1940–1980«, *American Journal of Sociology*, vol. 93, pp. 659–687.

Stier, H./Shavit, Y. (1994). »Age at marriage, sex ratio and assortative mating«, *European Sociological Review*, vol. 10, pp. 79–87.

Stier, H./Shavit, Y. (2003). »Two decades of educational intermarriage in Israel«, in H.-P. Blossfeld/A. Timm (eds.), *Who Marries Whom? Educational Systems as Marriage Markets in Modern Societies*, Dordrecht: Kluwer Academic Publisher, pp. 315–330.

Treas, J. (1987). »The effect of women's labor force participation on the distribution of income in the United States«, *Annual Review of Sociology*, vol. 13, pp. 259–288.

Containers, Europeanisation and individualisation: empirical implications of general descriptions of society

Ulrich Kohler

In 1983, in his essay »Beyond Status and Class«, Ulrich Beck described the structural development of Germany after World War II as a process during which »subcultural class identities have dissipated, class distinctions based on status have lost their traditional support, and processes for the ›diversification‹ and individualisation of lifestyles and ways of life have been set in motion« (cited from Beck 1992: 91; first published in Beck 1983). From this development he concluded that »the hierarchical model of social classes and stratification has increasingly been subverted« and therefore »no longer corresponds to reality«.

Beck's essay has been highly influential in the German debate on social inequality. German sociologists often refer to Beck's position, as stated above, as *the* individualisation hypothesis. In general, social researchers with an empirical orientation have been sceptical about the validity of the individualisation hypothesis (cf. Mayer and Blossfeld 1990, Jagodzinski and Quandt 1997, Burkhart 1998, Wirth and Lüttinger 1998, Huinink and Wagner 1998, Klein 1999, Simonson 2004). Walter Müller, in particular, is one of the more profiled critics (cf. Mayer and Müller 1994, Müller 1987, 1993, 1997, 1998). However, such empirically based criticism has not prevented the individualisation hypothesis from becoming widely accepted, especially outside sociology.

There are many reasons why empirical researchers have found it difficult to discredit a seemingly false hypothesis. For one, much empirical research highly relevant to the individualisation hypothesis has been carried out without reference to it. This is true for much of the research dealing with the »end of class politics« (Evans 1999, Brettschneider et al. 2002), education (Erikson and Jonsson 1996, Shavit and Müller 1998) or social mobility (Erikson and Goldthorpe 1992, Breen 2004). A more important reason is that the individualisation hypothesis is formulated somewhat ambiguously, and discussion about it has not made its meaning much clearer (Jagodzinski and Klein 1998). Because of the ambiguity of *the* individualisation hypothesis, empirical analysts have been forced to formulate their own specific individualisation hypotheses. One consequence of these reformulations is that negative results have not been accepted as a test of *the* individualisation hypothesis (Beck and Beck-Gernsheim 1993); on the other hand, at least some reformulated hypotheses were empirically supported (Schnell and Kohler 1995).

In recent years, interest in the individualisation hypothesis has receded, whereas the issue of the ›Europeanisation‹ of social inequality has gained more attention (Heidenreich 2006a). It is again Ulrich Beck who has articulated the point most vividly (Beck 2002, Beck and Grande 2004). In their recent book, Ulrich Beck and Edgar Grande (2004) criticise inequality research for its failure to address the European dimension. They claim that its concentration on societies in individual countries has distorted perception of inequalities by overemphasising inequalities within countries and downplaying the much greater inequalities between European countries. However, the distortion caused by the traditional »container model« of social inequality (Beck 2002: 390) will gradually disappear as a result of Europeanisation. Awareness of the huge disparities between countries is growing, and causing the poorer nations to demand a bigger share of the welfare cake. Thus, European integration can be expected to lead to the emergence of European-wide distribution conflicts that overlap with those already apparent at a national level.

There is some similarity between this Europeanisation hypothesis and the individualisation hypothesis. Both provide rather blanket descriptions of entire societies. Both offer a broadly drawn picture of how social inequalities structure societies, thus provoking the empirical question of which of them is more realistic. Is the structure of inequality of European society organised in containers, or is it Europeanised or individualised? Or is a society with Europeanised inequalities also an individualised one? Obviously, these questions cannot be answered without clarification of what the individualisation and the Europeanisation hypotheses stand for. What exactly are the properties of individualised societies? And what are the properties of societies suffering European-wide distribution conflicts?

This chapter is an attempt to compare to what extent these stylised depictions of societies correspond to reality. I therefore differentiate between four models of social inequality: the traditional »container model« of social inequality, the model of »individualisation«, a model of »supra-national« social inequality and a model of »national solidarity«. These four ideal types are oriented towards a specific understanding of what individualisation and Europeanisation of social inequality means. The understanding starts from the assumption that the level of individualisation and Europeanisation is a property of societies, not of individuals in societies. Of course, this is not the only possible understanding of what is meant with the respective terms. However, it is claimed to be *a* possible understanding, that one can derive implications from it that can be tested, and that these implications are of interest in a broader sociological sense.

Four Types of Societies

The sociology of social inequality is a sociology confined to nation-states. This predilection already starts with the definition of concepts, and is especially evident in poverty research. Poverty is most commonly defined with respect to national thresholds (Atkinson et al. 2002: 78–109): the poor are those at the margins of the society in which they live, no matter whether that society as a whole is rich or poor. Likewise, in research on educational inequality, educational groups are defined with respect to nation-specific norms and career opportunities (Brauns et al. 2003, Hoffmeyer-Zlotnik and Wolf 2003, UNESCO 2003), and not, for example, with respect to the absolute amount of knowledge and skills that people possess. Even the analysis of social classes, which tends to be carried out without particular regard for specific national circumstances, often remains within a national scope. For example, to maintain the significance of a class boundary, it is considered sufficient to claim that a class enjoys relatively good economic living conditions in comparison with those of other classes of the same nation-state (Goldthorpe and McKnight 2004). Whether or not the same class has the same »absolute« living conditions in other countries is not considered important.

The idea underlying this sort of sociology has been called the »container model« (Beck 2002: 390). The term denotes the idea that all forces that affect social life – living situations, attitudes, lifestyles, interactions – operate within the nation-state. According to this position, conditions in other countries are not relevant for how people live, feel and act, just as the living conditions of creatures from other galaxies are not likely to influence the social life of human beings. Thus, container models of social ine-

Figure 1. Models of social inequality

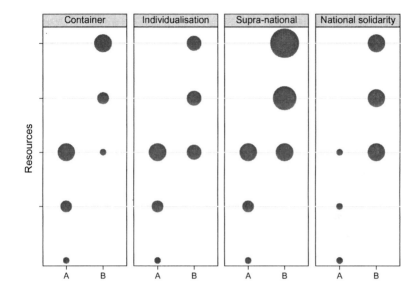

quality do examine social inequality within a society, but they maintain that social inequality does not affect social life beyond the borders of nation-states.

This chapter aims to show that the way in which social inequality structures social life within or between national borders can be reformulated in terms of the effects of *absolute* and *relative* amounts of resources. Assuming that all countries are in some way vertically structured by individuals who have or do not have certain resources, one can differentiate between an absolute vertical position and a relative vertical position. This approach is illustrated in Figure 1. The four panels of the figure depict four different societies, with each of them consisting of two sub-societies, A and B. (It might help to think of the four societies as Europe and of the two sub-societies as countries therein.) The resources that individuals have are plotted along the vertical axis; persons with more resources are placed higher. Within each sub-society, one can distinguish low and high vertical positions. It is evident that the people in sub-society A tend to have fewer resources than those in sub-society B: the highest vertical rank in sub-society A is as high as the lowest vertical rank in sub-society B. Both these

ranks can be regarded as high or low *relative* to those living in the same sub-
society, but they have an average amount of resources in an absolute sense
(or relative to the entire society).

The specific assumption of the container model of social inequality is
that only the relative amount of resources has consequences for certain
dependent characteristics. Relatively high positions are connected with
relatively good living situations, typical attitudes or lifestyles, or typical social connections. However, the absolute vertical position has no impact *per
se* on dependent characteristics. In Figure 1, this perspective is illustrated
through the use of differently sized plot symbols. The sizes reflect the typical values of an arbitrary dependent characteristic (e.g. living situations, attitudes, lifestyles) for the respective social strata. For the container model,
these symbols are of equal size for all persons who belong to the same *relative* position within a sub-society.

The individualisation hypothesis counters the container model of social
inequality on the inequality side. That is to say, the individualisation hypothesis also is a container model, but one with a different structure of
inequality. As Beck (1992: 95) has noted, »the distance between different
income groups has persisted«. However, as a result of »collective upward
mobility and increasing standards of living and higher income« (Beck 1992:
95), the position on the vertical dimension of social inequality has much
less influence on a person's living situation, attitudes or lifestyles (Beck
1992: 92, 95). This perspective is illustrated by symbol sizes that do not
vary between social strata in the sub-society that has higher values in absolute terms. Social strata only influence dependent characteristics in poorer
or less developed societies. Obviously, the same idea is inherent in general
modernisation theories, according to which increasing prosperity leads to a
decrease in the significance of materialistic goals (Maslow 1954, Inglehart
1977).

A different line of criticism of the container model of social inequality
is the hypothesis of the ›Europeanisation of social inequality‹. This time,
however, the criticism is directed at the container side. It begins with the
observation that countries have become Europeanised in two ways. The
increasing similarity of the legislative systems of European countries, or
»Europeanisation from above« (Heidenreich 2006b: 7), is the first form of
Europeanisation. Europeanisation from above is believed to be especially
strong among the European Union (EU) member states in which the EU
institutions and the so-called open method of coordination exert pressure

towards a convergence of institutional norms. The growing importance of interrelations between people from different countries (Beisheim et al. 1999, Gerhards and Rössel 1999) represents the other form of Europeanisation: »Europeanisation from below«. Both these developments are thought to have increased the visibility of inequalities between nation-states. Thus, differences in absolute vertical positions no longer can be neglected, neither by the individuals who recognise the striking dissimilarities between countries, nor by the European institutions that must manage these inequalities (also see Mau 2006: 115–118).

To make a long story short, the Europeanisation hypothesis amounts to the idea that the aliens of the past have joined the reference groups of today. These individuals have begun to recognise that they are not only better (or worse) than their co-nationals, but also better (or worse) than people from other countries (Delhey and Kohler 2006). In terms of absolute and relative amounts of resources, this development suggests that the absolute amount (i.e. the relative amount within a supra-national entity such as the EU) has gained in importance at the expense of the relative amount within nation-states (Fahey 2005). In the supra-national model of social inequality (see panel 3 of Figure 1), the vertical inequality position still affects living situations, attitudes and lifestyles. This time, however, the upper social strata of the poorer society have values with respect to specific dependent variables that are similar to those of the lowest social strata of the more affluent society.

So far I have shown how the container model of social inequality could be countered on the container side or on the social inequality side. What, then, about the logical possibility of criticising it from both sides? This approach requires a little detour: in the model of supra-national social inequality, all persons« have the same »production functions« (Lindenberg 1986, Ormel et al. 1999), that is, all people in the supra-national society have the same instrumental goals, which they seek to achieve by means of their resources. It is the individual amount of the resource that structures people's behaviour, regardless of the country in which they live. According to the supra-national model of social inequality, the fact of belonging together as citizens of the same nation is not significant for people in this respect. This situation, however, also implies that these resources cannot be meaningless in either of the two societies, as proposed by the individualisation hypothesis. How, then, should one envision a supra-national society with individualisation? Such a society has been illustrated in panel 4 of Figure 1. Here, the relative amount of resources within a country plays no role in the formation of living situations, attitudes or lifestyles (individualisation), whereas the overall absolute amount of resources within a country substantially influences people's behaviour: it is not ›being poor‹ that counts, but ›living in a poor country‹. It is obvious, though, that such a society is conceivable only if there are strong feelings of ›belonging together‹ among people in each nation. At the same time, however, individuals of the society as a whole should have the same combination of instrumental goals, for otherwise there is no reason why people from countries with different amounts of resources to achieve these goals should differ in their actual behaviour. Hence, this model implies a mixture of an internationalisation of production functions and strong national solidarity.[1] Paradoxically, this supra-national model is, at the same time, a container model.

The discussion so far has summarised recent thinking in sociology in terms of absolute and relative amounts of resources. This step is useful because it allows us to investigate the models of inequality in terms of the importance of relative and absolute effects of resources for selected dependent variables. The more important the relative amount becomes, the closer we are to the container model of social inequality. If the absolute amount becomes more important, we move in the direction of the supranational inequality model. For national solidarity, the average amount among one's co-nationals is more important than the individual amount; for the individualisation model, we would expect the resource-effect to decrease with countries' affluence.

Empirical Implications

The empirical implementation of the four models of social inequality can draw on the wealth of literature that investigates relative and absolute income effects on »utility«. As early as 1949, Duesenberry stressed the importance of relative income for individual consumption and savings behaviour. Easterlin (1974) has explained the puzzling result that economic growth has not increased people's happiness by drawing attention to what has become known as the »comparison income« or »relative utility« effect

---

1 The model is similar in some ways with Samuel Huntington's concept of national cultures.

(see also Easterlin 1995, Frank 1997, Easterlin 2001, 2005). He argues that raising individual income above the income of relevant others is more important for one's utility function than is the absolute level of that individual income. Increasing the income of all will, therefore, merely raise the aspiration levels rather than the levels of individual happiness. In a similar vein, Kahnemann and Tversky (1979) define a value function over gains and losses with respect to some natural reference point, and hence relative to this reference point; in the context of this study, the reference points are first and foremost the co-nationals. The notion of a comparison income has inspired a number of researchers carrying out econometric studies to compare the relative and the absolute income effect (McBride 2001, Stutzer 2004, Ferrer-i-Carbonell 2005, Vendrik and Woltjer 2006). These studies start from an econometric specification like the following:

$$Y = b_0 + b_1 \text{abspos}_i + b_2 \text{abspos}_r + \mathbf{b}\mathbf{X} + e_i, \tag{1}$$

where Y is the dependent characteristic, abspos_i is the absolute amount of resources of person i and abspos_r is the absolute amount of resources of a social reference group. $\mathbf{X}$ is a vector of control variables. b_0, b_1 and $\mathbf{b}$ are parameters to be estimated. The formula conceptualises the effect of the absolute amount of resources, controlling for the resources of a social reference group.

If the container model were true, the individual amount of resources should be of importance only *relative* to the resources of the co-nationals, who in this case constitute the social reference group. The term *relative* means that an absolute high individual income will not lead to high values of a dependent variable if it is low in comparison with those of co-nationals. Hence, the income of relevant others decreases the value of the dependent variable, which translates into a negative sign of the coefficient b_2 in the above specification:

Hypothesis 1 (Container)

$$b_1 > 0; \ b_2 < 0.$$

For the supra-national model of inequality, one expects an effect of the absolute vertical position regardless of the resources of relevant others. Translated into the estimated coefficients of specification (1), this becomes

Hypothesis 2 (Supra-nationalism)

$$b_1 > 0; \ b_2 \approx 0.$$

The model of national solidarity implies that all variance in the dependent variable is due to the resources of one's social reference group. How high one's personal income is does not matter; only what the social reference group has matters. Hence,

Hypothesis 3 (National solidarity)

$$b_1 \approx 0; \ b_2 > 0.$$

Finally, for the individualisation hypothesis, one would expect that the effect of the individual resources is moderated by the resources of the reference group. If a country is rich, personal income becomes less important. This can be expressed by expecting a negative sign of an interaction term between the individual income and the reference group's income:

Hypothesis 4 (Individualisation)

$$Y = b_0 + b_1 \text{abspos}_i + b_2 \text{abspos}_r + b_3 (\text{abspos}_r \times \text{abspos}_i) + \mathbf{b}\mathbf{X} + e_i,$$

with $b_1 > 0; \ b_3 < 0$

In what follows, I estimate the above specification in a slightly different form (cf. Vendrik and Woltjer 2006: 10). Adding the term $b_2\text{abspos}_i-b_2\text{abspos}_i$ to specification (1) and applying some simple algebra,[2] I attain the following specification:

$$Y=b_0+b_{\text{abs}}\text{abspos}_i+b_{\text{rel}}(\text{abspos}_i-\text{abspos}_r)+\mathbf{b}\mathbf{X}+e_i \qquad (2)$$

with $b_{\text{abs}} = b_1+b_2$ and $b_{\text{rel}} = -b_2$

Although this specification adds nothing to specification (1), it allows a somewhat more direct interpretation of the coefficients. The specification separates the effect of the individual resources (abspos_i) from the effect of the difference between the individual's and the reference group's resources ($\text{abspos}_i-\text{abspos}_r$). As the latter is a measure of *relative income*, the coefficients of this model allow one to directly compare the absolute and the relative income effect. In this specification, one expects $b_{\text{abs}}>b_{\text{rel}}$ for the supra-national model and $b_{\text{abs}}<b_{\text{rel}}$ for the container model. The model of national solidarity translates into $b_{\text{rel}}\times(-1)\approx b_{\text{abs}}$. For the individualisation hypothesis, one must add $b_3(\text{abspos}_i\times\text{abspos}_r)$ to (2), with the expectation that $b_1>0$ and $b_3<0$.

Empirical Applications

Whereas the empirical implications of the four types of society are straightforward, their empirical applications are not. It is obvious that empirical data from more than one country is needed in order to verify the different hypotheses. It is also necessary to have at least one comparable measured indicator of a dependent variable of interest. Moreover, and most important, one requires a data set in which the resources of the individuals and the reference groups vary substantially and independently from one another. That is to say, there must be enough observations in the data set which have amounts of resources that are relatively high but low in absolute terms. Ultimately, this requirement necessitates the collection of data from many nations that differ strongly in their overall amount of resources.

---

2 $ab+cd=ab+cd+cb-cb=(a+c)b-c(d-b)$

In what follows I have used data from the first two rounds of the European Social Survey (ESS) for an empirical application of the above specifications.[3] The two time points were chosen to check for the robustness of results, rather than to draw inferences about developments over time. I therefore have only taken into consideration those countries included in the ESS that were observed in both rounds.[4] Moreover, I have restricted the countries to the EU member countries because the supranationalism hypothesis applies primarily to them. These considerations led to the following set of 18 countries: Austria, Belgium, the Czech Republic, Germany, Denmark, Spain, Finland, France, the United Kingdom, Greece, Hungary, Ireland, Luxembourg, the Netherlands, Poland, Portugal, Sweden and Slovenia.

A further prerequisite for the empirical analysis of the four ideal types was the selection of suitable dependent variables. Given the universal character of the societal models, the number of possible dependent variables is just about limitless; it therefore becomes necessary to restrict the analysis to *important* dependent variables. An important dependent variable might be a variable that is directly mentioned by a proponent of one of the societal models, or a variable that represents a living situation, an attitude or a lifestyle that is of broader interest in a sociological sense. In the following applications, I have selected three dependent variables that are definitely important in the latter sense: general life-satisfaction, individual health and political participation. However, they are also closely connected with the thinking of originators of the models under consideration here. In a discussion of the early literature on the individualisation hypothesis, Haller (1986: 170) identified the diminishing influence of traditional social strata on other advantageous or disadvantageous living situations as one of two core elements of the individualisation hypothesis; health and general life-satisfaction can be seen as measures of such living situations (also see Kohler 2005). Others have proposed decreasing correlations of social strata with behaviour that is »not primarily based on material resources« (Schnell and Kohler 1995), or with indicators for social integration (Simonson 2004); political participation is an indicator for both.

Household income has been used as a dimension of vertical inequality in all models. In the ESS, household income was measured by a list of

3 The Stata do-file (*aness.do*), used for all analyses presented in this chapter, can be downloaded from http://www.wz-berlin.de/~kohler/publications/wmfest07/index.html.
4 Second-round data from Italy were not available at the time the analysis was carried out.

Figure 2. Log household income in euros (in thousands;purchasing power parities) by country and survey year

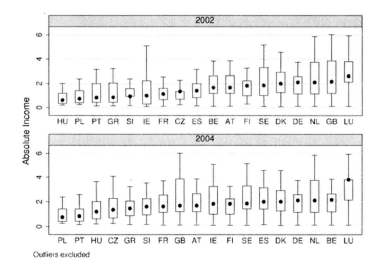

Outliers excluded

Do-File: aness.do

twelve income intervals, whereby the lowest and the highest intervals have been left open. To construct a variable for the absolute vertical position, the midpoints of the intervals have been calculated, whereby the lower bound of the lowest interval has been set to 90% of the upper bound of the lowest interval, and the upper bound of the highest interval to 110% of the lower bound of the highest interval. The midpoints have been divided by the »comparative price levels« in order to express them in purchasing power parities.[5] Finally, the values have been divided by 1,000, so that the regression coefficients express the change in the dependent variable associated with a thousand-euro increase of income.

The country-specific distribution of the income variables for the years 2002 and 2004 are shown in Figure 2. The figure reveals that the highest income quartiles of the poorest nations – Hungary and Poland – are about as high as the lowest income quartiles of the richest nations. Moreover, the highest quartiles of Portugal, Greece, Slovenia and the Czech Republic

5 Comparative levels were downloaded from Eurostat (http://epp.eurostat.ec.europa.eu) on Friday, 28 Aug 2006, 14:09:40.

tend to be below the median in quite a number of richer nations. Hence, it is guaranteed that there is some independent variation of relative and absolute income in the data. The variable for relative income has been calculated by subtracting the average absolute income of the ›reference group‹ from the absolute income; the reference group was defined as persons from the same country.

The correlation of relative and absolute income is about $r=.93$ in 2002 and $r=.95$ in 2004. This outcome suggests that the use of both variables in one regression model might cause problems of multi-collinearity. Although the problem itself is often a bit overstated (Goldberger 1991: 248–250), one should anticipate inflated standard errors and, as a consequence, results that are compatible with a diverse number of hypotheses (Gujarati 1995). One remedy against the increased probability of accepting an unjustified hypothesis is to check for the robustness of results in two different data sets.

All regression models described in the following sections have used centred versions of the income variables, which facilitates the interpretation of the constant terms and prevents artificially inflated values for the income effects in the models with interaction terms (cf. Aiken and West 1991). Moreover, all models control for gender and age as antecedent factors influencing the present socio-economic status. Finally, the models include a measure for household size in order to control for the fact that household income must be shared by all members of a household.

Subjective well-being

›Well-being‹, and its synonyms ›quality of life‹, ›happiness‹, and ›utility‹, can be viewed as the central goal of human activity (Ormel et al. 1999: 62). In the context of social inequality research, one question of obvious importance is whether and to what extent economic success produces such a favourable state of being. It therefore becomes necessary to measure well-being. One method is to ask the individuals to evaluate their well-being themselves. This evaluation is commonly called »subjective well-being«. In this section, I apply the specification outlined in equation (2) to a measure of subjective well-being.

Previous research on the relationship between subjective well-being and income has shown that income does indeed increase subjective well-being, but that this impact is relatively small in comparison with other factors, such as family and social life. Moreover, it has been argued that up to 60% of subjective well-being is driven by personality or genes (Lykken and Tellegen 1996), and hence cannot be changed by living situations. It has also been shown that the impact derived from changing living situations is only transitory. An increase in income might raise the level of subjective well-being for some time, but soon this level decreases to the original, personality-related level.[6]

Nevertheless, income has consistently shown a positive impact on subjective well-being in essentially all studies; it is therefore reasonable to conclude that subjective well-being can be at least slightly influenced by individual success. Yet the extent to which income modifies well-being might vary between societies, and the nature of this relationship can tell us something about the societal production functions. If the absolute income level strongly influences subjective well-being, we can conclude that income is a means to satisfy the need for goods that are valued by practically all persons. If it is relative income that counts, this is a sign that the production functions differ between countries. Finally, the weaker the relationship between income and life-satisfaction becomes, the lower the value of buyable goods is in the production-function of people. Thus, goods that cannot be bought with money are considered more important.

Several studies have investigated research questions that are related to, but yet different from the one I am occupied with here. On the basis of a meta-analysis of longitudinal studies, Veenhoven (1994) has found a positive relation between material resources and subjective well-being that becomes weaker in rich countries; this finding supports the individualisation model of social inequality. It also has been shown that the life-satisfaction difference between workers and non-workers decreases in richer countries (Kohler 2005). Several studies directly concerned with the comparison of relative and absolute income effects have demonstrated a higher relevance of relative income effects (McBride 2001, Stutzer 2004, Ferrer-i-Carbonell 2005, Vendrik and Woltjer 2006). However, these studies only compare relative and absolute income effects on a national level, and thus neglect the possibility that individual well-being might also be shaped by much greater country differences. Studies by Fahey (2005) and Delhey and Koh-

---

6 For an overview, see Frey and Stutzer 2002, Donovan and Halpern 2002.

Table 1. Unstandardised regression coefficients and t-values (in parentheses) of linear ordinary least square (OLS) and random intercept regression models for life-satisfaction

	2002			2004		
	(OLS)	(RE-1)	(RE-2)	(OLS)	(RE-1)	(RE-2)
Coefficients						
Men	-0.04	-0.07	-0.07	-0.05	-0.06	-0.06
	(-1.5)	(-2.7)	(-2.7)	(-1.8)	(-2.4)	(-2.5)
Age	-0.06	-0.06	-0.06	-0.06	-0.06	-0.06
(centred)	(-14.2)	(-15.9)	(-15.9)	(-15.2)	(-15.6)	(-15.6)
Age squared	0.00	0.00	0.00	0.00	0.00	0.00
(centred)	(14.3)	(16.5)	(16.5)	(15.4)	(15.9)	(15.9)
Household size	0.07	0.09	0.09	0.06	0.08	0.07
(centred)	(6.4)	(8.7)	(8.6)	(6.2)	(7.4)	(7.4)
Absolute income	0.95	0.96	0.99	1.05	1.01	1.03
(centred)	(41.8)	(4.9)	(5.5)	(42.6)	(3.5)	(3.9)
Relative income	-0.74	-0.75	-0.76	-0.87	-0.83	-0.84
(centred)	(-30.0)	(-3.8)	(-4.2)	(-33.3)	(-2.9)	(-3.2)
Abs. × Abs.Ref.Group			-0.08			-0.06
			(-6.3)			(-4.3)
Constant	6.99	7.00	7.03	7.02	7.00	7.02
	(381.5)	(57.2)	(62.2)	(396.8)	(42.2)	(46.7)
r^2	0.08	0.08	0.09	0.09	0.09	0.09
n	27250	27250	27250	26634	26634	26634
ρ		0.06	0.05		0.11	0.09

ler (2006) point towards the high relevance of absolute income; however, these studies use a completely different set of methods.

The ESS contains two measures of subjective well-being, namely, happiness and life-satisfaction. I have used the latter. The wording of the corresponding question was, »All things considered, how satisfied are you with your life as a whole currently?« Respondents could express their answers on an 11-point scale from 0 to 10. Table 1 shows unstandardised regression coefficients and their t-values from the regression models for the years 2002 and 2004. The results of the two survey years are not very different; I take this as an indication that the results are more than just accidental.

The columns labelled ›OLS‹ in Table 1 refer to an ordinary least square regression model.[7] In this model, the main interest is in the absolute and the relative income effects. It has been claimed above that for the model of supra-national social inequality to be true, the coefficient of the absolute income should be high, whereas the coefficient for the relative income should be small, if not zero. For the container model, one would expect the coefficient of the relative income to be larger than the coefficient of the absolute income; for the model of national solidarity, one would expect coefficients of the absolute and the relative income that work in the opposite direction. Given these expectations, the results strongly point towards the model of national solidarity. The absolute income effect is (significantly) positive, and the relative income effect is (significantly) negative. It seems that subjective well-being varies such that people living in poor countries are less satisfied with their lives than are people living in rich countries – regardless of whether they themselves are rich or poor.

It is, however, also clear from Table 1 that the effect of the absolute income has not vanished completely. In a pure version of national solidarity, one would expect that the effects of relative and absolute income are of approximately equal size, despite their different algebraic signs. Contrary to this expectation, the modulus of the absolute income coefficient is larger than that of the relative income coefficient. This result suggests that within countries, income still has an effect on life-satisfaction, although it must remain unclear whether one should call this an absolute or a relative income effect. It also suggests that overall well-being in poor countries is even lower than that in rich countries than one might expect from the individual incomes of their respective citizens alone.[8] If one wishes to depict these results in visual form, one might want to start with the third panel of Figure 1. In doing this, one would change this such that all the plot symbols of society A become smaller, and all the plot symbols of society B become larger. (Or one might start with the fourth panel and slightly increase the symbols for the highest stratum within each society.)

The columns labelled ›RE-1‹ in Table 1 contain a recalculation of the model by allowing a random effect on the intercepts of the previous model

---

7 The model includes a term for age-squared, which is common practice in econometric models of life-satisfaction (see, for example, Blanchflower and Oswald 2004).

8 This interpretation might be easier to see in a model that follows specification (1). To transform the results in Table 1 to specification (1), calculate $b_1 = b_{abs} + b_{rel}$ and $b_2 = b_{rel} \times (-1)$. For 2002, b_1 becomes $0.95 - 0.74 = 0.2$ and $b_2 = 0.74$.

(»random intercept model«; Snijders and Bosker 1999, Rabe-Hesketh and Skrondal 2005). These random effects are best interpreted as a latent variable capturing stable country characteristics that influence the dependent variable – one might call it ›culture‹. This ›culture‹ variable accounts for around 6% ($\rho=0.06$) of the variance in life-satisfaction, but the coefficients of the income variables more or less stay the same. Hence, the findings of the first model are not due to unobserved country characteristics. The random intercept specification, however, leads to larger standard errors, and hence to more conservative t-values.

Finally, the columns labelled ›RE-2‹ contain the coefficients (and t-values) of a random intercept model including an interaction term that captures the individualisation hypothesis. For the individualisation hypothesis, one would expect a negative coefficient of this interaction term, which is in fact the case. The individual income effect diminishes by 0.08 whenever the average country income increases by one thousand. Inserting the minimum or maximum value of the (centred) average country income leads to a predicted individual income effect of 1.03 for the poorest country, and 0.84 for the richest country.[9]

Health

Living in good health is definitely one of the more important aspects of human well-being. A vast body of research has shown that health conditions co-vary with socio-economic status (Maucher 1996, Marmot and Wilkinson 1999, Marmot and Bobak 2000, Wolf 2003, Alber and Kohler 2004). Lower-level social groups tend to be less well-nourished, to live more frequently in unhealthy environments and to have more dangerous jobs than the more affluent. But it is not just poverty at an individual level that can affect a person's state of health. The institutions of one's home country also play a crucial role. Environmental protection, maintenance of industrial health and safety standards, and the health system are just a few of the country-specific institutions and practices that might affect one's state of health. And these factors might influence not only the health of all

---

9 The formula for the above numbers is $b_{abs}+b_3\times abspos_r$, where b_{abs},b_3 and $abspos_r$ have the meanings as defined on page 300f. The minimum (centred) average country income is -1, the maximum (centred) average country income is 1.4. Hence: 0.95+ $(-0.08)\times(-1)=1.03$ and $0.95+(-0.08)\times(-1.4)=0.84$.

Table 2. Unstandardised regression coefficients and z-values (in parentheses) of logistic regression and random effects logistic regression for health

	2002			2004		
	(Logit)	(RE-1)	(RE-2)	(Logit)	(RE-1)	(RE-2)
Coefficients						
Men	0.04	0.04	0.04	0.07	0.07	0.07
	(0.7)	(0.7)	(0.7)	(1.2)	(1.2)	(1.2)
Age	-0.04	-0.04	-0.04	-0.04	-0.04	-0.04
(centred)	(-24.4)	(-24.5)	(-24.3)	(-23.3)	(-23.9)	(-23.8)
Household size	0.01	0.02	0.01	0.07	0.06	0.06
(centred)	(0.3)	(0.7)	(0.5)	(2.6)	(2.3)	(2.3)
Absolute income	0.24	0.23	0.12	0.21	0.19	0.19
(centred)	(5.4)	(3.9)	(2.4)	(4.1)	(1.9)	(1.7)
Relative income	0.06	0.07	0.22	0.01	0.03	0.04
(centred)	(1.2)	(1.1)	(3.6)	(0.2)	(0.3)	(0.4)
Abs. × Abs.Ref.Group			-0.12			-0.01
			(-3.2)			(-0.2)
Constant	3.03	3.18	3.04	3.03	3.13	3.13
	(73.2)	(47.6)	(63.4)	(72.7)	(52.5)	(52.3)
R^2_p	0.10	0.09	0.09	0.09	0.08	0.08
BIC	11808	11696	11696	11332	11223	11233
N	27291	27291	27291	26612	26612	26612
ρ		0.03	0.06		0.04	0.04

citizens in a country, but also the degree of social inequality with respect to health conditions.

The ESS contains two indicators for health. The first question asks whether the respondent is »strongly«, »somewhat« or »not at all hampered in his daily activities by illness, disability, infirmity or mental health problems«. The second question pertains to subjective general health, asking, »How is your health in general? Would you say it is very good, good, fair, bad or very bad?«. The latter refers more to a subjective evaluation of one's health; these measures have been shown to be closely related to personality and general satisfaction (Okun and George 1984). The former question pertains much more to objective health problems, and for this reason was used for the subsequent analysis.

Table 2 shows unstandardised regression coefficients from logistic regression models of general health. Therefore, persons »strongly« hampered in daily activities by illness were coded with zero, the others with one. The dichotomisation was designed to allow the use of a random intercept binary logit model. This model is computationally less complex than the random intercept ordered logit model, which would have to have been calculated otherwise. The interpretation of the coefficients in Table 2 essentially follows that of Table 1: For the model of supra-national inequality, the absolute income effect should be high, and the relative income effect should be about zero. For the container model, the coefficient of relative income should be larger than the coefficient of absolute income. For the model of national solidarity, the coefficients should work in the opposite direction.

The results presented in Table 2 almost perfectly fit expectations of the supra-national inequality model. The absolute income effect is much larger than the relative income effect, and, at least for 2002, it is only the former that shows significant z-values. Regardless of how affluent a country is, the higher the absolute income, the higher the probability becomes that one will not suffer serious health problems. Being rich in relative terms, but not in absolute terms, is not enough to be protected against serious health problems. Moreover, there is no indication of any additional effect of a country's affluence on its citizens' health. It is simply the case that rich countries do have more people who are affluent in an absolute sense, and that these people are healthier. Apart from this clear-cut result, there is ambiguous evidence on the individualisation model. The interaction terms in the RE-2 models are both negative, but significantly so only for 2002. The size of the interaction is considerable for 2002, but very small for 2004. It therefore must remain an open question as to whether or not health problems are more equally distributed in richer countries.

Political participation

A long-standing finding of political sociology is that the political participation of lower social strata is less frequent than that of higher social strata (Almond and Verba 1963, Brody and Sniderman 1977, Schlozman and Verba 1979, Lipset 1981, Rosenstone 1982, Powell 1986, Lijphart 1997). In the light of the pluralism theory of democracy (Dahl 1961, 1991), unequal political participation must be regarded as a problem, as it diminishes the chances that the political system reflects the interests of all social groups equally. Despite the normative desirability of equality of participation, there are several reasons why lower social strata do not participate. It has been argued that realisation of the consequences of policies requires insight into complex social problems, and that such insight is more widespread among higher social strata:»Most executives and business owners and many branches of the professions deal daily with complex legal, economic, and technical problems which develop their understanding of the workings of complex social and political mechanisms. Routine clerical and manual jobs, on the other hand, allow little opportunity for acquiring such insight« (Lipset 1981: 197–198). Moreover, people with financial difficulties are said to be less likely to turn out, because they spend their scare resources on »holding body and soul together«, not on remote concerns like politics (Rosenstone 1982). It also has been pointed out that factors that encourage political participation, such as group norms or the extent of one's social contacts, tend to be smaller among lower social strata (Lipset 1981). Piven and Cloward (2000: 28–29) even see a vicious circle with respect to an increasing gap in voter participation. In their view, lower levels of voter participation among working people will force parties to turn away from the issues needed to mobilise lower-class support. »The resulting marginalisation of poor and working people, not only from political influence but from the political culture created by the parties, in turn reinforces their tendency to abstain.«

Piven and Cloward's description of a vicious circle pertained to the political system in the United States. Yet it speaks to the point that turnout inequality is changeable, and might therefore vary between countries and at different times. The expansion of the educational system may have increased the insights of the under-classes; economic growth should liberate the poor from being preoccupied with pure survival; and ›individualisation‹ should increase cross-cutting group pressures. However, there are also reasons why inequality of political participation may increase. One could argue that the process of handing over political decisions to international institutions, such as the EU or even the United Nations, increases such inequality. This process broadens the gap between national interests and the decisions made by national elites, who must take international conditions into account. The further away a person's living conditions are from the logic of the international situation, the more he or she may become alienated from policies.

The ESS contains several measures of political participation, with electoral participation being one of the more important ones. Electoral participation in itself is not, however, well suited to the question at hand. For one reason, non-participation in an election can be interpreted either as politi-

Table 3. Unstandardised regression coefficients and z-values (in parentheses) of logistic regression and random effects logistic regression for political interest

| | 2002 | | | 2004 | | |
	(Logit)	(RE-1)	(RE-2)	(Logit)	(RE-1)	(RE-2)
Coefficients						
Men	0.52	0.60	0.60	0.50	0.56	0.56
	(20.7)	(8.6)	(8.5)	(19.6)	(7.2)	(7.2)
Age	0.01	0.01	0.01	0.01	0.02	0.02
(centred)	(13.6)	(3.6)	(3.7)	(16.6)	(7.2)	(7.1)
Household size	-0.06	-0.05	-0.05	-0.06	-0.04	-0.04
(centred)	(-6.4)	(-1.8)	(-1.8)	(-5.7)	(-1.2)	(-1.2)
Absolute income	0.51	0.38	0.41	0.49	0.60	0.61
(centred)	(23.2)	(8.7)	(8.2)	(19.9)	(7.5)	(6.2)
Relative income	-0.28	-0.15	-0.17	-0.31	-0.38	-0.38
(centred)	(-12.0)	(-3.1)	(-3.4)	(-11.9)	(-4.5)	(-4.2)
Abs. × Abs.Ref.Group			-0.03			-0.00
			(-1.4)			(-0.1)
Constant	-0.27	-0.33	-0.30	-0.41	-0.43	-0.43
	(-15.3)	(-3.9)	(-3.5)	(-23.1)	(-6.6)	(-6.0)
r^2_p	0.05	0.01	0.01	0.04	0.01	0.01
BIC	36048	24683	24691	35193	25202	25212
N	27300	27300	27300	26655	26655	26655
ρ		0.07	0.07		0.11	0.11

cal alienation or as protest. It therefore seems reasonable to differentiate between politically interested and politically uninterested non-voters, whereby the former represent the protest non-voters and the latter the alienated non-voters (Armingeon 1994). Another complication is that some of the countries participating in the ESS have a compulsory election system – Luxembourg, Belgium, Greece, parts of Austria – with the consequence that not voting means something completely different in these countries. Alternative measures of political participation are the indicators for specific forms of political participation. However, the use of these indicators would require further analysis to justify the combined (or selected) indicator. To circumvent these problems, I have reverted to political interest, which has proven to be one of the strongest predictors of political participation throughout Europe (Oppenhuis 1995: 69–85), and which might be interpreted as a sort of mental participation indicator. The ESS asked about political participation by posing the question: »How interested would you say you are in politics? Are you very interested, quite interested, hardly inter-

ested or not at all interested?«. As before, the variable has been dichoto-
mised (i.e. between being very or quite interested versus being minimally or
not at all interested) in order to allow use of the computationally simpler
random effects logistic regression. Results are presented in Table 3.
The results in Table 3 look very much like those from the models of
life-satisfaction (cf. Table 1). The absolute income effect is significantly
positive for each specification, whereas the relative income effect is negative throughout, albeit small in size. The results therefore again point towards a society in which people from poor countries have less political interest than one would expect from their individual income alone. However,
unlike the results for life-satisfaction, there is no indication for the individualisation hypothesis. Although the interaction terms are negative, the
coefficients are insignificant and very small in size. Even for the richest
countries, one does not obtain an effect of individual income such that it is
justified to speak of an individualised society. Hence, to depict these results
in visual form, one would start with the model of national solidarity
(panel 4 of Figure 1) and slightly increase the plot symbols according to the
socio-economic positions in both sub-societies.

Summary

In this chapter I have discussed four models of social inequality in Europe:
container, individualisation, supra-nationalism and national solidarity. The
four models differ with respect to how the absolute and the relative position of a vertical inequality structure influences a dependent variable. The
relative vertical position is important in the container model of social inequality, which is the implicit model of official EU statistics and of most sociological analyses of social inequality. The *absolute* vertical position is important in the model of supra-national inequality, promoted by Ulrich Beck
and others. Individualisation, also connected with the name of Ulrich Beck,
means that the individual vertical position becomes less important in countries that, on average, are better off. Finally, in the national solidarity model
– introduced as a logical possibility – belonging to a country that is disadvantaged on the whole affects a dependent variable more strongly than
does the individual position on the vertical inequality dimension.

Each of the four ideal types draws a very broad picture of European society. The empirical part of this chapter attempts to investigate whether these depictions are realistic and, if so, to what extent. To this end, theoretical expectations of the four ideal types were confronted with the results of a statistical model that disentangles the relative and the absolute effects of income. For this empirical application, three important dependent variables were selected, namely, general life-satisfaction, health and political interest. It turns out that the three applications support different societal models.

The results for life-satisfaction by and large support the model of national solidarity. People from poor societies tend to be less satisfied with their lives, regardless of whether they are rich or poor themselves, although some effect of individual income remains. As the effect of individual income decreases with the countries' affluence, there is also some evidence of a process of individualisation. The results for political interest are similar to the results for general life-satisfaction. Here, people from poorer countries tend to be less interested in politics than are people from more affluent ones. However, unlike the results for life-satisfaction, the remaining effect of individual income does not decrease with the countries' affluence. Hence, there is no indication for individualisation. Finally, the results for health support the supra-national model of social inequality. The affluence of one's country is not an important factor in whether or not one is healthy; it is only personal affluence that counts. The higher the income, the healthier one is. The results with respect to individualisation are ambiguous.

As it stands, none of the four models of European social inequality can claim to be generally true. This is the general crux of theories that describe societies in broad terms. They are too general to be true in every respect, but they are broad enough that something in them is true anyway. It is therefore difficult to criticise them in empirical terms, and this might be the reason for the widespread unwillingness of empirical sociologists to take them on. On the other hand, the example of the individualisation hypothesis shows that there is a market for sweeping representations of society. Empirical work may help identify the best among them.

Which of the four depictions of society is the best? Admittedly, this cannot be answered on the basis of the present analysis. But there is one model among the four that is supported by little or no empirical evidence in all the analyses: the container model of social inequality – that is, the model that more implicitly than explicitly forms the foundation of so many analyses of social inequality.

References

Aiken, L. S./West, S. G. (1991). *Multiple Regression: Testing and Interpreting Interactions*, Newbury Park: Sage.

Alber, J./Kohler, U. (2004). *Health and Care in an Enlarged Europe*, Luxembourg: Office for Official Publications of the European Communities.

Almond, G./Verba, S. (1963). *The civic culture. Political attitudes and democracy in five nations*, Princeton: Princeton University Press.

Armingeon, K. (1994). »Gründe und Folgen geringer Wahlbeteiligung«, *Kölner Zeitschrift für Soziologie und Sozialpsychologie*, vol. 46, pp. 43–64.

Atkinson, T./Cantillon, B./Marlier, E./Nolan, B. (2002). *Social Indicators. The EU and Social Inclusion*, Oxford and New York: Oxford University Press.

Beck, U. (1983). »Jenseits von Stand und Klasse. Soziale Ungleichheit, gesellschaftliche Individualisierungsprozesse und die Entstehung neuer sozialer Formationen und Identitäten«, in R. Kreckel (ed.), *Soziale Ungleichheiten*, Göttingen: Schwarz, pp. 35–74.

Beck, U. (1992). *Risk Society. Towards a New Modernity. Theory, Culture & Society* , London: Sage.

Beck, U. (2002). »The cosmopolitan society and its enemies«, *British Journal for Sociology*, vol. 51, pp. 79–106.

Beck, U./Beck-Gernsheim, E. (1993). »Nicht Autonomie, sondern Bastelbiographie. Anmerkungen zur Individualisierungsdiskussion am Beispiel des Aufsatzes von Günter Burkart«, *Kölner Zeitschrift für Soziologie und Sozialpsychologie*, vol. 22, pp. 178–187.

Beck, U./Grande, E. (2004). *Das kosmopolitische Europa*, Frankfurt: Suhrkamp.

Beisheim, M./Dreher, S./Walter, G./Zangl, B./Zürn, M. (1999). *Im Zeitalter der Globalisierung? Thesen und Daten zur gesellschaftlichen und politischen Denationalisierung*, Baden-Baden: Nomos.

Blanchflower, D. G./Oswald, A. J. (2004). »Well-being over time in Britain and the USA«, *Journal of Public Economics*, vol. 88, pp. 1359–1386.

Brauns, H./Scherer, S./Steinmann, S. (2003). »The CASMIN educational classification in international comparative research«, in J. H. Hoffmeyer-Zlodnik/ C. Wolf (eds.), *Advances in cross national comparison*, New York: Kluwer Academic, pp. 221–244.

Breen, R. (ed.) (2004). *Social Mobility in Europe*, Oxford: Oxford University Press.

Brettschneider, F./van Deth, J./Roller, E. (eds.) (2002). *Das Ende der politisierten Sozialstruktur?*, Opladen: Leske + Budrich.

Brody, R. A./Sniderman, P. M. (1977). »From life space to polling place: the relevance of personal concerns for voting behavior«, *British Journal of Political Science*, vol. 7, pp. 337–360.

Burkhart, G. (1998). »Individualisierung und Elternschaft. Eine empirische Überprüfung der Individualisierungsthese am Beispiel der USA und ein Systematisierungsvorschlag«, in J. Friedrichs (ed.), *Die Individualisierungshypothese*, Opladen: Leske + Budrich, pp. 85–106.

Dahl, R. A. (1961). *Who Governs? Democracy and Power in an American City*, New Haven: Yale University Press.

Dahl, R. A. (1991). *Modern Political Analysis* (5th ed.), Englewood Cliffs: Prentice Hall.

Delhey, J./Kohler, U. (2006). »From nationally bounded to pan-European inequalities? On the importance of foreign countries as reference groups«, *European Sociological Review*, vol. 22, pp. 125–140.

Donovan, N./Halpern, D. (2002). *Life Satisfaction: the State of Knowledge and Implications for Government*, http://www.strategy.gov.uk/downloads/seminars/ls/paper.pdf.

Duesenberry, J. S. (1949). *Income, Savings and the Theory of Consumer Behavior*, Cambridge: Harvard University Press.

Easterlin, R. A. (1974). »Does economic growth improve the human lot? Some empirical evidence«, in P. A. David/M. W. Reder (eds.), *Nations and Households in Economic Growth: Essays in Honour of Moses Abramowitz*, New York and London: Academic Press, pp. 89–125.

Easterlin, R. A. (1995). »Will raising the incomes of all increase the happiness of all?«, *Journal of Economic Behavior and Organization*, vol. 27, pp. 35–48.

Easterlin, R. A. (2001). »Income and happiness: towards a unified theory«, *Economic Journal*, vol. 111, pp. 465–484.

Easterlin, R. A. (2005). »Feeding the illusion of growth and happiness: a reply to Hagerty and Veenhoven«, *Social Indicators Research*, vol. 74, pp. 426–443.

Erikson, R./Goldthorpe, J. H. (1992). *The Constant Flux: a Study of Class Mobility in Industrial Societies*, Oxford: Clarendon Press.

Erikson, R./Jonsson, J. O. (eds.) (1996). *Can Education be Equalized? The Swedish Case in Comparative Perspective*, Boulder: Westview Press.

Evans, G. (ed.) (1999). *The End of Class Politics*, Oxford: Oxford University Press.

Fahey, T. (2005). *Rich and Poor in the Enlarged EU: an Expanded Approach to Measurement*. Dublin: European Foundation for the Improvement of Living and Working Conditions.

Ferrer-i-Carbonell, A. (2005). »Income and well-being: an empirical analysis of the comparison income effect«, *Journal of Public Economics*, vol. 89, pp. 997–1019.

Frank, R. H. (1997). »The frame of reference as a public good«, *Economic Journal*, vol. 107, pp. 1832–1847.

Frey, B. S./Stutzer, A. (2002). »What can economists learn from happiness research?«, *Journal of Economic Literature*, vol. 40, pp. 402–435.

Gerhards, J./Rössel, J. (1999). »Zur Transnationalisierung der Gesellschaft der Bundesrepublik. Entwicklungen, Ursachen und mögliche Folgen für die europäische Integration«, *Zeitschrift für Soziologie*, vol. 28, pp. 325–344.

Goldberger, A. S. (1991). *A Course in Econometrics*, Cambridge: Harvard University Press.

Goldthorpe, J. H./McKnight, A. (2004). *The Economic Basis of Social Class* (CASE paper 80), London: London School of Economics and Political Science, Centre for Analysis of Social Exclusion.

Gujarati, D. N. (1995). *Basic Econometrics*, New York: McGraw-Hill.

Haller, M. (1986). »Sozialstruktur und Schichtungshierarchie im Wohlfahrtsstaat. Zur Aktualität des vertikalen Paradigmas der Ungleichheitsforschung«, *Kölner Zeitschrift für Soziologie und Sozialpsychologie*, vol. 38, pp. 167–178.

Heidenreich, M. (ed.). (2006a). *Die Europäisierung sozialer Ungleichheit. Zur transnationalen Klassen- und Sozialstrukturanalyse*, Frankfurt/New York: Campus.

Heidenreich, M. (2006b). »Einleitung«, in M. Heidenreich (ed.), *Die Europäisierung sozialer Ungleichheit. Zur transnationalen Klassen- und Sozialstrukturanalyse*, Frankfurt: Campus, pp. 7–13.

Hoffmeyer-Zlotnik, J. H./Wolf, C. (eds.) (2003). *Advances in Cross-national Comparison. A European Working Book for Demographic and Socio-Economic Variables*, New York: Kluwer Academic/Plenum Publishers.

Huinink, J./Wagner, M. (1998). »Individualisierung und die Pluralisierung von Lebensformen«, in J. Friedrichs (ed.), *Die Individualisierungshypothese*, Opladen: Leske + Budrich, pp. 85–106.

Inglehart, R. (1977). *The Silent Revolution. Changing Values and Political Styles Among Western Publics*, Princeton: Princeton University Press.

Jagodzinski, W./Klein, M. (1998). »Individualisierungskonzepte aus individualistischer Perspektive. Ein erster Versuch, in das Dickicht der Individualisierungskonzepte einzudringen«, in J. Friedrichs (ed.), *Die Individualisierungshypothese*, Opladen: Leske + Budrich, pp. 13–31.

Jagodzinski, W./Quandt, M. (1997). »Wahlverhalten und Religion im Lichte der Individualisierungshypothese. Anmerkungen zu dem Beitrag von Schnell und Kohler«, *Kölner Zeitschrift für Soziologie und Sozialpsychologie*, vol. 49, pp. 761–782.

Kahnemann, D./Tversky, A. (1979). »Prospect theory: an analysis of decision under risk«, *Econometrica*, vol. 47, pp. 263–291.

Klein, T. (1999). »Pluralisierung versus Umstrukturierung am Beispiel partnerschaftlicher Lebensformen«, *Kölner Zeitschrift für Soziologie und Sozialpsychologie*, vol. 51, pp. 469–490.

Kohler, U. (2005). »Empirische Überprüfung zweier Individualisierungshypothesen mit Querschnittsdaten aus 28 Ländern«, *Kölner Zeitschrift für Soziologie und Sozialpsychologie*, vol 57, pp. 230–253.

Lijphart, A. (1997). »Unequal participation: democracy's unresolved dilemma – presidential address, American political science association, 1996«, *American Political Science Review*, vol. 91, pp. 1–14.

Lindenberg, S. (1986). »The paradox of privatization in consumption«, in A. Diekmann/P. Mitter (eds.), *Paradoxical Effects of Social Behavior. Essays in Honor of Anatol Rapoport*, Heidelberg: Physica-Verlag, pp. 297–310.

Lipset, S. M. (1981). *The Political Man: The Social Bases of Politics* (expanded edition), Baltimore, MD: Johns Hopkins University Press.

Lykken, D./Tellegen, A. (1996). »Happiness is a stochastic phenomenon«, *Psychological Science*, vol. 7, pp. 186–189.

Marmot, M./Bobak, M. (2000). »International comparators and poverty and health in Europe«, *British Medical Journal*, vol. 321, pp. 1124–1128.

Marmot, M./Wilkinson, R. G. (eds.) (1999). *Social Determinants of Health*, Oxford: Oxford University Press.

Maslow, A. H. (1954). *Motivation and Personality*, New York: Evanston.

Mau, S. (2006). »Grenzbildung, Homogenisierung, Strukturierung. Die politische Erzeugung einer europäischen Ungleichheitsstruktur«, in M. Heidenreich (ed.), *Die Europäisierung sozialer Ungleichheit. Zur transnationalen Klassen- und Sozialstrukturanalyse*, Frankfurt: Campus, pp. 109–136.

Maucher, M. (1996). *Sozial differentielle Mortalität – Analyse sozio-ökonomischer Unterschiede in Sterblichkeit und Lebenserwartung*, Konstanz: Diplomarbeit Universität Konstanz.

Mayer, K. U./Blossfeld, H.-P. (1990). »Die gesellschaftliche Konstruktion sozialer Ungleichheit im Lebensverlauf«, in P. A. Berger/S. Hradil (eds.), *Lebenslagen, Lebensläufe, Lebensstile*, Göttingen: Westdeutscher Verlag, pp. 615–665.

Mayer, K. U./Müller, W. (1994). »Individualisierung und Standardisierung im Strukturwandel der Moderne. Lebensverläufe im Wohlfahrtsstaat«, in U. Beck/E. Beck-Gernsheim (eds.), *Riskante Freiheiten. Individualisierung in modernen Gesellschaften*, Frankfurt: Suhrkamp, pp. 265–295.

McBride, M. (2001). »Relative-income effects on subjective well-being in the cross-section«, *Journal of Economic Behavior and Organization*, vol. 45, pp. 251–278.

Müller, W. (1987). »Ist die Klassenanalyse obsolet geworden?«, in J. Friedrichs (ed.), *23. Deutscher Soziologentag 1986, Beiträge der Sektions- und Ad-hoc-Gruppen*, Opladen: Westdeutscher Verlag, pp. 499–502.

Müller, W. (1993). »Social structure, perception and evaluation of social inequality and party preferences«, in D. Krebs/P. Schmidt (eds.), *New Directions in Attitude Measurement*, Berlin/New York: DeGruyter, pp. 94–117.

Müller, W. (1997). »Sozialstruktur und Wahlverhalten. Eine Widerrede gegen die Individualisierungsthese. Anmerkungen zu dem Beitrag von Schnell und Kohler«, *Kölner Zeitschrift für Soziologie und Sozialpsychologie*, vol. 49, pp. 747–761.

Müller, W. (1998). »Klassenstrukur und Parteiensystem. Zum Wandel der Klassenspaltung im Wahlverhalten«, *Kölner Zeitschrift für Soziologie und Sozialpsychologie*, vol. 50, pp. 3–47.

Okun, M. A./George, L. (1984). »Physician and self-ratings of health, neuroticism and subjective well-being among men and women«, *Personality Individual Differences*, vol. 5, pp. 533–540.

Oppenhuis, E. V. (1995). *Voting Behaviour in Europe: A Comparative Analysis of Electoral Participation and Party Choice*, Amsterdam: Het Spinhuis.

Ormel, J./Lindenberg, S./Steverink, N./Verbrugge, L. M. (1999). »Subjective wellbeing and social production functions«, *Social Indicators Research*, vol. 46, pp. 61–90.

Piven, F./Cloward, R. A. (2000). *Why Americans Still Don't Vote: And Why Politicians Want it that Way*, Boston: Beacon Press.

Powell, B. (1986). »American voter turnout in comparative perspective«, *American Political Science Review*, vol. 80, pp. 17–43.

Rabe-Hesketh, S./Skrondal, A. (2005). *Multilevel and Longitudinal Modeling Using Stata*, College Station: Stata-Press.

Rosenstone, S. (1982). »Economic adversity and voter turnout«, *American Journal of Political Science*, vol. 26, pp. 25–46.

Schlozman, K. L./Verba, S. (1979). *Injury to Insult*, Cambridge: Harvard University Press.

Schnell, R./Kohler, U. (1995). »Empirische Untersuchung einer Individualisierungshypothese am Beispiel der Parteipräferenz von 1953-1992«, *Kölner Zeitschrift für Soziologie und Sozialpsychologie*, vol. 47, pp. 634–658.

Shavit, Y./Müller, W. (eds.) (1998). *From School to Work. A Comparative Study of Qualifications and Occupations*, Oxford: Clarendon Press.

Simonson, J. (2004). *Individualisierung und soziale Integration*, Wiesbaden: DUV.

Snijders, T. A. B./Bosker, R. J. (1999). *Multilevel Analysis. An Introduction to Basic and Advanced Multilevel Modelling*, London: Sage.

Stutzer, A. (2004). »The role of income aspirations in individual happiness«, *Journal of Economic Behavior and Organization*, vol. 54, pp. 89–109.

UNESCO (2003). »International Standard Classification of Education, ISCED 1997«, in J. H. Hoffmeyer-Zlodnik (ed.), *Advances in Cross-National Comparison. A European Working Book for Demographic and Socio-Economic Variables*, New York: Kluwer Academic, pp. 195–220.

Veenhoven, R. (1994). »Is happiness a trait? Tests of the theory that a better society does not make people any happier«, *Social Indicators Research*, vol. 32, pp. 101–160.

Vendrik, M./Woltjer, G. (2006). *Happiness and Loss Aversion: When Social Participation Dominates Comparison* (Research Memoranda 026), Maastricht: Maastricht Research School of Economics of Technology and Organization.

Wirth, H./Lüttinger, P. (1998). »Klassenspezifische Heiratsbeziehungen im Wandel? Die Klassenzugehörigkeit von Ehepartnern 1970 und 1993«, *Kölner Zeitschrift für Soziologie und Sozialpsychologie*, vol. 50, pp. 47–77.

Wolf, C. (2003). *Soziale Ungleichheit, Krankheit und Gesundheit* (Abschlussbericht an die Deutsche Forschungsgemeinschaft, Projektnummer WO 739/3-1), Köln: Universität zu Köln, Forschungsinstitut für Soziologie.

Authors

Silke Aisenbrey is a postdoctoral associate at the Center for Research on Inequalities and the Life Course at Yale University, U.S.A. Her research interests lie in the areas of gender, social stratification and the life course.

Richard Arum is professor in the Department of Sociology (Faculty of Arts and Sciences) and professor in the Department of Humanities and Social Sciences in the Professions (Steinhardt School of Education) at New York University, U.S.A. His primary areas of interest are the sociology of education, social stratification and the sociology of organizations.

Eyal Bar-Haim is a graduate student at the Department of Sociology and Anthropology, Tel Aviv University, Israel. Using hierarchical models he analyses ISSP data to study the effects of educational expansion on inequality of educational opportunity in 23 countries.

Hans-Peter Blossfeld holds the Chair of Sociology I at Bamberg University and is director of the State Institute for Family Research at Bamberg University, Germany. Currently, he is interested in the flexibilisation of work in modern societies, the division of domestic work in the family, and the development of individual competences and the formation of educational decisions in early school careers.

Richard Breen is professor at the Department of Sociology at Yale University, U.S.A. His research interests are social stratification and inequality, and the application of formal models in the social sciences.

Robert Erikson is professor at the Swedish Institute for Social Research (SOFI) at Stockholm University, Sweden. His research interests include social stratification, education, family, and health, especially the study of individual change over the life course and how it can be understood with regard to individual and structural conditions.

Markus Gangl holds the Chair of Methods of Empirical Social Research and Applied Sociology at the University of Mannheim, Germany. His main fields of interest are social stratification and inequality, labour markets, poverty, welfare states and social policy, and the development of statistical methods for the analysis of longitudinal data.

John Goldthorpe is an emeritus fellow of Nuffield College, Oxford, UK, and a Fellow of the British Academy. His research interests are in social stratification and mobility, and he has also written on methodological problems, especially concerning the closer integration of sociological theory and research. His work on social class has led to the Goldthorpe class schema which is now widely used in empirical social research.

Nadia Granato is research associate at the Institute for Employment Research (IAB) of the German Federal Employment Agency. Her research interests are migration and labour market integration.

Johann Handl is professor of Sociology at the University Erlangen-Nuremberg, Germany. He has received his degrees in Sociology, Economics and Statistics at the Universities of Vienna and Mannheim. He has published on methodological and substantive problems in several areas of social stratification, e.g. labour force participation of women, demographic problems and aspects of ethnic inequality.

Frank Kalter is professor of Sociology at the University of Leipzig, Germany. His main research areas are migration and integration, esp. conditions and mechanisms of structural assimilation. He has also worked on the sociology of the family, formal models, and quantitative methods.

Irena Kogan is senior research fellow at the Mannheimer Zentrum für Europäische Sozialforschung (MZES), Germany. Her main research interests include immigration and ethnicity, transitions in youth, social stratification and inequality in comparative perspective.

Ulrich Kohler is senior research fellow at the Wissenschaftszentrum Berlin (WZB), Germany. His research interests include social inequality, political sociology, and empirical research methods. He has published on individualisation theory and on social bases of voting behaviour.

Cornelia Kristen is senior research fellow at the University of Leipzig, Germany. Her research is in the areas of migration and integration, educational sociology, and social inequality.

Ruud Luijkx is a lecturer of Sociology at Tilburg University, the Netherlands. He contributed to international benchmark studies on social mobility and published further in the field of (educational) heterogamy, social inequality, career mobility, and labour market transitions and on log-linear and latent class analysis. Recently his focus shifted partly towards research on (European) values.

Karl Ulrich Mayer is Chair of the Department of Sociology and director of the Center for Research on Inequalities and the Life Course (CIQLE) at Yale University, U.S.A. His research is in the areas of social stratification and mobility, sociology of aging and the life course, social demography, occupational structures and labour market processes, and methods of survey research.

Gunnar Otte is senior research fellow at the University of Leipzig, Germany. He received his doctoral degree in sociology at the University of Mannheim. His main research area is the interplay of social stratification and culture, i.e. the structural dimensions, origin and impact of values, lifestyles and preferences.

Reinhard Pollak is research fellow at the Wissenschaftszentrum Berlin (WZB), Germany. His main research areas include social mobility, social stratification, sociology of education, comparative welfare state analysis and measures of social inequality.

Ellu Saar is senior researcher at the Institute of International and Social Studies and Professor at Tallinn University, Estonia. She works on social stratification.

Stefani Scherer is research fellow at Milano-Bicocca University, Italy. She received her doctoral degree in sociology at the University of Mannheim. Her current research interests include social stratification and inequality, the analysis of life courses and labour market dynamics in comparative perspective.

Yossi Shavit is professor at the Department of Sociology and Anthropology, Tel Aviv University, Israel. He is also Head of the B. I. and Lucille Cohen Institute for Research on Public Opinion at Tel Aviv University. His main areas of interest are social stratification and sociology of education.

Stephanie Steinmetz is doctoral candidate at the Mannheimer Zentrum für Europäische Sozialforschung (MZES), Germany. Her research interests are social inequality, comparative labour market research, labour market segregation, comparative welfare state research, and gender studies.

Marge Unt is researcher at the Institute of International and Social Studies, Tallinn Pedagogical University, Estonia. Her research interests lie in social stratification and class analysis, methods of data analysis, labour markets, occupations and careers in comparative perspective.

Meir Yaish is senior lecturer at the Department of Sociology and Anthropology, University of Haifa, Israel. His research interests lie with social stratification and mobility, sociology of education, and the puzzle of altruism.